MONKS AND CIVILIZATION

WORK AND CIVILIZATION

I. ST BENEDICT. Panel in Perigueux Cathedral: fifteenth century.
(*Photo: Archives Phot.*)

MONKS AND
CIVILIZATION

*From the Barbarian Invasions
to the Reign of Charlemagne*

JEAN DÉCARREAUX

Translated by Charlotte Haldane

London
GEORGE ALLEN & UNWIN LTD
RUSKIN HOUSE   MUSEUM STREET

© *George Allen & Unwin Ltd,* 1964
This translation

Translated from
Les Moines et la Civilisation
© *B. Arthaud, Paris* 1962

PRINTED IN GREAT BRITAIN
in 10 *point Plantin type*
BY SIMSON SHAND LTD
LONDON, HERTFORD AND HARLOW

PREFACE

In the following pages the reader will find an account of the monastic institution in relationship to Western civilization. The formative and educational activities that resulted from it were those of great leaders and the centres of holiness and culture they created. That is why we have placed the main emphasis on the collective aspects of monachism. The way of life of the hermits and recluses did produce saints, but contributed little to civilization, and have therefore only been touched on incidentally and in the measure that they affected our principal theme. For a similar reason little has been said here with regard to the female monasteries. But whenever it appeared useful to our purpose we have dealt with our subject in the light of contemporary ecclesiastical and even political history, for although they lived in seclusion from the world the monks were men of their own day, and certain of them were directly involved in its affairs.

It has been our particular aim to highlight certain individuals who made a characteristic contribution to their times. Seen as a whole the monastic world, making a special virtue of humility, presents a picture of numbers of men who lived and died in anonymity, basically a little drab and uncouth. The work they accomplished might have remained a somewhat monotonous and unappreciated contribution to history had certain great leaders not at certain times set their stamp upon it. We have been less concerned to give an account of the careers of such leaders than to draw attention to their spiritual or intellectual qualities and the influence they exercised on their periods. From time to time we have dwelt more fully on a certain number of them, whose characteristics it seemed might be interesting to examine more closely.

In this first volume we have dealt with the settlement of the monks in the Western world, a new world, dominated by the Barbarians, and the work they accomplished there. This consisted on the one hand in the endeavour to consolidate institutions that had until then been merely provisional, and on the other, in missionary enterprises that were in due course to become missions of civilization. After an introduction in which certain general lines dominating the subject are laid down, the two following chapters appeared indispensable. Even at the risk of generalization it seemed necessary to recall in outline the collapse of one world at the very moment of the appearance of those who were to bring about its transformation. Secondly, in order to understand Western monachism, it seemed equally important to describe the origins of that institution in the East. Thus the reader, having become acquainted with their terminology, environment, and way of life, would be enabled more accurately to appreciate the differences that little by little arose between the two forms of basically the same institution of monachism. On such broad lines it would be possible to base a work of 700 pages.

In dealing with this subject two alternative methods were available; one, strictly chronological, the other, along geographical lines. The first of these would have presented the reader with the difficulty of having too often to jump over the frontier lines to find in certain places in the contemporary world individuals who were being studied at a given historical moment. This would have been a kind of piecemeal method, which by disturbing the integral cohesion of each chapter would have blurred the basic lines on which it was built. Following the example of some excellent historians we preferred the geographical order for the sake of clarity (Italy, Africa, Spain, Gaul, Britain, etc.) rather than to follow more profoundly, in a vertical direction, the scattered monastic institutions that had not yet come under the influence of the Rule of St Benedict. We have therefore included wherever possible, in one chapter or section of a chapter or another, everything within a given nation relative to our subject. In certain points the result of this has been to anticipate here or there some aspect of the subject to be dealt with at a later stage. But we took care to avoid this procedure if its use might have interfered with the account in general. A list of dates in the course of the book and a chronological table at the end should help to remedy any inconveniences that this arrangement might have produced.

In writing this book the author has been able to draw on many preceding works. As authors dealing with one and the same subject often tend to repeat one another, it is necessary to select among them the leading authorities, whether ancient or modern, and only these have been referred to in the bibliography. But whatever their merits, historians cannot replace first hand study of the original documents, to which it was necessary to refer. Yet it seemed unnecessary to overload the work with a mass of footnotes or to quote the documents in question in full; as a rule hagiographers were both longwinded and addicted to gossip, and repetitious quotations from them would merely have slowed down this account, which, with or without quotation marks, is based on those sources.

In meeting so many monks the reader, one hopes, may come to feel some sympathy for them. Although in spite of their greatness their faults may be found irritating or their achievements arouse some scepticism one cannot, nevertheless, help liking them. They are never boring in spite of the fact that their standards of conduct and the austerities they practised were occasionally positively alarming. In endeavouring to discover points of contact with them on the twofold level of holiness and civilization, and in applying to them the only constructive form of criticism, based on sympathy with their point of view, we will perhaps have been able to establish a certain degree of understanding between them and ourselves. 'History,' wrote Camille Jullian, 'is the science of recollection. It therefore contains an everlasting principle . . . carrying forward in time the ideas and aims of men who have disappeared . . . Between them and ourselves it creates a sense of devotional solidarity.'

CONTENTS

CONTENTS

ILLUSTRATIONS

MAPS

14

CHAPTER I

HUMANISM AND MONASTICISM

The aim of any intelligent traveller is to revivify, and if necessary to correct, his theories by personal contact with flesh-and-blood human beings. A journey undertaken to rediscover the fathers of our civilization should have a very special attraction. Yet before setting out on it, it appears necessary, nevertheless, to clear up, by as detailed an approach as possible, a certain number of ideas that very widespread usage has tended to devaluate and deprive of their importance. Yet such ideas, freshly re-stated if one may say so, will assist us in understanding the subject-matter and appreciating the personalities involved more correctly.

CIVILIZATION, PROGRESS, CULTURE, EDUCATION

In any given society civilization represents, in continuous terms, the sum total of its spiritual, intellectual, ethical and institutional values, which in varying degrees will permit those living in it to develop as completely and harmoniously as possible. Thus we recognize that there exist different civilizations, each one with its own particular character-istics—Western, Byzantine, Islamic, Hindu, Far Eastern, etc.—which have gradually ripened over a long period of time, although not an indefinite one, since all civilization is based on a certain degree of tradition. Based on and enriched by the past, it continues to enrich itself in the present, especially when it produces individuals who, emerging suddenly, at a given moment, provide it with apparently unexpected renown. And when, in addition, it happens that it reaches beyond its own frontiers, this will enable it to expand and increase its own inheritance. From the points of view of thought, literature, and art, this includes at one and the same time the inception, flowering, expansion, preservation, and handing-on of works which, after having proved the claim to fame of one nation in particular, by their universal character become the patrimony of the whole human race.

All civilization is a carrier and generator of progress. Leibnitz imagined progress to be a kind of passive depository of advancement, which, by successive impulsions, was gradually induced to develop toward perfectability. Progress makes demands on the resources of the human mind in various ways, in the guise of pure thought, scientific research and technical advances. Yet in these different spheres progress is not necessarily simultaneous; at the time when Plato was writing his dialogues Greek science, although young and vigorous, had not yet reached a similar stage of development. More precisely, under the general term of civilization, we must distinguish as being particularly relevant to progress, on the one hand scientific, economic, material and technical developments, and on the other, as the result particularly of culture and education, aesthetic and ethical advances.

The former, especially in their technical achievements, today seem to have no term set to them excepting by their own self-destruction; after bursts of genius, ingeniousness, the capacity for methodical research, the communication of discoveries and the sharing of them, their synthesis and chain reactions leading to further syntheses appear to be endless, *nec proinde unquam ad terminum progressus perveniri*, as Leibnitz also said. But the successes of literature and the arts, in so far as these depend on the individual, even although he be not segregated from his environment, do not reveal a similarly happy continuity. No other literary genius has re-created the poetry of *Phèdre* or the prose of Voltaire's tales, whatever one may think of them as individuals. After them, their tradition will not be carried on merely as imitation, which could only fall more or less flat, but rather by indirect reference or in individually formative elements. For although the general lines of progress tend to run constantly towards a higher individual stage, human values may be dispersed, become worn, vegetate or disappear, unless a renaissance, which may not even owe everything to them alone, arises to ensure their revival.

These values, ephemeral, delicate and fragile, belong to culture. Although the German word *Kultur* may be a fair translation of our idea of civilization, in the French sense of the term culture, as we have seen, has a more limited meaning. It refers to the efforts and methods adopted by mankind to emerge from every form of barbarism (including that of over-specialization) and to exploit every one of his spiritual resources as the cultivator employs his in order to fertilize his fields (*colere*, to cultivate). Viewed in the light of its results, culture is the sum total, the treasure, of intellect, good taste, judgment and qualitative development acquired by mankind during the course of its efforts towards full enlightenment. For its expression in time and space it will depend on the environment which has provided it with its essential elements—as there was a pagan culture, so there is a Christian culture. And Christian culture itself has taken diverse forms in producing the men of the Middle Ages, the Renaissance, or those of today. However, it may be with regard to these accidental differences that culture is essentially, in the happily phrased definition of M. Marrou, the personal form of the life of a mind that has reached the stage of full development.

It is curious to observe, as the same author has pointed out, that the Romans did not find a term corresponding precisely to the French word *culture*. To the ancient Romans *cultura* included fewer intellectual than ethical, traditional and athletic elements. After them, Cicero, who was well aware of it, hesitated in the use of words to define it. Those he suggested, *humanitas, doctrina, disciplina, studium, litterae, cultura animi, ingenii*, all reflect certain aspects of what we know as culture, but their very multiplicity reveals that he did not succeed in comprising them into one satisfactory definition. But on the contrary, the Greek *païdeia* corresponds fully to our idea of culture because it includes every aspect of education, with its results and its aristocratic ideal, which distinguished the cultured Greek not only from the barbarian, but also from the common herd (*idiotes*).

Culture is acquired through education. As the word indicates, (*e-ducere*, bring out, draw forth) it refers to a number of methods destined, through the graduated repetition of a number of exercises, to develop the capacities of a given individual in the direction of his best potentialities, to create in him habits that will facilitate his development and will enable him to do justice to his status as a man, a citizen, and eventually as a Christian. A product of civilization, education cannot be perceived in its totality until it has reached a certain stage of maturity and late enough for its values and methods to have been tested by experience.

In order to be efficacious, education must always remain rooted in reality. When it is divorced from it, it misses its aim and it is always a problem—when it is not a tragedy—for educationalists to have to adapt to the present what they have taken over from the past, or otherwise to provide an unsuitable system. This is not a matter of fashion but of living. If force of habit, a lack of imagination, the retention of dead wood, moral and intellectual timidity, cause an educational system to be imposed on the scholars against the grain, the young will instinctively look elsewhere for their true cultural stimuli. In our time, a pupil forced to endure the scholastic boredom of Corneille will spontaneously seek for less pompous and more authentic examples of greatness of soul from modern authors who do not appear in his teacher's curriculum. From a more general point of view, it is no longer at all certain that our traditional programme of study of the classics, which dates from the sixteenth century, is suitable to the atomic age into which we have entered. We may regret the disappearance of the famous 'disputations' between 'Romans' and 'Carthaginians' in which, from the Renaissance to our own childhood, generations of scholars contended for honours in Latin grammar, but it is a fact that some of those who teach it no longer know Latin very well, and that Greek is quietly dying away. It would be vain to endeavour to arrest an irreversible trend for the sake of nostalgia for the greatness of the past. And it is perhaps not sacrilegious to imagine a form of humanism that would give a greater prominence to mathematics and the sciences, grafting them on to the old tree after having cut out its dead branches, notably those concerned with trans- lating the ancient classics, which has become a merely sterile exercise, and with rhetoric of a certain rotundity, which has become merely ostentatious vacuity. In his educational programme Plato not only excluded the poets—in which he was wrong—but gave a pre-eminent place to mathematics, in his view the most precise instrument of intellectual acuity as a means of discovering truth by the dialectical method. The strange signboard of his school—'Entrance forbidden to those who are not geometrists'—was not, probably, his invention. But this does not affect the facts nor its successes; the teaching at the Academy was based on arithmetic, the geometry of planes, and the geometry of 'solid' objects, the higher course in which was entrusted to Theaetetus and Eudoxus.

Nor is it without interest to note with M. Marrou that in the Western world the classical method, founded in the fourth century B.C. with Plato and Isocrates, was not seriously threatened as an institution until the time of the Barbarian invasions. It subsisted in Africa under the Vandals (Carthage), in Spain under the Visigoths, and especially in Italy under the Ostrogoths (Ravenna, Milan, Rome), and even under the Lombardians (Pavia, Milan, Benevento, Salerno). Elsewhere, in the Danubian provinces and in Gaul (the Brittany Islands and Ireland are exceptions) teaching was kept going willy-nilly by preceptors or private schools. The Church, moreover, was beginning to play its part, pre- serving by the modest means at its disposal what it could, until such time as it could take over. Thanks to this tenuous and widespread continuity, a part of the old classical methods and examples survived the test and became part of the different phases of civilization. The universal spreading of Christianity and the new methods of the Middle Ages did not completely alter its substance nor disturb its stability. Its capacity for endurance was undoubtedly due to certain intrinsic characteristics suitable to the West, and also, in the fallow periods, to the sense of conformity of a lower pedagogical cast of mind, which easily sees in any innovation a revolution that must be condemned. In any case it is to this humble tradition that we owe the preservation of a scholastic humanism that until recently could still claim to be a theory of living even when those to whom it was handed down were strong enough to drive it from the schoolrooms and break through its formalism.

BARBARIANISM AND HUMANISM

We are all barbarians in someone else's view. In the fourth century B.C. Demosthenes sneered at Philip of Macedon, who was unable to pronounce his own name in a pure Attican accent. At the same period Isocrates, his opponent, stigmatized as a barbarian everyone who was unfamiliar with the language, customs, and institutions of Athens. After having been regarded as barbarian by the Greeks, for others Rome became the matrix, mother, and mistress city. The new Rome, Constantinople, on the shores of the Bosphorus, despised the metropolis and was scandalized when a Barbarian, Charlemagne, dared to usurp the title of Emperor. In the middle of the eleventh century, Peter III, the Patriarch of Antioch, stated without a trace of polemical meaning and even with a certain degree of pity, that the Latins were 'barbarian nations', especially when compared to the Byzantines, 'educated in all the refinements of culture'. In the eighteenth century Italy, England and Spain had produced the finest fruits of their civilizations, and after more than two centuries of the highest culture, around 1750, France had reached a point that might be regarded as its zenith. Yet in 1793 the Emperor of China, Kien-Long, replying to the inquiries of a merchant ambassador, informed King George III that although he appreciated that monarch's desire to 'participate in the benefits of Chinese civilization' 'barbarian products' imported from 'an island cut off from the rest of the world' did not interest him. And during the first half of the twentieth century, the German racialists took the view that there was no civilization worthy of the name apart from the German.

During the same period the French by no means discounted the existence of other civilizations, but left the study of them to specialists who had read little and when by chance they compared them with their own it was only in order to depreciate and sometimes even to deride them. They gladly proclaimed that there was only one civilization worthy of the name—their own—descended from Rome and Greece and modelled on their genius. Maurras, one of the masters of thought at that time, was a perfect example of that type of culture. Although a man of undeniable talent he ostracized everything that did not spring from the wisdom of Ulysses and the Roman system of which France was the heir. Beyond Delos he found nothing but obscurity, mystery, troubles and monstrous anarchy. A born Catholic and a prejudiced racialist, he found 'Hebrew Christianity' suspect, but it pleased him that the Roman Church, as distinct from that of the Evangelists, had inscribed 'the name of Minerva on more than one altar'. In his opinion, even Art was based only on one precept, eternal and absolute, to be followed undeviatingly, the Greek tradition of Pericles and Sophocles, according to his own particular definition of it; the rest having no validity except to the extent to which it depended on that principle. This academic kind of dogmatism, however comforting to his mind, was out of touch with historical reality by the fact that he deliberately discarded as barbarian everything that did not conform to it.

Those who, overcoming such sectarianisms, made at least an attempt to conceive of Europe as a whole, were satisfied by honouring in 'this little cape of the Asiatic Continent', as Valéry called it, that peak towering above the universe whose searchlights lit up a world of shadows, and whose power could dominate it. But even this definition ignored the rest.

The perturbations and upsets of two world wars brought Europe down to more modest claims. And as, in addition, the conquests of speed gradually made this earth appear to shrink in size and caused the blank spaces on our atlases little by little to disappear, and as more and more exact and valuable knowledge was gained from the new land that was being discovered, we became aware of a certain oecumenical unity reigning over our planet. Thus we discovered that the forgotten Celts, to whom, after all, we did owe something, were civilized people, that the Iranians had been so every bit as much as the Greeks, although in a different fashion, that even the nomadic hordes between the Black Sea and Outer Mongolia appreciated the rugged arts of the steppes and that primitive and even prehistoric peoples were capable of producing masterpieces. A more thorough reading of ancient texts, and archaeological excavation everywhere, revealed that there was not just one and only one mode of feeling, thinking, and expression, and that every civilization, whether it were barbarian or advanced, founded either on a warrior and athletic aristocracy or nurtured by learned men, had contributed to human development. Even although as early as the third century B.C. Polybius had already foreseen that the Western Mediterranean, the world known to him, and the unknown world of the East in fact formed one whole, our self-sufficiency and our pride in our privileged status were shaken by the revelation of a new concept of the universe. As Valéry also said, 'the oscillations were so violent that even the most firmly attached lamps were at last thrown down.' Free minds, dazzled by this discovery, revised their scale of values and accepted the facts.

But if this shock, which was a genuine intellectual and spiritual revolution, burst open the most firmly padlocked barriers, it should nevertheless not mislead us into a muddled syncretism or to dissipate the best of our inheritance. Whilst we may accept riches that are not of our making we do not have to renounce the substance of our own tradition. Whether we be Celtic or Germanic, nourished at the source of Rome and through her by Greece, we are neither Persian nor Chinese. If we attempted to become so, in the end we would risk becoming no more than bastards. But faced with the enormous field that lies before us, our task is to endeavour, without ceasing to be ourselves, to measure up to the new world dimensions, to respect what in the past appeared to us to have been barbarianism, and to assimilate, according to the degree to which we can do so, the treasures which until now we had not known existed. Thus history, by teaching us the lessons of humility, justice, and wisdom, opens up infinite new perspectives.

True humanism consists not only in an exclusive and punctilious attachment to certain special texts or to certain ways of feeling and thinking of which we have reason to be proud. Properly understood, these same texts, from which their more intelligent interpreters have often drawn the lesson of universalism, invite us to go beyond them if we wish fully to realize our capacities. Securely based on its original sources, humanism must always remain open-minded towards everything that, although not intrinsically part of it, yet in one way or another redounds to the credit of mankind, so that it becomes, if it does not include it, a point of departure for a complete vision of the world, with the many relationships and analogies that reveal its unity, diversity, and universality. In such intercourse with a different one our own civilization is enriched both by what it has to give and to receive. Thus we will gain full access to complete humanism, which does not of course mean the knowledge of such or such a man, nor even that abstract knowledge of man in general that the Greeks handed down to us, but which includes every grand and noble human activity in any and every degree of longitude and latitude, in the domains of achievement, liberty, justice, and love. Man, as the old adage said, is in some sort part of all things. *Homo est quodammodo omnia.*

CHRISTIAN HUMANISM

From an historical point of view, detached from the abstractions of the philosophers, man has never ceased to be religious-minded. The pagan Greeks, although certain of their rhetorical systems only praised the sense of orderliness, measure, and serenity, were also concerned about religion. To be convinced of this it is only necessary carefully to read Aeschylus, to enter into the forest of mythology, or to glance through the door of a chapel of initiates. Graeco-Roman humanism, even within the confines of the city or the state, was never as rationalistic as has been claimed.

Faced with pagan civilization, Christianity was compelled to take up a certain definite position. From the beginning there was conflict between them; the complete monotheism of the Gospels could not but reject polytheism and the ethics of paganism. Lost in an environment in which they were unable to recognize one another, the first Christians only accepted from the ancient civilization what they could not avoid. We know, on the other hand, St Paul's vehement invectives against the wisdom of the philosophers, but in favour of the ecstasy of the Cross. After him, especially among the monks, the Church always included a certain number of the faithful who withdrew from the world because they hated all that it stood for, and in face of the philosophy of their century posed as champions of the 'philosophy' of asceticism, with all the exclusivity that implied.

But St Paul himself, a Jew by origin, but a Greek culturally, in his own person provided the kernel of what afterwards was to become Christian humanism. By studying the men of the ancient world the Christian soon realized that in their company he might enrich his own mind. In his eyes all the higher human values were already regarded as a gift from God, even if those on whom they were bestowed did not know whence they came. The Oracle of Delphi's 'know thyself' was good advice, and following a logical course the Christians were able to apprehend the outstanding nobility of human nature when fitted into the scheme of the Redemption. To know mankind was at the same time a means of fitting it into its proper place in the scheme of things; if the pagans vaunted the natural order of things, the God whom they ignored was nevertheless its creator. Their virtues, even when insecurely based, were to the credit of humanity, and their magnificent achievements in literature and the arts were, whether or not they themselves realized it, a hymn to the Creator. Erasmus expressed it thus: 'Remember that every truth which you may find in a book comes from Christ and belongs to Him.' Deeply impaired as it was by original sin, human nature, controlled by powers from which a certain degree of grace was not excluded, was capable of producing works that, far from being sinful, only required ordination to enable it to participate in the renewed harmony of the cosmos. It was not a question of baptizing Homer or Antigone, but of putting them in their place, not the first in the new order of things, of learning the lessons they taught, incomplete but valid, as a contribution of imperfect man to the perfectibility of man redeemed. In redeeming man from the Fall the work of re-creation (*opus recreationis*) placed the work of creation (*opus creationis*) in its final position and, allowance being made for original sin and grace, provided the bases for a Christian optimism; although fallen, man was still created in the image of God and still in spite of everything retained the imprint of the hands that formed him. All the more as when redeemed, a part of what he had lost was restored to him by virtue of grace. St Bernard said of him that he was an elevated being, capable of majesty (*celsa creatura in capacitate majestatis*). Despite the problems and disturbances that arose during the course of history Christian humanism was based on such optimistic foundations.[1] Far from claiming to repudiate the contribution of the ancients, it took it over in order to ennoble it still further. After the operation described by

[1] The fear of falling into Pelagianism, which tends to suppress or underrate the influence of original sin, has often led Catholics to adopt a pessimistic point of view which may falsify their view of the world. 'The popular concept of a Christian universe the nature of which is corrupted by sin owes much of the ready acceptance it has found to the influence of Luther, Calvin, or Jansenius; but to see Christianity through their eyes is to do so in an entirely different light from that of Thomism or even authentic Augustinism. No one, in fact, is further than St Augustine from regarding the world since the Fall as valueless . . . Although he deplores what mankind thereby lost, he never thought to despise what remains to us; the very misery of our present state is not in his opinion without a certain magnificence . . . How much good must there still remain in human nature for man to have invented clothing, agriculture, industry, and navigation! The arts of language, poetry, music, and finally, moral science, to lead humanity back on to the path of its eternal destiny.' (E. Gilson, *L'Esprit de la Philosophie médievale*, Paris 1932, Vol. I, p. 126 s.)

Origenes as the transition of the wisdom of flesh-and-blood to divine wisdom, there was to ensue a wider world outlook and on the human plane a radical transformation of civilization. In the domain of literature and the arts alone Christianity, after the unavoidable transmutation had taken place, revealed itself capable of producing masterpieces as great as the best of the ancient ones and of transcending them.

HUMANISM AND EVANGELISM

More easily than any human discipline, Christianity, whilst remaining unchanged, overflowed every frontier. Hebraic in origin, the message of the Gospels was proclaimed to all nations. From the beginning, St Paul broke down the narrow confines of the earliest Christian setting in Jerusalem and aspired to the vastest conquests. In his eyes there were no longer either Jews, nor Greeks, nor Barbarians. His genius, working within the Graeco-Latin social order, fertilized it in such a manner that a new vision of the world was imposed on it. After him it was predominantly in the manner and terminology of Greek thought that the doctors of the first important schools and the first councils developed the core of doctrine that had been revealed to them. The formulation of these inner advances bore the marks of the environment in which they were elaborated. Yet in a world in which minds and languages were already on the point of parting company, the Egyptian, Athanasius, the Syrian, John Chrysostom, the Cappadocian, Gregory of Nazianza, the Illyrian, Jerome, the Roman, Ambrose, the African, Augustine, all belonged to the same spiritual family. In the thirteenth century, certain axioms of St Thomas Aquinas, emerging from the centres of Parisian scholasticism, acquired universal significance. Better still, the doctrines of St Thomas, if not his methods, became the norm of all teaching in Catholic schools.

When religion was restricted to the Mediterranean or European world it could only express itself according to the means at its disposal. But when the discovery of other continents opened a wider field to the message of the Gospels they were able to travel far beyond the bounds of their place of origin in order to adapt and transmit their message to new climates, and did so in much a manner that its substance remained unchanged. This was a considerable task, in the carrying-out of which the early pioneers met setbacks, but which was—and remains—within the pattern of universal Evangelicism.

The message of the Church was not confined to any particular civilization. Whatever the origins of its missionaries, it was never, even in the slightest degree, the religion of one people or one period. The gospeller, without ever forgetting the message he was bringing, had to forget whence he came. If his mind had been formed by any given culture he was called to put it to the service of the environment he intended to labour in, after a 'conversion' that might call for the final sacrifice, that of his intelligence. Unless he first discarded his own prejudices even to the extent of adopting those of his chosen field, his message might run the risk of being regarded, not as an oecumenical or Catholic one, but as a foreign importation. After all his predecessors since Benedict XV, John XXIII, as soon as he had ascended the pontifical throne, took care to remind the Black intellectuals of this: 'The Church does not identify itself with any culture, not even with Western culture, with which its history is closely linked.' (April 1959.) In effect it is a matter of two separate orders of things: all civilization, even Christian civilization, is rooted in the human, temporal, and perishable, but the Catholic religion, of divine origin according to its Founder, is rooted in the supernatural, the non-temporal, and the eternal.

To an even greater extent the missionary must not be a member of a nation of conquerors. Even if its initial successes were to be numerically increased thereby, in the last resort religion has everything to lose by sheltering behind the sword. If it has been imposed by force, or violence, it can only appear as imported in the baggage-train of a conquering army, and imposed on the vanquished by the victorious party. Protected and defended by politicians and merchants, it will in due course by a gradual and often unnoticed series of compromises become an instrument of States and a flag of protection under which may shelter for their own advantage those unconnected with its vocation. Not all the heroically endured persecutions can be explained away only on the grounds of hatred of Christianity. When new paths have been hacked out by force, it is the duty of the Church to rush into them, but once engaged in them it has the further and no less imperious duty of practising the virtues of independence with complete disinterestedness. This, too, may call for sacrifices, especially that of keeping her hands bare and clean.

Since Pius XI gave the native clergy the most vigorous encouragement in contemporary times, religion, remaining unaltered even on the most distant shores, has more and more tended to lose, if one may put it so, the complexion of its place of origin and to take over that of those countries where it has become implanted, the aim of the European missionaries being less to remain there themselves than to train their local successors. Thus Europe, which for a short time succeeded in conquering or in 'protecting' vast stretches of the earth, may recall its diplomats, armies, and merchants. European priests may be expelled under the generally fallacious pretext of having played a political game, yet the Church, even when persecuted, does not renounce her task. The virulent fanaticism she must then face up to, successive xenophobias resisting a foreign occupation, temporary changes in her discipline, the weakening or damaging of her authority, all form part of the dangers that she has always had to face. Strong in her thousand-year-old experience, assured that she will endure forever, she will then proclaim more loudly and firmly than ever her independence of all nations which pass, and her universal character.

In those regions that still remain to be converted she will accept everything that, born of their particular historical circumstances, does not conflict with her message. In the seventeenth century, Father Ricci in China and Father De Nobili in India, both of them genuine Christian humanists anxious to adapt themselves perfectly to their new environment, opened up paths which in time and in spite of the obstacles that can be imagined, were to prove themselves fruitful. Their decision, entirely in the Pauline tradition, to become Chinese with the Chinese or Hindu with the Hindus, was considered scandalous. This was the period when the Hispano-Portuguese 'patronate', joining together 'pepper and souls' to its own greater advantage, was aiming towards denationalizing its conquered subjects in order to assimilate them. It was, in fact, in order to free himself from the practices of the 'patronate' and to concentrate in his own hands all mission work that in 1622 Pope Gregory XV founded the Congregation of the Propaganda. Thirty-seven years later (1659) the methods to be adopted were set out in the *Instruction for the usage of Apostolic Vicars leaving for the Chinese kingdoms of Tonkin and Cambodia*:

'Refuse absolutely to sow in their kingdoms the seeds of any party, whether Spanish, French, Turkish, Persian or other . . . Use no zeal and advance no arguments, in order to persuade the people to change their rites, their customs, or their habits, unless these are obviously contrary to religion and morality. It is absurd to try to transplant to China, France, Spain, Italy, or any other European country. Do not introduce our countries to them, but our faith . . . It is, so to speak, inscribed in human beings to love and place above all else on earth the traditions of their own country and that country itself. Thus there is no stronger cause of withdrawal and hatred than to bring about changes in the customs proper to a nation . . . What would it be like if, having abrogated them, you were to try to set in their place the customs of your country, introduced from without? Do not, therefore, ever make a parallel between the usages of those peoples with those of Europe. Quite to the contrary, you should hasten to get used to them. Admire and praise everything that merits praise.'[1]

This charter of respect for other peoples, a genuine monument to Christian humanism, was capable of arousing the strongest generosities, but it interfered with too many prejudices, interests and established positions to be always generally and everywhere applied. Then as today men were lacking in both the necessary methods and understanding, not to mention good faith and heroism. On the spot, the spirit of the *Instruction* might often be dismissed as Utopian and forgotten. Nevertheless this document remains the evangelical and humanist code of all missionary work. In addition, John XXIII said, on April 3, 1959, that 'the Church is always ready to recognize, accept and love everything that does honour to the human heart and mind in the regions of the world that are not those of the Mediterranean'.

That is the doctrine. At the period with which we are concerned it was still far from being laid down. In the Western Roman Empire, shaken by the Germanic invasions, the Church, although still remaining, had above all to preserve its message. The clerics or the monks, Romans by upbringing, had to retain all of the original bases that could be saved, although latinized by the Roman conquests and already encroached upon by the Evangelical conquest. They had, moreover, to approach the pagans, still very numerous far from towns and roads, and the Barbarians, themselves pagans or Arians. The methods they used differed little in either case. The prestige of the preacher, his ascetic virtues, the fame he achieved, the real or supposed thaumaturgical gifts he possessed, provided him with a halo. Their apologetics were rudimentary. The God of Clovis or the 'druid' of St Patrick having proved themselves the stronger, there was no reason why the Franks or the Irish should not join the better side.

As regards the methods of approach, it is interesting to note that a little later, the monastic missionaries sent out from Ireland failed in spite of their high saintliness, because they remained narrowly nationalistic, whilst in England the Benedictines sent from Rome by Gregory I succeeded by adapting themselves to their new environment. Elsewhere, at other times and in another way, under Charlemagne, the missionaries accompanied the troops when an army crossed over a frontier and began its campaign. This type of action had its own characteristics. The King,

[1] Cf. A. Rétif, in *Etudes*, January 1959.

later the Emperor, blessed by the Church, and by virtue of his sacrament, regarded it as his duty, not only to protect his faith but to propagate it by force of arms. In those circumstances every military action against the pagans took on the appearance of a crusade. The conqueror imposed his faith on the vanquished and the latter was not considered as completely conquered until he had been immersed in the baptismal font. Thus the sacrament became a gauge of political loyalty, that is, an instrument of subjection. At one moment Charlemagne even decreed the death penalty for any Saxon who refused baptism. Compulsion and violence in the name of Christ were inherent in the period. At the end of the tenth century St Vladimir converted the people of Kiev entirely by force of arms, and a little later, the region of Novgorod was 'baptized by iron and fire'. For a long time this was the policy of princes inclined to confuse God's will with their own and in the interests of their policies. A certain number of Churchmen thought with better sense that it was necessary to introduce civilization before proselytization if baptism was to have its full effect.

PREJUDICES AND TRUTHS

This plan was evolved by the clerics of the episcopal schools and the monks. Whilst the former were chiefly attached to the bishopric, the latter were first settled in the countryside, where there were also lay priests, and after the end of the fifth century, beneath the ramparts of the cities.

As regards the monks, it is indispensable to underline heavily the fact that their basic vocation was never either to civilize nor even to proselytize, but, far from the world, to devote themselves to asceticism, to prayer, and the love of God, without any other kind of specialization. Nevertheless, since virtue is not invariably unrecognized, owing to their renown, the monasteries became reception centres to which the peasants (*pagani*—pagans) came to beg for the charity of a Christian order. There they were then taught the rudiments of religion and later of grammar, as they were in more recent times by our humbler village schoolmasters. From that point onwards only a step needed to be taken, as it soon was, to pass beyond the monastery walls in order to visit neophytes, complete the training of the catechumens, give baptisms and go on missions. Thus the disciples of St Martin travelled through Western Gaul. Later, St Benedict, imposing restrictions on his Order, found it necessary to confine its members to their walls, restricted even their missionary sorties, but nevertheless did not close his gates to the rude peasantry.

The general impression regarding the activities of the monks does not always conform to this historical point: whether they were priests or not, these contemplative religious became by accident catechists and roving missionaries.

Another misconception, a romantic counterpart of the former one, sees the monks first and foremost as scholars, bent over manuscripts, scratching away on vellum, or working on uncials. At a given period this was the case, but originally this kind of work seems to have been mostly occasional, even in Benedictine monasteries. In withdrawing from the world a monk divested himself completely of the trappings of the world, even those that were cultural. It also happened that he was completely ignorant and unlettered, for the attainment of perfection placed less value on knowledge than on virtue and the pursuit of sanctity. From that point of view the best of the monks were perhaps those of whom we know nothing, not even their names. Those who did have some education were enjoined not to waste their time over it, but to devote themselves to following the rule of obedience. When their services were required it was initially in order to serve their community; either to transcribe one of the Gospels, or a liturgical book, a religious work or a commentary needed for immediate use and difficult to obtain outside the monastic walls. In addition the work of a good copyist could bring in some revenue to the monastery. It follows that in themselves such activities had not been foreseen as essential to the institution. As regards profane literature, it was only at a fairly late stage that the monks became the guardians of such works as had not disappeared in the upheavals of successive invasions. Before the sixth century the culture of the clerics and the monks was above all ecclesiastical. The monastery, a house of prayer, was never an academy. If, at certain historical moments it did become one, this was by force of circumstance which without in any degree infringing its original aims, added to them a supplementary form of activity which had not been foreseen by its founders. On this point also it was necessary to make this indispensable distinction, whilst, however, always bearing in mind that every monastery, whether a cultural centre or not, was a centre of civilization.

Moreover, throughout the course of history and in spite of their considerable scientific achievements, even in the Western monasteries there was always a certain active anti-intellectual trend. The reader may perhaps be surprised to know that even today, in certain foundations that have a high reputation, the contribution of the community to profane science is nil—which need not be stressed—but that it is sometimes also negligible with regard to ecclesiastical knowledge. The classics of our youth, even when expurgated *ad usum Delphini*, are mercilessly relegated to 'hell', that section of the library to which are relegated those books regarded as unnecessary or dangerous, and cannot be taken out of it without the express and rarely-given permission of the Father Abbot; as a rule Virgil or Corneille may only be read under such conditions. Study or research in ecclesiastical literature may only be undertaken if they do not in any way impede divine service or prayer. The same monks also remain averse from any kind of missionary activity; for instance, many of them have never preached, nor heard confessions. This deliberately adopted attitude is only in appearance paradoxical. It simply reflects a close loyalty to primitive monastic ideals, which from this point of view have been more carefully cherished in the East than in the West.

The true function of the monks is to follow the example of the saints and their heroic virtues, and in prayer. In doing so they do not always reveal their most praiseworthy side to us; that special aspect of grace which we would like to have a share in, which is the treasure of the King. 'All hearts of a certain kind,' said Mauriac, 'will have had the same history.' We must therefore content ourselves by approaching them only through the fringe of their lives that we can perceive, and through those visible works that, issuing from their private sanctuaries, are but a reflection of them. Although, truly, that is enough to arouse our admiration and provide us with instruction.

As we study their lives we find to our surprise that what we can see of them resembles our own, and that in that respect they are our brothers. If they tower above us like giants they also occasionally reveal to us simple human qualities such as common sense, equanimity, sound education, and gentleness. When they step down from their pedestals they inspire confidence in us and it is no abuse of it to endeavour to know them as they are. Like ourselves, they have a body that suffers, faults, weaknesses, enmities, humours, which their powerful personalities do not always keep under control. But virtuous as they are, they also teach us that virtue is not always synonymous with sanctity, but can become so. As saints, they are the witnesses and bearers of grace. And they would not, probably, recognize themselves under the mawkish daubings, almost caricatures of themselves with which we are presented by certain of their pious admirers. They would be the first to reject them. Silliness, they would tell us, has never brought credit to sanctity. If, in order to rediscover their truths, we attempt to strip them of attitudes by which they would have been the first to be disgusted, we do not fear to endanger their reputation, but by becoming on familiar terms with them with no loss of respect, by their true example we are encouraged to imitate them. They can be paid no greater homage than to be reconstituted in their entirety. 'The greatest charity towards the dead,' Mauriac also said, 'is not to kill them a second time by lending them sublime attitudes.'

We do not therefore need to conceal the fact that when we see them face to face with their adversaries they sometimes give us a point against them. Against those who claimed to be followers of Christ although declared enemies of the Church, their orthodoxy was without doubt a source of grace and strength, but they did not by any means always express this orthodoxy pleasantly. Some of them sprang with such enthusiasm over the narrow barrier that in theory separates the hatred of an idea from the hatred of its holder that they bore in the eyes of their adversaries all the exaggerations of heretics. Moreover these energetic characters expressed themselves in language which had not yet been softened or toned down by our so-called well-mannered puritanism. One is always sure that in their company faith will remain intact, but not always good manners as well. There are wide shades of difference from Jerome to Augustine and Bernard. As always, Augustine is exemplary—well-behaved in all circumstances, he had no difficulty in recognizing the good qualities of his enemies. Le Nain of Tillemont informed us that 'he could always judge with much frankness what was good even in the wickedest'. It is easy for us posthumously to denounce heresy when the Church settled the question so long ago. But at the height of the dispute, when authority was occasionally slow in giving its decision, matters were not always so simple. The combatants had a free field. Those under suspicion had not yet been found guilty. Although they were obstinate and litigious, they were neither fools nor ignoramuses. They might be of good faith, and lead honest lives. They had disciples, many of whom were bishops. If we ourselves had been engaged in those long-drawn quarrels, can we in all honesty say which side we might have taken?

These statements are made in a general context which it is useful to remember. It would be false to present history, including that of the Church, surrounded by a conventional halo, as if it were the subject of a stained-glass window. In the great story of our past there are shining pages, but also black ones. The former may cause the latter to be forgotten, but they will not suppress them. Linked together day by day, they form an interlocked whole of which the historian must take account. To isolate or stress certain episodes because they are of a

31

flattering nature, whilst ignoring or blotting out others that may be embarrassing, is not the way to deal with history, and such a procedure would only discredit those who adopt it and the end they claim to have in view. To judge Protestantism by Luther's dinner-table talk would have as little relevance as if one were to judge the Christian thirteenth century on the basis of the police methods of the Inquisition, or the Renaissance in Rome according to the morals of some of the Popes. A lie, whether pious or impious, however qualifying, is still a lie. In history as in apologetics honesty is always the best policy. In the fifteenth century the humanist Lorenzo Valla stated that 'The Church has not to protect falsehood'. In the same way but in a different sense Leo XIII wrote in 1883 that 'the first law of history is not to dare to lie; the second, not to fear to tell the truth. In addition, the historian must not be suspect either of flattery or of animosity.' This does not imply that the historian should remain indifferent to his subject; he should be impartial, if that quality does not merely represent a point of view. But at least he must be honest, loyal, equitable, and in his own way, respectful towards his material, whatever it be, not merely on aesthetic grounds, as if he were painting a picture in which the light plays upon carefully arranged shadows, but in tribute to truth, of which he is the servant.

This question is of prime importance to Christians. They want their Church to be the pure Church of God. It saddens them to see her face occasionally lined or covered with pimples, and her holiness dimmed. Without mentioning those who are always ready to denounce in others what they allow themselves without stint, and who should at least be decently silent, many honest people expect from Churchmen in this world what they will only be granted in the next. A little reflection on the forgotten words of the simple Catechism would teach a vast number of well-intentioned but ignorant people that if the toleration of evil is connivance in sin the terrestial life of the Church is not fixed in the absolute, but takes place in relation to its environment. The divine creation of its Founder, the source, receptacle and channel of grace, the Church is served by men redeemed, yet fallen, and thus, at varying degree, by sinners, all of whom, however, are expected to imitate Christ and participate in His holiness. In a good man an invisible ferment may be taking place, of which nothing is seen; the common man limps along as best he may; the wicked man may sometimes cause a scandal to reveal him, allowing that the most wicked are never altogether evil, and that even the best can change. The Church on earth is, in fact, no more than militant, that is to say engaged in the vicissitudes of daily

2. BAPTISM OF PAGANS. From St Peter's antiphonary: twelfth
century. *(Austrian Nat. Mus., Vienna)*

ST BASIL AND
ST GREGORY
OF NAZIANZA.
From Greek MS no. 55,
Bibl. de Paris.
(Photo: Archives Phot.)

SCS·SIMEON

3. ST SIMEON STYLITES. Mosaic in the narthex of St Mark's, Venice: thirteenth century.

(Photo: J. Décarreaux)

combat, with its heroes and camp-followers, its alternating victories and defeats, of glorious exploits and small actions. To expect these combat troops to appear as if on a parade with no slackers is not only to demand that the Church should take up a position which was never promised her here below, but also to misunderstand her role. The Church as we see her today is a traveller who must face, even when she cannot overcome them, all the hazards along her way (*viator*).

The greatest of the saints do not escape the laws of human nature. Grace, whether visible or invisible, produces them, and it is they who save the rest of humanity. But they do not float along their way like pure spirits who do not belong to this earth. They, like everyone else, occasionally stumble, and if they do know better than others how to rise up again, the trail of light they leave behind them, from their point of view, was most of the time darkness and peril, without ever giving them that peace which comes of a good conscience. Like all truly brave men, they knew fear. Seen from afar, their numbers dazzle us, and their works bear the stamp of success. We admire them, although, preferably, posthumously. But had we actually met them—as they bore no labels and were quite often insignificant-looking little men—we, after searching everywhere for them, might easily have passed them by, unrecognized, possibly cold-shouldered them, and, very probably, ignored them. For, interesting though they were, they did not, according to the example of their Master among the Pharisees (all of us), hesitate to proclaim home-truths, embarrassing in distinguished company. (Which of us today, as Herod nevertheless did, would feel honoured to invite a modern John-the-Baptist, with his ragged beard, his dusty feet, his uncouth language; a tiresome person, obviously coming to no good end? And even St Francis of Assisi, a ragged tramp, with his embalming in the *Fioretti*?) In the course of their daily lives our saints were mixed up in the quarrels of those, far more numerous than themselves and some-times their conquerors, whose desires, even within the Church itself, were close to the soil or even spattered with mud. Whether above it, or below in the mire, the Church lived only in an atmosphere of struggle; around her, within her, or above her. Rare, indeed, were her periods of calm, and this is as it should be.

Nevertheless, as everywhere else, the law of compensation also played its part in this. The ground the Church lost in one direction she regained in another. At the end of the fifth century and the beginning of the sixth, she was going through a particularly discouraging phase, but at that precise moment St Benedict founded his monastic institu-tion. Ignatius Loyola was born in 1491, one year before Alexander

Borgia, Alexander VI, ascended the papal throne. Loyola is still remembered, Borgia much less so, although a little later his family was to give a General to the Society of Jesus and a saint to the Church— Francisco di Borgia, Duke of Gandia. Huysmans, who was always ready to point to the warts on the faces of the clergy, expressed this common-place rather well: 'When one side of the balance sinks too low (God) throws the tears of his saints into the other.' Thus each generation seeks to do what it can as best it can; makes the attempt, either fails or succeeds, and day after day continues to build its edifice from very diverse materials. In danger at every moment, whether from time to time clean or contaminated, in spite of everything saintly in general and finally fruitful, the Church, by hard labour, in the face of passing set-backs or temporary successes, nevertheless continues on her course until the end of the road, where she knows that the last stage will lead to the triumph of her universal restoration. However beautiful she may from time to time appear, only in Holy Jerusalem will the gates of the city shine like flawless gems, and the walls be of unsullied gold. Here below even the most priceless mosaics contain some very ordinary pebbles.

Civilization, grafted on to the tree of the Church, or emerging from her creations, follows from day to day the same way of laborious growth, even if sometimes out of gear. Taking advantage of the successes of the few in order, by a long process, to arrive at an ever higher ideal of humanity, it also remains, like the peacefulness that encourages its development, vulnerable and fragile, since at any given moment it may be undermined, or collapse, or retreat owing to a too hasty advance, human contempt for its values or lack of care for what has been won. As it is specifically the work of man, he himself may kill it. But whilst it remains it is the outward and visible sign of human progress. Shadows are not wanting, since if there exist sins against God there are also crimes against civilization. But until now the scourges of folly and evil-doing have not yet impeded the handing-on of the torch.

LEGENDS AND MIRACLES

The holy monks, like their brethren in this century, in the past pro-duced a whole crop of manuscripts which it is desirable to describe in some detail.

When reading their biographies one is generally immersed in an extraordinary world, simple, naïve, sometimes picturesque, charming or comical, sometimes, also, extremely boring, but in which miracles appear as everyday incidents. The man of ordinary common sense staggers back from such a picture, composed for the most part entirely of marvels. In certain cases he asks himself whether he is looking at a novel, a work of panegyrics, a collection of commonplaces, or a list of virtues that can be affixed to any given one of the characters. We are, in fact, faced with a particular literary form, hagiography, which is based on legend as well as on a certain amount of fiction, which a reasonable critic owes it to himself to investigate.

Recently still, a certain part of it which claimed to be based on tradition, was regarded as immune from investigation. Any marvel referred to in the texts as a miracle was above discussion. Any suspicion or rejection of it was considered as a lack of respect, an attack on piety and a menace to religion as a whole. If, in addition, one allowed oneself to be diverted by some episode that did seem rather far-fetched, certain people were positively shocked that the ridiculous could occasionally produce a smile. At most they would agree that some scabrous or absurd detail would seem improbable; a concession, incidentally, that was a risky one from their own point of view, since once one starts to make any it is always difficult to know where to stop.

Faced with those who accepted each and every miracle as inviolable, the hypercritical had a fine chance. They did not fail, so to speak, to prise out many a saint. But whilst often putting forward reasonable and genuinely scientific objections it happened that they pulled to pieces certain accounts that were in part valid until nothing was left of them. In consequence certain genuine biographical facts were either queried or discarded, or the very existence of their subjects might be so strongly challenged that they became relegated to the world of mythology.

Others, however, like the Bollandists, among them Father Delehaye, a real authority, investigated the material calmly, with intelligence and discernment. They were careful 'not to fail to discriminate between the saints and everything concerning them', noting that great men have not always found historians worthy of them, and that hagiographers, whose critical talents might be discussed without irreverence, in their turn had spoken more frankly of their superiors. To those who clung tenaciously to 'tradition' they strove to explain that the Church was not obliged to guarantee the truth of all these accounts. And in answer to the hypercritical they clarified the laws of that literary form known as hagiography, which differs from biography as such.

The unacceptable term, legends, when applied to the lives of the saints, becomes much less so when it is more closely examined; legends in fact are no more than accounts to be read (*legenda*) during the celebration of the liturgy or the reciting of the official prayers of the Church. By including them in its books the Church never intended to suggest that they were historical texts, nor to give any judgment as to their value. She refrained with all the more reason from doing so with regard to certain works which we may, generally speaking, classify as hagiographical novels, pious fictions embroidered around an historical kernel or even entirely fictitious. The *Life of St Hilarion* by St Jerome belongs to the former category. The *Life of St Paul of Thebes* by the same author is based on such slight foundations that it has been supposed—although erroneously—that its hero never existed. Still more curious is the *Life of Saints Barlaam and Joasaph*; the former only existed in his biographer's imagination and the second reproduces the story of a transformation of the Buddha. We may legitimately doubt whether St Martial of Limoges was in fact the child whom Jesus referred to as worthy of the kingdom of heaven and who handed Him the basket containing the loaves that multiplied themselves. The Church, when canonizing men, never thought of canonizing all these pretty tales.

We may make the same observations with regard to the term 'miracle', an extraordinary manifestation of God's power through the intervention of a saint in our affairs. When such an event is guaranteed by its character, its conclusive value and a 'tradition' without a flaw between the intercessor and the narrator, it would be foolhardy to doubt it, even if such a 'tradition' has been difficult to establish. But in the type of literature with which we are dealing, and which is ruled by the marvellous, miracles are so abundant and often of such a nature that the powers of the thaumaturgists (*virtus*) appear literally as a kind of exhibition of virtuosity. Incontestably it contains exaggerations, fascinating no doubt, but more than suspect when it comes to matters of fact. And not only did men perform miracles, but animals and inanimate objects as well. The Abbé Aigrain, a learned and reliable author, made a fine collection of such *virtutes*. Against all theological teaching, St Gregory and St Malo were said to have saved the damned by pulling them out of hell. The same St Gregory reported that a horse he had mounted refused to carry the body of a woman on its back. St Malo taking the chalice to celebrate Mass, changed a stone into a vase of rock crystal. St Gildas ordered a dangerous monster to die and it obediently killed itself. It was a hind that guided Clovis against Alaric. St Hubert was converted by a ten-antlered stag that he was pursuing, and between whose horns was a cross. Other stags had the same powers, although without crosses. St Martial and St Frontus used St Peter's staff to resuscitate the dead. The staff of St Gildas had the same powers. The coffins containing relics of dead saints are alternately so heavy that no power can move them, or so light that they float on the waters. One thinks in spite of oneself of good old La Fontaine, who, by the way, adored such tales—'Men, gods, animals, all of them are a part of it.' They are all very poetical, too, but it is obvious that the Church could not be responsible for fantasies which, even when they are not simply absurd, prove nothing.

The hagiographer inventing such stories was essentially concerned with edifying his readers. He was addicted to panegyrics, which as we know, make considerable use of exaggeration and over-statement. And this was, in fact, what his audience demanded. In those days, far more than in ours, the saints were expected to have all the virtues. Even when this was the case the author did not fail to present them in the manner expected of him. At other times—for instance in the case of Gregory of Tours—all he had to do was, quite honestly, to put together the oral or written accounts which, as they were handed down, became more and more prolix, enlarged, and adulterated, which he then enlivened yet still further in a manner similar to that still favoured by our own society reporters, sensational journalists, or writers of flattering obituaries. It is easy to imagine what in those circumstances might happen to a text that, originally more or less a reasonable record, passed through the hands of a succession of compilers who were by no means all literary fakers, but very often well-meaning and of good faith, and simply of their period. If their material was meagre and their imagination was weak, they had at their disposal all the clichés they needed with which to clothe their hero. For they were always expected to provide good measure. Eagerly awaited and demanded by avid readers, the 'real miracle', whether it might seem probable or absurd, was the rule. It was as much a part of this literary genre as his pitchfork was one of the attributes of Lucifer.

In texts that have been dealt with in this manner it is often impossible to disentangle the truth from falsehood. The Church, which is so extremely thorough when examining the claims to sanctity of any given person, microscopically examining the miracles he is alleged to have performed, gives the historian a lesson in caution, honesty and strictness which it is his duty to follow. To verify and classify these collections of extraordinary events is in many cases a difficult task and, granting the premises on which the material was based, often a useless one. But neither is one entitled to deny the existence or the influence of a thaumaturgist, simply because he has thus been given a halo, if there is other than mere literary evidence in his favour, which gives a definite corroboration to writings of lesser importance. And therefore when a methodical examination of inscriptions, liturgical books, itineraries of pilgrimages, and all available material—over and above the stories which have not been proved incontestably authentic—has made it possible to establish that at a given date and in a definite place a certain person became the centre of a cult born of popular devotion and ratified by the Church, the historian will have conscientiously fulfilled his task and served a tradition his opponents reproached him for having attacked. 'When a saint is genuinely deserving of his niche, i.e. his traditional cult, even if nothing else were known about him, no hagiographer worthy of the name would challenge his right to it; and even the accounts that might be most damaging to his memory should not prevent the critic from firmly according him this right. . . . If the result of such an inquiry be definitely negative, and if the tradition of such a cult has not definitely been established, traceable to a date fairly close to his death or to a canonization or an accepted "elevation", it would be impossible to remove from his niche a saint who did not possess one.'[1]

One must accept the situation that the historical period with which we are concerned has been to a large extent worked over by the hagiographers and laden with doubtful 'miracles'. In most cases, even after having dug out certain indubitable facts or at least those which have a certain likelihood, one is compelled to remain unsatisfied. Careful though we may be to retain only the truth, despising all exaggeration of it, we should nevertheless not forget that legends form part of our subject-matter. We cannot, therefore, altogether refrain from presenting our heroes as they appeared, at a given moment in their history, in the eyes of their hagiographers, who bear witness, not only to the facts, but to a certain method of presenting them. Once the truth, even if it be fragmentary, has been carefully defined, in order to understand it the best method is still to follow the story-teller and with him to visit for a brief moment the earthly paradise he has created for his subject. And if by chance one has been able to enjoy a good tale met with on the way, one seldom departs from it without some gain. It is enough not to have been taken in by it.

[1] R. Agrain.

CHAPTER II

CIVILIZATION IN PERIL

In A.D. 161 the Emperor Antonius died in his villa at Lorium; his last word, *aequanimitas*, summing up his ideal as a great Roman. The following century was to become known as the Antonine.

Rome was then at the height of her power and glory. From that day in 753 B.C. when Romulus, having harnessed an ox and a cow to a cart, marked out the first boundaries of the future city on the ground, nine centuries of heroic perseverance had built up on the confines of the Mediterranean an Empire that reached to the ends of the then known world. Sixty million people—some say one hundred—lived there, their eyes turned towards the Imperial City, 'shrine of courage and greatness'. Rich in temples and monuments and distinguished by the prestige of unrivalled success, the city itself contained half-a-million inhabitants.

The days of the Republic were over. Thenceforward the Emperor or first magistrate of the State held the ruling power, which tended more and more to become absolute and sacrosanct. From time to time he still consulted the Senate, but as the authority of one man became greater, that great institution played a smaller and smaller part in affairs. In return the ruler filled the ranks of an administration that was still youthful with the most able members of the Equestrian order. The succession was assured by a system of adoption, association, or choice, i.e. in principle, by the promotion of the most suitable successor. When the Emperor had children, it was usual for the hereditary system to prevail, but not inevitably with successful results. Many such princes were unworthy, but it is only fair to note that their folly or their cruelty, even in the case of a Nero, never went beyond the confines of their own circle, or the periphery of Rome. Tiberius, suspicious and bloodthirsty, was nevertheless a hard worker. Thus the world in general enjoyed a degree of stability that was ensured by a succession of able men, anxious to preserve the greatness of their city and the general welfare of the Empire. The love of one's fellow-men, the 'philanthropy' of the philosophers, was no mere phrase.

The legions completed the great conquests. In theory 350,000 strong, more or less, the army, a professional army, although owing to lack of money not up to full strength, was an excellent instrument. It consisted mostly of volunteers and provincials, proud to serve under the Eagles, and garrisoned the frontiers of the Empire, then a matter of 9,000 kilometres. Along those 9,000 kilometres, the Army engineers built 3,400 kilometres of fortifications, continuous in many places, vast systems of trenches topped by palisades, earthworks or stone ramparts, and watch-towers. The Rhine and the Danube were thus protected along their whole length. Elsewhere, to the south and east, where the frontier was on the edge of the desert, carefully selected strongpoints were constantly manned. Begun under Augustus, and methodically continued under his successors, the *limes*, or great shield, was completed in the third century. Within the enclosure that it protected, reigned the majestic *Pax Romana, immensa pacis Romanae majestas.*

On land, by means of the Empire's splendid roads, on the inland waters that had also become a means of communication, in the many ports bulging with merchandise, business went on without any fear of bandits or pirates. The gold currency, invariably honoured, was the rule everywhere. The laws, which were equitable and considering the period humane, were far ahead of those of Lycurgus and Solon. Agriculture, which was the basis of the respectability and moral sanity of the ancient Romans of the Latium, made little technical progress, but spread throughout the Empire. Industry, which remained at the stage of artisanship, easily satisfied the modest demands on it. Business, banking, the earning of huge profits, and usury, were developing. Enormous fortunes were accumulated and spent on luxurious properties, distinguished by the numbers of slaves kept on them. Everywhere new towns were arising and the older ones were being transformed and enlarged. Many of them were collectively entitled to the rights of cities. Adorned with monuments, temples, amphitheatres, and baths, well equipped with great works which were also works of art, from Rheims to Timgad, from the bridge of Alcantara to Baalbek, all of them recognized what they owed to the genius of Rome. Everywhere people endeavoured to live according to the ways of the capital. Although Greek was still held in honour and inspired authors who remained faithful to the past glories of Athens, Latin was producing masterpieces that rivalled the great writings of Attica. Moreover, Gaul, Spain and Africa could measure up to Rome as regarded their literature and the excellence of their authors. Rome at that period, according to the elder Pliny, was 'the pupil and mother of the whole world, chosen by the providence of the gods to add even to the sun's brilliance, to unite once again peoples who had been dispersed, through the community of language to bring together other peoples, however discordant and barbarian their own tongues might be; to enable men to understand one another, to civilize them; in a word to become the sole fatherland of all the nations on earth.' This picture, although idyllic and somewhat uninformed, nevertheless contained a good deal of truth.

ROME IN THE TWILIGHT OF HER GLORY

Yet towards the end of the second century, even in the midst of its splendours, the majestic edifice of the Empire revealed certain cracks which were not shock-proof.

At that time the ruler tended to replace the cult of Rome, which not long previously had still been a source of civic pride, by the cult of his own personality. Although *de jure* the first magistrate of the State, in fact he was an absolute monarch, and sometimes a tyrant whom a palace revolution might overthrow. The Senate was not resigned to the amputation of its prerogatives and its traditional role in order to become too often a merely discontented and symbolical institution. Against its will it was obliged to agree to the creation and to watch the emergence of a new caste, that of Captains (*equites*) who supplanted it by forming the cadres of the administration. Below them the idle populace of Rome drew from the provinces both its nourishment and its distractions, which were guaranteed by the State. Children, of whom there were already not very many, especially among the rich, grew fewer still. As was the case of Sparta in the past, Rome was suffering from 'oliganthropy'. The rights of citizenship, granted indiscriminately by Caracalla, were abused. Those on whom they were conferred were quick to take advantage of their privileges, but were less anxious to shoulder their responsibilities. In religious affairs, scepticism was spreading with regard to the local deities; only a small number of believers remained loyal to them; their devotion based on nostalgia for the past. The cult of Mithras was arousing interest, and shortly afterwards, the Christian religion, in spite of the fact that it was still suspect as 'the enemy of the human race', which meant the Roman civilization. The leading intellectuals, meanwhile, had become a prey to syncretism, a sign of spiritual decadence. Literature itself had degenerated into meaningless verbiage, whilst art—apart from architecture, which still remained grandiose—had become commonplace.

The army itself, which was the cornerstone of the whole Imperial structure, revealed an even more alarming state of affairs. Its leadership, drawn from the Senatorial ranks, was too often inadequate in the field. It was necessary to replace it by professional officers, promoted from the ranks, most of whom made excellent generals, but who were dangerously inclined towards the *pronunciamiento*. Conscription was failing to produce the required number of new recruits, for too many citizens were able to claim exemption from it, and the middle classes who in the past had provided most of the legionaries did so no longer, because they had simply ceased to exist. Volunteers, who in the past had remained in the service for twenty or twenty-five years or even longer, came forward in fewer and fewer numbers. In order to remedy the situation, efforts were made to recruit the vigorous and martial-minded inhabitants of the middle and lower Danube basins, in the province of Illyria, where there was a high birth-rate. The army was even reduced to recruiting mercenaries from among prisoners and the barbarian tribes, a situation which as it became more general was to have serious consequences. These auxiliary corps became so numerous that soon the Empire's best troops were no longer Romans. Even then the army was never sufficiently strong to provide protection everywhere at one and the same time.

Behind the *limes*, constantly strengthened and fortified, the defence troops, although their high quality was maintained for a long time, gradually lost the mobility in which their chief strength had lain. Men recruited from amongst the peasantry and given permission to marry disliked leaving their wives, their homes, their land in order to defend threatened positions elsewhere. The garrisons, spread out behind the fortifications, led lives of idleness weakening to aggressive militancy. As for the interior, no big or general defence plan had as yet been drawn up to provide for massive troop movements in case of the frontiers being breached at any given points.

Even worse, the armies, which in the great days of the Empire had occasionally been troublesome, were now working towards its ruin. They might decide to proclaim their generals Emperors when, indeed, they did not assassinate them, either because they decided that their leaders had run their course, or had no more money with which to pay them; in the end result, much the same. In disastrous sequence emperor succeeded emperor, some of them retaining the title for merely a few months, or even days, and the chiefs who had been proclaimed as such were from the outset no more than usurpers, so much so that, in fact, whichever among them happened to become emperor was merely for a short time luckier than the rest.

Inevitably such a state of anarchy could only hasten disaster. The economy that had been a flourishing one during the preceding century was badly shaken. The currency depreciated. Speculation was rife, to the detriment of army supplies, the public coffers, and private fortunes. Piracy and banditry arose. There was an alarming commercial crisis. Manual labour flagged for lack of slaves. Financial affairs, already precarious ever since, the conquests having been made, there were no more vanquished to pillage, deteriorated still further. The treasury existed merely by expedients. Taxes, although increasingly heavy, were no longer adequate, and became difficult to collect, even under duress. In order to avoid them and to shed the load of civic duties which every day were becoming more onerous, although still referred to as honourable, many important people were thinking of retiring permanently to the countryside.

This crisis, which was to last for seventy years (268–337), was nevertheless to some extent mitigated by courageous statesmen, devoted to the public welfare, the best among whom not only succeeded in avoiding anarchy but proved themselves worthy of their hard task. During those perilous times Rome still had great servants—Aurelius, an excellent general, who might have done even better had he not been assassinated; Diocletian, a politician and administrator of genius; Constantine, deservedly called 'the Great'; men such as these would have saved the Empire had it been possible to do so. At least they did for a time reorganize it, maintain and prolong its duration.

As it was nevertheless too vast to be administered and defended by only one man, it was at first ruled by two, then by four sovereigns, of whom Diocletian was both the brains and the strength: two Augustuses and two Caesars. Each of them had his seat within reach of the frontiers; at Treves, Milan, Sirmium (Mitrovitza), Nicomedia. The inevitable result of this state of affairs was the cleavage of the Empire into two halves, the *pars orientalis* and the *pars occidentalis*. As a result, Rome was to lose even more of its importance.

The army, the chief problem of all successive governments, was reorganized. Its effective forces were strengthened. They were still insufficiently strong, but, on paper at any rate, they rose to half-a-million men. Of these the less efficient formed the garrison troops of the *limes*. The more active forces, spread out in depth, were held ready for immediate action, but the combat strength of the best of them was never more than 15,000. Volunteers were constantly sought for, even through dealers in mercenaries, but as enough could never be obtained it was decreed that the sons of soldiers could follow no other activity than their fathers'. Slaves were also enrolled, after having first been enfranchised, since only a freeman could be a Roman soldier. The big landowners were called upon to levy recruits and took the opportunity to rid themselves of undesirable characters. As these individuals did not make good soldiers, the landowners were then obliged to make monetary payments for the purpose of obtaining the services of mercenaries. The latter were mostly Barbarians, who, although they were recalcitrant to the older discipline and regular training, were nevertheless excellent fighters when it came to the offensive; they also cost less than the regular troops. The high command, which since Gallienus had become more specialized by separating the civilian from the military authorities, had remained efficient. All the regular officers, the chiefs or *comites* (companions of the Emperor), or *duces*, remained worthy of their great traditions. Many of them, as the result of their bravery, were proclaimed emperors, and after their elevation many of them preferred to remain with their troops as long as possible, instead of immediately retiring to their palaces.

In face of the dangers that threatened from without, the towns, which during the *Pax Romana* had remained open and defenceless, surrounded themselves with walls, leaving their suburbs to the mercy of any later aggressor. Most of them covered from five to eleven hectares, six or seven at Senlis, ten at Autun and at Tours, sixteen at Nantes and Rouen, and thus contained very few inhabitants, if one allows only 3,000 to every ten hectares. A city of the importance of Verona was less than 1,000 yards in circumference; Paris was twice as large. The largest cities, such as Bordeaux (twenty-three hectares), covered barely a mile and a half. Rome itself, anxious for its security, was surrounded by exceptionally long walls, of about twelve miles in length, which for a time rendered it impregnable. All were garrisoned.

The bureaucracy formed a second army, in which, as has been said, the pen replaced the sword. It was commanded, supervised, formed into cadres and hierarchies along similar lines to the army, and was well paid, enjoying numerous exemptions, and in due course came to form a new aristocracy with ever greater influence. The provinces, which had become too large, were broken up into smaller administrative districts, of which there were in due course 115. Grouped into fifteen dioceses, they were ruled by delegates who transmitted the orders of the supreme power to them. The whole edifice was topped by three entirely civilian prefectures. It was significant that none of the prefects were resident in Rome, where the Senate, although still held in high honour, was now definitely inactive. Around the monarch were grouped his court, his 'friends', or favourites, his chief servants, his officers, the guard, a bunch of intriguing women, the spies, who were very active, informers and stoolpigeons of all kinds, the entire household surrounding the emperor who, seated on a heavily decorated throne around which revolved the whole palace ceremonial, no longer received the homage of the people of Rome, but that of his own subjects (*subjecti*).

This enormous military, administrative and Aulic apparatus, which during the reign of Diocletian alone was based on 1,200 edicts or rescripts, was extremely expensive to maintain, and the financial situation was further worsened by the fact that the State had to struggle to overcome the continuing economic crisis. The measures that were then adopted were Draconian. A totalitarian system was introduced to control all exchanges, restrict the professions, establish a detailed land registry, crush the more prosperous under heavy taxation, and cleanse the currency, but these measures led to gigantic inflation.

At that moment the signs of a radical change began to appear. There were still towns, but there were no more cities. And the towns themselves began to disintegrate. The plebeians, or lower orders, ever famished, lazy and turbulent, were a heavy liability on the municipal budgets. In order to control them their provider, the State, was obliged to keep them supplied with bread, oil and bacon, and with free entertainment on 175 days a year, this consisting of spectacles that were either bloody or obscene and debased them still further. The middle-class was exhausted to vanishing-point. The civilian posts it should have filled either remained vacant or were in incompetent hands. The artisans worked little and traders sold at a loss. The wealthy landed gentry, still with plenty in reserve, especially in the form of real estate, and powerful enough to avoid their duties with impunity, lived on their own soil. The villa, the traditional residence of any important personage, whether he were of Roman origin or had been assimilated, became more than ever before a self-supporting unit based on a closed economy, and with no need of currency. The landowners, who lived on the grand scale, were autonomous to the extent of levying their own taxes, dispensing justice, raising their own private men-at-arms and forbidding entry to their property to the tax-collectors. The poor, reduced to penury by the State and usury, were able to exist only by begging for the protection of the powerful, in exchange for their own tiny plots, which, incidentally, they were unable to leave. Having sought protection more often than not they only found themselves under further oppression. Yet the

smaller landowners were never completely absorbed by the villa-
owners; the free peasants in the villages, registered as rural landowners,
never ceased altogether to exist. The large estates themselves consisted
of several different categories; the best land being cultivated by the
masters, the rest being made up of smaller farms worked by free
farmers (*coloni*) or 'settled' slaves (*casati*), subject to rural taxation and
subject to certain onerous working obligations and fines.

Yet the villages still retained something of their character. The
schools had not yet lost all educational value, although teaching had
degenerated into a welter of pedantry, consisting of exercises, commentaries, compilations and rhetoric. In spite of certain honourable exceptions and a few admired individuals the traditional cultural sources had
turned in another direction; glimpses of the city of God were distracting
people's attention from the terrestrial city, which was more than dis-
appointing. Art, too, was in course of transformation. Nor were art and
culture any longer the same everywhere; East and West were beginning
to evolve, each in a different direction. In the West, for the time being,
literary activities tended to be restricted to the villas, whose owners
remained faithful to their earlier education by continuing to practise
them and perfecting their correspondence. Their style, differing more
and more from that of every day, was becoming artificial, and they
could not be certain that their sons, entrusted to preceptors, would,
like themselves, retain a predilection for their ancient culture.

Beginning in the third century, this exodus to the countryside was
a real turning-point in the history of a civilization that until then had
been almost exclusively urban. If, as was the case, thousands of cities in
the Empire had modelled their political, administrative, and economic
institutions, as well as their cultural and social structures on those of
Rome, the capital had had very little influence on the countryside. From
the day when the city's leading citizens abandoned it, leaving it empty of
cadres, it was Rome's own tradition that they were giving up. By settling
down on their lands, which had become the only remaining bases of
wealth, they adopted a way of life that was completely to overthrow the
previous order of things. And it is no exaggeration to maintain that even
without the invasions— which one might rather have expected to cause
the country folk to surge back behind the protection of the city walls—
the face of civilization would still have been changed by this sole change
in values. The nobility of the Middle Ages, leading, as they did, exclusively rural lives, in fact hark back to the fourth century. Juilly was
the domain of a Julius, Savigny that of a Sabinus, Vitry of a Victor.

In the midst of these upheavals and in spite of the transferring of the capital to Constantinople (330) and the effective division of the Empire into two halves after Theodosius (395), even in such crises the idea of Rome's eternity and universality still inspired a certain number of minds filled with the tradition of her past grandeur. Nevertheless Rome, once the queen of cities, had thenceforward lost her position as such. At the beginning of the fifth century, certain poets, under the sway of a name and a myth, could, like Claudius, still write that the domination of Rome would never know any bounds, or, like Rutilius Namatianus, that the city's glory would be reborn out of her own trials, but their loyalty to a conservative point of view through which they obstinately clung to the idea of an eternal world order, only prevented them from seeing that the grandiose edifice was cracking everywhere. Only eighty-one years elapsed between the death of Theodosius and the deposition of Romulus Augustulus (476). No lengthier period was needed by the Barbarians, whose hordes had for so long been battering against the *limes*, to overrun it finally. Their booty was to be the Western Roman Empire.

THE BARBARIAN ATTACK ON THE EMPIRE

As we know, to the ancient Graeco-Roman world, the Barbarians were those who spoke an unintelligible language and who were despised because they were ignorant of the culture, customs, and ideals taught and spread by the Athenians and the Romans. At the period with which we are now concerned the term had lost some of its pejorative meaning and was used more in a geographical sense. All those who were not citizens of Rome and lived outside the boundaries of the Empire were Barbarians. It therefore included, as well as really backward peoples, certain others who nevertheless were highly civilized. China was a Barbarian country, although not altogether unknown, thanks to the Silk Road and the maritime routes of the Persian Gulf and the Black Sea. The Iranian nations were also Barbarians, in spite of the fact that they had reached a high state of development and, although antagonistic to Hellenic civilization, together with the Romans, 'one of the two eyes of the universe'. But those peoples who lived beyond or along the frontiers of the *limes* were more particularly Barbarians. *Barbaricum*, the neutral term, was used to describe these vague and indeterminate hordes, as opposed to the feminine *Romania*, which, gravitating around Rome, was clearly delimited and possessed a clearly defined organization, institutions and regulations.

Centred on the 'dangerous islands' of the Baltic and Scandinavia, the most numerous of the Barbarians were the Germanic tribes. In the

47

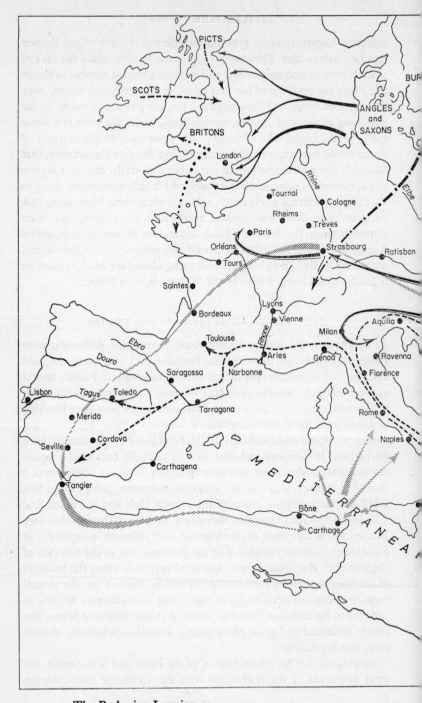

PICTS

SCOTS

BURG...

ANGLES
and
SAXONS

BRITONS

London

Tournai

Rhine

Cologne

Rheims

Trèves

Paris

Strasbourg

Ratisbon

Orléans

Tours

Elbe

Saintes

Lyons

Vienne

Milan

Aquilia

Bordeaux

Ravenna

Ebro

Toulouse

Rhône

Arles

Genoa

Douro

Saragossa

Narbonne

Florence

Tagus

Toledo

Rome

Lisbon

Merida

Tarragona

Naples

Cordova

Seville

Carthagena

Tangier

MEDITERRANEAN

Bône

Carthage

1. The Barbarian Invasion

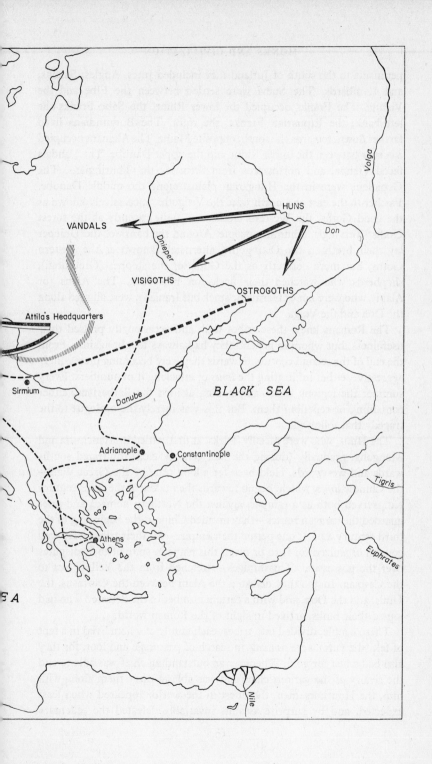

HUNS

Volga

VANDALS

Dnieper

Don

VISIGOTHS

OSTROGOTHS

Attila's Headquarters

Sirmium

Danube

BLACK SEA

Adrianople

Constantinople

Tigris

Athens

Euphrates

S A

A 5

Nile

peninsula to the south of Jutland they included Jutes, Angles, Saxons, and Lombards. The Suevi were settled between the Elbe and the Vistula. The Franks occupied the lower Rhine, the Salic Franks the left bank, the Ripuarian Franks, the right. The Burgundians lived farther down, towards the south, opposite Mainz. The Alemans occupied a corner between the upper Rhine and the upper Danube. The Vandals faced Vienna, and northwards from them lay the Thuringians. The Gepidians were in the Hungarian plains, along the middle Danube. Farther to the east and north were the Visigoths, successively known as the good Goths, the Western Goths, and quite recently as the forest Goths (Tervingi), a hunting people. Around the banks of the Dnieper lay their brethren the Ostrogoths, alternately known as the Eastern Goths, but more correctly as the Goths of the steppes (Greutungi), shepherds who watched their flocks on horseback. The Alans (or Alani), who were not of Germanic stock but Iranians, were aligned along the Don and the Volga.

The Romans knew these tribes well, and occasionally praised their usefulness, but whom in general they had always fought against. From the end of the second century onwards they were becoming increasingly aggressive, either infiltrating the *limes* or attacking it in numbers. Every summer the legions were campaigning against the Barbarians, either containing or repelling them. But this was merely the prologue to the tragedy that followed.

The Huns, who were racially Turks, at first settled in Manchuria and Mongolia, gradually (during the first century B.C.), infiltrated southwards and westwards. Held back for a long time by the Great Wall— the Chinese *limes*, which, begun towards the middle of the third century B.C., served both as a rampart against the Northern nomads and safeguarded the caravan routes—they invaded China at the beginning of the third century A.D. At one period their empire—for their tribes were well enough organized for it to be given this name in spite of their disputes over the possession of pasturages—stretched from the Yellow Sea to the Caspian. In 370 they defeated the Alani between the Caucasus, the Urals, and the Don, and with a certain number of the defeated who had joined their ranks, arrived in sight of the Roman world.

These people, divided into tribes, each family of whom lived in a tent of felt (the yurt) were nomads in search of pasturage and loot, for they also had a lust for gold. Whenever an outstanding chief was able to end the rivalry of the various clans and was able to carry them along with him, the Hun horsemen, the finest in the world, appeared when least expected, and by surprise assaults invariably defeated the sedentary peoples whom they attacked. They moved so rapidly, wrote Amminius Marcellinus, that they would leap a trench or ravage a camp before their victims had time to defend themselves. They then gathered up their loot, piled it into carts in which their wives were awaiting them, destroyed what they could not carry off, and disappeared into the steppes which they alone could traverse and the climate which no one but they could bear.

From the middle of the fourth century their activities to a large extent undermined the Germanic tribes. Between 370 and 376 they swooped down on the Ostrogoths settled to the south of Russia. A number of survivors were forcibly taken off by the victors. Others, moving towards the West, joined up with the Visigoths and with them obtained a passage into the territory of the Empire on the right bank of the Danube. All of them crossed the river in great haste and disorder, tumbling into boats and rafts, clinging to hollowed-out tree trunks and some even swimming. From that day onwards the 'Gothic poison' penetrated into the Empire. Settled for a time in Moesia on the lower Danube the newcomers soon became discontented with their lot, and were in fact so ill-treated that in exchange for slaves of their race they were given dogs to feed themselves. So the Gothic horsemen, together with Sarmatians and led by Alani chiefs, set out again, ravaging Thrace and defeating the imperial troops at Adrianople (378). Their victory, which was mainly due to the new tactics of the massive employment of cavalry, was so striking that the Emperor Theodosius entered into an alliance with these Barbarians, and by granting them the title of 'federated' troops hoped to make use in the service of the Empire of fighters whom he could not help admiring.

One of them, a young Visigoth chief called Alaric, fought loyally for Rome against other Barbarians, the Franks and Germans. But when his ambitions were frustrated he preferred to act on his own account, like the Ostrogoth Gainas, of a related race, who at one time commanded all the Eastern armies and claimed to make emperors. It was then that the Visigoths began their extraordinary trek through the 'western part' of the Empire. Alaric pillaged Greece, with the exception of Athens, which he respected, then moved northwards along the Dalmatian coast and arrived in Italy (401). He did not tire during nine years of marching and countermarching, achieving a succession of victories and only partial reverses. He appeared before Rome on two occasions, but was repelled. The third time he succeeded in entering the City and according to custom delivered it over to the soldiery during three days (410).

Thus, wearing the insignia of a Roman commander, master, first, of

51

the cavalry and subsequently of both cavalry and infantry, a Goth thus allowed himself to act towards ancient Rome, and even to take away the sister of the Emperor, Galla Placidia, among his hostages. The civilized world regarded such profanation with horror. The pagans blamed it on the Christians, who were the enemies of the Imperial gods. At Hippo St Augustine considered replying to them and raising the human soul above History by meditation on the great pages of *The City of God*. St Jerome, unable to continue his learned studies in his retreat at Bethlehem, cried out: 'My voice is choked with sobs as I dictate these words. She is conquered, the City that conquered the universe. Even more, she is dying of hunger ere she be conquered by the sword. Barely a few men are left to be led away as captives.' Sensitive and imaginative as he was, St Jerome was exaggerating the tragedy, but as regarded the facts he was expressing the feelings of the entire civilized world; never had anyone believed it possible that Rome, that since her foundation had only on one previous occasion been violated, by the Gauls, in 390, could ever again be humiliated, and by the Barbarians.

Unmoved, Alaric continued on his march until he came in sight of the Straits of Messina, whence he unsuccessfully attempted to cross into Africa. But his profanation of Rome brought him ill-luck and he died in the same year. He was buried with his treasures, his furs and his slaves, in the bed of the river Busento, which was first turned out of its course for this purpose, and then restored to it. The prisoners employed on this task were all massacred—no Roman would ever know where lay the corpse of the great *condottiere*.

His brother-in-law Athaulf, who succeeded him, returned up the whole length of the peninsula, and for some time jostled the elbows of the troops of the Emperor Honorius, after which he received permission to settle in the Narbonne district as a 'federal'. He then proceeded on his own account to seize Narbonne, Toulouse, and Bordeaux, in the most fertile districts. He was convinced that he was striving to restore Rome's greatness, and married his Roman captive, Galla Placida, the sister of Honorius, but he was assassinated in 415. The new chief, Wallia, was delegated by the Emperor to restore order in Spain, where the Vandals and Suevi were causing trouble. He then moved northwards, towards Toulouse and Bordeaux where, having also been recognized as a 'federal' chief, Rome maintained and supplied him with foodstuffs. The Visigoths, having exhausted the rich soil of Aquitania, were once more drawn towards Spain. After the deposition of Romulus Augustulus, in 476, their kingdom reached from the Loire to Gibraltar, from the ocean to the Cévennes and the Alps. The kings resided at

Toulouse. After the battle of Vouillé in 507, they were forced back, however, and only retained the Iberian peninsula and a part of the Narbonnaise.

Whilst Alaric was ravaging Italy, other tribesmen swathed in furs—Vandals, Suevi and Alani, pursued by the Huns—crossed over the Rhine, which no doubt was then frozen over, in large hordes. Penetrating through the defences manned by the Salic Franks and the Ripuarians, in the service of Rome, without striking a blow they took Mayence, Treves, Tournai, Arras, and Rheims, crossed the Loire and reached Bordeaux and the Narbonnaise. They moved with great speed along the Romans' roads which to this very day still constitute our own main roads or railway lines. The local populations fled before them, but first buried their gold, and it was the discovery of these hoards that enabled later historians to track down their route.

The march of the Vandals was also an epic achievement. Pouring down from Scandinavia, they remained for a time between the Vistula and the Oder, only to be halted later on by the Pyrenees. The tale of their atrocities went before them, and their cruelty was such that posterity, although at a much later date, coined the word 'vandalism' to describe the havoc they wrought. Compared to the other Barbarians they did not altogether deserve the bad reputation they had already acquired in the first century: 'They are fierce men, and their native savagery is reinforced by cunning and the circumstances of which they take advantage. They carry black shields, and their bodies also are blackened. They prefer to fight in the dark. The dread and horror aroused by this army of death and the darkness in which it moves inspire panic.' In the east St Jerome compared the irruption of these Barbarians to the Assyrian invasion described by Isaiah. It was generally thought that this cataclysm was the beginning of the end of the world. But it was only the end of a world.

The Vandals were followed by a second wave. Gunther and his Burgundians occupied the Rhinelands south of Mayence; the Alemans took Alsatia, the Suevi and the Alani bore down into Spain, where they were permitted to settle as 'federals' in 409. The latter were scalp-hunters, but this practice was more or less general. The Vandals gave their name to Andalusia, for the flames that had scorched Gaul now spread throughout Spain.

The Vandals, harried by the Visigoths, who exterminated them in the Emperor's name, sought to free themselves from all Imperial service and to become independent. Having learned shipbuilding and navigation—probably from deserters to their side—they occupied the Balearic

Islands, crossed the Straits of Gibraltar, skirted the North African coast, took Hippo, where in 430 St Augustine died during the siege, and arrived before Carthage; yet after these exploits they were recognized as 'federals'. In land warfare they were unlucky rather than incompetent, but they were excellent sailors, and by their raids they were able to overrun most of the Mediterranean coastal districts, threaten the Empire up to the walls of Byzantium, and to pillage Rome thoroughly, without, however, murder or incendiarism, thanks to the intervention of the bishop, Pope Leo, in 455 (*sine ferro et igne*). Their booty nevertheless included Eudoxia, wife of the Emperor Valentinian III, her two daughters, Eudoxia and Placida, and the Imperial insignia. At the height of their power the Vandals formed an independent kingdom which stretched along the coast from Oran to Tripoli, and included all the islands of the Western Mediterranean, including, at one time, Sicily. The Empire had lost its Mediterranean hegemony, and Italy her reserves of corn and oil.

The patrician, Aëtius, meanwhile, succeeded in restoring order in Gaul: Aëtius, an odd Roman, who had served in Alaric's squadrons and spent several years with the Huns, with many of whom he was on friendly terms. At this time his own troops consisted entirely of Barbarians, including Huns. Thanks to them he held back the Visigoths in the south-west of Gaul; successively defeated the Ripuarian and Salic Franks in 443; retained the Burgundians as his 'guests' in Savoy; and with the Alani repressed a peasant insurrection by the Bagaudes. Aëtius, 'the last of the Romans', for thirty years, from 424 until 454, held together the remnants of the Empire in Gaul.

Towards the middle of the fifth century it appeared likely that after so many trials the Western Empire would at last enjoy some respite. It seemed as if the Barbarians, who had gradually settled down, had at last satisfied their land-hunger, and would gradually advance towards some kind of enduring civilization. But in 451 the peoples were again terrified by hordes of Huns.

After having caused tremendous upheavals among the local populations, they were now settled in the plains of the Theiss, in Hungary, when in their turn they planned to push further forward towards the West. They also had lost something of their original primitive savagery through contact with Rome, and often enlisted in her service. Like the rest these nomads, people of the plains and the winds, had to some extent adapted themselves to sedentary living. They no longer spent their entire lives on horseback. In many cases their felt tents had been exchanged for wooden huts. In the Hungarian plain, between the Theiss and the Körös, their king, Attila, 'the greatest of the gods', had founded a kind of capital, where he lived surrounded by a court that endeavoured to ape the refinements of civilization. He himself had retained his simple way of life, dressing casually and eating out of wooden bowls. But his relatives were richly apparelled, their weapons encrusted with gold and jewels, and they had a predilection for carpets of wool. At public feasts and banquets their couches were sumptuously adorned, their vessels of gold, and the finest wines were drunk. Attila was above all a diplomat; he kept up relations with Ravenna and Constantinople; received tribute from the Empire, and bore the title of Master of the Militia. He knew how to assert himself, and even went so far as to demand that Honoria, the Emperor's sister and grand-daughter of the great Theodosius, who had placed herself under his protection, should not only become his wife, but as dowry should bestow upon him half of the Empire. His kingdom formed a vast rectangle between the Alps and the Don, and its southern part crossed the Danube as far as Niš. Within this area the conquerors, although they were the minority, ruled over the Germanic populations attached to the soil. The languages spoken there were Hunnic, Gothic and Latin. When Attila died in 453, his Empire disintegrated into fragments held by 'an army of descendants'. His own descendants were the Bulgarians. The Avars, who were Turks, succeeded him in Central Europe in the middle of the sixth century.

For the time being, however, the Huns terrorized the world. Attila, humiliated by the setbacks to his matrimonial plans, was resolved to annihilate the Visigoths of Aquitania, whom he claimed the right to punish as fugitive slaves. Under the pretext of a delay in their payment of tribute he hurled his hordes into Gaul. Their numbers increased by Germans, they swooped on Metz, Rheims, and Troyes. They avoided Paris, which would have held up their charge, and arrived before Orleans, the gate to Visigothic Gaul. There the bishop, Ainianus, played for time. The arrival of Aëtius and the Visigoths drove the Huns from the city as they were about to enter it. Attila retreated towards Troyes. Near this city, an indecisive battle was fought at the Campus Mauriacus, which enabled him to resume his march towards Pannonia, followed at a distance by the 'Roman' armies.

But the Barbarian chieftain had not abandoned his dreams. He decided once again to attack the West, this time through Italy. In 452 Aquilea, the gate to the peninsula, fell to him. Its inhabitants fled to the Adriatic lagoons, where the island of Rivo Alto (Rialto) was later to become Venice. Milan and Pavia fell in turn. The road to Rome lay open to him, when a delegation, that included Pope Leo, arrived near to

Mantua to treat with the Hun. At the price of gold and the promise—which was never kept—of Honoria's hand, he agreed to evacuate Italy, and the Western world was rid of the nightmare of the Huns.

Nevertheless, stability was not yet achieved. The Franks, whom the Romans had themselves in the past settled on the banks of the Rhine, in Toxandria, were restless. The Alamanni were gaining ground towards the north, and the Burgundians, especially, were widening their domains around Savoy. Along almost the whole course of the Rhône, between Italy, Gaul, and Germania, they were in occupation of a central position which was of great importance in the mutual relations of these countries. Italy, meanwhile, was delivered over to the intrigues of the Court of Ravenna. Ricimer, a German, was in power behind a succession of emperors whom he raised up or overthrew according to his whim. A little later the Imperial rule was suppressed in the West by Odoacer. Finally, in 489, Theodoric marched into Italy with his Ostrogoths, seized Ravenna and ruled the peninsula in the name of the Emperor Zeno, who could find no other way to get rid of him.

The young chief of the Salic Franks in Gaul, in the region of Tournai, called Chlodovech or Clovis, lacked neither intelligence, ambition, nor courage. He hated the Romans, whose subjects his ancestors had been in the past, and began by suppressing what remained of the nominal power of the Empire, represented in 486 by Syagrius, between the Somme, the Moselle, and the Loire. He then occupied nearly all the lands of the Alamanni to the east, in Alsatia, the Palatinate, and the right bank of the Rhine. In 507, allied to the Burgundians, whom he was unable to overthrow, he destroyed the Visigoth armies south of the Loire, in the battle of Vouillé. When he died in 511, his kingdom extended from the Rhine, and a long way beyond it on the right bank, to the Pyrenees. The capital of this new kingdom was Paris.

The insular Britons, who had only been very superficially romanized, and were also invaded, very soon forgot the Latin language. The Anglo-Saxon Barbarians, descending from Jutland, succeeded with some difficulty in founding small kingdoms all hostile to one another, and at the time of their conquest in the fifth century, what was later called the heptarchy consisted of far more than seven little kinglets. A real kingdom was not founded there until the ninth century. For it was in fact there, owing to the obstinate resistance of the natives, that the Germanic cadres were the strongest and best preserved, with their hierarchy of an ancient and aristocratic warrior caste, a new administrative aristocracy, free peasants, and slaves.

The Western Empire had ceased to exist. Instead, the Barbarians, having completed their conquests, gradually transformed their possessions into national entities.

THE 'NATIONS' WITHIN THEIR FRONTIERS

Under Theodoric Italy enjoyed a period of peace such as she had not known for a long time. Whilst his Goths formed the soldiery that protected the kingdom, he very intelligently left the administration of the State to the Romans. All the ancient institutions, including even the Senate, were preserved. He had spent part of his youth as a hostage in Byzantium, and in Ravenna he modelled his court on its example; drawing into it the chief administrators, distinguished intellectuals, and the notables of the Roman and Barbarian worlds. The king organized games, drained the marshes of Ravenna, cleansed the Roman campagna, and in his capital raised monuments that were comparable to those of Constantinople. He very cleverly came to terms with the Barbarian chieftains that ensured power and stability to his throne and prosperity to his subjects. Under his reign Italy was reborn. As the Goths, mostly segregated in the north, had their own quarters and churches and retained their laws and customs there, the occupation did not weigh too heavily on the country. Many Romans were won over by the liberal rule of the Barbarian, and he himself knew how to make use of those who believed in reconciliation between Goths and Romans; the question of fusion did not yet arise. Of all the Barbarians now settled in the Empire, Theodoric was the most famous.

Amongst the Visigoths, who since the battle of Vouillé were restricted to Spain itself, and the Vandals of North Africa, the other Barbarian nations were also organizing themselves. Actually, the Visigoths still had to battle against the Suevi of the north-east until they absorbed them, around 585. And the Vandals, forced constantly into fighting the mountaineers of the Aures, were only able to occupy Tunisia itself in depth. But there, as elsewhere, thanks to the old administrative cadres which the conquerors had not replaced, stability was gradually established. The kings had 'Roman' courts, where the rules of hierarchy were observed. There the old Romans met leaders of the occupation, who like themselves had become landed proprietors. Literature and the arts were encouraged, although politics did not flag. The Barbarians still held on to their own laws, but in spite of juridical differences the time was approaching when fusion would occur through intermarriage. And thus, in spite of many trials, a certain degree of civilization was enabled to survive.

In the valley of the Rhône the Kingdom of Burgundy also knew the beginnings of prosperity. At the end of the fifth century, King Gondebaud, allied to the Empire, enjoyed a well-earned reputation for liberalism, and although observing separate laws and customs, the occupying powers and the inhabitants were on fairly good terms. But for a long time their neighbours, the Franks, had been scheming to destroy this great enclave which prevented them from having any direct access to Italy. Sigismond, Gondebaud's heir, was unable to resist the coalition of the Ostrogoths, who attacked him from the south, and the sons of Clovis, who quite simply suppressed the Kingdom of Burgundy, and by taking Marseilles in 536 and thus giving themselves an outlet on the Mediterranean, came best out of the business.

For the time being the Franks, the least civilized of the Barbarians, were everywhere the stronger. Even although they were 'federals' they clung more tenaciously than any of the other tribes to their ancestral ways. The king was above all else a warrior chief, an absolute monarch, master of all he conquered, and distributed at his own will. In the lands he overran, he found an administrative machine ready to hand and retained it, especially when it brought him in taxes, which he collected for his own benefit. Thus the *res publica*, which even in the Empire's darkest hours was regarded as common property, now became *res privata*, to the sole benefit of one individual. This changeover from the service of the State to that of only one individual was symptomatic of the profound changes that had occurred in the State, and was to be followed by a rupture leading to a very serious decline in morality, and in social and economic conditions.

The Barbarians had transformed the Western world, yet for many of them Rome, although in decay, was still a power that counted. Most of their chieftains had in their youth been soldiers of the Empire, and so long as they were well treated, served it well. They were still as it were fascinated by the prestige of Rome, and proud to have become part of her system. By entrusting them as 'federals' with the defence of Rome, and by recognizing their occupation of territories that could not be defended against them, the Emperors thought to entrust to them some responsibilities for maintaining the Imperial system. Of this the Barbarians were well aware. Taking into account the occasions for playing at politics that this system provided, their mutual relationships, although difficulties often arose, were sometimes quite friendly ones. Thus the Vandal chief, Stilicon, married Serena, the niece of the Emperor Theodosius. Whilst working towards his own ends the Ostrogoth Theodoric was never in doubt that he was serving the glory of Rome. He wrote to the Emperor that he was 'his servant and his son', and that his reign was 'an imitation of the Imperial reign, example of the one and only, the unique Empire'. The Emperor's portrait was stamped on his coinage. The Visigoth Alaric first served under Theodosius, who thought highly of him, and he was later to be honoured with resounding military titles. After the indecisive battle of the Campus Mauriacus, the title of 'Saviour of the Western State' (*occidentalis Reipublicae salus*) was bestowed on Aëtius, the Illyrian. Whether he meant it or not, Sigismund, King of the Burgundians, wrote to the Emperor Anastasius: 'My people belong to you. When I command them, I obey you, and I have more pleasure in obeying you than in commanding them. To them I am a king, but in fact I am only your soldier.' Attila himself provided the Empire with mercenaries. All these chieftains were filled with ambition, but they only became a source of danger owing to the impotence of those who, failing to subjugate or control them, only required that they help them to survive.

However powerful, ambitious, and independent these tiresome servants may have been, not one of them ever aspired to the purple. From 456 to 472 the Suevian, Ricimer, made emperors at his will, but never attempted to usurp the position himself. When Odoacer, a Romanized Pannonian, who was Attila's former secretary, master of the militia, and king of the Scyrri, decided that there should no longer be a Western emperor, he did not himself ascend the vacant throne, but made a parcel of the Imperial insignia and despatched it to the Emperor of Constantinople. This could have been a gesture of contempt. Perhaps, too, the Scyrrian, convinced as everyone then was of the universality of the Empire, by doing so recognized that if there could no longer be a co-Emperor in Ravenna, Italy must nevertheless still be governed in the name of the Emperor of Byzantium, the one and only true master of the civilized world. Clovis despised the Empire. Yet even he regarded the bestowal on him of the title of consul by the Emperor Anastasius as increasing his prestige amongst his own people. Anything connected with the Emperor induced respect.

It is clear that the establishment of the Germans in the West caused confusion and anguish. Even if one must allow for eloquence and imagination in the accounts of it by contemporary eye-witnesses, the fact remained that when the Barbarians captured a city, even when respecting its churches, it was given over to appalling pillage. At that period this was everywhere—not excepting amongst the Romans themselves—the traditional prize awarded to the soldiery. But the Barbarians looted so many places and so often that their descents took on the proportions of a universal catastrophe. At the slightest sound the local populations would flee along the roads in a streaming procession, which the pursuing cavalry soon overtook. The rich endeavoured to reach their properties in the south, hoping them to be out of range. They buried their gold, and its recent discovery proves that no one returned to dig it up again. Those who remained generally lived on in misery and humiliation. Elsewhere the refugees, a pitiful sight on arrival, and in consequence spontaneously given assistance, became more and more demanding, and having nothing more to lose loudly proclaimed their own indifference to the disastrous situation. They adored the Carthaginian spectacles and shocked the inhabitants. Some of them, who were more simple-minded, were shamelessly exploited by those who always know how to take advantage of the misfortunes of others. Pagans and Christians mutually blamed one another for the general collapse.

If one were to believe the contemporary accounts one might imagine that a tidal wave had swept over the Western world. But in fact the situation was a very different one. In Gaul, for instance, the Barbarians had only occupied one-seventh of the entire country, i.e. many of the Gauls had probably never set eyes on a Barbarian. And in the other countries it was more or less the same. Regarding the numbers of those who occupied them it is necessary to discount figures swollen by the fears or the imaginations of those who gave them. Present-day historians have brought them down to a more reasonable estimate. It is considered that around 10,000 Goths conquered Adrianople in 378. At the battle of the Campus Mauriacus the Huns were probably not much more numerous, and did not amount to 500,000, as claimed by the Gothic historian Jordanus, and those who followed his reckoning. The Burgundians probably numbered no more than 25,000, of whom only a few thousand would have been fighters. When the Vandals crossed into Africa there were about 80,000 of them, including slaves, which would give around 15,000 soldiers. When they entered Italy Alaric's Visigoths counted probably more than 100,000, of whom 20,000 to 25,000 may have been men-at-arms. At the time of the final battles against Byzantium the Ostrogoths had been reduced to only 7,000 men, plus a few garrisons. The Franks, Salics and Ripuarians, were reckoned at 100,000 to 150,000. This would have amounted to about 30,000 warriors, but in fact far fewer if one subtracts the 3,000 who, baptized at the same time as Clovis, were said to have conquered Gaul, the larger part of the population having remained in the region of Tournai. Clovis, certainly, never disposed of any but small forces.

Their languages, religion and laws separated these minorities from those they conquered. Their kings were absolute rulers, both in peace and war. The freemen were attached to him by personal bonds that were the precursers of feudal customs. The duty of the family, completely under the control of its head, was above all to produce warriors. If a man between the ages of twenty and fifty was murdered, the fine imposed for his killing was 300 gold sous, a considerable sum; but the nation was in that case deprived of a combatant. If the victim had reached the age of sixty-five, at which he was no longer fighting fit, the fine was only 100 sous—the same rate as for a middle-aged Roman. The articles of the same legal code also stated that the loss of the second finger, which pulled the bow, was valued at 35 sous, but the fine imposed 'if someone was hit on the head in such a manner that the brains burst through and the three bones covering them were laid bare', was only 30 sous. This was the *Wergeld*, or a man's price, the aim of which was to suppress the habit of personal revenge or vendetta, as the result of personal enmities between families.

At first all the conquerors lived beside but not with the original populations. The Barbarians, most of whom had been accepted as 'federals', were entrusted with the defence of the sector to which they had been assigned. In return, similarly to the civilian officials and the soldiers of the Empire, they received a 'billet-paper' entitling them to lodgings with the local inhabitants and to victuals drawn from the official stores. They were housed far away from the towns, in cantonments provided for them by the local landowners. But they did not long remain there and soon found means of obtaining a greater degree of hospitality. They then had the right to occupy a third—which often became a half or even two-thirds—of the estate, side by side with the staff, the tenants, and the slaves. All the landowners were not burdened with the duty of providing such 'hospitality', but whenever they were, there was nearly always trouble with their 'furry' neighbours, who in such cases were more often than not simply turned out. Only a certain number of peasants and slaves declared themselves satisfied by the changeover; for new masters are sometimes less demanding than old ones.

Nevertheless, by ensuring a reserve supply of troops and attaching these restless foreigners to the soil, the whole system of 'hospitality' did reduce destruction and damage to a considerable degree. It also encouraged the settlement in the Roman world of Barbarian tribes who, as they gradually lost their nomadic habits and fell under the spell of civilization, were only too pleased to remain sedentary and gradually to become integrated in it. It is, however, true, that most of them very quickly came to regard this so-called hospitality in the Empire's service as a mere fiction and made themselves independent of all obligations in return for it.

The force of circumstances inevitably drew them closer to the local inhabitants. The clearest evidence of this was linguistic. Nearly everywhere, in the courts and administration especially, the conquerors adopted the language of the conquered. Only 300 Germanic words are incorporated in Latin. Onomastically, the prefix Alan is the name of the Iranian tribe settled in the Orleans region. There is an Allaines in the Eure-et-Loire. Sermaize, in the Marne, designates a cantonment of Iranian Sarmatians. Gourville in Charante was originally a property (villa) occupied by a 'guest' or Goth. Courtabon was that (*curtis*) of an Abbon, Bettencourt that of a Betton, Hermonville that of an Herimond. Around Rheims, on the *Chemin de Barbarie*, one finds Sarmatian settlements at Sermiers, Goths at Gueux, Burgundians in Burgundy, Franks at Villers-Franqueux. Again, in the Marne and also in the Aisne, Fère and La Fère derive from the Germanic *fara*, meaning family, clan, domain. Houdan, Dourdan and Gazeran are Frankish. These vestigial Frankish names are particularly numerous around Paris.

As we have seen, all civilization and even all court life were by no means abolished by the Barbarians. In spite of the scarcity of gold the same was true of commerce; the Syrians and Jewish merchants, and the pilgrims, still travelled the ancient Roman roads. Anglo-Saxon slaves were much in demand in Byzantium. In spite of Vandal piracy the Mediterranean was never closed. Although they became less frequent and more haphazard exchanges still continued.

In spite of the respect in which it was held by the Ostrogoth Theodoric in Ravenna, the Visigoth Athanalgild in Toledo, and the Vandal Thrasamond in Carthage, intellectual activity suffered more severely. Only in the world of art did a certain vigorous degree of invention exist. But such art was chiefly metallurgical and in the main consisted of polychrome jewellery and stylized ornaments, based on the figures of animals. It was probably on the one hand inspired at a distance by Celtic influences, and on the other, certainly, the far more important influences of the Iranians and the tribes of the steppes. In Gaul the construction and decoration of the churches, in Spain, the ironwork architecture, which was not of Moorish origin, and in Britain works in bone, gold, and miniatures, owed something to Barbarian influences.

THE CHURCH AT THE HEAD OF A NEW ORDER

During the periods of invasion and occupation the basic problem confronting churchmen was whether, as they survived it, they could preserve in face of the Barbarians something of the system which they almost alone continued to represent?

The Church had incorporated itself into the Roman system as soon as the number of its adherents became large enough for it to become organized. The seats of the more important ecclesiastical centres were gradually founded in the former cities of the Imperial administration. Inside the town walls were the churches, the baptisteries, and the clergy houses. Under the rule of its religious head, with his staff and administration, the city became a centre of Christianity, and, as well, a kernel of civilization. The heads, having received a Latin education, remained faithful to the traditional culture. Ambrosius, Augustine, Pope Leo and, to mention less important figures, Paulinus of Nola, Avitius of Vienne, knew how much they owed to Cicero and Virgil. In the midst of the tumult he was witnessing, Sidonius Apollinarius even declared that 'the only mark of nobility that remains is literacy'. Face to face with the Barbarians the prime necessity, therefore, was to preserve as far as possible the institutional, legal and cultural heritage to which the bishops owed so much, and which was to benefit their religion.

Circumstances gave the churchmen the opportunity to take the lead in municipal life. The secular leaders, on giving up their town residences, deserted from the responsibilities that lay on them. There remained no longer anyone in the old cities except magistrates whose powers were ineffective and civil servants discredited by the very nature of their calling. Among this group, in 375, the treasury agents had become so generally hated that Valentinian I was obliged to create a special corps whose task it was to redress on behalf of the exploited the abuses committed by these extortioners who could not be suppressed because only they provided the funds needed by the treasury. These new officials, given the title of 'defenders of the city' (*defensores civitatis*), very quickly became influential personages. Thus a certain number of bishops became *defensores civitatis*, either by collaborating with those who held this title or by themselves of necessity assuming it. The first bishop of Angers was referred to as Defensor. The chronicler who noted the fact, in his ignorance assumed that this was his name, when actually it was only his appellation. But this confusion is significant of the fact that the bishop's own name was dropped and that of his office substituted for it. Later on the word took on a wider meaning. When the Barbarians arrived at the gates of a city from which either all its inhabitants and officials had fled, or which had become disorganized owing to the temporary influx of refugees, they were often met by a bishop who having taken the interests of his city in hand, became its 'defender,' not as regarded fiscal matters but in order to save the lives or property of the citizens. Thus his powers were widened to include the most varied activities, and he even dispensed justice. If the Barbarians were 'federated' it was he who provided their cantonments, their upkeep, and their pay. If they were the enemies of Rome he would endeavour to negotiate with them, and if he were unable to turn them away, to limit their depredations. For better or worse, the bishop, head of the city, was the preserver of the remaining Imperial institutions and, in any event, the protector of the population.

Everywhere the pastors set an example in their sermons and lived up to their responsibilities. Many declared themselves against the Huns. Ananius of Orleans urged his flock on to the ramparts and went to Arles to beg Aëtius to send troops to the rescue. Whilst in Paris Geneviève quelled the panicking population whilst those same Huns, in a hurry to reach Orleans, by-passed it; in Turin Maximus was the soul of the resistance to the hordes of Attila. And when the dreaded Barbarians were threatening to march on Rome, one of the most important members of the delegation charged to treat with them, near Mantua, was Pope Leo, bishop of Rome. In order to ransom the prisoners, Caesarius of Arles, who was an ally of Theodoric, sold his sacred vessels and even the presents he had received from the Ostrogoth chief. All of them, more or less, in one way or another, realized that in saving souls, lives, and property, they were accomplishing deeds that were not only humanitarian but religious, patriotic, and civilizing. It was their initiative that saved what still could be saved of Rome at that period.

Once the country had been conquered, they had another problem to solve. Catholicism having been saved, would it be possible to conquer the conquerors by inducing them to join the true religion and civilization?

This question, a tricky one enough, was complicated in a rather singular way. When the Germans arrived, most of them were Christians who were facing Christians. Some of them had become converted as early as the third century, but most of them had been so by the Arian heresy.

Their apostle was a German, the Goth Ulfila (d. 383) who was

64

4. CHURCH OF THE MONASTERY OF KALAAT-SEMAAN (SYRIA). Built c.480 around the column on which St Simeon lived for thirty years.

(Photo: J. L. Colas)

5. ST AUGUSTINE SHOWING THE PSALMS. Initial from a MS in the Bibl. de Tours. (Photo: Archives Phot.)

consecrated as an Arian bishop by Eusebius of Nicodemus. Arianism, a Platonic interpretation of the doctrine of the Trinity, was condemned by the Council of Nicea in 325, but for a long time afterwards held sway in many parts of the Empire and as far as Gaul. It held that Christ, one of God's creatures and half divine, half human, was of other than divine origin. Thus Ulfila held that alone God the Father, uncreated, was the only 'God above' and that the other two Persons of the Trinity were inferior to Him. Ulfila, a cultured man, who spoke Gothic, Greek and Latin, translated a great part of the Bible into Gothic and also celebrated the liturgy in that language, and thus to some extent introduced Christian civilization to his compatriots. The simplicity of his doctrines, freed from all subtleties, held no mystery for unsubtle minds to grapple with, and so, thanks to Ulfila, Arianism having taken root in the lower Danube region, spread from there to all the neighbouring tribes. One after the other the Visigoths, Ostrogoths, Gepidae, Alans, Vandals, Ruges, Alamanni, Thuringians and Lombards went over from paganism to Arianism. And similarly to the orthodox Christians the Arians believed in the Bible, recognized the same hierarchy and practised the same rites. Belief in the Trinity was the only difference between them. This intrinsic difference would have been enough to set these two religious groups against one another, but their mutual antagonism was still further reinforced by nationalist antagonisms which were irreconcilable. Thus the two camps—Romanism and Catholicism, Barbarism and Arianism—opposed one another almost instinctively.

Many among the Catholics who had suffered from the Barbarians were strongly inclined to let them remain in a state of sin. No doubt Sidonius Apollinarius, when he wrote that 'you may shun the Barbarians because they are said to be wicked, but I shun them even if they are said to be good', was expressing the feelings of many of his fellows. Others, however, who above all were seeking to come to terms with them, found that the invaders possessed certain qualities that, to say the least, were surprising. St Augustine's friend Orosius regarded their descent as a well-deserved punishment, and thought that their innate qualities offered good ground for the work of Evangelization. Salvinus, a priest of Marseilles, went even further, claiming that the Barbarians offered the Romans, i.e. the Christians, an example worth imitating; for if their vices differed little from those of the Romans, their virtues were more obvious. Rising above the controversy, St Augustine was to formulate the great solution that was to win through. Although owing so much to Rome, he did not confuse the future of religion with that of the Empire.

In his view the City of God was far above the cities built by man. 'Its call reaches out to the citizens of all nations . . . it does not seek to know whether or not they possess different customs, laws, or institutions. It seeks to abolish nothing, nor to destroy existing practices, but even to preserve them and retain everything that, although differing amongst the different nations, is aimed at one and the same end, peace on earth.' These were the prophetic words of a farseeing mind and an authentically Christian genius. Christianity, being universal, i.e. catholic, is tied to no particular kind of human organization, and if it is temporally linked to one or another, this is only in order that it may ultimately transcend it.

And apart from doctrine, the churchmen very quickly came to accept the facts before them. Knowing that their own flocks were more numerous than the Barbarians, and would not, therefore, be absorbed by the occupying forces, they constantly asked themselves how they could bring the Arian masses into the Catholic fold. The answer was not a simple one. In the long run the intermingling of the Teutons with the local populations would inevitably occur, but as regarded the actual religious fusion, the outcome was uncertain, since mixed marriages were merely a compromise in which both parties generally lost something. It was true that the conversion of the chiefs would lead to that of their subjects. But in the minds of the chiefs, particularly, Arianism was not merely a matter of religion; it was also a form and source of nationalism, which it was their duty to nourish and provoke. And the bishops realized that the prejudices inherent in such nationalism would be as difficult to break down as those of Ulfila's faith. They set about it, nevertheless. Yet the pagans, who had fewer basic values to cling to, offered an easier field for their labours. If the heads of the Church did not explicitly see the problem from this point of view, events in Gaul certainly developed as if they had done so.

For there these pagans were, and—a far from negligible point—they were everywhere victorious. And by approaching them the Church was to achieve its most striking success in the Barbarian world.

For some time the Silesian Franks had been in the forefront of the pagan Teutons. Sidonius Apollinarius left us a striking description of them: 'Their fair hair falls over their foreheads. . . . Their eyes are green and white, their pupils glassy, their faces are completely shaven. Their beards consist of little combed-out tufts. The limbs of their warriors are long, encased in close-fitting garments.' In warfare, which was their delight, they threw their spears and battle-axes—shaped like a shoulder-blade (the *francaise*)—with unerring aim, twirled their shields and fell on the enemy as fast as their arrows. After being beaten by Aëtius, their infantry—for alone among the Teutons they were not a race of horsemen—took service under the Empire. They were cruel, 'savages of a wild and stupid nature', but occasionally their leaders behaved as decently towards the local populations as might be hoped for from Barbarians. They were considered preferable to the Visigoths. It is understandable that having begun by ravaging the north of Gaul they came to respect religion. When, after having destroyed the last Roman army at Soissons (486) young Clovis came into contact with the Bishop of Rheims, Remi, the latter, farsighted and wise, advised him to win over the bishops. The Frank, also persuaded by his wife Clothilde, who was a Burgundian Catholic, thought well of it. The Ripuarians having been defeated Clovis went to their aid with the Silesians, and gained a victory on a battlefield that possibly was not Zülpich (Tolbiac). According to tradition, it was Clothilde's God, invoked just in time, who helped him to it. This success, by which the God of Remi became the God of the conquerors, confirmed the young king in a plan that was favoured by circumstances. Clovis, who was intelligent, realized that his conversion to Catholicism—which was not necessarily insincere—would place him in a position that the other Barbarian chieftains, committed to Arian nationalism, would be unable to achieve. Thus, encouraged by Clothilde, advised and gladly received by Remi, he was baptized at Rheims on a Christmas Day, probably in 506. It was claimed that three thousand of his men followed his example.

From the political point of view his baptism had a decisive result. Supported by the bishops and congratulated by the Emperor of Byzantium—who sent him the consular insignia consisting of the purple tunic, the Chlamys and the diadem, the 'new Constantine', thanks to the Church, was able now to fulfill his ambitions with regard to Gaul. Compared with those of his rivals, the Visigoths and the Burgundians, his forces were small, but backed by moral prestige, and his campaigns, nearly all of which were victorious, were regarded as providential. This young chieftain was trustworthy. One by one, hostile barriers disappeared. Not only the gates of the cities were opened to him, but also those of the treasuries and Imperial possessions. Better still, the collaboration between the Catholics and the Barbarians, which from that moment took place without mental reservation on either side, had nothing more to fear, and could now await the complete fusion that would in due course ensue between the local inhabitants and the conquering tribes. And the Church, its prestige enhanced by this victory over a tribe that was until then farthest from religion and the least influenced by civilization, had proved that it alone was strong enough to absorb the whole of the Barbarian world.

In this connection it is inaccurate to maintain, as has been done, that failing the baptism of Clovis a large part of the Western world would have remained of the Arian faith. The Arian church was a minority, deliberately set apart by its chiefs, its laws and customs. It never sought actively to impose itself on others, whereas, for its part, the Catholic Church was daily conquering new ground. The Vandals, the only tribes that actively persecuted the Catholics, were never able to destroy the orthodoxy of Nicea. If the Arians in Ostrogothic Italy had continued in power, they would finally have had to emerge from their isolation, and in order to do so would have had to amalgamate with external forces and by doing so enter into contact with the Catholic church. This is what actually happened in Visigothic Spain, in Burgundy, and later in Italy with the Lombards. Even without Clovis the Western world would not have become Arian. The conversion of the Suevi of Galicia and Lusitania in the middle of the fifth century, e.g. before that of the Franks, would be enough to prove this. Clovis's baptism merely accelerated the general process.

Thus, whilst the ruins of the Empire were still smouldering, a new world was gradually emerging. Although there was still much confusion the game was won. Imperial Rome was dead. In its place were young nations with their future before them, installed within natural frontiers. Pagan Rome was dead, also, and was to be succeeded by Christian Rome. From a material point of view, the City was so exhausted as to have become insignificant, but gradually and with much travail, its spirit was preserved, transformed, broadened by the Church, and survived in a new form. After having endured the long tempest without losing any of its essentials, the Church conquered and knew that a new and immense field lay before it. By baptizing the Barbarians the bishops would one day bring them into the orbit of civilization.

But in this respect they were still a long way from their ends. Their new tasks were too many and too urgent to allow them to be, as well as evangelists and organizers, the mainstay of culture. The world with which they were dealing still from time to time passed through periods of anarchy as bad as the worst moments of the invasions. Even the baptized Franks were far from being true Christians. Greater Barbarians than any of the other Aryans, even the Vandals, they were the first to put to the test the budding civilization that might have been hoped to flower as the result of their conversion, and to bring to the brink of ruin all that until then had been saved. Even the churchmen themselves did not all escape the contagion surrounding them. In the midst of such confusion the monks were called upon to play the leading part in the maintenance and spread of religion and the safeguarding and transformation of civilization.

CHAPTER III

THE EPIC OF THE DESERT

When the monastic orders first originated, there was no indication that they were destined to become the saviours of a civilization and the preservers of its monuments. When, towards the end of the third and the beginning of the fourth centuries, certain Christians felt the call to put into practice a sentence from the Gospels (Mark x. 21) on the perfect life, they left the world for the desert partly as a gesture of denial. Their civilization, entirely directed towards human aggrandisement, presided over by an insensible pantheon without moral uplift, or, at best exemplified by philosophers whose conduct bore little evidence of their precepts, even in such brilliant examples as Athens and Rome, only in the end led to vice, pride, and domination. It was inimical to the Gospel, and the faithful were cruelly persecuted.

Even among the Christians there were a certain number who were imbued with the doctrines of pagan philosophy. They attempted to combine the teachings of Plato with the truths of religion, and even when they escaped the Gnostic heresy they formed within the Church itself a class of privileged initiates apart from the mass of the faithful; or else gave an intellectual interpretation to the articles of faith which bore little evidence of the original simplicity of Christ's teachings.

It was necessary to show contempt for the spurious gifts of the pagans and to prove to the philosophers that their niggling 'autarchy' was a mere mockery of true philosophy, by leading an heroic life as an example of a wholly new spirit. To those Christians seduced by profane literature it would be shown that those who would genuinely follow the Gospels were not to be won over by professorial chairs or librarianships. The teachings of Platonic universities were not to be trusted, and would be opposed by those of the desert school, which had proved itself by long experience. By ruthlessly rejecting all physical and mental indulgences the gauntlet was to be thrown down by those who, far from the corruption of cities, would practise complete poverty and pitiless asceticism, complete charity and genuine contemplation, in imitation of Christ, who had preached segregation from worldly affairs and inspired the remorseless search for the spiritual life. By doing so an implacable war, such as he had never yet known, would be launched against the devil. Persecution could be escaped in the desert, but if one day it were to cease in the Church of God, it would be replaced by mortification to such a degree that this would be equivalent to a whole life of martyrdom, and thus would rank with the blood heroically shed by others, by its severity, constancy, and duration. Finally, if in times of peace that same Church were to run the risk of losing its standards as its adherents became more numerous, richer, and more powerful, a new generation of witnesses would arise to remind the world of the great lessons taught by the pure Gospel.

It is a marvellous story. Somewhere in Egypt, in a palm-grove, near a grotto, perhaps, or in the stony sand dunes of the desert, we may watch a procession of giants, who frighten us a little, of animals, the tame ones, even although dumb, seeming to have escaped from Aesop's garden, and the wild ones, roaring and snarling, vomited up by the infernal regions. There are sinners, saints, angels, devils, miracles by the dozen, and quite simple stories. Faced with these, in which the most extraordinary events are of daily occurrence, our own minds, trained to investigation and sceptical by preference, boggle. We are enchanted by the *Golden Legend*, but do not take it too seriously. But the epic of the desert is a very different matter. That it is partly fictional is indubitable; but behind the screen of romanticism we feel an authentic reality at which we can only guess, an echo, possibly, or examples, from a way of life that, were we ourselves of the race of heroes, we might still follow today. In this sense these stories of the monks carry far more weight and worth than the least unlikely tales of the *Golden Legend*. It would be absurd to take them all literally, but to rebut them altogether would make it impossible to understand anything of them at all. Even the extraordinary is not so very extraordinary. Anyone who, at Mount Athos or elsewhere, has known something of the Eastern monks, and has witnessed what a degree of abnegation, endurance and lucidity they can attain by methodical and rigorous exercises, would be much less likely to doubt the achievements of our saints. If we wish to understand their behaviour, perhaps the best thing would be to endeavour to divest ourselves of all prejudice and to accept them as they were. This was the approach to them of the austere Gentlemen of Port-Royal, who, whilst deploring their own inability to live up to them, delighted in them. So let us do the same, on their recommendation.

THE PIONEERS OF ASCETISM

The proper definition of the word 'monk' is a man by himself (from the Greek, *monos*). But the term was very soon used in a generic sense to describe all those called upon to live, for one reason or another, out of contact with the world. The solitaries were indiscriminately known as hermits (*eremos*, solitude, desert), or anchorites (*anachoresis*, retreat) When assembled into communities the monks were known as cenobites (*koinon*, common). The ascetic was the monk, whether an anchorite or a cenobite, who trained himself to carry out his vocation (*askesis*, exercise).

Etymologically, therefore, a monastery was the dwelling of one individual, living in isolation. It was only later that the word took on the meaning of a number of buildings that harboured a group. After a certain period of vagueness in the use of the term the primitive monastery, in fact a hut or a grotto, was called a cell (*kellion*).

The first great anchorite was a certain Paul. An earnest and gentle youth, learned in Greek and Egyptian, e.g. Coptic, at that time, he had a comfortable inheritance. He was anxious to flee both from persecution and family troubles, and in the distant region of Thebes he discovered a mountain, a cave, a palm-tree and a spring, all that was needed for living alone in sanctity. There he lived for 113 years, clothed in the leaves of his palm-tree, and for sixty years he was fed by a crow, that every day punctually brought him half a loaf of bread, which together with the fruits of his tree was quite enough nourishment for an anchorite in heroic times. Paul, living far away as he did from commerce with evil men, was in fact able to make friends with the animals. When he died in 347, two lions arrived, with flying manes, and crouching beside his corpse, endeavoured to revive it by sweeping their tails over it, making their funereal moans in loud howlings. Finally, with their claws they dug their friend's grave, and having accomplished these duties craved his blessing from a solitary man passing that way, who, having paid a first visit to the anchorite, on his second found only a corpse. They licked his hands and feet, wiggled their ears, and having obtained their wish, disappeared into the sands.

This visitor, who himself was a monk of some renown, had for a long time sought out the hermit's refuge. Anthony was then more than eighty years old. More than seventy years previously, in Middle Egypt, south of Memphis, he had abandoned the 300 measures of good fertile land that were his heritage, given his possessions to the poor, and gone away to lead a solitary life. With no interest in literature, unable to read either Greek or Coptic, he remained all his life an ignoramus according to worldly standards, but was to penetrate deeply into understanding of the Scriptures. During fifteen years he lived in a tomb, in contact with an experienced teacher, and thus learned his doctrine. He then crossed the Nile and settled near a spring, in the ruins of a small fort. He spent another twenty years in the terrible desert of Pispir, struggling with demons,[1] training himself for a life of perfection. He wished for solitude, but his fame attracted crowds, who begged him to become their teacher. In spite of his love of solitude, he knew that he could not abandon them, but finding in the end that his mind was being too much distracted from essentials he one day joined a caravan with which he proceeded eastwards. About twenty-five miles from the Red Sea, in the desert of Mount Qolzum, he found a suitable site, with an excellent fresh-water spring, a few wild palm-trees, a narrow strip of land that would provide him with a little corn and green-stuff (salads?). In this faraway spot he would be much less disturbed, although from time to time he visited his disciples at Pispir, who once a month, 'because he was old', brought him a few olives, vegetables, and some oil. Later on two brethren were allowed to live with him, no doubt more from filial devotion than to look after him, for at 105 years of age Anthony's asceticism had kept him hale and hearty, with excellent eyesight and all his teeth, although they were worn down to the gums by age. Nor did his declining strength ever induce him to change his habit or to wash his feet. When he died in 356, he left as his heirlooms an old cloak, two sack-like garments, and a desertful of monks.

We may imagine Anthony's life as that of an old man who was hard on himself, good to others, and outwardly uneventful except for the interference of demons; an old man who reached the heights of experience and spiritual wisdom. His disciple Ammon was forced into marriage against his will. On his wedding day, as soon as the ceremonies were

[1] The representation of St Anthony and his pig does not belong to the literature of the Desert Fathers. It is a purely Western concept, dating from the end of the fourteenth century, and the sign of a confraternity. In the Middle Ages an epidemic of swine fever ceased thanks to the intercession of St Anthony, and the Anthonines, a charitable organization of brethren originating in the Dauphinois, having been allowed by the police to let their pigs circulate in the streets, the picture-makers had the idea of representing the Anthonine confraternity by the portrait of the hermit from whom they took their name, and the privileges they were granted by a pig with a bell around its neck. (E. Male, *L'Art religieux du XIIIᵉ siècle en France*, p. 292.)

over and the spouses bedded down, he suddenly rose, bolted the door, and said to his wife: 'Come, Madam, I will explain my trick to thee; our fine marriage was not worth much. It will therefore be better if each of us sleeps separately.'[1] Madam agreed. Ammon continued to grow his balsam in the garden, whilst Madam kept house, and thus they lived very virtuously until the day they agreed to separate. Ammon then made his way to the north-west side of the Delta, south of Alexandria, to the barren Wadi Natrûn, where he built himself a two-roomed cell which sheltered him for twenty-two years, from 315 to 337. His wife, meanwhile, filled their former conjugal dwelling with pious virgins. And twice a year, Ammon, remembering that he was a married man, left the Desert of Nitria to visit his sister-wife.

His disciples became so numerous that forty years after his death there were 5,000 monks in the barren wastes of the Natrûn. There was then a church for the Saturday and Sunday services, conducted by eight priests. On Saturdays, around midday, from the surrounding huts would emerge a crowd of thin, bearded men, not exactly filthy, but in that dried-out state produced by entirely refraining from ablution under an Eastern sun. They were all dressed more or less similarly. Their bodies were enveloped in a kind of sack, known as a tunic, belted around the waist. Their heads and necks were hooded, or cowled. A few of them wore sandals. Those who had hired themselves out for harvesting, or travellers in search of edification, also wore on their shoulders a goatskin that fell to their knees, or a cloak. Most of them carried a basket of plaited palm leaves or osiers. They had woven these during the week, in their retreats, and were now bringing them to the store, to be sold in the market of Alexandria, and in exchange for which they were given their weekly ration of bread and salt from the bakehouse. Visitors were lodged at a hostelry. During their first days they were favoured with a more varied diet; to their hunk of bread the friendly brethren would add a few salted olives, a few drops of oil, a handful of chickpeas, some plums or figs. If the guest was familiar with desert customs, he took good care to eat only a small quantity of this appetising meal. And as he was travelling in search of a life of holiness, after sundown he did not fail to sit down on a bundle of reeds in order to cull words of wisdom from his hosts. He was told that if he were willing to work like everyone else, he might stay as long as he liked. On those same Saturday evenings the brethren, after sharing a communal meal, also listened to the wisdom of their elders, took part in the liturgy, and on the following day, if necessary, were punished for their sins. Three palm-trees stood

[1] Draguet.

74

next to the church, on each of which hung a whip. There was one for the monks, one for robbers, and one for wayfarers. Whoever had sinned went to the tree-trunk reserved for his own group, flung his arms around it, and received the number of strokes which he had been allotted.

Between 320 and 330 the desert of Skete in the region of Nitria also began to fill up. Although it contained fewer than its nearby colony, there were nonetheless 2,000 monks at Skete. The grand old man of this group was Macarius the Egyptian. At thirty he had given up his little pastrycook's business to go into the wilderness, where he remained for sixty years. Macarius was a great saviour of souls, but also a magician. A man had one day found his wife in his bed, transformed into a filly by the evil machinations of a jealous rival. The husband was obliged to drag the unfortunate creature as far as Skete by a halter, but Macarius gave her back her true form. This saint also performed less startling miracles.

There were many other Macariuses in the valley of the Nile, according to the *Histoire Lausiaque* no fewer than six. The most famous of these was Macarius of Alexandria, who generally lived in the cells, where, not far from their main centre, the Nitriots went to train themselves for the harshest kind of anchorite life. But Macarius enjoyed travelling and wandered all over the desert, where he had his own hut in all the most important monastic centres. He was not an amiable man, and knew how to find the most cutting and least charitable phrase with which finally to put a brother in his place, especially if the latter was prone to vainglory. His great speciality was asceticism, which he had raised to such a degree of virtuosity that Dom Butler, who knew all about it, called him 'the record-holder of the desert'. Not satisfied by exceeding his own records, every time Macarius heard of another's, he would go into training in order to beat it, and achieved astounding results, that were worthy of a champion. He had not once spat on the ground since his baptism, which when the sandstorms blew may have been remarkable; for seven years his only diet was of raw vegetables; for three years his bread ration was minimal; he never slept for twenty days and nights; for seven months he was exposed to the mosquitoes of the swamps near Skete; for forty days he fasted altogether, remaining in one corner without either speaking or moving, except (so the record states) in order to relieve himself, and during the same period he ate only a few leaves of raw cabbage, on Sundays, just for a change. When he was 100 years old, having lost all his teeth, he was still training like a novice, but as the result of his austere life this thickset little man had become more or less non-existent. Even his beard no longer grew normally and only a few hairs around his lips and at the top of his chin proved him to be a genuine monk. Like many of his kind, Macarius, who had a rough way with people, was kind to animals. One day a hyena pushed open his door with her snout, bringing him her young one. As the baby hyena was blind, Macarius instantly gave it back its sight. Next day the ladylike mother hyena did not fail to pay him a visit of thanks, bringing him as a present a fresh, fine, large, and warm sheepskin to wear as a cloak. Another time, in the course of his many wanderings, Macarius, in order to find his way back, had laid along his way not stones, but reeds. When he awoke he was surprised to find his reeds, tied in a neat bundle, over his head. The demons had paid him this kind attention, but now he could no longer find his way back. He had no bread, his goatskin was empty, and he was tortured by the mirage of a young person carrying a water-jar. Even such an athlete as he was about to give way to exhaustion when a herd of antelope arrived. One female, her udder swollen with milk, left the herd and 'having lain down beneath her and sucked at it, his thirst was quenched'. And the antelope not only fed him, but was kind enough to lead him back to his cell.

Although all the anchorites were not Macariuses, a good few of them had rather original ways. It was both one of the advantages and the inconveniences of the life of a hermit that in the hut he had built himself with a few stakes and palm-branches held together with lumps of clay, in his grotto or deserted tomb, the ascetic, living alone, obeyed no rules except his self-imposed discipline. Such discipline was always very harsh, and also, if he who practised it was not wholly well-balanced, dangerous. We should therefore not be too surprised if some of our holy men were slightly eccentric.

In the favourite regions the swarms of hermits soon changed the face of the anchorites' lives. Certain of them, whose huts were close together, began to visit one another. They lived alone, but if they observed, watched, and possibly even spied on one another, they also vied with each other in doing good and practising charity, one of the particular and by no means the least important forms of asceticism, which the anchorite's life by its very nature excluded. In fact the material needs of a huge colony made social relations necessary. We have seen that at Nitria, where life was semi-anchoristic, there was a kind of council of elders, there were common buildings, a common church, a common whip, although there were no superiors in the ordinary sense and the individual more or less retained his freedom of action. Such a grouping around a common centre was called a laura, although this term was also applied to more homogeneous assemblages.

Thus matters were moving towards a more complete system, in which the community, having become one, would operate under a chief whose authority it accepted. Personal initiative was to give way to obedience. The mutual contact with others, constantly watched over by their superiors, would develop the souls and personalities of the monks by enabling them to practise a larger number of virtues. Pachomius was the man of genius who by organizing such communities of cenobites, instituted a way of life that was to be more favourable than that of the anchorites.

When young Pachomius was pressed into military service, but had no taste for it. He was a pagan. On the look-out for the first opportunity to escape, one day the young conscript met a party of monks, and as soon as he could leave the service was baptized. Then, under the direction of Palemon, a wise elder, he spent his solitary years as an anchorite. This happened towards 307, north of Thebes in Upper Egypt, where the Nile makes its big bend.

When he parted from his guide he settled at Tabennesi, a deserted village on the edge of the desert. He had a plan, inspired by a heavenly visitant. As a hermit he had thought only of himself, but now it seemed to him that if he were able to gather some brethren around him he would serve them without neglecting his own salvation. For this purpose he decided to build a kind of monastic village, surrounded by walls as a protection against brigands, who in those parts were always numerous. There they would all pray together, work together, eat together, and together achieve salvation.

The attempt was made, but from the start it turned out to be difficult. His brother John joined Pachomius but the first two cenobites soon learned that to live together their characters must be, in the words of an elder, rounded, not angular. But in spite of their evident goodwill these two Egyptians were still somewhat too angular. And John soon died.

The experiment was even less successful with other brethren who at first accepted the new regime. Pachomius might feed them, serve them as well as possible, take on the most menial tasks, but those full-blooded fellows, if one may say so, made a mug of their superior. One day when they were working out of doors and Pachomius had brought them their food on the back of a donkey, they played a trick on him, as the result of which the Abbot was obliged to carry home all the kitchen utensils. They continued to play such pranks more and more frequently. When Pachomius finally decided to assert himself the monks became so threatening that he picked up a bolt, in his turn threatened them, and finally threw them out. But those five years taught him more than he would have learned in the same time spent as an anchorite. He did not give up, however, and at his third attempt, begun with three new disciples, was so successful that the small foundation of Tabennesi soon numbered 100, with more to follow.

Now at last the way of life he had dreamed of was realized. It was humanitarian, each member of the foundation giving according to his means, scrupulously obedient and as fraternal as in the early days of the Church. Strangely enough, the demons were much less obstreperous. Within the walls the monks' houses, or quarters, were arranged fairly methodically. Each of them had a head, and contained a certain number of monks, three to a cell, all of them organized to fulfil similar tasks, for the community had to be entirely self-supporting. There was a church, a refectory, and a hostelry. There were cooks, bakers, gardeners, potters, and even scribes. Like the anchorites, the cenobites were obliged to perform certain duties. The doorkeeper was a careful guardian, 'whose tongue was salty', who received the pilgrims and subjected postulants to a detailed examination. The monks were even classified according to their personalities; each category being listed under a number, or, rather, a letter of the alphabet. The least intelligent were grouped under the letter i, the best under an x. With his genius for organization and mental capacity Pachomius divided his disciples into as many intellectual categories as there were letters in the alphabet, namely twenty-four. Yet he wisely only gave such lettering on good grounds, to those monks with a genuine spiritual vocation. On his hood each monk wore in red the sign of his monastery and his house. At regular hours, which of necessity were not the same times for all of them, they took their vegetarian meals, which consisted of olives, vegetables, and cheese. Their portions were carefully restricted, especially during Lent, but each one received according to his needs. Experience had proved that excessive fasting might be injurious to health and that if a little wine were drunk with humility a great deal of water might be drunk with ostentation. On one occasion, even, a sick brother, was, with the Abbot's permission, allowed a small chicken, a unique event in the annals of the desert, and chronicled for that reason. During mealtimes, which occurred after noon, there was complete silence. The monks wore their hoods and saw nothing but their bowls, so that if they wished to deprive themselves of food there was no witness to their abstention. If they felt an obligation to fast they were able to obtain a dispensation from attending refectory. The rest of the day was of course divided into periods for prayers, which were relatively few, and communal; twelve prayers to be said at matins; and a similar number at noon, sundown, and in the middle of the night. The elect—not those who claimed to be so, but those accepted as such—were allowed to pray for longer periods without interference. Lectures on religious subjects took place weekly. On Saturdays and Sundays the whole community attended divine service, which was generally celebrated by visiting priests. For Pachomius, although he venerated the priesthood and, if they were willing to accept the common rule, received priests into his monastery, had certain mental reservations with regard to this matter. With a high degree of good sense he feared that their superiority over the ordinary brethren might lead to false pride, envy, jealousy, and contention, all of which were the perdition of monasteries. 'It is as if one were to throw a burning coal on to the threshing-floor; unless it were quickly put out it might destroy the labours of a whole year.'[1] Like Anthony, Pachomius himself remained throughout his life a pious layman.

This new system soon had a tremendous success. It had proved that one might become an excellent monk and yet remain an anchorite. Palladius, the delightful author of the *Histoire Lausiaque*, heard that in the founder's own lifetime there were already 7,000 Pachomians scattered around in nine monasteries, of whom 1,300 were living at Tabennesi and 300 at Panopolis, all, like a modern congregation, under the rule of the one superior authority. These figures are exaggerated, but it is certain that the monks of Tabennesi were very numerous.

It is not surprising that schisms occurred among such great numbers. It is only human that the heirs of great founders, whilst doing their best to preserve their inheritance as intact as possible, should yet interpret its rule according to their own views. Such are the quarrels of holy men, who, although specialists in charity, sometimes forget to practise it. In this case they were also Egyptian holy men, of a race that we know to have been stiffnecked and intransigent. Pachomius' successors, after 346, were faced with the problems inherent in all monastical systems.

Amongst them one of the foremost was the highly coloured figure of Shenute—383—who was the head of 2,000 men in the 'white monastery' of Atripe, to-day Sohag. Shenute possessed certain highly estimable monastic qualities, but also some very human failings. A ruler of iron, meticulous in matters of detail, intransigent in general, irascible beyond measure, incredibly austere himself, like the Frenchman Rancé and others he was anxious to confer on his neighbour the benefits of his own rigorous discipline. Needless to say, his monastery was autonomous, entirely separate from the Pachomian congregations. Lacking a sense of proportion in his vocational activities he emphasized the wise precepts

[1] Draguet, p. 100.

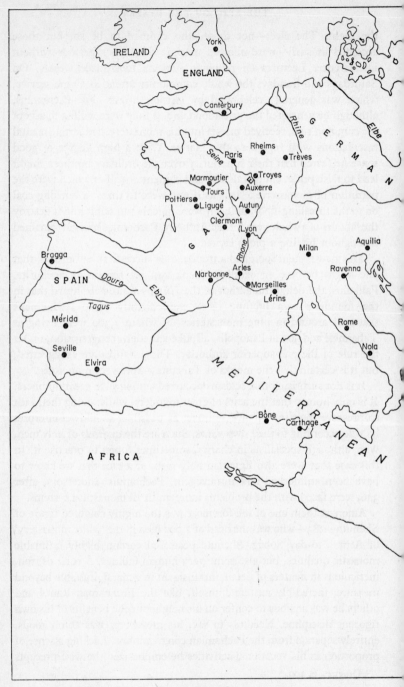

2. The Near East and the Christian West before the sixth century

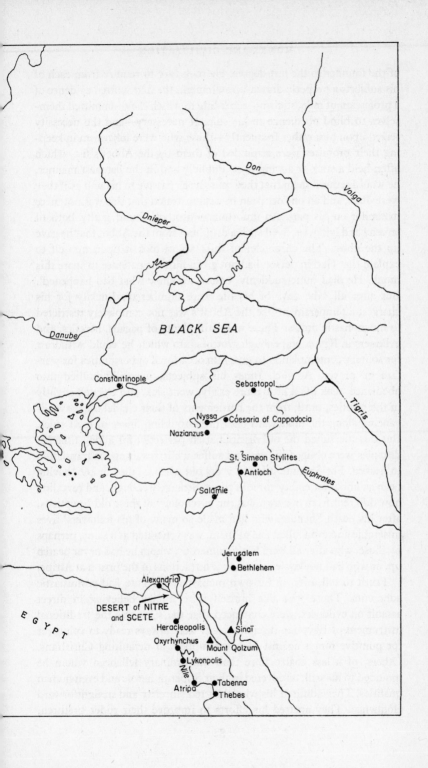

of the founder to the last degree. He took care to require from each of his subjects a properly drawn-up statement, the first written evidence of a profession of monasticism—according to which they committed themselves to blind obedience to his rule. If necessary—and the necessity seized upon him rather frequently—those who were lukewarm in keeping their promises were reminded of them by the Abbot's fist, which often held a stick or a whip in it. Publicly and in the harshest manner, he would remind them that they must be as passive to his will as if they were dead, and on one occasion he demonstrated that this was not mere metaphor on his part. An unfortunate brother, found guilty both of larceny and lying, received such a drubbing from the Abbot that he gave up the ghost. The chronicler of this exploit took it upon himself to explain that God in person had not given him the patience to spare this monk. He died quite suddenly 'before we knew what had happened'. But after all, 'the days of his life were numbered'. Luckily for his charges, a temperament like the Abbot's was not completely restricted to his monastic duties. There were still plenty of pagans, heretics, and evildoers in Egypt, and enough grottoes into which he could withdraw for solitary contemplation to give him occasional opportunities for warfare or prayer. At such times his subjects, normally bullied into obedience, took life a little more easily, went sick, and cheated slightly in their duties, until, from the battlements of their citadel they saw advancing along the homeward path the forbidding figure of their ruler. But this life suited the old disciplinarian perfectly; for a long time his disciples were obliged to pray and suffer whilst awaiting his translation to heaven. For Shenute was 118 years old when he died in 466, having been an abbot for eighty-three of them. Strangely enough, and revealing how different from our own was the psychology of these old Egyptians, after his death Shenute, who had made so many of his followers' lives miserable and even killed one of them, was venerated as a saint, perhaps by those, who after all were fairly numerous, whom he had never beaten up, or who had not known the unique attractions of the prison at Atripe.

Truth to tell, even in his own monastery Shenute had enthusiastic adherents. Those who like himself were monks believing in direct assault on evildoers, were convinced that the stick was the traditional instrument of Egyptian discipline, and were always ready to volunteer for punitive forays against idol-worshippers or defaulting Christians. Others, of a less coarse fibre than the ordinary fellaheen whom he moulded to his will, discovered in their Superior heroic and even human qualities. They admired his wholehearted sincerity and straightforward eloquence. They abetted his efforts to improve their ruder brethren.

They were touched when their Superior, momentarily wearying of the struggle, went so far as to admit his failures. They knew that he was generous, anxious for the common welfare, and occasionally even able to unbend to the extent of revealing a strange kind of gentleness. They admired his asceticism, his praying, and, perhaps with good reason, his miracles. Had he possessed no other qualities than his too obvious faults, Shenute would never have recruited a regular monastic army— more than 2,000 monks and 1,800 nuns.

In organizing these battalions the Abbot showed exceptional ability. The monastery-fortress was the hub of the community. Even today it still consists of a great stone square, 130 yards by 110, pierced by two deep passages, each leading to a gate. Within, near one of these gates, was a large domed church, a second Holy Jerusalem. Beyond it the houses and cells lay scattered around more or less haphazardly, amongst larger buildings used as meeting-places. As this enclave could not contain a very large community, it is probable that semi-cenobitic colonies stood on the slopes of the neighbouring mountain, and that outhouses, stables, bakehouses, and various workshops were built closer at hand, just outside the walls. When robber bands, large enough to frighten even the Father Abbot, were seen approaching, all the inhabitants of the village took refuge within the walls; but when things were normal activities were minutely regulated.

At dawn and sunset the brethren, marching in long silent files, attended service in the church. All of them crossed themselves, carefully refraining from moving their hands below their beards. During prayers they all knelt down without giving the slightest glance to their neighbours, and with their heads held high and their feet hidden by their gowns, listened to the reading of the Lessons that provided the subject for the day's meditation; these readings being broken off at least six times for prayer. At a given signal the head of each section would distribute their tasks amongst the monks in his group. The most important of these organizers was the steward, whose responsibilities were considerable. It was he who presided over or appointed deputies to preside over the preparation of their daily bread, to which particular care was given. The kneading of the dough and the baking were done at the word of command. He also decided the amount of salt water to be used, the mixing of the date-water, which was their usual drink, the collecting of wood, which at the edge of the desert was available only in small quantities, the manure which, when dried, provided the fuel for the eleven bread-ovens, and the general provisioning and cleanliness necessary so that each of the brethren might receive small, but healthy and adequate rations, for these monks washed their utensils. Outside, other teams took charge of the irrigation of the black soil, the harvest and the threshing, or, more precisely, the gleaning. The hospital, the hostelry, and the refectory services were also carefully organized. Towards midday all the workers came to the refectory and silently ate their meal, mostly of bread. There was a second meal in the evening, before bedtime, which was not obligatory, after which the monks might either go to bed, read, or learn Holy Scripture. The sequence and ordering of these multifarious activities were carefully watched over by the Abbot.

Women also were attracted to the cenobitic life. When one day Maria, Pachomius' sister, arrived at the gate of Tabennesi her brother informed her through the porter that he would not receive her, but that if she wished to live far from the world, they would be glad to build her a hut. Soon an organized nunnery centred around Maria. Two more became necessary, both of them crowded, since one of them contained 400 nuns, under the direction of one of Pachomius' trusted old colleagues. And the 'red monastery' which stemmed from Shenute contained, as we have seen, 1,800 nuns.

The hagiographers, who were generally discreet in their accounts, occasionally went into greater detail regarding certain aspects of monastic life, even more difficult for women to lead than for men. It appears that among these ladies some bickered, quarrelled or spied, and on one occasion, at least, the consequences were dramatic. A sister who had been denounced threw herself into the Nile, and her accuser hanged herself. This was an exceptional case, but daily intercourse between all these women living together did not always proceed smoothly. In one Pachomian convent a nun pretended to be seized by divine madness, as a number of Russian saints did, later on. In many individual cases this deliberate choice of such a humble vocation was an eccentricity. In a community it was bound to be a disruptive influence, since those who claimed to be the victims of divine madness had not previously informed anyone of their personal inclinations. In this particular case the nun in question was quiet, silent, practised extreme self-mortification, and gave offence to no one, never complaining and living on scraps and dishwater. But although the chronicles do not mention the fact she was obviously inclined to be peculiar. She succeeded strikingly in her aim, since her companions were all taken in by her, and teased her mercilessly. One day, as if by accident, a bucket of dirty water was spilled over her; another day, her nose was stuffed with mustard, on a third occasion one of the sisters felled blows on her face. The entire convent took part in the game, no doubt egged on by the victim's unprotesting acquiescence, until one day, a passing holy man restored order by declaring that the alleged madwoman was the saint of the community. Thereupon, greatly distressed by such high honour, embarrassed by the apologies she received, and unable any longer to practise her self-immolation, the poor girl who by then, probably, was no longer quite sane, disappeared without a trace.

In general, however, convent life was more edifying, both among the female Pachomians as well as in the twelve convents of Antinoë, in the district of Sheikh Abadiah. There, a certain Abbess, 'amma' Thalis, was an ascetic for eighty years. Another, who for thirty years had never taken off her rags, preferred to continue her menial tasks even on Sundays, to deny herself the pleasure of attending services on that day. And, to boot, she was strikingly beautiful and could have turned all heads, had it not been, as the chronicle tells, 'for her chastity'.

All these accounts lead one to assume that apart from certain exceptional groups such as those at Skete and Nitria these armies of monks and nuns were mostly humble fellaheen, many of whom, even on the heights, continued to bear the marks of their origins. Their motives in fleeing to the desert were not always heroic ones. Some of them fled from persecution, or military service, or the tax-gatherers, for all of them knew that the police did not venture far into the sandy wastes. Others, quite simply, were seeking to quit life's complications. And in fact the schools of holiness included all manner of men; slaves breaking their bonds—which in Egypt was possible—a former brigand who at least on one occasion managed to keep his hand in, knife-grinders, a merchant who was good-for-nothing, not even as a copyist, and ordinary folk with no qualifications at all. Some of them were gentle, like that friar who, noticing during the service that his neighbour was dozing, took him on his knees to allow him to sleep more comfortably. Some were boors. We have already met a certain number of Macariuses. Then there was Arsenius, a boor but a good psychologist, who, when visited by a rich and pious female tourist with the highest recommendations, told her bluntly: 'Well, now you've seen me . . . Back in Rome you'll boast of it, and soon there won't be enough ships to bring the other women here.' Amongst this crowd, the Egyptians—who would have thought it?—had a general reputation for nonchalance, whereas those of Jerusalem were considered accessible and discreet. There were few intellectuals, especially, it seems, in the south, and even fewer priests. Holy men were not lacking. On the whole, however, the desert population was still more or less a lay one, even if heroic. It was to cause formidable developments.

For the time being these peasant masses, who had no status in the Church, did not seek to intervene in its affairs. But in a little while, when Christological quarrels aroused violent passions, it was enough for only one saint to raise his voice to mobilize what Duchesne called the democracy of the cells. These monastic battalions, composed of all the wandering monks prowling around the cities, reinforced by those of the backwoods itching to be on the roads, spurred on the local inhabitants, clamorously, with sticks and rioting, either to support or to denounce the tenets worked out by the theologians in the silence of their studies. Men of action rather than of intellect, these simple people, many of whom were illiterate, defended the purity of their faith—or what they took to be so—for whole colonies went over to heresy, with a degree of zeal only equalled by their ignorance. Occasionally they handled their own bishops as roughly as the meanest priests. St Jerome, who was himself a monk, occasionally fell into the very evils he denounced, but he rightly complained of those who, vowed to humility, sackcloth and ashes, hastened to condemn the bishops and the world in general, if the bishops and the whole world were not of their opinion. There is no documentary evidence to inform us whether, once they had returned to their solitudes, these fanatics ever asked themselves whether certain malicious devils, masquerading as upholders of the truth, had not led them rather far along the road of intolerance, vainglory, self-righteousness, and contentiousness. Upheld by the public authorities the Eastern bishops tried, rather late in the day, to quell them, but they never completely got the better of these self-appointed guardians of the faith of others (Council of Chalcedon, 451).

The few figures given above lead us to think that they were very numerous. All along the Nile, in the Delta, along the Delta, and as far as Thebes, over a distance of 700 kilometres, the desert on the edge of the Nile valley was a mass of anchorites' huts and cenobitic monasteries. In one town alone, Oxyrincx, there were apparently more monks than laymen. The men of God perched everywhere, in holes in the walls, unused temples, ruined towers, in every nook and cranny. The streets and public squares were full of bearded men. Twelve churches were hardly enough for the lay population, but the monks had many more, so much so that when they chanted their prayers 'this city seemed like a church consecrated to Divine Majesty'. The hagiographer noted with satisfaction in passing that in this hothouse where tolerance was held within very narrow limits, neither pagans nor heretics dared to show themselves. The description of this earthly paradise may be accepted with some reservation, and the same applies to the figures given by the chroniclers. Nevertheless, during the fourth and fifth centuries there must have been considerable numbers of these monks there. The following figures may perhaps be roughly correct: about 10,000 in and around the Delta, rather fewer in the south, between Akhmim and Thebes, and, dispersed between these two very dense groups, several thousand more along the course of the Nile.

THE PATH OF TRANSFIGURATION

Hell owed it to itself to assign for special duties among those who specialized in self-mortification, devils who were specialists in temptation. The monks who peopled the desert were well aware of the fact that they had settled in spots where devils whirled around their huts like sandstorms. There were enough of them to keep them all busy, although most of the wiliest plots misfired because, as is well known, the Devil is a fool. Nevertheless, their main attacks were centred on the most hard-bitten ascetics. For the Satanic forces it was an important issue; asceticism was growing too fast, it had too bright a future, and therefore had to be attacked wholeheartedly. They were even wily enough to choose their prey among the hermits who, they thought with good reason, were less carefully watched over than the cenobites.

They were not to be recognized by the horns and other characteristics they were alleged to possess in the Middle Ages, from the eleventh and twelfth centuries onwards, but preferably chose either the usual or hybrid forms of animals, such as bulls, leopards, bears, lions, scorpions and serpents, that with evil intent prowled around the anchorites. They also tended to appear as visions of voluptuous females. They very often disguised themselves as a little black Ethiopian, coming from the mysterious regions to the south. They all behaved and danced around in the same kind of way, sometimes artful enough only to play little pranks, for a saint who would smile at those was already half won over.

It would be easy, and it was in fact done,[1] to imagine the desert of the monks as a huge and absurd menagerie, in which they were either the victims or the tamers. The cells certainly did often echo to animal roars,

[1] Flaubert, we know, tried his hand at it in his *Tentation de saint Antoine*, but with less success than the two Breughels or Callot. Apart from its sumptuous style, nothing could be more false and boring than this unsuccessful book. Among the tempters only the courtesans, whom the author knew well enough, have any life. The rest, who each in turn perform an act in front of the saint, are like marionettes on strings as clumsily thick as cables. In order to create this endless and monotonous procession Flaubert had read a great deal, but only elementarily. His *Saint Antoine*, we are shamefacedly compelled to admit, is only a monastic version of *Bouvard et Pécuchet*.

whines, and other noises, but we should no more be taken in by these than were their occupants. All these devilries were part of a literary style that had its laws, its procedure, and its protagonists. Its authors merely had to remember the symbolic representations in the idolatrous temples all around them, to detach them from the walls in order to provide themselves with a ready-made gallery of devil images. No doubt they wished to provide us with good measure, but being of the same period they knew their subject-matter. When they tell us quite seriously that when a friar yawned during the service this was because a devil had poked his finger into his mouth they do not take us in for a moment, but they also knew that, in spite of the effects of insomnia, fasting, and solitude, the great men of their time never nodded.

Some of them were certainly heavy-handed in dealing with their subject. These fellaheen, born under a torrid sun, in a country that was still a heathen one, were greatly tormented by the flesh. Fortunately for ourselves, their accounts were mostly given in Coptic, Greek, or Latin, in terms that proved embarrassing to all their translators. They did not always remember that an obstinate refusal to dwell on their temptations was only another way of dwelling on them, and tried to deal with their obsessions by measures which in their way were equally obsessive. Those who had not yet attained to the requisite degree of indifference to sex were thrown into a frenzy by any haphazard and innocent meeting with a woman. One of them, who had been tempted rather too far, bluntly declared that he would be capable of coping with at least ten women, and gave up his asceticism on the spot. In fact one proved quite enough for him and the poor fellow had so much trouble with her that he preferred to return to Skete. But with women they at least knew where they were. Young lads, even when wearing the habits of novices, were far more disturbing. Some of the anchorites, whose former memories were awakened by these, were unable to hold out and returned to the sailors' brothels of Alexandria. Yet the majority of them held out successfully, sometimes by means which were both strikingly simple and original, sometimes disconcerting, but always heroic. When they felt themselves in danger of falling these stout fellows did not, if one may say so, resort to half-measures.

The most dangerous devils, however, were not those who left the imprint of their cloven hooves around the huts. There were artists in their Satanic ranks who were prepared to bide their time, to touch up and perfect their craftsmanship, for it was a fine victory if, instead of tiring themselves out by vulgar uproariousness they succeeded, by long and patient strategy, in bringing about the downfall of a veteran. If after many years an aged ascetic, having come to the end of his training in self-discipline, felt the least satisfaction in having done so, this was enough to unleash a whole cohort of devils around him. Others were so artful that in order to deceive their prey more completely they would appear to him in the guise of saints, or even bishops. Thus seven holy bishops came to visit Father Nathaniel, who had spent thirty-seven years without setting foot outside his cell, only in order to tempt him to emerge from it. Not a very serious matter as such, but which would have nullified all his long years of asceticism. Nathaniel understood this quite clearly. 'I am dead,' he informed the deacons of the holy procession, 'both as regards Their Lordships the Bishops and the world in general. I have my own reasons . . . and I cannot return with them.'[1] Others were even more careful; the forerunners of those who in the nineteenth century tormented the soul of René, they scattered little grains of sand in all the machinery of everyday life.

Towards midday, when the sun was blazing on the leaden rocks, it might be that the recluse, tired of keeping his vigils, fasting, working, reading and praying in turn, walked about his cell restlessly, his soul in torment. He contemplated himself, compared himself to some recent arrival, and sighed: after all those years of self-discipline he had made no progress. Then he might glance out of the window, and in the dreary and familiar landscape notice some other cabin. Immediately the evil one would whisper in his ear: 'Perhaps a neighbouring friar, who is sick, would be consoled if you were to visit him, or it would console you to have speech with him,' for he was one of those who did not have many visitors. But on thinking it over he concluded that his own total solitude, which he was not obliged to share with another who might covet his meagre rations, was preferable, since one knew that all around one untrustworthy or rude individuals were legion. Elsewhere matters might be differently organized; there were ardently religious communities, that contained men of a better stamp, whose reputation was high. The wandering Father Abbots, of whom there were large numbers, told of the many marvels they witnessed during their visits to the great anchorites, and praised the disciplined lives of the cenobites. According to their accounts certain corners of the desert were a veritable paradise. To see such sights with one's own eyes was obviously edifying. In like manner a pilgrim might take rest at a convent of goodly nuns, where once his own sister had taken the veil. But as he turned such thoughts over in his mind, muttering in his beard, he would yawn, sadly and flaccidly, his spirits had sunk into a kind of torpor, his heart was heavy,

[1] Draguet, p. 135.

his resolution weak, he was bored and sick of himself. For a long time his gaze would follow the path to the Nile. The midday demon was at work on him.

It was no more than that, but that was enough. The temptations of the noonday, inseparable from monastic life, provided good and hypocritical excuses to lead the saint from the straight road. They all experienced them, in a greater or lesser degree, but at the final stage, when they had overcome both their flesh and their feelings and extended their charity to the last stretch, the best of them were able to ascend the final rungs of the ladder leading to the borderline between this world and the next. Freed as far as could be from their fleshly bonds, ethereal and diaphanous in body and soul, they had reached a world of peace such as even the heathen philosophers had longed for when they wrote of the serene regions where all passions are stilled. The 'apathy' of the Stoics and Epicureans was sublimated and transfigured by these anchorites, who on the highest spiritual level attained to that special state of grace, where a kind of vacuity, motionless quietude, calm, serenity, security, even invulnerability, or in any event harmony, balance, and peace, placed the Christian sage in a state of the purest and simplest contemplation. The true philosopher, i.e. the perfect monk, was then close to God, the simplest Being of all, the final aim of his first setting-out into the desert, in the appeasement of his passion and silent contemplation (*haesychia*): although only as far as human nature could bear and still capable of temptation, which would always be threatening him.

Only the elite attained such spiritual heights, and in order to gain them both anchorites and cenobites had to go into long and hard years of training. They had to endure fasting and vigils, work at their matting and basket-making to earn their food. They must never cease to guard their souls, remain obdurately faithful to their cellular or monastic lives, set a good example to their brethren, and what was more, love them. They must punctiliously mumble their Scriptures and even if they could not read, memorize most of them; recite the prescribed Psalms and take part in the services. They must obey their elders, pray unceasingly, and endeavour to attain to that degree of worship that is less an activity than a state of mind. These were not tasks for children. A few of them accomplished prodigies, but most of them remained within the rules of their everyday lives, which themselves were very severe. All of them, whether elbow to elbow or alone, followed the same stony path, panting, stumbling, sometimes falling by the wayside, but always advancing towards their metamorphosis, i.e. their transfiguration.

The documents which tell us of them, and most of which were written by the monks themselves, provide us with innumerable sources. They include *The Life of Anthony*, by St Athanasius, the stern bishop of Alexandria who knew his hero well; the *Life of Paul, Life of Hilarion, Life of Malchus* by St Jerome; the *History of the Monks* by an anonymous author; the *Lives of Pachomius* in Greek, Coptic, Arabic and Syrian; the *History* by Bishop Palladius, who spent years in the desert and still hankered for it; the *Conferences* and *Institutions* of Cassianus, a monk of Marseilles who, with his inseparable companion Germanius, for many years visited the saints in northern Egypt, the *Religious History* of Bishop Theodoret on Syrian monachism, the rare *Apophthegms* in which the teaching and examples of the heroes are briefly related, the *Lives of the Fathers*, a composite collection as detailed as the preceding ones. These early works compose the *corpus* of a whole ascetic and mystical literature one of the masters of which was Evagius the Pontician (d. 399).

As we have already mentioned, they are full of truth and poetry. They contain sentence after sentence firmly and concisely written, corrected and polished over many years, and which, after having lasted for centuries, have come down to us still fresh and glowing, continuing to be used by our most genuinely spiritual contemporaries. We may regret that too many of those monks, by excessive vigils and fasting, weakened the intensity of the very contemplative powers they were seeking to attain, and that their deliberately non-intellectual proclivities did not always favour such contemplation. But if, on reflection, the term civilization includes both education and a higher degree of development, we must concede that those old monks, illiterate, hirsute, and occasionally even foul-mouthed, did, sometimes in spite of themselves, but undeniably work out a psychological approach and a form of wisdom that laid the foundations for further spiritual development.

THE SPREAD OF ASCETICISM

Monachism spread rapidly from Egypt into Palestine. As early as 307 Hilarion, after a spell at the school of Anthony, lived as a hermit in the region of Gaza, the point of junction between Palestine and Egypt. There he received disciples who for twenty-two years never left him, or rather knew where to find him either in Egypt, Sicily, or Dalmatia, for Hilarion belonged to the itinerant anchorites. All his life he practised the most meticulous asceticism. From the age of twenty-one to twenty-four he ate only half a measure of lentils daily; from twenty-four to twenty-seven, only bread, salt, and water; from twenty-seven to thirty, wild herbs and raw roots; from thirty-one to thirty-seven, rye bread and boiled herbs, without oil; from thirty-seven to sixty-three the same diet, with a little oil added for health reasons; and from sixty-four to eighty still the same, but with no bread, for an old man should have no need to take care of his health which, as one can see, was the case. Hilarion was a thaumaturgist who ruled the elements and exorcized both men and beasts. At his command a boa-constrictor obediently went and roasted itself in the flames. The holy man died in Cyprus, which was within the ecclesiastical jurisdiction of his friend Saint Epiphanius, Bishop of Salamis.

Epiphanius had no doubt met Hilarion during a sojourn in Egypt. At first a monk, he later ruled over a Pachomian monastery at Besanduc in the diocese of Eleutheropolis, near that of Jerusalem. He was a learned man who spoke five languages more or less, and his saintliness was legendary, but in addition to his natural gifts and grace Epiphanius had certain obvious faults—narrowmindedness, tenaciousness, a lack of judgment, a tendency to making scandals, violent scenes, and quarrelling, which, whilst his motives were undoubtedly sincere, were given full rein when he became Bishop of Cyprus. This man of God tended to make a great deal of fuss to impose on the Church certain obligations which it did not always wish to assume. Having become entirely on his own account a heresy-hunter, he ceaselessly endeavoured to hunt out more of them. His passion for orthodoxy which, let us admit it, was due to an almost morbid degree of theological prejudice, led him to discover no less than eighty heresies, some of them of course entirely imaginary, and twenty preceding the time of Christ. But in his eyes anyone who aroused his suspicion was automatically suspect in the eyes of the Church. The friends of John Chrysostom, the holy Archbishop of Constantinople, whom Epiphanius caused to be decreed a heretic, spent a great deal of time and charity in forgiving the latter the hostile, provocative and entirely gratuitous attitude he adopted towards their bishop, even in Constantinople itself; combined with other matters, the Cypriot's tempestuous intervention contributed to the iniquitous condemnation, followed by banishment, of his victim. This was his final act of injustice, but it had been preceded by several others. Thinking to have smelled out a heretic in the person of another John, bishop of Jerusalem, one fine day Epiphanius disembarked in Palestine. John received him kindly, but his guest proceeded to attack him in the Church of the Holy Sepulchre itself. John hit back, and their parting, as may be imagined, was not exactly friendly. But the zealous bishop of Salamis did not stop at that. His finest exploit would be hard to credit, had he not himself reported it. Some time later he decided to consecrate as priest to a community that was on good terms with the same John of Jerusalem, a pious layman who, however, was not agreeable to the decision that Epiphanius had taken regarding him. As he remained recalcitrant, his consecrator had him bound and gagged, and having thus put him at his ease, ordained him as deacon and priest on the spot. This priest in spite of himself, who by the way was a monk and an excellent man, was the brother of Saint Jerome. It is only fair to add that Epiphanius had enough sense not to stage this remarkable performance in the diocese of Jerusalem. The affair clearly made a certain sensation, but the first person to be astonished by it was he who had caused this scandal. Although he was nearing eighty, the old bishop was still very naïve, and was never able to learn anything by his mistakes. Shortly afterwards in fact he delivered himself of some new invectives against the holy images, for our heresy-hunter was also an iconoclast. The strangest thing about him was that having on numerous occasions burnt his bridges, he invariably found a ship to carry him home to Salamis, bored but incorrigible, so great was his prestige. He died in 403. The vitality of the Church was strong enough to allow it to absorb without difficulty such troublesome characters, provided that they were sufficiently saintly to make up for the violence of their temperaments, and this was the case especially among the ascetics.

In Syria, meanwhile, monachism was prospering to a degree great enough to daunt the stoutest champions of Egypt. In large numbers and possessing inventive minds, the Syrians were remarkable for ascetic activities that in all reverence can only be described as ridiculous. 'I am wearing what is wearing me out,' said Macarius of Alexandria when carrying a heavy load of sand in order to quell the temptation he felt to journey rather too far. The Syrians also wore themselves out, adding to the classical practices of asceticism iron chains and other instruments of exhaustion unknown in Egypt. Father Draguet, whom one is obliged constantly to quote, mentions three well known examples. One ascetic bore such a heavy load of iron that he could only crawl on all fours when he went to fetch his ration of water. Another insisted on remaining in a cell that was so low that he could only live there doubled up. A third spent ten years crouching in a cage shaped like a wheel. The Dendrites perched in trees. The Grazers lived in the forests and ate like wild animals, whom they imitated too well. And just in passing we may mention those who went completely naked, except for a loin-cloth of thorns that was providentially long and thick. By these new forms of asceticism the monks gained great renown among the simple peasantry.

Original as he was, St Simeon Stylites did not go quite so far. Younger than his Egyptian colleagues, this illiterate shepherd, born on the borders of Syria and Cilicia towards 389, began like many others, as an anchorite and then spent ten years as a cenobite at Telada, whence he was dismissed for his asceticism. Free to choose his own way of life, he then dwelt in a cistern, out of which he was with great difficulty persuaded to emerge. He then endeavoured to have himself walled up with no food during the whole of Lent, but as his friends refused to oblige him he compromised to the extent of accepting ten loaves and a jug of water, which he took good care not to touch. When he was excavated forty days later he was half-dead, but he nevertheless continued the exercise during every subsequent Lent. Simeon also trained himself by using a chain, a very heavy one, attached to a stone, allowing him only a dozen yards for his daily walk. When he was freed from it he barely noticed the worms that had lodged between the iron and his skin.

But all these were merely preliminaries. His true ascetic vocation was quite a different one. In default of a natural rock, Simeon had the idea of having himself hoisted on to a column a short distance from Antioch: not the kind of baptismal font on a pedestal shown in the iconograph, but a fairly massive stele, the first model being ten feet high, but the last, the tallest, at least sixty. At its summit, on a platform two square yards in size, the saint daily prostrated himself 1,244 times, ignoring ophthalmia, sickness, heat or cold. He spent Lent as already described, but in addition, chained to a stake. A ladder was provided for special occasions, but as a rule communication with the ground took place by means of a basket. When he had finished his exercises Simeon would preach and direct the souls of his congregation from the top of his column. His reputation as a specialist in the curing of infertility won him large numbers of devoted followers amongst the local peasantry. One day when Bishop Theodoret—who had endeavoured to count the number of his daily prostrations—visited him and the saint suggested to his flock that they should ask for the bishop's blessings, these good but over-enthusiastic people nearly tore the clothes off the episcopal pilgrim. When Simeon died in 459, after spending thirty-seven years on the top of his column, the 600 men-at-arms sent by the Emperor to retrieve his remains had the greatest difficulty in snatching them from the hands of the Bedouins, who had rushed to the spot from all over the desert for the same purpose.

In order to put matters in the right light one might no doubt affirm that God had never asked such things of men. That is true, but it pleased his servants to offer them to Him. Yet such eccentricities undoubtedly tended to lower the status of monasticism. The monks of the Wadi Natrûn, beaten and disgruntled, were severely critical of them. Yet everyone who went to visit him was won over by St Simeon Stylites' saintliness. His fame spread as far as Gaul and in Syria he had many imitators, even to female stylites.

His memory is preserved in 'Simeon's castle', Kalaat-Semaan, between Antioch and Aleppo. This is a huge church in the form of a cross, 360 yards by 325, with columns and porticos. At the point of intersection of the two halves there is a space for a central court in which are fragments of his famous column. The four arms of the cross, separated by the courtyard, each contain a basilica with three naves, and today still form the magnificent ruins of a unique edifice in the history of Syrian art. It was built between 476 and 490.

THE INTELLECTUAL AND MONASTIC EQUILIBRIUM:
ST BASIL

Before the strange asceticism of the stylites emerged, the rules of wiser forms of cenobitism were already laid down. On January 1, 379, Basil, Bishop of Caesaria in Cappadocia, died at the age of forty-nine,[1] worn out by merely nine years of his episcopate. Too often ill-served, the life-work he left behind him was unfinished owing to ill-health. His person-ality aroused a great deal of discussion and many ill-informed Christians feared that this bishop might become a kind of Oriental pope. A cham-pion of Nicaean orthodoxy against Arianism, an incomparable adminis-trator, a watchful dispenser of charity, St Basil was, as well, a great monk and one of the most perfect writers of ecclesiastical Greek.

Physically he was tall, thin, with deep-set eyes, bald but with a thick beard. His slow manner of speech might have confirmed a proverb then circulating: 'In Cappadocia, a good orator is as rare as a white crow.' But this slowness, which was partly due to shyness and partly to his habit of long reflection, gave way to genuine eloquence when he was moved by a great theme. Basil was discreet and reserved but a man of action and strong character, belonging to that race of prelates who having nothing to fear or to ask for, had no need to beat about the bush, and knew how to speak plainly to the great ones of their day. This timid

[1] Born in 329 or 330 at Caesaria in Cappadocia; 351–56 lived in Constantinople, then Athens; baptism and visits to monastic centres, around 357; priest from 362; bishop of Caesaria in Cappadocia in 370.

man was even able to assume surprising responsibilities. One day, needing a bishop, he consecrated his best friend, Gregory of Nazianza, as such. Gregory, unable to resist Basil's moral domination over him, allowed him to proceed whilst complaining bitterly and sincerely of his action. Basil was clever and even jolly at times, with perfect manners and always in command of himself. He knew which way he meant to go and did so without deviating from it, although like all of us he occasionally made mistakes.

Like many of his contemporaries, even in the most Christian families, he was not baptized until he came of age and almost immediately entered wholeheartedly into his new way of life; he would be a 'philosopher', i.e. a monk, and to prove he meant it set out to visit the hermits and the communities of Egypt and Palestine, Coelesyria and Mesopotamia. Through meeting so many holy men he discovered that 'lofty and indomitable disposition of the soul' of which he himself was to be a perfect example. But he was even more deeply influenced by a meeting in Cappadocia with a famous monk, who had carried the Gospels to Roman Armenia, Paphlagonia, and the Pontus—Eustathius, later Bishop of Sebaste. He was still not a very well-known theologian, but apparently spoke movingly, and willingly gave away his autograph when asked for a profession of faith. Presumably, in the violent quarrels raging around the Arian controversy, Eustathius merely wanted to avoid going to extremes. Basil broke with him later, and to some extent unfairly challenged his Nicaean orthodoxy, but as regarded the monastic rule he owed him a great deal. During fifteen years Eustathius was Basil's spiritual father, model, and mentor, with all the mutual esteem and affection such a relationship implies. Austerity, vitality, indestructible virtue, frankness towards oneself, and experience in the particular ways of their vocation—Basil admired all these qualities in Eustathius.

In Pontus, close to the Annesi family estate, he found an enchanting retreat; there were meadows surrounded by mountains, a river, the Iris, filled with fish, tumbling over the rocks and the water-mists of which pleasantly cooled the atmosphere. The rich soil was spangled with wild flowers and provided a splendid vegetable garden. It was an ideal spot in which to pursue one's highest aspirations. Basil had been bored in another place where he had stayed with his friend Gregory, and begged him to join him. As he invariably did, Gregory at first hesitated, then agreed, but finally changed his mind. He spent a happy visit at Annesi but finally left there, not having found Basil's ideal monastic site to his taste. The refreshing mists were, according to him, a thick fog, and as the mountains hid the sun it was damp. The Iris contained more stones than fish, the famous garden was simply a manure-heap spread on rubble, and the living-quarters were downright sordid.

Whether Basil's enthusiasm was exaggerated and Gregory's criticisms equally so, it was at Annesi that Basil created his own stamp of monasticism. During his pilgrimages he had known hermits and learnt the secrets of the desert by heart. Whilst he admired the feats of the ascetics he was wary of the adventures into which an individual without discipline could stray. His sense of proportion told him that one might become a holy man without so much ostentation and at a different price. He astutely observed that the hermit working only for himself had no opportunity to practise charity, highest of the virtues, and that left to his own judgment he was in danger of sinning through pride and vainglorious complacency. Fasting and vigil-keeping, even for record times, seemed to him quite unimportant. This had been the view of St Pachomius and Basil had taken a great interest in the Pachomian cenobites. But their organization into large colonies seemed too often to transform the monasteries into miniature towns, in which a monk, even when enclosed, was liable to lose his identity amongst the crowd of workers, and in which the superior often became merely an administrator, spending most of his time in keeping an eye on what might almost have been his business—the carrying-out of orders, deliveries, diverse exchanges and travelling, all of which occupations were very far removed from a life of holiness. According to St Basil a cenobite monastery was only justified if it were small enough for each monk to be in easy and regular contact with his superior, and in which the daily tasks, exclusively undertaken for serving the needs of the community, were carried on within the walls or in their immediate vicinity. In such cases the superior, assisted by a council of elders, would be more like the father of a family than the head of a business. This was a view of it that went far beyond Shenute or even Pachomius; a golden rule which today seems a normal one, but was then entirely new.

To all outward appearances the monks led a life of poverty. Even if it meant that they did not smell very clean, they were restricted to one sole garment, the tunic, a kind of robe with sleeves, neither too heavy nor too light, but suitable to be worn in all seasons. It was belted around the waist. Their buskins were coarsely made but solid. They slept on boards or mats and their food, although sufficient for remaining healthy, was strictly frugal. No doubt they did not wash very often, and they were particularly enjoined not to comb their hair. They prayed before sunrise, several times daily, and at bedtime, and they were to sleep only lightly and for short stretches. As he was not one of those who held that the good monk should do nothing when he was not attending either chapel or the refectory, Basil set his monks to manual labour from dawn onwards. Study formed another activity of his rule, i.e. the reading of the Bible in such a way as to train the memory, the imagination, and the intellect. They had no opportunities to indulge in exaggerated or fantastic forms of austerity, and no devilries occurred. They were expected to be serious-minded, but absolute silence was not enjoined on them. A monk might have been married, but in that case was not admitted unless the spouses had previously agreed before witnesses to separate. Slaves were only rarely accepted. The slave might be more anxious to join in order to lead an easier life than to perfect himself, and if on knocking at the door he were to be taken in, the monastery would be technically guilty of receiving stolen property. Basil may have known of the depositions of the Council of Gangra (in Paphalonia in 340 to 341) which condemned 'whosoever under the pretext of pity, encouraged a slave to despise his master, to escape from his servitude, or not to serve him willingly and respectfully'. With prudence and humanitarianism he followed the universal practice of the Church since the time of St Paul, which did not oppose the lawful institution of slavery, but endeavoured to humanize the relationship between masters and servants, and encouraged the emancipation of the slaves. Only if their faith and morals were endangered was he prepared to risk contravening the law regarding fugitives.

This way of life was based on experience, good sense, and a sense of proportion, yet it was not a monastic rule in the meaning of the term in the Western world of today. The Easterners were not as legally-minded as we are, and adapted themselves more easily than we would have been able to do, to a general way of life grafted on to existing customs and traditions, not as a precise and detailed code emanating from a centralized organization, but as a loose body of general directives and observances, the interpretation of which was left to the superior of each monastery. Thus, what is called the Rule of St Basil, i.e. the two collections of the *Extended Rules* and *Abridged Rules*, are no more than a series of answers to actual questions, giving rise to longer or shorter explanations and a certain number of which are as extended as lectures. These precepts are not even laid down according to a definite plan. It has been noted that certain of his ideas were influenced by the mystical Platonism of the Alexandrians, but basically his precepts simply rested on the interpretation of Christianity at the time; of faith, ecclesiastical dogma, and the Gospels. As it stood, the so-called Rule of St Basil spread via Constantinople throughout the Byzantine Empire. The hundred thousand monks who, apparently, encumbered the State at the time of the Iconoclastic feuds (eighth and ninth centuries) based themselves on St Basil.

As a centre of contemplation in the world and outside it as well, Basil's monastery was open to pilgrims, visitors—even heathen ones— and especially to children. Basil was clearsighted enough to realize that the pupils he trained would be of far greater service to his community than casual applicants. This—another fruitful concept of his—laid the foundations of the monastic schools. It even seems that he inaugurated two different kinds of school, one organized as a preliminary to the religious novitiate, the other, under certain provisions, opened for children whose lives would be spent in the outer world. Under experienced masters, preferably monks, the scholars lived separately from the community, only coming into contact with it for certain religious services. They were all taught according to 'an easy, pleasant method, refreshing to the spirit but without either constraint or fatigue'. Yet the traditional beatings were not eliminated from it. If one may say so, it was a very Aristotelian method, introducing knowledge to the mind through physical sensations: 'The teaching which had previously remained a dead letter was suddenly heard and memorized, as if the pain induced by beatings suddenly awoke the sense of hearing.' (*Homily XII.*)

At that turning-point of civilization heathenism, having nothing more to contribute either to thought or to letters, was giving ground to the Church, which having now come into its own, was about to produce a whole new crop of first-class minds, most of which had step by step progressed from the pagan schools to the monastic rule, and this state of affairs was reflected in the educational programmes of these early schools.

At that time religious education was entirely a family matter. Parents set their children an example and taught them the rudiments of their faith; the clergy prepared them for baptism during a period of three years, and this specialized teaching was often of a very high grade. The Catechetic lessons which have come down to us in part went far beyond our modern 'preparations'. And as M. Marrou has pointed out, the Christian religion, with its sacred texts, its liturgy, its disciplinary regulations, was based on writings, and for that reason required a certain amount of mental training before it could be understood.

It is rather curious that in countries with a Graeco-Latin cultural background the Church never aimed at a broader kind of education, in addition to its purely ecclesiastical schools, to compete with the heathen schools. By deliberately sending its children to sit on the benches of the heathen schools it acquiesced in this non-Christian training of their minds. It suffered them to be given an interpretation of the universe that it abhorred, and to be educated in a cultural and philosophical tradition that it wholly condemned. The Christians, as M. Marrou also pointed out, 'were satisfied by carrying on their specifically religious education . . . side by side with the classical teachings their pupils were given in the traditional schools, together with the heathen pupils'. In the Western world the Barbarian occupations to some extent shook them out of this habit, but no one in the Byzantine world ever thought of changing the old educational traditions, in spite of the fact that the Church was so powerful there, social life so penetrated by theological interests, the 'Holy' Emperors so 'orthodox' and the Christian scribes so famous. This system lasted for a thousand years, until the Turks took Constantinople. Educational systems die hard.

There were, nevertheless, certain opponents of this educational collaboration. In the third century the African, Tertullian, who died in 240, although he himself owed so much to the classical tradition, declared that 'there is nothing in common between Athens and Jerusalem, between the Academia and the Church.' Most of the monks shared his view. And they could base this opinion on an illustrious example—their Father, St Anthony, who, although illiterate, was able to refute certain alien philosophers, and to prove to them in dialectical debate that showed no trace of illiteracy the futility of all worldly wisdom compared to the folly of the Cross, wiser than all wisdom, although it must be borne in mind that in reporting this his biographer, St Athanasius, may have been laying it on a little. And when they founded a school they took care that for their pupils the Bible came to mean as much as Homer and Virgil had meant to the heathens. Pachomius arranged that his illiterate young monks should receive three hours' elementary education daily. And in his monastic school Basil also laid down an educational curriculum in accordance with his aims. Instead of learning their vocabulary from a list of heathen names they did so from the Gospels. He replaced the risky or impure tales and stories formerly taught by stories of the Biblical miracles, and rules of everyday life were taken from the Book of Proverbs. These efforts were nevertheless only on a small scale and had little future. The schools of the Eastern monasteries were only rarely pedagogical or intellectual centres.

Those who, rather than remain in a state of pious ignorance, preferred to acquire some learning at heathen sources were numerous. They in fact include all the intellectuals of the Church, students of Homer, Isocrates—the pastmaster of oratory—Plato, Cicero, and Virgil; among their pupils were Clement of Alexandria, Origen, Gregory of Nazianza —a holy man of letters with all the faults and qualities of that company —Basil, who, with Gregory, spent long years in Athens deeply immersed in the heathen masters; John Chrysostomus, pupil of the famous Libanius; Jerome, with his liking for Plautus; Augustine, who wept at the death of Dido; all the great names of the Christianized Graeco-Roman world.

Yet all of them, at some stage of their maturity, were highly critical of the disciplines in which they had been trained. Jerome's dream, even although he himself did not always take it seriously, apart from its vividness reveals a genuine conflict. Augustine found the Bible all-sufficing; it already contained everything of value that might be found in classical works, and rejected everything in them that was of no good. Gregory of Nazianza himself occasionally used very effective rhetoric to denounce rhetoric—'painted like the face of a courtesan'. Basil regretted the time 'spent in the past on vanity, his entire youth, almost, wasted in the useless labours of endeavouring to acquire the teachings of a science declared by God to be vain'. John Chrysostomus declared that Athens was nothing but a city of gossipers, and that the schools of the philosophers were a combination of lies, trickery and hypocrisy.

In order to explain these rebuttals by the very men who owed so much to the classics, one need only point out that the acceptance of the curricula and methods of classical pedagogy does not in any way imply the acceptance, also, of that particular culture, its ideals and world outlook. This basic distinction made by M. Marrou is supported by the texts themselves. But on the other hand it is indubitable that all human culture, whether it be heathen or not, and especially if it be regarded as a step towards the throne of Divine wisdom, has its uses. The examples of these Christian classicists is sufficient proof of it.

But bearing in mind the fact that Greek and Latin were at that time living languages, another train of thought is opened up. Is it wise to inculcate growing children with a 'poison' (that very word was used) in the hope that when they reach maturity they will of their own volition seek and take an antidote to it? Having sown the seeds of a certain culture in virgin soil, would it be logical not to expect to have to gather its fruits? Having developed their liking for certain ways of thinking and speaking, is it reasonable to suppose that one will be able to change it by presenting them with another literature, the very forms of which, they maintain, displease them, however true it may be? Whether we like it or not such a compromise contains a paradox, for, deciding that there was nothing else to put in its place, the Churchmen agreed to share in the general culture of their time, and whatever they wrote against it later, they were never in fact 'wholly freed from it'.[1] This was so much the case that when in 362 the Emperor Julian the Apostate forbade Christians to teach classical literature, allegedly because they did not believe in the works that they were expounding, the Christians them-selves were the first to protest against this measure, and their position was already so far consolidated that on the Emperor's death the Imperial edicts became a dead letter.

These early authorities found some ingenious excuses in justification of their attitude. St Jerome, who was always highly original, quoted the Bible itself (Deut. xxi. 12). It was usual, before presenting a female captive to her future husband, to shave her head and eyebrows, pluck out other hairs, and cut her nails so that she should be worthy of her spouse; and profane knowledge should be similarly groomed to prepare it for serving God. St Augustine used another analogy: when they departed from Egypt the Hebrews took away with them the precious vestments and gold and silver utensils of the heathens; why, then, should it be forbidden to Christians in their turn to despoil all the treasures of Antiquity?

St Basil dealt with the matter with less imagery and more closely in a little work addressed to his nephews, *To young men on the uses of Hellenism*. This little book was somewhat excessively welcomed by Humanists, who claimed that it recommended, even although perhaps somewhat shamefacedly, classical culture. Others with better reason claimed it to be a warning against the acceptance of profane wisdom; although certain elements of such a culture, either in word or deed, might be useful to Christians, there were certain others that should definitely be rejected. Whatever the rights or wrongs of such an interpretation, like all the leading thinkers of his time, St Basil did not envisage a different curriculum for the pupils selected for a regular study course, although definitely on condition that the teacher made a careful selection of the works presented to them. He himself set the example by compiling a number of extracts with a skill that proved his own familiarity over a considerable period with those authors he regarded as unsuitable.

This method, which consisted in eliminating everything that might undermine the faith, whilst retaining those elements conducive to virtue, has always been the guiding principle of pedagogues, but it is a

[1] M. Marrou.

fact that ours only applied it to classical literature. They were all convinced that the study of it constituted the only proper intellectual training and that an intensification of the Christian way of life provided a sufficient antidote to the dangers inherent in it. This, again, might be a source of embarrassment. It might happen that a pupil used to the carefully edited works *ad usum Delphini*, would one day find out that the divine Plato was not as divine as he had been led to believe, and that even in certain of Virgil's *Eclogues*, a very strange morality can be apprehended in spite of the magic of his poetry. It was only necessary to be able to read. Thus, even after such a long tradition of vigilant censorship a selection from these works could inevitably only constitute a half-measure. Ironically enough, after Christian teaching had for centuries reached a compromise with classicism, around 1900 those teachers who agreed that the great Christian classics were worthy to be placed on an equal footing with the heathen ones were not, in fact, all Churchmen.

Basil owed a great deal to the traditional education he had received at Caesarea in Cappadocia, at Constantinople, and above all at Athens. Whilst by no means a man of letters he wrote frequently, for owing to his interpretation of his responsibilities he was involved in all the great religious events of his period. Less metaphysical than the other two great Cappadocians—Gregory of Nyssa, his brother, and Gregory of Nazianza, he attempted to solve the problems of his time on the dual basis of dogma and practice. His attack on Arianism, following on that launched by Athanasius of Alexandria, the invincible champion of Nicaean orthodoxy, was a decisive blow to heresy. His works on the subject remain one of the sources of Christian dogma. We have seen how important his monastic activities were. His homilies on certain portions of the Bible and his lectures prove to what a height he was able to lead his listeners, even although Cappadocian, and when necessary present them with certain truths that in other times it might be dangerous to proclaim. What preacher today, for instance, would, without shocking his congregation, state that 'the most difficult virtue for the rich man to practise is the very one that he should find easiest—charity'? Even the liturgy engaged his attention. It is difficult to give exact details of his activities in this domain; nevertheless, in the Eastern Church a certain number of texts bearing his name are still used, concurrently with the liturgy of St John Chrysostom. His correspondence is of great value with regard to his period, his environment, and even more, the man.

It is our best source for estimating his rectitude, his levelheadedness, his practical and realistic intelligence, the greatness of his soul and his sense of responsibility. Certain of these letters are carefully composed, showing that their writer was thoroughly well educated. But most of them get to the point as quickly as was possible for a writer of the fourth century. His style, which is less varied and less spontaneous than those of Gregory of Nazianza or John Chrysostom, is more vigorous, competent, and possibly truer. It avoids the pedantic purism that was then the fashion, and for its period is excellent. Here, too, Basil showed his good sense and sense of proportion. His teachings have been described as 'A great but disciplined force'. It would not be an exaggeration to extend this praise to the man himself.

A LATIN MONK IN THE EASTERN WORLD: ST JEROME, FATHER OF THE LEARNED MONKS

In the autumn of 374 there arrived at Antioch a frail little man, loaded with books, and weary to death. Having come from Aquilaea, the big Italian city nearest to his native town, Stridon, which today no longer exists, Jerome had had a difficult voyage on his way to the desert, where he was hoping to perfect himself. He hoped to become one of those great monks whose lives had inspired him, but in addition to solitude and asceticism he was seeking opportunities for spiritual labours, a new activity in so intense a form in the monastic world.

Jerome was a burning soul who enlightened, warmed, and occasionally scorched and branded those who came close to him. The man was a mass of contradictions. As an author he produced a gigantic collection of works. As a monk he clung inflexibly to his vocation.[1] This saint like the others was of stern stuff, but he showed his metal more clearly than most. A man of quite extraordinary gifts, his defects were as outstanding as his great qualities. His heart was of gold but his teeth sharp as steel; he was as tender as a child yet he could be carried away to the point of fury; both sensitive and unjust, trusting and suspicious— Jerome was all those things. He both attracted and repelled people, overwhelming them one day with friendship and the next discarding them like so much rubbish.

His friends were always the best a man could have, but he had few of them, at least among men. On the other hand his friendships with women became famous. For three years he was received in the highest

[1] Youth and education in Rome, 347–74; lived in Antioch and in the desert of Chalcis, 375–79; lived in Constantinople and translated the Homilies of Origen, 379–82; visited Rome, monastic propaganda and scriptural works, 382–85; Bethlehem, Biblical works, polemics against John of Jerusalem and Rufinus, 385–419; died at Bethlehem, 419.

social circles in Rome. Intelligent and cultured Patrician women of the highest rank, devoted to sanctity in a society in which religion was not taken too seriously, converted their palaces on the Aventine hills into near-monasteries. Jerome became their teacher, guide, and friend, for those women were anxious that their faith should be enlightened and well founded. The Bible was their Book and Jerome expounded it to them. He worked hard on their behalf and never had need to regret it, for the devotion tinged with tenderness that he gave them was rewarded by their faithfulness, attachment and admiration, to which he was not at all insensible. There is nothing purer or clearer than those colloquies held on the Aventine between Marcella, Paula, and her children, whom Jerome taught to chant the psalms in Hebrew. When he took ship for the East some of the family left to join him in Bethlehem in order to continue to perfect themselves in the life of asceticism they had begun to lead in Rome. The discussions were continued between the monastery under Jerome's direction and the nunnery where those noble women did not think it beneath their dignity to sweep and wash the dishes, and their souls were sanctified in the footsteps of Christ. Several of them, consumed by the bright flame that their teacher had lit in them, died before their time, and Jerome, whose capacity for work was ordinarily insatiable, grieved so much for them that he was unable to write. Already an old man, he expressed his sorrow as emotionally as an adolescent might weep over his first love, but with such pure and dignified eloquence that his elegies for them remain amongst the masterpieces of Christian elegy.

But this tenderness had its counterpart in the saint's complex nature. Sensitive, imaginative, moody, sharp in debate and never at a loss in ridiculing his opponents, Jerome could hate as well as love.

He was the pastmaster of those polemecists who, during the fifteenth and sixteenth centuries especially, showed the highest skill in revivifying the old tradition of scholarly invective, not always from similarly high motives. 'Any adversary of his,' said Le Nain of Tillemont in the seventeenth century, 'was nearly always denounced as the lowest of the low.' And this is so true that an important book was written on Jerome's enemies.

His relations with the Aventine circle attracted the malignant attentions of those souls who, whilst themselves certainly not being above criticism, were the most quickly shocked and malicious when someone else's virtue was in question. Bespattered but unstained by the mud cast at him, Jerome furiously and superbly defended in acid terms the purity of his women friends. On whatever matter he might be attacked he always had at his command ready and ample means of counter-attack. This Christian Lucilius needed only to describe what he had seen with his own eyes to provide an edifying spectacle—over-dressed women, their faces covered with powder and rouge, so that when they wept their tears left dirty runnels on their cheeks; women who tried to conceal their age and who might have been less ridiculous had they not vainly attempted to hide their wrinkles; Tartuffes of all sorts, deliberately affecting a sleazy piety, and under their sordid rags going to church with their bellies distended by rich dinners; clerics of feeble virtue, with artificially waved hair, bowing and scraping, scrambling for honours and profits with which to deck out their own mediocrity; detractors of monastic life who, when unmasked, fell under the weight of their own ignorance; adversaries of learned works, those ignorant embryos (*homunculi*), two-footed donkeys—this was Rome, the whole of Rome, that Babylon, that 'purple-clad courtesan'. It was a large social group, a section of society that did not forgive such insults. Jerome tasted to the full the bitter fruits of its hatred. There is no doubt that he felt honoured by their insults, nor that it gave him pleasure to launch his barbed arrows into the 'Senate of the Pharisees'. But he had made so many enemies who were after his blood that one day, nearly having had his throat cut, he was obliged to quit 'Babylon'. He never again set foot in it, but he always kept an eye on it.

All his life Jerome gave way to his weakness for controversy. Although he was brilliant at it, one must regret that he wasted so much time over it and that he went as far as he at times did. On one occasion even, this saint who prized friendship so highly sinned so deeply against his own best friend that even his most faithful admirers could not forgive him for it.

One of the most widely read authors in the Eastern world at that time was a writer whose undeniable genius was of the greatest honour to the Church. Origen, the Egyptian, was a philosopher, an exponent of the Scriptures, a theologian, apologist, preacher, and master of the famous school of Alexandria, a monk living in the world and of immovable faith. He left on his death a first attempt at a synthesis of the Catholic dogma as well as scriptural works to which our modern authorities are still obliged to refer, and such a high example that he died, a firm witness to his faith, after an inquisition to which he did not yield an inch. 'According to his admirers, no one listened to God more intelligently . . . He had received the most precious gift, a splendid portion, that of being the one who explained God's ways to men.' Nevertheless, a certain degree of daring and rashness in his outlook, errors, even, that were later condemned, had already during his lifetime attracted the attention of theologians, so that after his death, according to their own views, certain of the saints were for, and certain others against Origen, an unsatisfactory situation.

Yet at the end of the fourth century he was assiduously read by all the intellectuals, and even, as far as they were able to understand him, by the monks of Nitria, whilst the rest only followed, occasionally with a good deal of noise, those who led them into one camp or the other. Jerome constantly used him in his Biblical studies, and when the master was attacked defended him sharply—'Neither because he has introduced a new interpretation of dogma, nor for heresy, as these mad dogs pretend, but because they cannot bear the power of his eloquence and knowledge. When Origen speaks all the rest should hold their tongues.'

Jerome's love for the master was shared by a friend of his youth, Rufinus of Aquilaea, like himself a monk and in love with friendship, equally devoted to the monastic and studious life. Rufinus, although not outstandingly brilliant, had taken on the more modest but very useful task of translating the great works of the Greek Orthodox Church and the lives of the holy monks in order to spread the knowledge of them in the Western world, which stood badly in need of it. Nothing does humanity greater credit than the communion of two such men, both of them sharing the same outlook, the same interests in scholarship, the same ideals and faith. Jerome and Rufinus were the Christian equivalent to the famous friends of heathen antiquity—Achilles and Patrocles, Orestes and Pylades, Nisus and Euryalis.

But one day, sad to relate, on being challenged to renounce Origen, Jerome lapsed from his usual rectitude. He prized his reputation for orthodoxy very highly; he was no theologian but a mere exponent— those were his excuses. But when a man as intelligent and cultured as he was, of so enlightened a faith, who for thirty years had followed an intellectual leader, translated dozens of his homilies, defended and proclaimed him 'the master of the Church after the Apostles', suddenly realizes that he is a heretic, such a change of tune is, to say the least, surprising, even when, as Jerome did, he uneasily claims that he only retained from him what was useful.

At that precise moment Epiphanius of Salamis arrived in Palestine. When that holy man, whose apostolic zeal was so gladly exercised at the expense of others, arrived anywhere, it was generally as a troublemaker. This time he was determined to add a particularly distinguished trophy to his past successes; to bring down Origen would be to crown his own career. He wasted no time in persuading Jerome to break with his bishop, John of Jerusalem, who as we know, was already suspected of heresy. Their relations soon became such that when John demanded of him that Jerome should make his submission to him, the latter replied by demanding that he should address to him, a simple monk, his profession of his Catholic and episcopal faith. This was quite rightly refused, to the great indignation of Jerome. 'Has there ever been such arrogance,' he wrote, 'as to refuse one's profession of faith to those who ask for it?' On the Mount of Olives Rufinus, better advised, closed his door to Origen's inquisitors. He was soon to learn the consequences of his loyalty, for Jerome, on the warpath against Origen, was to make Rufinus, his friend of all time, his principal target.

And so the 'brother' whom he had so well loved became a 'Sardanapolis, whose vices were more shameful than his name', a monk whose 'religion was mere lucre', a greedy-guts who stuffed himself at banquets, a hypocrite, 'a Cato without, but a Nero within', and finally, a 'swine'—(*grunnius*). It was the usual custom to blacken one's adversary before destroying him, but unworthy of Jerome, who was great enough to have dispensed with such arguments, even if his brand-new zeal might be regarded as an excuse for his denunciation of Origen.

This unfortunately famous quarrel was to continue to perturb Christianity during ten years, fanned when it appeared to be subsiding by clumsy or malevolent friends, who were not particular as to the methods they used to do so. Rufinus had no difficulty in pointing out the contradictions in his attitude to Jerome, which only annoyed him even more. But Rufinus was not up to the situation and, wiser than his old friend, took refuge in silence. When an argument reaches such proportions there are bound to be wrongs on both sides. Rufinus had his faults but in this affair it seems that Jerome's behaviour was the less pleasant, ill-served as he was both by his weaknesses of character and his evil genius. St Augustine, who was a heartbroken witness of this scandal, could not help commenting: 'What friend would not fear to become an enemy, if what we so much deplore could happen between Jerome and Rufinus?'

But it would be a mistake to judge Jerome only by his ill-humour, which was more than compensated for by the excellence of his other qualities. His ability as a humanist alone would suffice to do so.

Christianity very early included in its ranks writers who had been trained in the excellent literary tradition inherited from Athens and Rome. Among the Latins there were two particularly distinguished Africans—Tertullian, who in certain characteristic excesses resembled Jerome; and Cyprian, the martyr-bishop of Carthage. But none of the others reached such heights as Jerome, who was a true humanist. An exceptionally gifted student, in Rome he had the good fortune to meet two famous teachers, Victorinus and especially Donatius. His marvellous memory served him well in his ambition to read endlessly, intensely, all the works in his curriculum. Cicero held no secrets for him; he knew his Virgil by heart, and his Horace nearly as well, and these literary treasures remained with him all his life. His style, formed by such knowledge of the great masters, but reinforced by his own powerful personality, even in his hastiest improvisations retained the mark of a master. As a disputant he is sometimes irritating, but without forfeiting our affection. His erudition is seldom boring, even when he dwelt on certain points that no longer interest us. Occasionally, in works where one least expects a personal touch, his whole personality suddenly emerges, and in spite of ourselves we are drawn into his preoccupations at that time. It may be surprising, but one soon forgives such lapses on the part of a man of letters, since what he has to say is nearly always as interesting as his manner of saying it, and if Jerome had left himself out of it he would no longer have been Jerome. His sentences are well-shaped, solid and clear, with relatively little eloquence considering his period, yet occasionally they vibrate, burn, or sparkle. He could enter into details, find the correct analogies, get the best out of his reader and his subject-matter. He had, as one says, a presence. His translations have been highly praised. They form a considerable volume of his works, yet however eminent and useful they may be, from a literary point of view they are far inferior to his correspondence, his prefaces, and those numerous pages in which lyricism, romanticism and verve are suddenly projected. Latin literature, which in the classical tradition had petered out, in him irrevocably changed sides to occupy in future a pre-eminent place in the Church.

In Palestine he learned Greek thoroughly, but wasting no time in the garden of the Muses he only used it for his studies. He also thoroughly knew all the ecclesiastical literature of the Eastern world, and did not conceal from St Augustine his opinion that a good commentator of the psalms needed to know more Greek than a pious bishop of Hippo. In the desert of Chalcis he struggled with the refractory sounds of Hebrew, asking the help of a Jewish convert to learn it. Later on, at Bethlehem, he had recourse to another Jew, Baranima—whom Rufinus naughtily called Barabbas—who, as he had not been converted, was obliged to receive his caller at night, in secret. Finally, he learned Chaldean. If we add to all this the exegetical training he had received at Antioch, and at Constantinople from St Gregory of Nazianza, it is clear that his grounding would enable him to apply himself successfully to the most knotty points of ecclesiastical knowledge.

With his keen intellect, as a Christian humanist whose faith was so strong, it was to be expected that Jerome would be among the first to take up the problem which periodically confronted Churchmen, and to which from time to time he gave a very characteristic solution: namely, what should be the attitude of a Christian and even more so of a monk, towards classical literature, the product of a civilization so contrary to his own estate?

Jerome dealt with this question at a very early stage. Having decided to devote himself to Christian thought whilst living the life of a hermit, he provided himself with a library and settled down to work on the Bible. But as frequently happened, when he found his researches impeded by the uncouth language with which he was dealing he would have recourse to the rolls or codexes on his shelves of Horace or Plautus, two authors who were always carefully stored away in the monastic 'hells'. He deplored the fact that time and again he gave way to the temptation, due to his intellectual blindness, for, as he said, seeing no light, he did not blame his own eyes but the sun. At Antioch Jerome was once so desperately ill that almost nothing remained of him but skin and bones, and even his bones barely held together. He imagined himself to have died, and, before his Judge, claiming to be a Christian. 'You lie,' was the reply, 'you are a Ciceronian, not a Christian,' and having been given a thorough hiding he was only forgiven when he swore to renounce the perusal of heathen writings. And, he declared, this was no mere dream.

It was certainly an intellectual sacrifice. When he set out to master Greek, nothing was more natural to a mind like his than to lose himself in the pleasures of those passages of Homer, Plato, or Demosthenes far more subtly delightful than their Latin imitators. He renounced this pleasure and it has been correctly pointed out that when he quotes an ancient Greek author he often does so at second-hand. On that point he certainly kept his word. When Rufinus reproached him for having broken the promise he had made in his dream Jerome in some embarrassment attempted to minimize the importance of it. He told him, which in his own case was true, that a good memory could replace a library, that one might write down something one had remembered even without intent, and that, after all, this would never happen to Rufinus, since Rufinus was only a second-rate writer. And if he did in fact occasionally sin as regarded Plautus or Virgil he was generally too deeply preoccupied with other matters to spare much time for reading the classics.

During decades he worked away in his cell on his life's task, revising, translating, and commenting on the Bible with an ardour that never slackened.

This vocation began in his Roman period. Urged on to it by his friend, Pope St Damasus, he undertook to revise according to the Greek texts the numerous Latin translations of the New Testament then in circulation, the diversity and divergences of which were troublesome to the Western Church. It was a tricky task, the importance and dangers of which he well realized, since he, a mere private individual, was alone taking upon himself the responsibility of weighing and retouching a venerable work, whilst under the obligation not to offend those who with good reason did not wish to see it altered. This work, which had accrued from a revision of the Psaltery, he accomplished carefully and reverently, without too much trouble.

On his return to the East Jerome, as he studied the monumental work of Origen on the Gospels, realized that any revision of the Latin texts based on the Greek versions would be inadequate unless it had also been correlated with the original Hebrew. If this were possible, it would provide, in the Latin translation of the Old Testament, a direct version of the original, and, in apologetic debate, a marked advantage over the Jews, who then could no longer claim to be the sole authentic possessors of the Word. Once he had formed this view, it became for Jerome a plan from which he never diverged. Using the best manuscripts available, he once again returned to the Latin versions, compared them with the original texts, and retranslated them directly from the Hebrew. He worked on this with minute care, although on certain occasions he did allow himself to dictate rather quickly. The result was a work that was to become the book for all mankind, and which only a writer of genius could have produced—clear, firm in language, without ornamentation, as close as possible to the 'Hebraic truth' and sometimes, even, deliberately incorrect as it followed the original text.

In doing so, although he made considerable use of the Greek Bible, Jerome relegated to second place that version, which in the entire Eastern world was accepted as the paramount authority, and as a prime work of reference in the West. A great many, in fact, venerated it as the result of a miracle and accepted it as divinely inspired. But this translation, which was already in widespread use at the beginning of the third century B.C., was the work of Alexandrine Jews who had been charged with bringing the sacred books within reach of their coreligionists, who were becoming less and less familiar with Hebrew. Legend, however, had it that it had been carried out in seventy-two days by seventy-two exegetists, who had expressly arrived from Jerusalem in the island of Pharos with a Hebrew manuscript in letters of gold. Thence its name, the Septuagint.

This translation, incorrect but widely used, backed up the authority of the Greek text in the universal Church. But here, now, was an audacious individual who, on his own sole authority, even although referring to the Greek version as an indispensable source, discovered mistakes in it and in doing so lowered part of its prestige. However carefully he worked at the truthfulness and stylistic distinction of his own version, however respectfully he dealt with the Hebrew text and that of the Septuagint, Jerome was still regarded with suspicion. Rufinus, under the influence of those feelings which we have seen he held towards his former friend, regarded him as a forger and a heretic. St Augustine, who would have preferred a revision based merely on the Greek version, was more moderate in his views, but he also had reservations. He did not think that Jerome could improve on the Alexandrians, and because of the divergencies between the two versions—the ancient Greek and the new Latin—feared that difficulties might arise between the Eastern and Western Churches; he also feared that in the West the inevitable difficulties arising out of the fight against the heretics would be increased by yet another Latin translation. To the reasonable objectors were added those who, reinforced by Jerome's enemies, declared as revolutionary and therefore to be condemned, anything new that might be disturbing to their peace of mind.

Jerome defended himself as well as he could, and without an excess of charity, against the barking of those mad dogs who rushed around, thinking themselves clever in tearing others to pieces. After all, he concluded, 'those whom my work displeases are not obliged to read it'. He had confidence in his genius, and it was not misplaced. In the Western world his translation was to have an ever-growing influence on its civilization, on ecclesiastical research and piety, since from the fifth century onwards his version became the accepted one for all, and all prayers were based on his verses. The old fighter and untiring man of learning grumbled when his tired eyes could no longer read manuscripts, but he did not then know how many other eyes would wear themselves out over his own works. Better still, his translation, with the addition of four volumes of the original Latin version, was to receive the highest official consecration bestowed in honour of a human achievement; the Bible in Jerome's version became our Vulgate, i.e. the universal version of the Book (*vulgus*), proclaimed by the Council of Trent in 1546 as the authentic version of the Roman Church. On that day, in Heaven, Jerome must have given Rufinus a very knowing look.

If, however, such a work had been accomplished under conditions that did not include the supernatural, it would have gone for nothing in the order of sanctity; the exegetist and theologian are not necessarily sanctified by their work. Jerome's character was such that too often his behaviour was anything but saintly, yet however much noise his vehemences made in the world, and however much they indeed upset him, they did him no lasting harm. On the contrary, just because they created such a stir, they were an intrinsic element of his unceasing striving for saintliness. Except on the occasions when some irrepressible spark would fly from his pen, Jerome left few records of his own piety, yet there is little doubt that at the time of his tussles with Rufinus his prayers must have reflected his inner turmoil and difficulties, and that he often suffered through his own inability to restrain his feelings and his imagination. His struggles, harder than those of any other mortal, only gained the greater glory thereby.

Frail, in constant ill-health, and easily tired, in solitude he accomplished a task far more exhausting than any basket-weaving. He was constantly complaining of his sicknesses. 'Even when in good health,' he conceded, 'my poor body is a weak one.' Yet he kept strictly to the monastic rule and persevered all the more relentlessly in his task. He did not practise all the ascetic ruthlessness of the Egyptian way of life, which would have been incompatible with his work, but he was, nevertheless, very hard on himself. He would really have loved the desert, if he had been left to himself in it, or if there he had been able to find inner tranquillity. 'The desert, studded with the flowers of Christ. A solitude embellished by the precious stones of which the city of the King of Kings of the Apocalypse is built. The desert of the hermits, of which God is the host.' He might have repeated these slightly too poetical words of his youth truly at any moment of his life in the monastery of Bethlehem. Black as an Ethiopian under his habit, ill-nourished, he at first suffered from certain vivid personal memories, which were obsessive but not always chaste. Broken by fasting, he half-killed himself with work, but came triumphantly out of his trials. Whenever the monastic life came under fire Jerome was always at the breach, impelled thereto by his fine courage. His keenness even went so far that it caused him to denounce the marriage bond more strongly than was reasonable. His *Life of Saint Paul as a Hermit*, his *Life of Malchus*, which in 1673, at the suggestion of the Gentlemen of Port-Royal was used by La Fontaine, his *Life of Hilarion*, although a little too full of classical quotations for our taste, are all works of propaganda in favour of the desert life and as such must have had a great success on account of their style, content, and moral teaching. His own asceticism did not involve perpetual silence, fasting, the wearing of chains or sitting on a column, but in working incessantly, a harder test than is generally supposed, and which gradually drew him on to a higher plane without, however, completely altering his nature.

Thus, rising above his distressing quarrels, Jerome remains for us the outstanding and always human example among the monks of those who endeavoured fully to live the difficult monastic life whilst wholly devoting themselves to the service of ecclesiastical scholarship. It has not, perhaps, been sufficiently appreciated that at a time when the two halves of the Christian world were already setting out on separate paths Jerome, the Latin, by dwelling in the East, by his powerful personality and the importance of his works, was a bridge-builder between these two worlds. If he had had fewer enemies he would have succeeded his friend Damasus as Pontiff; in which case, if one may say so, we would have had an incomparable Pope. Towards the end of the Middle Ages pious artists bestowed a fine cardinal's hat on him. But he had no need of it, and we may permit ourselves to prefer to this distinguished ecclesiastic our own tempestuous and learned Jerome, a simple priest who went so far as to refuse 'respectfully and humbly'—and also for the sake of his independence—to carry out his sacerdotal duties in order to remain completely faithful to his ideal life of a monk and a scholar.

A great deal more might have been added to this deliberately restricted but indispensable account of the monastic estate in the East. There were a great many holy monks in Palestine, crowded with *laura*, on Sinaï, in Mesopotamia, even in Constantinople, who deserve not to have been excluded from it. But a more detailed description of them would not add any more fresh information to it; the anchorites everywhere were individualists, and amongst the 230 monasteries that Dom Leclercq counted in Palestine and Egypt alone, the cenobites all more or less led a similar communal life. But in Palestine three names must at the least be mentioned: those of Chariton, whose dates are uncertain; Euthymis (d. 457), and Saba (d. 532).

Even today, this way of life has hardly changed at all in the East. There are no monastic orders there as we in the West understand them, i.e. various groups of specific kinds serving the same ideal, as, for instance, our Benedictines, Cistercians, Trappists, or lay monks, all followers of St Benedict. There are simply vast groups of monks all living according to their vocation either as anchorites, semi-anchorites, and cenobites, or sometimes adopting each of these monachal forms alternately. As we have observed, the most perfect rule is a spiritual state rather than the following of a set of rules. It has always been so. At the end of the eighth century and the beginning of the ninth St Theodore, when reorganizing monastic life in his famous monastery of the Studion at Constantinople, did not think either in terms of a regular charter for all, so to speak. To this very day the monks of Mount Athos, whilst basing themselves on St Basil and St Theodore, live above all according to secular customs which have not altered. If outwardly the cenobitic communities more or less resemble one another, taking into account the general concept of cenobitism, as in the past every monastery is autonomous, with its own peculiarities. Although there are not now many of them the anchorites do still exist. The aim everywhere is to attain perfection, without troubling much about culture or scholarship. A few monks who are also priests conduct the services, but in theory this does not entitle them to any particular privileges, since in the East a monk who is not a priest may rule a community and have priests under his orders.

Taken as a whole, in the Eastern world far more than in the Western the monastic institution has remained much closer to its origins, consisting of, on the whole, the predominantly plebeian classes, of a crude saintliness, often ignorant, sometimes illiterate, and for that reason all the more narrow-minded and intransigent. But through its leaders it did exercise a definite influence on civilization. It gave the Church a number of saints, visionaries, and most of its bishops. Among the latter in particular were men of the status of Basil, the two Gregories, John Chrysostom, and these outstanding heads had many successors. The influence of the monks on the arts was always considerable, especially after the middle of the ninth century. Having from the end of the fourth century organized the times of the offices around the services, they created masterpieces which are amongst the highest achievements of art in general. Their theological and mystical writings were given out thanks to ateliers in which there were copyists, translators, and illuminators who illustrated them. If their educational efforts were limited, they practised charity on a wide scale, especially when their monasteries lay near the gates of cities. Many of them directed great missionary enterprises, which deserve to be better known. Only to refer to the most important of these, the labours of Cyril, the 'philosopher', and Methodius, the monk, won first Serbia and Bulgaria and then the whole of Russia over to civilization. There were large numbers of monks to be found wherever Byzantine influence spread. The Holy Mountain of

Athos had dependencies in Poland, in Russia, and all over the Eastern world.

It is, nevertheless, a fact that by inclination, temperament and tradition, and because the idea of efficiency was never as highly thought of in the East as it was in the West, the monks in the former half of the world were above all contemplatives and in general less educated, and never took part in outside activities to the same extent. During a thousand years, in spite of the Arabs, the Romans and the Turks, in spite of recurring crises, the relative stability of the Byzantine State, its social life and cultural developments, were such that those monks did not have the same opportunities as their Western brethren to direct their vocational activities towards specific works of civilization. On this side of the world matters developed very differently—everything, or nearly everything, had to be rebuilt on new foundations.

CHAPTER IV

THE CONQUEST OF THE WEST

From the earliest days of Eastern monachism the saints of the West looked towards Egypt and Palestine. The fame of the desert was so great that a stream of pious pilgrims set out from the farthest shores in order to collect the famous apophthegms on the spot. Egypt was a mere detour on the sea-route to Jerusalem, and once on their way, the pilgrims did not look to a month or two's delay. They would thus in fact reap a double harvest by both following in the steps of the Saviour and discovering the secrets of complete initiation from the ascetics. This lure of the desert was emphasized by Jerome, who when it suited his mood could be irresistibly persuasive, and who at that time sang the praises of such solitudes where, he then declared, people did not tear one another to pieces as they did elsewhere. Another very odd witness was the nun Silvia, Etheria, or Egeria, who, at the end of the fourth century, in no hurry to return to her convent, at every moment discovered new monks to visit in Jerusalem, Sinaï, Arabia, Mesopotamia, Cappadocia and elsewhere, describing her pious travels for her Western sisters, probably Spanish, with satisfaction and a wealth of detail, but not at all romantically.

Yet these travellers were still a minority. Very many others told themselves that in order to attain perfection it was unnecessary to voyage so far. They considered that such an aim, inspired by the eternal Gospels, was not linked with geographical exploration. Living humble lives, either singly or in small groups, history ignores most of their activities.

In Rome from an early date asceticism was practised privately, at home. When, towards the end of 339 Athanasius of Alexandria, a disciple of the Egyptian Anthony, and a bishop obliged to flee on account of his heroism in the service of the doctrine of the Trinity, disembarked there accompanied by two authentic desert Fathers, he did not feel entirely out of place. The saintly people and especially the women, received him joyfully. Athanasius told them stories of the marvels of Egypt, confirmed by the amiable monk Theodore and the behaviour of the silent and surly monk Ammonius. Marcella, a young Roman lady of high degree, was so filled with love of asceticism by these tales that she wore the dress of those who had taken their vows of renunciation. As we have seen, her palace on the Aventine Hill housed a kind of convent, before this was moved to a villa in the suburbs. There was also a woman called Melanie, who became the follower of the monk Rufinus, Jerome's brother and later adversary. In Marcella's circle they pointed out the charming young Asella, a girl who, having heard of the marvels of Egypt, sold her pretty golden chain in order to buy the brown garment of the ascetic virgins. She trained herself in an uncomfortable cell to protracted fasting, to living on bread and salt, and she prayed for so long that her delicate knees were covered with callouses. When Jerome arrived in Rome soon afterwards he merely had to enrich a little the soil prepared by domestic asceticism to cause a number of the members of the community to transfer themselves to Palestine.

ST PAULINUS OF NOLA, SCRIBE AND ASCETIC

Whilst they were inspired by the great lessons they learned from the Easterners, some of these initiates were already adopting a somewhat different attitude, and in certain cases, rather tentatively, a new style. St Paulinus of Nola, although too exceptional to be regarded as typical, nevertheless provides an example of a somewhat broader kind of ascetic idealism.

He was not a poor devil of a fellah seeking for the Absolute in a desert, but a person who would have been completely at home in the distinguished company of the Aventine ladies. Paulinus, who lived around 354 to 431, had in fact everything necessary to achieve what is called a career. He was born at Bordeaux, a member of a family claiming to be descended from the Anicii, and which had given the Empire a number of high officials. He, too, made his way quickly, since at the age of twenty-six he was governor of Campania. He was also extremely rich. His large estates in Aquitania, Campania, and after his marriage, in Spain, assured him of a leading position in that powerful class that lived sumptuously in its palaces or villas. And in addition he was a man of culture.

His teacher was Ausonius, one of the great names of intellectual Gaul. Ausonius was still a mere professor, but in those days, when a man was honoured by his calling, he was to end as Consul, after having been Prefect of the Praetorium and Governor of the Gauls. At that time, however, he was impressing his pupils and Aquitanian society by his poems, although in his case good craftsmanship rather than genius was their mainspring. His was a minor talent, clear and elegant, that observed all the rules of the Schools, but although Ausonius, as one might say, lived among the shallows of the poetic world, he gained a devoted following.

Paulinus, an impeccable pupil, who had similar gifts, was his teacher's favourite friend. He was kind-hearted, good-tempered, and jolly, quite at ease in the lesser poetic forms, and amused his correspondents with the ingenious trivialities then in fashion.

Suddenly one day Ausonius heard that his pupil, who had been baptized, as was customary, rather late in life, had sold his own estates as well as his wife's property, had, apparently to his own satisfaction, become a poor man, was ordained, although a little in spite of himself, and had chosen the monastic life. The high society to which he belonged was shocked that one of its members, arrived at the age of final success—Paulinus was nearly forty—should refuse to play the game. In the eyes of those to whom he said good-bye, he was not only a deserter from the city that needed intelligent, influential, and rich leaders, but his action appeared to them as unpleasantly critical of a society that did not enjoy being compared, in its futility, to a spider's web. Ausonius was one of those Christians who assigned to God the precise, or rather, the smallest portion due to Him, and for that very reason was incapable of appreciating Paulinus's resolution, for which he blamed him bitterly.

Paulinus, quietly but obstinately, let him talk. With his wife Theresia, thenceforward his sister, he retired to Nola in Campania, near to the tomb of St Felix, an obscure martyr of the third century. Installed there towards 395, they remained there for the next thirty-five years, eating the 'bread' of the Scriptures and living lives of the strictest asceticism, including the wearing of hairshirts, in the midst of two little communities, more on the lines of family life than cenobitic, one of men, the other of women. They ate only one frugal meal daily, preferably vegetarian, with a little wine, which was not enough for a certain Cardamas, who was inclined to the bottle. Nola was not so inaccessible that the priestly monk, Paulinus, now a bishop, was unable to receive many visitors. On these occasions his saintliness was reinforced by his good breeding as a man of the world, which he never lost. Whilst there was precious little politeness in the deserts of the East, at Nola it was prized as a monastic virtue, it being by no means the least of the characteristics of humility to show every courtesy to one's brethren. Thus life passed peaceably although not without strict discipline around the amiable Paulinus.

It was only from time to time troubled by the menace of Alaric, which then lay heavily over Italy. Things might indeed have turned out very badly when the Ostrogoths, in their southward march, destroyed part of the city, had not the saint shown his innate equanimity when threatened with adversity. 'Only those who do not believe in Christ our Saviour trust in the legions and take refuge behind the ramparts.' When this danger threatened, the favour he asked of God, that he should not be tortured 'either for his gold or his silver'—which he no longer possessed—was granted him. St Felix was taking care of his own.

In normal times Paulinus's duties did not prevent him from following his earlier loves. When he was converted he did not cease to be a man of letters, but the tools of his trade were hallowed instead of being broken. Paulinus thoroughly enjoyed the written intercourse which was one of a bishop's duties. He corresponded with Jerome, Rufinus, Augustine, Sulpicius Severus, his great friend, and other Church leaders. He was unable to write treatises of theology or philosophy, since he was not particularly well acquainted with the problems of the Scriptures, knew little Greek and detested Hellenic culture. His offerings chiefly consisted of the flowers of his gentle piety. He even found time to flirt with the Muse. He remained all his life a good student, especially of Lucretius, Virgil, and Horace, but the dramatic reactions aroused in a Jerome by the perusal of the classics never affected him. Thus he continued to rhyme at his ease, satisfied to 'season' his poems 'with faith and religion'. He even dared write an epithalamium, usually a very indecent poetic form, but which his pen adorned with chastity. His principal subject, however, was St Felix, whose panegyrist Paulinus could well claim to be, on the basis of a total of 5,000 verses in his praise. His lack of inventive powers was compensated for by oratorical amplifications and utter constancy in his devotion. On January 14th of every year, or nearly so, the saint's birthday, the bishop-monk produced his annual poem. In this activity Ausonius's disciple came into his own, in slightly precious descriptions and accounts of the miracles performed with open hands by his local saint; chiefly, it would appear, on behalf of cattle or pigs. And many pilgrims came in January, more or less from all over the place, but chiefly from the surrounding countryside. These Campanian peasants still preserved the old pagan custom of junketing on the sacred occasions of the Church. Paulinus viewed their feasting indulgently. In order to distract their attention he had pictures of certain Biblical episodes painted on the porticos under which rather less holy scenes were taking place, and whilst the good people gazed delightedly at them, their bishop, with a hidden smile, told himself that for a few hours, at any rate, their wassails were halted. And when the glad summons of the bells rang out, the whole people rushed to church; and to this very day it is still asserted at Nola that the Campanian Paulinus was the inventor of bells (*Campana*).

This was the life of Paulinus, monk, bishop, and man of letters. The rich and fertile Campania, where he lived so happily, was not the Thebaid. We may easily guess what a Macarius would have thought of so many hours wasted in pious niceties in the midst of a beautiful landscape. But that was only one side of the real Paulinus, and we should not be taken in by his man-of-the-world manners. The fact that he drew to Nola so many distinguished personages from Italy, Gaul, and Spain, as well as the Balkans, proves that in matters of saintliness and asceticism he had something to say and set an example. Paulinus occupies a place apart and possibly rather far below the leaders in the hierarchy of the monks. Had he stayed in the world he would merely have remained a witty man of leisure. When he was converted to the Christian rule he became the least fierce of the ascetics, but was nevertheless an ascetic first and foremost. As his contribution to civilization he introduced classical literature to the Western world; he did so by making a place in Christian literature for certain minor forms of it, maybe, but although they had all the faults of their fashion and period, at that time they were admired as among the best. Whilst in Milan Ambrosius was laying the foundations of Christian poetry, at Nola Paulinus evolved a form of devout humanism which in certain aspects could be compared to the works of St Francis of Sales.

ST AUGUSTINE, MONK AND MASTER OF CHRISTIAN HUMANISM

In Africa monastic life was also being developed by individual initiative. There, as elsewhere, its origins are uncertain, and for more precise evidence in this matter we look to St Augustine, but it must be understood that this only represents one facet of his personality, and that he cannot be confined to any limited framework.[1] The plans for a communal life occurred to him fairly early on. In Milan, at the age of thirty, where, as he said, he was following his trade as a merchant in words, in

[1] Born 354 at Tagaste (Suuk-Ahras); student at Carthage, 370; visits to Rome and Milan 383–84; baptism at Milan and return to Africa, 387; became priest at Hippo (*Bône*), 391; bishop of Hippo, 396; died at Hippo, 430.

one of those moments of fatigue that overtook him occasionally in his struggle for grace, he had the idea of founding a philosophical and friendly community in which an intendant, elected like the magistrates for two years, would take over the administration in order that the rest of the group might be free to devote themselves to their studies. But the problem of the women (Augustine was not referring to married women, *uxores*, but to little women, *mulierculae*), prevented his plans from maturing. Some of the members of the proposed group already had a female attachment, others wished to have one, and we know Augustine's own situation at that time.

About two years later the question was raised again. One day, still at Milan, he had a visitor, a compatriot called Pontitian, an officer of the Imperial court who was then stationed at Treves, on the German frontier. During their conversation Pontitian noticed an open book lying on a gaming table. He picked it up, leafed through it, and not without a touch of humour remarked that it was very serious reading, on which he congratulated Augustine. Pontitian, who was a Christian, had recognized the Epistles of St Paul. He then told Augustine that an Egyptian monk called Anthony was the founder of monachism, and that right there in Milan there was a monastery directed by bishop Ambrose. Augustine listened with even greater interest as his visitor told him of an adventure of his own at Treves. One day when the Emperor was presiding over the circus games, a few officers, including Pontitian, to pass the time went for a walk in the gardens near the ramparts. In a cabin there they discovered a hermit who had in his possession, in the Latin text of Evagrius of Antioch, the biography of Anthony by bishop Athanasius, who was formerly banished to Treves. Two of them read it, no doubt rather hurriedly, and on the spot decided to become monks. They were both engaged, but their fiancées were simply informed that the engagements were off, whereupon the two girls decided to become nuns. Augustine was deeply moved by this story and the famous scene in the garden led to his final decision. We know that on the same day, opening St Paul's book, that was still lying on the table, at random, his eyes lit on the decisive passage. St Augustine, too, had gained his victory.

One cannot exactly describe the place he chose for his retreat, shortly before his baptism, at Cassiciacum, not far from Milan, as a monastic house. It is true that Augustine had been joined by a group of friends in the villa belonging to Verecundus. Monica was the mistress of the house and presided at table, whilst her son went into deep meditation. Having decided to become a Christian he enjoyed a spring-like period of anticipation whilst his mind was absorbed in the passive contemplation of disincarnate Beauty. But although life at Cassiciacum was carefully ordered, it was not in any way monastic. Its intellectual activities and metaphysical discussions, even when they touched on the young master's preoccupations, were more in the nature of a study group, slightly resembling the conferences formerly held at Pontigny, or, rather, the moving experiment at Littlemore of Newman before his conversion.

The idea, nevertheless, developed little by little. On his return to Thagastus Augustine developed the attempts made at Cassiciacum in a monastic direction. He had consulted the saints in Milan, and visited cenobites in other parts of Italy, preferring them to the anchorites. He admired their virtues, their fasts, their humble and practical daily labours, the wisdom of their superiors. In the small community of Thagastus they led a life of poverty and sobriety, prayed a great deal, read the Bible, no longer shocked by its crudities, went on philosophizing and receiving numerous visits, for Augustine was born there, and people were talking about him. But the monastery thus established did not endure.

Having become a priest and then a bishop, Augustine was obliged to leave his natal town for Hippo (Bône). There the ideas he had tried out at Thagastus were put into final practice; the bishop turned his house into a clerical monastery, which was at one and the same time a centre for contemplation as well as propagation of the faith, a seminary and a parish. Under the Master's direction the priestly monks were made to study the methods of the profane Schools, along with the Bible and divine teaching. Contemplation was regarded as on a higher level than action; the search for truth must never be relaxed, and however pressing apostolic needs might be, they must not ever be put before it. It was a fertile method and quickly bore fruit. Augustine's companions trained in this school not only settled down all around Hippo, providing local parish priests, but a good number of them in their turn became bishops and founders of monasteries. It was a definite departure from previous Eastern monachism, which had been strictly contemplative, and very much inclined to pious ignorance, even although certain episcopal monks like Basil and Gregory of Nazianza had conscientiously devoted themselves to works as well. Yet it was not altogether a new departure. Eusebius at Verceil, Martin at Tours, and especially Ambrose at Milan, had already introduced a similar rule. Augustine, meanwhile, with his new method in mind, founded a second monastery on classical lines at Hippo, destined for laymen who felt themselves unsuitable for the priesthood or rejected it as a vocation.

The Augustinian monastery was run on cenobitic lines and all activities were devoted to the common good. All the inmates collaborated closely in their striving for sanctity and in their apostolic mission. To enter the monastery was by no means to enter the heavenly gates, as some over-enthusiastic apologists might have led one to suppose. It was more like serving in a ship, in which everyone was assigned to his post, and which normally sailed through calm waters. But when storms arose they clung tightly to one another, sheltering against the tempest. They were always together.

Augustine never assumed the name of abbot. The role of the superior was firstly to ensure that unanimity and harmony prevailed, that the rule was rigidly observed, especially with regard to work both within and outside the walls, that poverty and chastity were practised, and that the attendance at services, which were celebrated in the Eastern fashion and sung as simply as possible, was punctiliously observed. He did not spend his time keeping a ceaseless watch on his monks. His aim was a rule that was both punctilious and broadminded, trusting and without pettiness, allowing certain reasonable exemptions, but severe towards any delinquency. He set the precedent of a golden rule for abbots which in his own case he made an iron one; he found happiness, not by using his authority in order to dominate, but by service in the spirit of charity. This leads one to assume that Augustine had had some very definite experiences in the matter or else that his intuition was infallible.

The community must have been a considerable one, since the abbot was assisted by a number of officers or deacons (*decani*) who were in charge of the laundry, the refectory, the infirmary, and the library, for in the Western monastic world there was far less illiteracy than in the Eastern. They all had to cater for the needs of the brethren, but on the basis of poverty, for the rule of poverty was the general one. The monastery was poor rather than rich, and in any case never, as happened elsewhere, run on business lines.

Both rich and poor, however, were accepted there. Those who had been 'powerful' men were to forget it, and re-model their souls, without expecting any advantages from the monastery on account of their choice of poverty nor endeavour to enjoy on a small scale any of the comforts they had given up. And the poor man, now elbow to elbow with his former master, was not to take advantage of the equal status they enjoyed in monastic life in order to work off on him grievances which he was formerly obliged to repress. Everyone laboured according to his abilities; systematic harrying or trials of strength, however useful they might be thought as tests of the victim's virtue, were not conducive to the harmonious equilibrium necessary to communal living. Those who were capable of writing sermons might do so, but this was not to be an excuse for scamping their manual tasks. Brethren of the peasant class (*rusticius*) were not to envy those who did no manual work and if they were able to read they were not to pose as intellectuals, arguing that the study of the Bible was far more useful than any physical labour. Who would eat must work, was the general rule. The monastery was not at all an almshouse for those who were tired of living—a romantic notion that was as widespread as it was false—nor for those who, having nothing to eat at home, imagined that there they would at all hours find a well-laid table awaiting them.

Around the refectory table, however, all the brethren gathered. Nobody 'dined out', but it was a law of hospitality that all who wished to come to it should be allowed in. Meals were frugal but filling, for the Superior frowned on exaggerated asceticism. There was occasionally meat and also wine, both of which were sternly forbidden in Eastern monasteries. It was even permitted to enjoy the tasty little dishes that the pious nuns in the neighbouring convent from time to time sent across. The table service was of common materials, either wooden or earthenware, but the spoons which had come from no one knew where, were silver ones, for the Master could, when he liked, behave like a lord. On certain occasions even conversation was allowed at table, but there was an inscription in the refectory which stated both with authority and humour that gossip was forbidden (*absentium rodere vitam*).

They dressed like any other monks, wearing the same habit fastened by a belt around the waist, with a cloak in bad weather (*casula*, hence our chasuble). All of them, including their Superior, had shaven heads. Ablutions were not too frequent; visits to the baths were only permitted to those who were sick, and they were only allowed to make them in groups of three at a time, not on the initiative of those who did so, but on the orders of their Abbot. Augustine had good reasons to be suspicious of the behaviour of his Numidians in public places, which were not at that time temples of virtue. For the same reason a monk was never allowed to receive a female visitor in the parlour alone. In general it was regarded as advisable to keep all women out, for if one were allowed in she would bring others, and there would be no end to it.

These general principles, counsels, and style of living were far removed from the severity customary in most monastic institutions, especially the Eastern, at that period. The monks who lived in the Bishop's residence at Hippo were clerics, partly active in the outside world, and as such obliged to combine unequivocally and with the least possible expense the obligations of the monastic life with the requirements of their apostolate, the latter depending on the former. Others who dwelt in the cloister obviously led more closely regulated lives.

But the account that has been given above must not be over-estimated. It would be incorrect to include Augustine among the founders of an order. The experiment at Hippo was conducted along certain definite lines, but it was entirely empirical. What is known as the Rule of St Augustine was only a formal letter addressed to the nuns of Hippo, whose Superior, a sister of the bishop, had got into difficulties with her nuns. This letter was complemented by the treatise on *Monastic Works*, another formal document written for Aurelius, bishop of Carthage, who was encumbered with a monastery in which the male inmates were strongly fighting to retain their right to inactivity, basing their claim on the Gospel stories of the lilies of the field and the birds in the heavens. These two documents were designed to correct bad behaviour and to suggest general rules, and cannot be regarded as forming a complete code of monastic life as a whole. They are nevertheless very valuable and might have contributed to establishing a tradition as lasting as the rules of Pachomius and Basil in the East, had not the African church, after Augustine, been shattered by the Vandal invasion and finally destroyed by Arab colonization.

We have seen that everything was not always for the best in Augustine's monasteries. There, as in Egypt, the devils were active, although not on so spectacular a scale. In his treatise on *Monastic Works* Augustine condemned a race of hypocrites who, under the guise of saints, overran the provinces, with no charge and no fixed domicile, in a disorderly manner. Some of them sold relics, supposing that they in fact were relics; others pretended to be learned, and others again falsely claimed that they were obliged to visit relatives a long way off. But all of them demanded and insisted on the money to be earned by a lucrative poverty (*sumptus lucrosae egestatis*), or else as the price of a pretended holiness (*simulatae pretium sanctitatis*). And when they were caught the entire world of monks had to bear the brunt of it.

In addition to his multifarious tasks as an apostolic bishop and a monk, as well as those of a secular judge which at that time were carried out by the bishop, Augustine was an orator, philosopher, moralist, theologian and polemicist—a complete cleric, and as such a worker in the cause of civilization. His works comprise eleven in-folios in the Benedictine edition. This intellectual, as he would be called today, acquired considerable learning almost unaided, a method that a genius sometimes finds useful. But, helped by a marvellous memory and no less marvellous intelligence, he assimilated all his learning without difficulty, and transmuted it into a body of knowledge that was stamped with his own characteristic warmth. Augustine, in fact, sought for truth not only with his mind, but, as Plato advised, with his whole soul. Slowly he advanced along his road to discovery. When he made a mistake he admitted it, and retracted, and this innate honesty is one of the most attractive characteristics of the greatest among all the Doctors of the Church. 'May those who read these lines,' he wrote at the beginning of his treatise on the Trinity, 'advance with me when they share my certainty, seek with me when they find themselves sharing the same doubts, return to my interpretation when they admit that they are in error, and win me over to theirs if it is I who am wrong.'[1] No one could have been more respectful of the feelings of others, aware of the pitfalls of research, and less filled with theological pride. Having been graced by faith, Augustine endeavoured to find evidence of Godliness in mankind, and for this alone, had he done nothing else, would have the right to be ranked as the most complete humanist. With deference towards authority and tradition he still wished to investigate the bases of his faith, and finding it confirmed by them went ever further into both his faith and his reasons for holding it. To believe in order to understand, and to understand in order to believe was his incessant aim, for he knew that the way of Christ was not one of perpetual security but a divine adventure, and that it was 'with perishable means that the architect must build an imperishable dwelling'. Thus he was able to enjoy that Sovereign Good which through grace victorious leads to love, mysticism, and the gift of tears. In Augustine's case Truth entire entered into the whole man.

In spite of the heights to which he leads us he always remained one of ourselves. Himself a lord of the Church he knew how to stoop down towards those beneath him, and without lowering himself, gradually raise them up to him. The most eminent of all the learned, he took care to expound the truth to them in simple terms, and not as a Doctor. As a witness to God—and this is the true meaning of the word confession—he bemoaned his own faults. They were both of mind and of body, and perhaps he attached too much importance to the latter, which misled some of his superficial readers, for in his days the unconverted committed far greater ones. Even as a bishop he had his faults like the rest of us. It has been noted that when it was a case of fighting against heresy he occasionally threw himself into the arena rather too quickly and without the necessary calm of mind, as a result of which he

[1] Fr. Trad. Labriolle; Eng. C.H.

sometimes voiced exaggerated views, that fell from him in the heat of discussion, and, especially, on the subject of grace, showed a hardened mental attitude that might have turned the most human of saints into the most inhuman of theologians. He was by nature sensitive, and the more he towered above his colleagues, the more clearly he realized his own abilities; isolated by his very genius he may occasionally have mistrusted others, even, maybe, to the verge of arrogance. It seems certain that he found it difficult to forgive Jerome for the rebuffs dealt out by the old master, with no consideration for a young colleague. But all this only endears both of them all the more to us.

Before his time Christian erudition had produced two very great Africans, Tertullian and St Cyprian; a Roman intellectual and innovator, St Ambrose, and an Illyrian, St Jerome. Augustine, alone, carried it several stages further. Trained like his predecessors in the classical school, he knew Cicero thoroughly and Virgil moved him to tears. In addition he had assimilated the greater part of the knowledge available in his time, although later on he disdained it as mere vanity. He was a sufficiently expert master of his own language to include in it deliberately certain inaccuracies from the Latin version of the Bible, roundly declaring that he would prefer to be blamed for doing so by the grammarians rather than to be misunderstood by his listeners. Without giving it particular thought, he created ecclesiastical Latin, based on the ample sources that preceded it. Ignoramuses for a long time denigrated this as a bastard language, as if Cicero's Latin had been the same as that used by Tacitus or Pliny. He was a born writer, and used his gifts to their fullest extent; his style was entirely his own, with that warmth and liveliness that invested everything he touched. His *Confessions*, his *Treatise on The Trinity*, waft us on to lofty and sometimes breathtaking heights. It is restful to return from them to the rambling simplicity of his sermons and commentaries, full of human and spiritual experience; one feels appeased and relaxed, returning from the enjoyment of such incomparable riches.

He was a new phenomenon in the world of letters. We know that for the Ancients eloquence was the hallmark of culture. The good orator was assured of a career, particularly and especially in politics, although, if he did not want to lose himself in mere verbiage, he should also have completed a full course of studies, of which the essentials were known as the seven liberal arts. Over and above this special knowledge was required by the professional man, particularly of the law, and the best of them had sufficient general culture to be able rapidly to grasp the most varied problems. 'The learned orator' was Cicero's ideal. A

6. ISIDORE OF SEVILLE AND BRAULION. From the *Codex Monacensis* Lat. (13031). *(Bay. Staatsbib., Munich)*

THE LEGEND OF ST MARTIN. From the MS Life of St Martin in the Bibl. de Tours. *(Photo: Archives Phot.)*

7. ST MARTIN. Latin MS no. 9448. Bibl. de Paris.

(Photo: Archives Phot.)

century later Quintilian added ethical problems to the rest. His ideal man had first been trained by reading and poetical commentaries, then by the study of oratory and the Stoic philosophy—'an able man and a good speaker'—a formula that today is outworn but which nevertheless produced generations of thinkers and writers.

Augustine was educated by these methods. As a teacher of literature and oratory, he remained all his life influenced by this early training, to which, however, he gave a new meaning. As the old methods had proved their value, the thing to do was to use them, not in order better to understand Homer or Virgil, but God's word. These techniques could be used to go more deeply into it, and to expound it more worthily. And his Commentaries reveal the methods he had learned in the Schools. So that even when he pronounced strong criticisms of the sources of Latin culture, he continued to apply in his own way a part of what he had been taught. The 'learned orator' of Cicero and the 'able man and good speaker' of Quintilian with him became the 'able Christian and good speaker', and this formula was to be accepted during part of the Middle Ages.[1]

Yet Augustine's system nevertheless had its limitations. It was only a Western one. If one dare say so it would have been even more far-reaching had he known Greek well. He was a hard-working student and unable to afford the customary trip throughout the Eastern Greek world. Only little by little, forced by circumstances to do so, and by dint of perseverance was he able to read without difficulty, but as if it were a dead language, the Greek texts he required. His Platonism, which he took as far as was consistent in a religious sense, was mainly based on Latin translations or accepted at second-hand. His knowledge of ecclesiastical Greek, which he acquired late in life, was limited to what was indispensable for a knowledge of the Bible. Augustine never actually read the great works, such important theological sources, of Basil, Gregory of Nazianza, John Chrysostom, in spite of the fact that they were his contemporaries. This was undoubtedly a gap in his knowledge, but at that time it had not been filled throughout the Western world. It is only fair to add that in the Eastern, where Western thought was never very highly esteemed, Augustine himself did not become well-known.

When Alaric captured Rome in 410, unlike the heathens, Augustine immediately realized that the fate of the world was not bound up with the Empire, and as far as Christians were concerned that neither did the existence of Christianity depend on this same Empire. Having expressed

[1] Cf. E. Gilson, *La Philosophie au Moyen Age.*

this new sense of values which, barely a couple of years after the profanation of Rome, shocked the heathens and disturbed the Christians, Augustine rose above all temporal conflicts to immerse himself in historical theology. This is even today the chief point of interest in *The City of God*, a dense and occasionally difficult work to follow.

Because there are in the world, as it slowly moves towards its end, two kinds of love, there are the just and the sinners. The terrestrial city is built by man's self-love, as was promised to Gehenna. But in fact the two cities overlap one another, since owing to their sins there are Christians who belong to the terrestrial city, whilst through grace, certain heathens may attain to the celestial city. Everything in human society is not absolutely evil. For although the Christian must serve God in a city in which 'truth is king, charity the law, and eternity the measure', yet he is also living in a State of which he must be a good citizen. The State, which is the terrestrial city, must for its part, far from opposing the celestial city, by keeping the peace and practising civic virtues lead the citizens towards a future happiness which it cannot itself offer them, for the uneasy peace it can at best achieve is only the foreshadowing of eternal peace.

In *The City of God* Augustine, who was never a politician, yet provided the groundwork of a Christian political attitude which was further worked out and practised throughout the Middle Ages. What he did was to lay down 'the principle of a supernatural state of society founded on Christian wisdom, essentially separate from the State but compatible with it.'[1] The Church was to work out his ideas, in a direction which he had not foreseen. In the City of God, which is none other than the Church, in view of the fact that the civil and religious authorities were entirely separate, the authority of the priesthood was agreed to be above that of the laity. On that principle it followed logically that as regarded spiritual affairs and on their behalf, the Church had the right to intervene in temporal matters. This axiom was carried even further—the Pope would hand over one of the two swords in his possession for the purpose of leading the world towards God to the civil power, but would be entitled to withdraw it if the latter were unworthy of bearing it. 'It is the prerogative of the spiritual power,' wrote Hugues de Saint-Victor, 'to create the terrestrial power, and to judge it if it be guilty.' The application of this principle, designed to give the world peace and stability under the aegis of the Cross, was not always to create that harmony between princes and Churchmen so ardently hoped for by the author of *The City of God*.

[1] E. Gilson, *op. cit.*

Augustine was a distinguished figure in those early years of the fifth century that were not, as has been claimed, a period of decadence, but marked a phase in a continuous process of change. As he expressed the thoughts and to a large extent embodied the erudition of his period, inspired by a still young and vigorous Christian outlook, his point of view was no longer altogether bounded by Antiquity. His mind transformed every idea it touched upon, and directed it more strongly than any of his contemporaries towards the future, always in a Catholic tradition that was already very marked. With him and to a large extent through him civilization was to take on a new aspect lasting for several centuries.

His death in 430 coincided with the colonization of Africa by the Vandals. These Barbarians, who were aggressive Arians, were especially ruthless in their humiliation of everything that bore the label Roman, and cruelly persecuted the Catholics who, in their eyes, formed part of the order against which they were fighting. During this time of trial the monasteries led a precarious life.

The man of the moment was Fulgencius. He was an austere monk, who did not seek the limelight, but who nevertheless was intelligent, well-mannered, and cultured. According to his pious biographer he even spoke Greek without a trace of accent, and could recite the whole of his Homer without a break. Certain critics frowned on these claims, and as a matter of fact Fulgencius had thoroughly studied the Graeco-Latin glossaries of the period and his erudition was purely scholastic, but that was enough for his admirers to talk of miracles. He himself had more important things on his mind. In spite of himself, for he shunned all honours, he became bishop of Ruspe. He was a great admirer of Augustine and stretched that Master's theories on predestination to their farthest point. In spite of joining the Vandals he was banished to Sardinia for his Catholic faith, and taking advantage of this situation returned to strictly monastic life and an investigation of the theology of the Trinity. His exile was more a sentence of banishment than of deportation, and he was so highly esteemed that King Thrasamund, a convinced and erudite Arian, who prided himself on his acquaintance with theology, recalled him from Sardinia in order to debate with him— as the king thought, to his own advantage—on Arianism versus orthodoxy. Fulgencius, with respect for his sovereign but even more so for the truth, did not give him the satisfaction he had expected, and shortly afterwards was again exiled. Having thus rid himself of his burdensome prestige, he now roundly denounced the Vandals, their brutality, rapine, and perseverance in promoting apostasy, as well as the vulgarity and ignorance of their clergy. After Thrasamund's death his diocese was restored to him, but he always regretted not having been able wholly to devote himself to monasticism. When he died, in 533, the Byzantines were engaged in finally overthrowing the domination of the Vandals. Peace once again returned to the monasteries, protected by the Imperial government and gradually but increasingly released from apostolic duties. But the work began in Africa by Augustine was destroyed by the Arab invasion in 709.

A strange fate awaits those writers whose important works are numerous, for posterity invariably finds a means of claiming a famous precedent or leading the most highly venerated masters along ways which they themselves would be hard put to recognize. In adapting to their own ends certain works written in a very definite frame of mind, and in certain given circumstances, their most fervent disciples tend to distort these when setting them in a new light, separating them from their general context, or else forcing them into some new and narrow system. Augustine did not escape this ordeal his admirers put upon him. Sensitive as he was, had he been present at some of their doctrinal debates, he would surely have complained of their excessive zeal. The astonishing thing is that in spite of having time and again been treated as a disputatious writer his achievement was never thereby diminished.

He was read everywhere, and everywhere he made a deep impression, in Spain, Italy, Gaul, and in the far regions of the Danube. And as always, the polemics made more noise than the slow, obscure, but solid work that went on among the Augustinians unknown to history. After his death the discussions on grace were centred in the isles of Lérins. At a later date, under Charlemagne, Augustine most strongly influenced what became known as the Carolingian Renaissance. In the twelfth century he reigned over the humanists of Chartres, inspired the first Schoolmen and the regular Canons of the famous Abbey of Saint-Victor. Like many others, St Dominic, founder of an order, stemmed from him. Although in the thirteenth century his influence was challenged by the discovery of Aristotle, in the eyes of St Thomas he remained a fundamental authority, whom he constantly consulted, even although occasionally distorting his teachings to fit in with his own views. After the hard-won victory of Christian Aristotelianism, Augustinism still remained a considerable influence, thanks to the Franciscan St Bonaventure. We have already seen its important bearing on political ideas. During the Renaissance Augustine still exercised the same attraction, although in a rather different way. In the sixteenth century Luther made use of him, and the Council of Trent reproved this exacerbated Augustinian. Among the humanists, Petrarch, at the beginning of the fourteenth century, used him as his bedside book, Erasmus edited him, and after him, magnificently, the theologians of Louvain. In the seventeenth century Bérulle founded the French Oratory under his patronage, the great quarrels concerning grace were fought out in his name, the Jansenist controversy revolved around the *Augustinus*, and not without difficulties the Benedictines produced an edition of his works that is a masterpiece of erudition. It is not surprising that the eighteenth century should have passed him by. The philosophers of the nineteenth made use of him, although they often misused him, but the twentieth understood Augustine more and more fully, and the most enlightened leaders of modern Christian culture are today inspired by him.[1]

Fifty years ago, Mgr Duchesne—whose historical knowledge was perfect, even although he did not always stick to the facts—wrote with a depth of feeling he did not generally show—'Augustine illumined the whole of Christianity. He taught those of his own day all they needed to know. He taught them to know themselves, consoled them for the world's sorrows, and led them to an understanding of the mysteries. He calmed the fanatics, enlightened the ignorant, and kept the learned in the right tradition. He was the teacher of the whole of the Middle Ages. And even today, after the passage of time has inevitably rubbed off some of the freshness of his teaching, he still remains the greatest theological authority. He is our foremost link with the ancient Christian world, and in certain respects he belongs to every age of time. His soul—and what a soul!—was greater than his works; it still lives in them, and on certain of his pages our tears will always continue to fall.'

THE IBERIAN PENINSULA CONVERTED BY THE MONKS

Spain, at the farthest end of the Roman world, and therefore somewhat isolated from the rest of Christianity, by the sea and the mountains, has provided us with even less documentary evidence on the origins of monachism than other countries. One of the first of these was the account of her travels by Egeria, the pilgrim nun. From this we may rightly deduce that there were a certain number of monasteries in Spain at the end of the fourth century. It was exactly at this period that there

---

[1] This paragraph is a summary of the last chapter of *Saint Augustin* by M. Marrou (Paris, 1955). This little book, the result of years of thought and study, is a masterpiece of unpretentious erudition and fervour in the Augustinian tradition.

arose in the Church a scandal which from certain points of view concerned the whole monastic world, revealing as it did the dangers then threatening this new kind of institution. This was the Priscillian affair, which to this very day has never been cleared up.

Priscillian was a member of a good family in the region of Cordoba, cultured, well-spoken, rich and pious. Like many others, one day Priscillian decided to become an ascetic, but he did so in a very particular fashion of his own. He has been charged with half-a-dozen different kinds of heresy, quite a few for one man. But certain facts seem to prove that he did have a disturbing influence on his followers. After having, as was usual, renounced all their earthly goods, they formed a secret sect, ruled over by a superior class of initiates who received certain esoteric instructions and were even permitted to lie rather than reveal the secrets of their doctrine. Priscillian, basing himself on the Bible, St Paul, and the Apocrypha, was their prophet and mentor. He stressed to excess the difference between fleshly and spiritual acts, denounced any love for the things of this world as idolatrous, upheld celibacy to the extent of condemning marriage altogether, and rejected any kind of authority. These ideas were combined with odd practices. Fasting was carried to extremes, even on Sundays, which did not occur even in Egypt. The consecrated wafers received in church were taken home. At certain times of the year he and his followers disappeared from their dwellings to hidden retreats. He claimed that when they had reached the end of their term of asceticism they would become like the angels, a point of view that was always a dangerous one, and which, before the famous words of Pascal, might have led them to fall very low, although this was not so in Priscillian's case.

He had an extraordinary vogue in the whole of western and northern Spain and in Aquitania. After he became Bishop of Avila his followers included bishops, monks, and women, the latter of whom were always eager to tread in the footsteps of the prophets. His success brought about his fall.

Although at that time the monks were held in general esteem they did not lack enemies. They were accused by the heathens of deserting the cities and the established order and at the same time, when it suited their interests to do so, of noisily intervening in public affairs. These grievances against them were also reinforced by spite. They were mocked at for making themselves miserable for fear of becoming so. False monks, who deceived the populace, were pointed out as evidence against them all. The entire race of 'men in black'—already—was denounced as a horde of hypocrites who made themselves up to look pale, wan, and grubby, whilst in fact they stuffed themselves like elephants and wore out the arms of the barmen, or, more simply, they were described as swine. And as is always the case, these rumours spread. Many of the bishops who had risen from the monastic ranks continued to practise asceticism. Others, who were not monks, noted with regret that the enthusiasm aroused by the holy men diminished their own influence. Even without going into the matter of inevitable lapses or eccentricities they had little enthusiasm for the kind of pious laziness of those who remained apart from the ecclesiastical world and did nothing to prove their apostolic love of their neighbours. And others, although few in numbers, were all the more antagonistic to the monks on account of their own lapses. Such zeal, even when it claims to be orthodox, is always dangerous, since those who show it generally overdo it, and in due course find it turning against themselves. It was people of this kind whom Priscillian offended, and it is only right to point out that whatever his faults may have been, their criticisms helped to justify him.

He had two enemies in particular, who were determined to bring matters to a head. One of them was Ithacus, Bishop of Ossonoba (today, Faro), who thoroughly enjoyed the good things of this world, luxury, high living, and other less innocent amusements. The other was Hydacus, Bishop of Emerita (Merida), who was not much better. The latter was the leader. Priscillian was fair game for them, yet he held his ground. Nevertheless they pursued him obstinately and finally brought him down with much scandal. Ithacus, who had an almost insane hatred of anyone wearing a monk's robe, forgot himself to the point of insulting the irreproachable Martin of Tours, by whose sole existence he was condemned. Worse still, as the result of a mistake on the part of Priscillian, the matter was referred to the tribunals of the Empire, an unheard-of occurrence in the Church, which invariably settled its own quarrels. A Council at Bordeaux having already passed judgment in the matter of heresy, at the instigation of the two plotters the lay judges had to deal on their own account with the charges of immorality, as well as of magical and maleficent practices, which were strictly forbidden under the Imperial laws. After having been tortured, Priscillian and several of his disciples were executed in 385. Others were deported and a manhunt was organized against the remainder.

However much they approved of asceticism, the most thoughtful minds of the day were not in favour of Priscillian. The monk, Martin of Tours, Bishop Ambrose of Milan, Pope Damasius and his successor

Siricus had good reason to mistrust this sect. But in face of the impudence of the hanging bishops and the dragging of a religious quarrel before the Imperial courts, Martin and Ambrose voiced their disapproval in a firm and Christian manner; whilst desiring the repression of heresy they condemned the physical punishment of heretics, and on no account agreed to the handing-over of churchmen to the secular authorities. They were fully aware of the characters of the two bishops and unequivocally voiced their contempt and disgust for them. And both of them came to a bad end; Hydacus was obliged to resign his see, Ithacus was deposed, and a prison in Naples was their common lot.

After their disappearance monachism in Spain and Aquitania took some time still to settle down. In the eyes of many decent folk Priscillian appeared as the victim of those unworthy bishops, whilst further discords, due to personal rivalries, led to a schism which the churches of Milan and Rome only brought to an end with a great deal of trouble towards 400. Even after this date, Priscillianism still remained strong and popular for a great number of years before it disappeared. It did not even do so as a result of the Swabian, Alanian and Vandal invasions in 409, and only after 563 was it no longer mentioned.

Under the Barbarian occupation not merely the good names of the ascetics were threatened, but their very lives. During two years the Vandals left a trail of horrors in their wake—pillage, pestilence, famine, cannibalism, and general savagery. After them the Suerians and Visigoths, 'federals' of the Empire, settled in the country protected by the Pyrenees. Although they, too, were Arians, they were less brutal than the Visigoths, and after a period of anxiety the monasteries were again safe.

Towards 560, a Pannonian monk, Martin (not St Martin of Tours), was to make them even more secure in the north-west part of the peninsula, where the Suevians had settled. They were at first heathens, then Catholics, but at that moment had become Arians. Martin had lived in the East, where he had learned from the hermits and anchorites. Immediately on his arrival in Spain he founded a monastery at Dumio, near Braga. He was said to be a man of learning and even to know Greek, but he was particularly impressed by Seneca, whom he imitated perfectly. He was the talk of the country.

From the moment of his appearance among the Suevians an extraordinary event proved that Heaven was on his side. Towards 550, a son of King Cacaric's fell ill. The king's quacks having in vain tried to cure him, Cacaric, good Arian though he was, decided to send a delegation to Tours, to pray for the invalid's recovery at the tomb of bishop Martin, the great thaumaturgist of the time. Their first journey was unsuccessful, but their second met with better results. The messengers spread a silken cloth over the tomb, prayed all night, and the next morning noticed that it was heavier than on the previous evening, weighted down with the 'virtue' of the saint. The royal child was cured. As they were leaving Tours, the other Martin, in the East, was embarking in the ship that was to carry him to Galicia, and at the very moment when the messengers, after a relatively short trip, were arriving at Oporto, Martin also arrived, after a voyage that was no doubt a little longer. Perhaps the messengers had taken the longest way round, and no doubt Martin's ship had flown over the waves, but they all met simultaneously at the place where the miracle occurred, or so we are told by Gregory of Tours, whose memory we know was occasionally extremely good.

The good Gregory had better reason for calling Martin of Braga the greatest man of his day. His holiness, his goodness, his friendly relations with the Barbarian court, whose king he converted, and with him the whole nation, entitle him to this claim. He was the inspiration of the many councils in which the day-to-day affairs of Spain were then settled. As Bishop of Dumio and later Archbishop of Braga, the capital, he ensured the authenticity of the doctrines followed, watched over the morals of the clergy, and wiped out the last traces of Priscillianism. He wrote a little work for the use of the people which placed his reputation on as high a level as that of the apostles. From it we can deduce that the faith of his flock was still very much encumbered with witchcraft and demons. His Suevians, who like the indigenous inhabitants had been baptized, still made sacrifices to the streams, burned candles to the trees, made Thursdays a holiday in honour of Jupiter, and, more understandably, got married on Fridays in honour of Venus. This gives one an idea of his environment and of the pioneering missionary work he had to do. Whether or not his results were superficial or went fairly deep, Martin established the Catholic religion on a firm basis in the country held by the Suevians, and in doing so, under the sign of the Cross strengthened the good relations, which always tended to be on a precarious basis, between the indigenous inhabitants, those Romans who had remained in the country, and the Barbarian conquerors of it. He died in 580.

The Visigoths, who had settled near the Suevians, did not renounce Arianism until 587, under the influence of one of Martin's imitators, Leander, Bishop of Seville, a friend of the young king Reccared, and a supporter of the Visigoths' cause. He died in 601. Once again, the king's conversion brought about that of the Arian bishops and the people, religion uniting all souls with no racial distinctions. Leander even went so far as to take sides with the Barbarians against the very Christian Byzantines who then occupied the south-east part of the peninsula. He played a leading part in the various councils that at that period regulated the religious life of Spain. These not only included the bishops, but also the princes who had often appointed them, and thanks to their collaboration Christian influence could be brought to bear on the Barbarian laws, slavery diminished or became less inhuman, and morality improved. The intervention of the rulers in such gatherings might have—and later on did have—serious drawbacks, but Leander's personality dominated all the assemblies in which he took part.

Like many of the bishops he had been a monk. He to some extent drew on his experiences at that time in a memorandum to his sister Florentina, who was a nun. Like nearly all the Western monks Leander had realized that true asceticism must be rooted in the heart and mind. For instance, he pointed out to her, if in a convent the sisters resolved to refrain from idle talk with one another and to keep silence, this would be a much greater test of their asceticism than the resolution required to observe the fasting that was a matter of everyday routine. Such advice was more or less all he left us in writing, for Leander did not have much time to spare for recording his meditations. But this did not apply to his brother Isidore, who died in 636.

He, too, was a monk before becoming in his turn Bishop of Seville. When he held that see he directed all the religious life of his time through the local councils which by then had become regular institutions. Yet his fame rests as much on his erudition as on his saintliness. He saw clearly that education was one of the fundamental bases of apostolic work, even in still backward regions. 'Ignorance,' he wrote, 'is the mother of error. Ignorance encourages vice.' In Seville he founded a kind of seminary for those entering the priesthood and took it upon himself to provide them with plenty of reading-matter. His own output was enormous, consisting of encyclopaedias, learned treatises, grammars, chronologies and histories—or what then passed as such—commentaries on the Scriptures, works on theology, ethics, canonical law, and a rule of life for cenobites adapted from the Benedictine rule. He never finished his *Etymologies* or *Origins*. They nevertheless comprised twenty volumes, ranging from the liberal arts to domestic utensils, through the world above, the State, the family, languages, monsters, metals, games, ships, buildings, clothing. Isidore read everything that came to hand, sacred as well as profane. Although he knew no Greek he was the Picco della Mirandola of his age.

As one might expect, he was not an original thinker. He read everything, transcribed everything, collected everything, but uncritically,
in armsful, wherever he found it, in spite of what he himself claimed,
and as Duchesne has pointed out, more frequently used the scissors than
the pen. Nor was he ever at a loss; if he lacked knowledge he did not
lack ingenuity. Somewhere he wrote that he picked the flowers he had
chosen in various fields. But although he wanted to offer us a bouquet,
it must be admitted that all he gave us was an herbarium. In another
place he briefly (*brevi expositione*) recommended one of his works to
'studious readers and at the same time to those who dread an excessive
number of words'. But from our point of view, this work, which is not
in fact too long, seems endless. No doubt his contemporaries found it to
their taste, and Isidore's production must be judged from their point of
view—he placed all the knowledge available in his time in the hands
of those who very badly needed it, and in him they literally found a
mine of information.

His conscience was not troubled by his perusal of profane works.
Like all Christians he had reason to beware of their immorality, but
as he mainly read them in the versions of their commentators and the
Schoolmen, their perilous charms made no direct impact on him and he
judged them to be vain rather than dangerous. As a pedagogue he
realized their educational value. As a grammarian in the general,
classical meaning of the term, he considered that these works, fully
annotated by the School, taught beginners how to express themselves
correctly, and laid a proper foundation for scholarship. His grammatical
predilection was such that M. Fontaine, the learned editor of Isidore's
works, classified his thoughts in general purely and simply into grammatical categories. And even in his grammar, everything is reduced to
etymology. In this, of course, Isidore fulfilled the most urgent need of
his time—the protection and illustration of language as the instrument
for maintaining and developing culture.

When he took the trouble, Isidore wrote good Latin, a little precious
and flowery, but better than that of many Italians and all Gauls. His
preface to his *Histories* is deserving of inclusion in any anthology, well-
rounded although rather too florid, in praise of Spain, the loveliest spot
on earth, on whose fertile soil grew vines, grass, olive trees, with forests
on her mountains, and metals and precious stones in the bosom of her
earth; even the climate was temperate. Isidore could see no wrinkles on
the face of his dear 'Mother Spain', queen of all the provinces, the most
beautiful, holy and happy of all lands, reaching from the confines of the
West to the Indies. The fast-breeding Visigoth nation populated it

extensively. Far from regretting the days of Rome, they looked back on them only as a glorious memory. Its time was past, and the present was in no way unworthy of it. In singing the praises of Spain he became positively rhapsodical: 'Golden Rome, capital of the nations, did right in the past to desire thee, and if, at first victorious, the virtuous Romulus took thee for spouse, since then, after innumerable victories in the world the Gothic nation has gathered thee up in the splendour of its power, and now, among the royal insignia and vast resources of the Empire enjoys an assured happiness.' The climate of patriotism had definitely changed and we are indeed far from Jerome's lamentations on the rape of the queen of cities by the ancestors of these same Visigoths now so firmly rooted in Spain.

Isidore founded a library in Seville about which not a great deal is now known, but which, in view of its founder's mentality, must have contained an impressive number of glossaries, encyclopaedias, manuals, scrolls and commentaries. On the walls of this room he ordered nineteen little poems to be transcribed, in rather poor verse and somewhat halting prosody. We do not know whether they were meant to be ornamental or served as references to the contents of various coffers or bookcases. In the latter case we would have an idea of some of the contents of Isidore's library—a dozen or so of the great classics of Christianity in Latin, chief among them Augustine ('If he be there it will suffice'), Leander of Seville, naturally; two Greeks, Origen and John Chrysostom, almost certainly in Latin versions; works on law, history and medicine, a few Latin poems including the three greatest—*Maro* (Virgil), *Flaccus* (Horace), and *Naso* (Ovid, the very unchaste Persian)—Lucan and Prudentius, both of them Spaniards. Isidore obviously provided his readers with a wide selection of sacred and profane literature. Another of the poems in this library was almost an invitation to eclecticism: 'There are here a goodly number of works, both sacred and profane. If some poem amongst them should tempt thee, take it out and read it. Thou wilt see meadows full of thorns and flowers. If thou dost not wish to take the thorns, take the roses.'

In this hall, where the clerics trained by the Master often compiled the materials of his works for him, good behaviour and silence were the rule, at least according to the inscriptions decorating the walls. Inscribing parchments was compared to a battle (*mortua pelle*). Whoever lost half-an-hour through day-dreaming earned two strokes of the whip, and chatterers were shown the door. Isidore's books were all good ones: 'These coffers (*scrinia*) contain no deceitful works. If thou desirest them, here then they are. If they satisfy thy desires, read them.

Here thou mayest drive away sluggishness and banish thy spirit's weariness. Believe me, brother, thou wilt emerge a wiser man.'

Thanks to Isidore, the episcopal palace of Seville became the centre of an intellectual movement that perhaps was not quite a renaissance, but which appears at least to have been an efflorescence. At that period the Barbarians had for a long time been in occupation of Spain and it had become their home. Having from the start been attracted by Roman culture, by now they were all Catholics and politically independent. The conquered Provinces had been unified, and their geographical position protected them against the troubles that were convulsing the remainder of the Empire. The Visigoth kings inaugurated an era of stability, during which, thanks to the Churchmen, the guardians of knowledge, civilization gradually reconquered its victors. King Sisibut, a cultured Barbarian, encouraged this development. Modest though it was, the movement was headed by an elite, who, like their master, depended on the past, but were already, without clearly realizing it, moving towards the as yet tenuous dawn of a new world. Thanks to Isidore, the teacher of Spain, Baetica, the country of which Seville was the centre, had its poets, prose writers, grammarians and liturgists, and if only as yet on a minor scale this was in its own day an important development.

As the first personage in the Spanish Church and a Doctor of the Universal Church, Isidore occupies a distinguished position amongst the Fathers of the Western Church, of whom he is the last. At a time when the new learning was laboriously groping for contact with classical science, it was he who provided it; and this should always be remembered in his favour. He stood on the threshold of the Middle Ages and provided them so copiously with this knowledge of the classics that many subsequent writers found it unnecessary to turn back to those of the original sources which had not been lost trace of. E. Gilson remarked that his *Etymologies* served the same purpose in mediaeval libraries as the *Encyclopaedia Britannica* or *Larousse* do in those of today. And this is by no means faint praise. Generations of later thinkers relied on their 'Isidore'.

At the time of his death Spain appeared to be heading towards a religious and intellectual future in which the institution of monasticism was to have a share. She had many leading prelates, such as Braulion and Tayon of Saragossa; the abbot Valerius, Eugene, Ildefonso, and Julian of Toledo, several of whom had passed through the cloister before becoming bishops. They were all of them distinguished ecclesiastical authors. But when Julian died in 690 a new invasion threatened the Peninsula.

Barely seventy years had passed since the death of Mahomet in 632, yet already the legions of Allah had conquered twice as many kingdoms as once had Alexander the Great. When they arrived on the shores of the Atlantic they saw no more lands to conquer except those that lay across the sea, at the northern end of the Maghreb. Only a few miles separated them from their new prey. In 711 Tarik, on the orders of Mousaa, crossed the straits and landed at the foot of the rock which later was called Djebel Tarik (Gibraltar). His army, which included 7,000 Berbers and Arabs, was soon to be increased by the addition of another 5,000 warriors under the sign of the Crescent. With these he was able to defeat the Visigoth king Roderick on the Guadalete. Seville, Cordoba and Toledo capitulated one after the other, and except for a narrow strip along the Asturian coast in the north, Christian Spain became a province of Islam. Thenceforward and for several centuries the Christians were only able to retain their faith by paying tribute to it.

THE MIRACLES OF ST MARTIN IN GAUL

The results of persecutions are often unexpected. Five times Bishop Athanasius of Alexandria was driven for a total of seventeen years into exile in the West. And thanks to these he was able to achieve according to his own ideas a work of propaganda that would never have been possible had he retained his patriarchate. We know that in Rome he was able to introduce the Egyptian, Anthony, to the eminent group of feminine ascetics. Five years later, in 336, he brought his little book to the district of Treves, and Pontitian in his turn was able to show it to Augustine. Thanks to Athanasius, the *Life of Anthony* had already been re-copied several times in Gaul by the time that Martin entered the monastic world.

Martin himself enjoyed the unusual good fortune of having a distinguished hagiographer, his friend and admirer Sulpicius Severus, who died between 420 and 425.

Born in Bordeaux, a friend of Paulinus of Nola and like him a member of the highest society, Sulpicius Severus, who enjoyed the good things of this world, only decided after many postponements to take the startling step of choosing a life of poverty. He then organized at Primuliacum, an unidentified spot in Aquitania, a type of simple asceticism which, after the usual discarding of profane authors, included the study of literature. His doctrines were not very precise, and he was said to have been somewhat heretical in questions of grace and also to have had

Priscillian leanings. But he was an excellent man of lettsrs and devoted his talents to the service of asceticism.

His *Life of St Martin* made both his own reputation and that of his hero, whose fame he spread as Athanasius had spread Anthony's. He brought to the West a new literary form, that of aretalogy or the panegyric of the virtues, in St Martin's case based on certain historical facts. The term 'best-seller' would come to mind in connection with this book, were it not used merely to describe the sensation of a season, whereas his was the success of the century. And the author knew his business, both as writer and editor, for in sending his manuscript in strict confidence to his friend Desiderius, he had recourse to the most effective publicity methods, admitting that even in the East his little book was making the fortunes of the librarians at black market prices.

Apart from propaganda he had another motive, for he took an extreme-ly pessimistic view of the state of the clergy and meant to teach them a lesson, nor were all the members of the Church of the Gauls by any means at that time virtuous men. As in Spain, there were undoubtedly among them irreproachable prelates, who had their own reasons for not approving of everything that stemmed from the institution of monasticism. This is a well-known subject of Church controversy, which periodically sets against one another the upholders of absolutism and those who favour a certain moderation, and at that period it even for a short time caused Martin to be suspected of Priscillianism. The mistake Sulpicius Severus made was to accuse all those whom he knew not to be on Martin's side of being against Heaven. He was something of a zealot, and highly imaginative. Too many clerics, he claimed, would have remained mere clodhoppers had they not entered the Church, and having once arrived at success in it, behaved like parvenus, surrounding themselves with luxury and making exorbitant demands. Instead of travelling on a donkey they insisted on well-upholstered coaches, instead of a simple cell they dwelt in marble halls with decora-ted ceilings and sculptured doors, instead of a poor habit they wore gowns of sumptuous materials. Many of the bishops were not much better: 'If one knows how they behave, better not to talk about it; if one does not, better to leave it at that.' Oddly enough, he was inexhaustible on the subject. He denounced, for instance, a priest called Brice or Brisson, who, saved from the depths by Martin, had the impudence to breed horses, and to buy slaves, young boys and pretty girls. According to him the man of God only tolerated this individual because Christ had tolerated Judas. One is ashamed of the 'historian' who deals in such 'facts' when, as we know, this Brice was none other than St Brice in person. No doubt he had made the mistake of being a man of independent and difficult character, and the even greater one of not taking the miracles attributed to Martin the thaumathurgist too seriously. Whatever life he may have led, he was not only completely exonerated but became, even in face of a certain amount of opposition, Martin's own successor, appointed as such by him, to the see of Tours. A good prince of the Church and a grateful one, before accepting this, Brice very properly had a chapel built over Martin's tomb.

Whether in all sincerity or not Sulpicius Severus contrasted the behaviour of those he condemned with the highly coloured portrait of his hero. In his *Life*, *Epistles*, and *Dialogues*, all those humble men of goodwill whose patron saint above all was Martin, were ranked among the impeccable ones. And as he performed miracles, his biographer provided us with plenty of examples of them, so numerous and extraordinary that like Martin's own disciples we remain astounded, slightly giddied, and very embarrassed by them. These accounts, if we accept them unquestioningly, are undoubtedly perplexing. To swallow them whole may cause us to be unfair towards the innocent, but to reject them would be unfair to Martin, who was also an innocent. When hypercritically investigated nothing remains of them, nor of Martin's personality. In 1912 E.-Ch. Babut was even given a bad name for representing Martin as a doubtful monk whose reputation only rested on tendentious publicity. The Bollandists, cautious and unemotional men of learning, put the matter in its proper light. And Paul Monceaux was also wise in writing that: 'It is not a matter of knowing whether or not Martin really did perform such and such a miracle, but of knowing whether, during his lifetime, it was in fact believed that he had done so.' Certainly Martin was not as negligible as has been claimed, since even apart from his legend he made a deep impression on his whole period. He died in 397.

He was born at Sabaria in Pannonia (Szombathely, the region of Raab, in Hungary, not far from the site of the present monastery of St Martin of Pannonia), the son of a junior officer. Whilst still a youth and in accordance with the old law by which sons were obliged to follow their father's profession, he entered the cavalry, rising to a higher grade in the Imperial Guard. He was a good, obliging, and sometimes an odd soldier; although he was an officer he in all humility polished the boots of his orderly. After sharing his cloak with the beggar he applied for baptism. Although he had become a soldier in spite of himself, he was punctilious in carrying out his duties and popular with his comrades. But now he refused any longer to fight in order not to take his neighbour's life. On the eve of a battle, he, who was to become the patron saint of horsemen, declared himself to be a conscientious objector; yet in order to prove that he was no coward he volunteered to stand alone and unarmed next day between the lines. And on that day the Barbarians surrendered without a fight, and without any other miracle having occurred. Whereupon Martin 'threw his swordbelt into the Church'.

From early childhood he had intended to become a monk. He was a great admirer of bishop St Hilary, and now he withdrew into the solitude of Licugé, not far from Poitiers. He refused the priesthood but significantly for his future career agreed to become an exorcist. At Licugé he was happy in his solitude and the company of his disciples. Nevertheless, he was obliged to leave them, for a bishop was needed at Tours, where the populace clamoured for Martin the monk. He himself of course refused this offer and withdrew into still deeper solitude.[1] There was a posthumous legend that claimed that a flock of geese—the great-granddaughters of those that lived on the Capitol—revealed the stable in which the hermit had hidden himself to the people of Tours, but it should not be taken seriously since it was merely told in connection with the feasting that at that time of the year always included a St Martin's goose.

Sulpicius Severus claimed that he was only induced to emerge from his hiding-place by being asked to perform a miracle, which he could never refuse, and that when he then came out to them, all the people rushed at him and bore him off to their good city. So his Touraine flock had their wishes granted. The neighbouring bishops were not so delighted. According to his hagiographer, they were punctilious in matters of outward appearance, and were not enthusiastic in their reception of their future colleague, plebeian in appearance, 'small, badly dressed and uncombed', and who, in spite of a certain affability, never laughed or showed anger. They also knew (although we are not told so) that from the point of view of canonical law it was a difficult matter for them to consecrate a former soldier in this office. Later, even the most charitable of them did not show him more than 'that conventional brotherliness required of Churchmen in order to keep up appearances'.[2] For his part,

---

[1] This detail enables us to pin down a hagiographical theme which we find almost everywhere in this kind of literature. A holy man would never voluntarily accept a bishopric; his hand had to be forced. This ritualistic behaviour, which in many cases was genuine and sincere, was an indispensable subject on which every author felt obliged to dwell. When the future monk was to some extent a man of education it was equally obligatory to emphasize his farewell to profane literature.

[2] E.-Ch. Babut.

Martin thought little enough of them. All he wanted, after he had been enthroned, was to withdraw to Marmoutier, near Tours, and live there in a hut around which eighty of his disciples settled near him, as badly installed as he himself was, either in similar huts or else in the troglodyte type of grottos which still abound there.

But Marmoutier was merely his base, for Martin's episcopate kept him constantly on the move. In his vast diocese and elsewhere there were pagan temples to be overthrown, peasants to be converted, clerics who needed his support, and rulers requiring his advice. And now miracles followed everywhere in his footsteps. He began his career as a thaumaturgist by two resurrections, one of a man who had been hanged. Each military milestone became the site or some marvel or other. On his way to Treves he stopped at Chartres to bring a child back to life, and at Lutetia in order to cure a leper. At Treves itself he performed a double miracle, curing a leper and a man possessed by devils. At Vienne he cured Paulinus of Nola 'whose pupil was already covered by a thick veil'. He was also interested in animals; a cow was freed of a demon. He confined the carts in a circle from which they were unable to move, as, it appears the '*marcous*' of Touraine do to this day. He even showed his prowess in the face of Emperors. As Valentinian refused to receive him, Martin entered the palace as if it were his own, went straight up to the Master of the World, and as the latter did not deign to rise in honour of the man of God, 'his seat was covered with fire and the Emperor was burnt in that part of his body that sat upon it'. St Martin even occasionally made a mistake, although he never rejoiced. One day, on meeting a group of peasants in whose behaviour he seemed to detect some heathenish traces, he made the sign of the Cross, whereupon the peasants 'became as stony as rocks', and in spite of their efforts to struggle out of the magic circle could only 'turn on their own heels, in ridiculous pirouettes'. In actual fact it was a perfectly good Christian funeral. Another sign of the Cross and these harmless folk were set free to carry away their corpse. After such exercises Martin was sufficiently powerful to dare to attack the very source of all evil, the devil in person, with whom he entered into a forcible argument. 'If thou wilt repent of thy misdeeds, I have such faith in the Lord that I would promise thee mercy.' But this adversary was too strong for him and Martin failed to move him.

At Marmoutier, which according to his biographer, was a real desert, he founded a group of near-hermits without a very clearly defined rule. Their lives were hard but they were allowed a certain amount of freedom. They were permitted to emerge, take over apostolic responsibilities, and even, after having spent a certain time in a monastery, join the secular clergy. But so long as they were under the rule of asceticism they were strictly confined to their cells excepting for prayers and meals. Their clothing was rough, consisting of a kind of sack or habit, a black cloak distinguished by the name of pallium, and many of them also wore a camel's hair cassock similar to that worn by the Eastern monks. They did no manual labour. The younger ones transcribed sacred texts, a rather remarkable occupation in view of the fact that their Superior was often described as an ignoramus. The older of them were enjoined un-remittingly to practise prayer and contemplation. Martin set them an example by wearing a hair-shirt and sleeping on the bare ground, without even a bed of straw. The most he allowed himself was occasion-ally to take the air, sitting on his stool in a little courtyard near to his cabin, in order at the day's end to enjoy the softly roseate light of the country of the Loire. As an apostle he devoted a great deal of his time to the peasants, with whom his somewhat boorish nature made him feel at home; in that part of Gaul where Christianity had as yet not penetrated much further than the cities Martin became a rural missionary, travel-ling on foot, by boat, or riding on a donkey, surrounded by a walking monastery. He attacked all the monuments that commemorated pagan superstitions and his preaching was frequently backed up by the pickaxe. In western and central Gaul his war on idolatry, which in principle had been abolished by Imperial decree by the middle of the fourth century, consisted to a considerable extent in demolishing the remnants of paganism in the minds of the people. 'He was a simple, forceful, hard-working man; obstinate, strong-willed and right-minded; a slave to duty, a very good man, always ready to come to his neighbour's aid; if he became a great apostle, a great bishop and a great saint that was because in him these simple and strong characteristics were on a heroic scale. And that was the real miracle of his life . . . The miracle of his destiny was the work of his faith.'[1]

Whatever may have been said about it, his example was infectious. Before him there had been nobody, but with him and after him the roads of western Gaul were littered with ascetics, monastic wayfarers or episcopal processions in humble array. Almighty God's good saints did many strange things, sometimes with odd results amongst people whose minds were still more than a little unenlightened. St Lubinus, or Leobinus, who was first a monk and later Bishop of Chartres, compelled one night to ask for shelter in a convent, was obliged to sleep in the nuns' dormitory, and was suddenly awakened in the middle of the night

[1] P. Monceaux.

by a very odd sensation—to find that the female in the bed next to his was licking his feet in somewhat excessive devotion. Lubinus's reaction was saintly, but healthy and vigorous. But many monks not under obedience to a fixed rule were not Lubinuses, and followed their own whims or else were just vagabonds.

A whole literature came into being to proclaim Martin's greater glory. After Sulpicius Severus, his praises were sung by the poet Fortunatus. Gregory of Tours added to the list of his miracles; Alcuinus, abbot of St-Martin de Tours, took up the story. The whole of the Middle Ages rejoiced in Sire St Martin, and works of art swelled the popularity of this most popular of bishops. Innumerable villages were called after him, such as Dammartin, Martigné, Martigny, Martignac, Martincourt, Martineau, Martinet. In France alone there are nearly 3,900 parishes bearing his name. Crowds of Christians and Barbarians came from the most distant places to pray at his tomb. The imagination of the populace added still more wonders to those performed by their favourite saint. At one bound Martin's donkey leapt over the most dangerous precipice, leaving his hoof-marks in the stone, which ever since was known as St Martin's stone. The ascetic who never touched a drop of wine even became the patron saint of innkeepers because the work of the vintners finished as a rule around November 11th, the anniversary of his death. *Martiner* was a synonym for tippling and drunkenness was known as St Martin's sickness. In Touraine, tapping the barrel is known as *martiner le vin*. In Provence they say, 'On St Martin's Day close down your casks and taste your wine'. And on the banks of the Rhine—'Martin, Martin, must tonight, wine tomorrow'. Joan of Arc swore by her martin, i.e. by her stick. And everyone knows that St Martin continues his benevolence towards us by regularly sending us every year an extra allowance of sunshine for St Martin's summer.[1]

PROVENCE, A CENTRE OF MONASTIC CULTURE AND BISHOPS' NURSERY

Whilst the monks of Touraine still remained somewhat bucolic and barbarian those of Provence, if one may say so, had more polished manners. The ancient 'province' of Narbonnaise, of which one part became French Provence, was at that time still highly civilized. It was incorporated into the Roman order in the year 125 of the City, and at first, owing to the settlements along the coast, was Greek. The Phoceans founded Marseilles in 600 B.C.; Nice (*Nike*, meaning Victory) and Antibes

[1] Cf. A. Lecoy de la Marche, *Saint Martin*.

(*Antipolis*, 'the city opposite' to Nice) date from the third century B.C. These cities, as they were seaports, were the first to be visited by the Christian preachers coming from the south-east. Opposite the ancient *Castrum Marcellinum* of the Romans (Cannes) the archipelago of Lérins housed the most flourishing monastic centre of Western Christianity at the beginning of the fifth century. The two main islands, of which the most important was Lero (today Ste Marguerite), and Lerina (today St Honorat), were then only a mass of chalky rocks covered in brambles, the home of vipers. But these wild spots quickly became cultivated, for only thirty years after the monks settled there one of them, Eucherius, spoke of them as a paradise, with abundant fresh water, grassy slopes studded with flowers, sweet-scented and covered with vineyards. Thirteen centuries later the learned Benedictine Denys de Sainte-Marthe, founder of the *Gallia Christiana* at the beginning of the eighteenth century, forgot his austere labours for a brief moment. He, too, was almost lyrical in recollecting those monastic spots, where the sea air was healthy, the outlook pleasant, with a wide view of the sea; where fish were abundant and trees, shrubs and all kinds of plants grew naturally. The pines, especially, were magnificent, the palm-trees fluttered, there were plump olives and the laurels of victory. The soil was rich and fertile, many-coloured, and 'constantly exuding perfumes'. Everyone who visited these luminous isles loved them with as much fervour.

Towards 410 Honoratius (died in 429) landed with his friend Caprasius at Lerina, on returning from a journey to the land of the monks, and after a stay at a *baume* (grotto) on Cap Roux, which was too much overrun by pious but importunate visitors. He planned to organize in small huts at Lerina a monastic rule combining hermits and cenobites, and he succeeded splendidly in doing so. Following his example and under his direction a population of holy men soon settled on all the islands along the coast. The large island of Lero lay at a distance of only a few cable's lengths. Provençal legend claims that a nun, Marguerite, a sister of Honoratius, settled there. She was very fond of her brother and disappointed that she was not allowed to set foot on Lerina, where only men were allowed and which like Mount Athos was sealed off from the world by the sea. She begged her brother to visit her. He, who no doubt was more devoted to God than to his family, vaguely promised to do so when the almond-trees came into blossom, meaning thereby to put it off indefinitely or until the day of some saint not mentioned in the calendar. But the saintly nun prayed so hard that the almond-trees began to blossom every month. It could also be that

St Marguerite was the name of a martyr of Antioch in the third century, which does not appear in the martyriologies until the eleventh.

Shortly afterwards, Honoratius founded the line of the great bishops of Lerina by accepting the see of Arles, the capital of the 'Province' not far from Vienne, its neighbour and rival, which was the see of the Burgundians. Arles was then an important geographical centre. Its exchanges attracted a mixed population consisting of Gallo-Romans, Latins, Barbarians, Greeks and Syrians, and commerce between them was lively. 'All the riches of the East, the perfumes of Araby, the refinements of Assyria, the produce of Africa, the craftsmanship of Spain and the noteworthy products of Gaul' were to be found at this meeting-place of the river and the sea, as Honorius wrote to Agricola, the Prefect of Gaul. The resulting prosperity was a contributory cause of the prestige of the bishop, the leading personage in this provincial capital. His ecclesiastical diocese—an assignment rather than a jurisdiction, precisely—extended into Gaul and as far as Spain. In the many councils of the period the Arlesian Metropolitan was very often the leader and promotor.

After Honoratius Hilary, who was also a Lerinian, a well-loved disciple of the founder, was by him appointed to the bishopric without having first become abbot. He had a strong personality and as far as he was able on his appointment still followed the good and harsh discipline of the monastery. He was learned, read a great deal, dictated a voluminous correspondence, and in order not to lose a moment at the same time used his fingers in making nets. Occasionally he dug the soil, a healthy occupation which did not distract him from prayer. He preached very well but at great length; in Lent four hours at a stretch did not tire him out. His flock had less endurance, even in spite of the seats he had placed in the church for them—a comfort which until then had never been provided. One day even, at the very moment when he was about to pour out 'the torrent of his eloquence' they all of them, to a man, left the church. It was then that their preacher gave them what no doubt was his shortest and best sermon—'That's right, off you go; when you are in hell you won't be able to leave'. Above all he kept an untiring and very monastic watch on his bishopric, which occasionally led him into misadventures. He was an indefatigable traveller, but invariably went on foot, and had a habit of turning up where he was least expected. In his case the problem of the conflicting views on the role of the episcopate was raised again; on the one hand the monastic, haloed by its professional asceticism, was suspicious of the more worldly and temporal outlook of the other, regarded as a not highly desirable relation, and in spite of worthy and great bishops as being too partial to worldly advantages; whilst on the other, the saintly but authoritarian zeal of the ascetics was looked at askance and feared to be unsuitable to administrative duties.

Hilary, clinging obstinately to his own view of what was in the best interests of the Church, mercilessly deposed those candidates whom he regarded as unsuitable, replacing them with his own, preferably chosen in the monasteries. Recriminations left him unmoved, for in his own opinion he was always right. If necessary, his decisions were powerfully backed up by public opinion, which he controlled. Informed of his actions, however saintly and worthy his intentions might be, Rome showed little enthusiasm for a policy that was, nevertheless, unreasonable. The Pope was Leo, who was also a saint, and who knew how to live up to his responsibilities. When he was informed of the fact that the Archbishop of Arles had gone too far in unjustly deposing the Bishop of Besançon, Leo gave him a good scolding and forbade him to leave his diocese. Summoned to Rome, Hilary held his ground, refused communion to the reinstated bishop, and so thoroughly annoyed everyone that he was thrown into gaol. He escaped, returned to his diocese as he had come from it—on foot—and went on as before. Arriving suddenly at the deathbed of a dying bishop, he consecrated the successor he had chosen for him on the spot, but as the sick man refused to die, on his recovery the diocese found itself simultaneously under the orders of two bishops. In Rome Leo now was really angry. He charged Hilary with 'placing all the bishops of Gaul under his own authority and making himself their judge and head'. He excluded him from his communion with the additional—and wise—interdiction of even in future taking part in the consecration of a bishop. Hilary only just managed to escape deposition, yet this over-zealous prelate, on account of his great merits, was nevertheless canonized as St Hilary of Arles. He died in 449.

After Honoratius two great abbots succeeded one another at Lérins—Maximus, who died in 460, and especially Faustus (died some time after 485); both of them also successively became bishops of Riez. Faustus was a man of high character, a Breton and an enterprising monk, who declared and proved that the monastery was not a place of retirement but a training camp for the spiritual battlefield. A highly esteemed preacher and an able theologian, he played an authoritative part in all the discussions of his day. He also seems to have been something of a diplomat, for we find him on a mission to Rome and afterwards to Euric, King of the Visigoths, who, incidentally, exiled him. He was also a man of culture, and unlike most of the learned men of his time he had something to say. He did so in excellent style, rounded and well-scanned, and was an author who could fully express himself. Speaking to his monks, of whose faults he was well aware, he told them: 'We should bear in mind that our way of life should be harmful to none, that our own lukewarmness should not temper another's fervour, that our irascibility does not impair his patience, that our own stains do not soil his spotlessness, and that the lamps lit by others be not put out by us if we are incapable of lighting our own.' These words of wisdom and truth were addressed to those who, specializing in saintliness, might on the heights be tempted to stray from the path of simple Christianity.

His friend Sidonius Apollinarius, secular Bishop of Clermont in Auvergne, wrote to him in the fashion of his day: 'In everything thou doest, wherever thou mayest be, for me thou art always happy (*faustus*), always honoured (Honoratius, the first abbot), always very great (Maximus, Faustus's predecessor at Lérins).' This same Sidonius, who combined virtue and wit, elsewhere wrote to him of a magnificent female whom the revered monk-bishop was supposed to have loved in the camp of the enemy and torn from the arms of the conquerors. Fortunately he was merely referring to philosophy. According to the classical commentary of Deuteronomy xxi. 10, the Christians took this beautiful captive, cut her hair, shaved her eyebrows and pared her nails in order to prepare her for entering the service of Christ. History has not reported to us Faustus's opinion of this literary effort.

At Lérins the lords of the Church were legion. Among them Lupus was to become Bishop of Troyes (d. 479), Eucherius Bishop of Lyons (d. between 450 and 455). Eucherius had left his wife and entrusted his children to his friend Hilarius, but preferred Lero (Ste Marguerite) to Lérins. He remained, however, in close relations with the neighbouring isle, praising 'the holy old men who brought the Egyptian Fathers to Gaul'. Until the Middle Ages generations of believers followed his ascetic writings and his rules for the interpretation of the Scriptures. Erasmus, who edited him in the sixteenth century, praised his style, his precise knowledge of his craft as a writer, and 'the construction of his discourse'.

St Vincent, about whom almost nothing is known, became without having striven for it the theologian of the Lérinian colony (450). His was not an original mind, but as a writer he could select, simplify and round off a formula. His famous 'aide-mémoire' (*Commonitorium*) provided theologists with two great ideas—the criterion of traditional faith and the Catholic principle of dogmatic development. The former is famous: 'In the Catholic Church we must carefully watch that we take into account what has been everywhere believed, forever, and by everyone.'

This admirably concise formula has been more often repeated than actually studied. The simultaneous application of the triple criterion is not, as a matter of fact, as easy to verify as may be thought. Even in Vincent's own time the growth of Arianism, which counted more followers than the Nicaean orthodoxy, restricted the meaning of the word 'everywhere'. The cautious Church, in view of these difficulties, has always used this formula with a certain reserve. But on the other hand the idea of the development of dogma is lucid and fertile: the progress one can observe in the life of dogmas is not the result of outside elements that are added to them, but results from the inherent wealth of the revelation itself, which grows and develops by virtue of its own inner strength, as one gradually goes more deeply into it and circumstances require its reappraisal.

Lérins, still sheltered from the world into which at that period the Barbarians were advancing, and boasting such a galaxy of intellectuals, was then a centre of the highest culture. About fifty-five years elapsed from the death of Honoratius to that of Faustus of Riez. It has been claimed that there was at that time at Lérins a school of hagiography, as well as a kind of theological faculty, but that suggestion only rests on insufficient premises. On arriving in the islands those distinguished monks had already had a basic training, partly due to their origins and partly to their previous education, and thus these aristocrats of learning and religion, united by their similar social or intellectual background, simply founded a kind of monastic university. Further than that the known facts do not entitle us to go. The actual 'school' of Lérins, on a much lower intellectual level, consisted merely of children to whom they taught the rudiments of knowledge.

But the story of the islands by no means came to an end with the passing of this first generation. St Caesarius (d. 543), who had never known them, was even to excel them. Born of an undistinguished Burgundian family he did not have the intellectual training of his predecessors, but as soon as he entered the monastery he became an example to all others in his practice of austerity. Appointed cellarer by the abbot Porcarius, he rationed the community to such an extent that 'his holy circumspection'—as his hagiographer put it—led to general discontentment and his superior was obliged to remove him from his post. He retired to a cell and lived on a weekly handful of boiled herbs. This regime exhausted him and he was sent to Arles to recuperate. He read a great deal there and even endeavoured, unsuccessfully, to study profane literature. One evening, when he was reading in bed and before going to sleep had placed his book under his pillow, he noticed during his slumbers that a dragon, i.e. a serpent, was devouring both the pillow and the book. It was only a dream, but it taught him a lesson.

Towards 502 he was appointed Primate of Arles, which was by no means an easy post. Caesarius was faced with one crisis after another, for the 'Province', until then Roman, was now passing successively under the domination of the Visigoths, the Ostrogoths and the Franks, and this did not by any means smooth the path of a bishop who was already contending with Barbarians, whether Arians or Catholics. The neighbouring Burgundians, whose bishop was St Avitius, provided him with further problems. Avitius, a distinguished prelate of the century, both learned and politically-minded, after having converted the Burgundians attempted to extend his diocese of Vienne at the expense of the neighbouring bishopric of Arles, but Pope Symmachus put a stop to his attempted encroachment on it.

Caesarius was above all a man of action. Apart from his fairly rare interventions in politics—a fault common to all the bishops at that period—and his preponderating influence in the local councils, at Arles he created an ecclesiastical city which included both a hospital and a nunnery. He reprimanded certain of the clergy for their partiality to luxury, watched over the morals of his flock, and insisted that they all attended Mass until the end. He enjoyed the liturgy, which was a source of joy, for however austere one might be sorrow was in God's eyes an offence. He wanted the people, like the clergy, to learn and sing the psalms, the verses, and the anthems in Latin and in Greek. In that way everyone would be praying and, his hagiographer added, no one would have time for gossiping in church. The bishop was praised for his miracles, but he preferred to perform them behind the scenes and generally through his clergy. He attached basic importance to preaching, which he did often but briefly, in the simplest and most easily understood terms. 'I know that you do not understand everything; why, then, do you not ask questions? The cows do not always go to the calves, but the calves come to the cows, to satisfy their hunger at their mothers' udders. That is exactly what you should do.' His distinguished neighbour, Avitius, was more ceremonious. But Caesarius knew that a bishop or a priest—contrary to custom he ordered his priests to preach—might be too busy or too uneducated to carry out the task of preaching himself. In such a case he could do no better than to read or have read other people's good sermons, especially those of Augustine, whom he thought of very highly. Following his own advice he made no bones about taking what he needed wherever he found it. He arranged, transcribed, or had copied out any compilation or original work he judged to be of use for his purposes, and the priests were instructed to copy out his manuscripts in their turn, as he pointed out to them, at their own expense. Such writings were always fertile and, it seems, with fewer references to St Augustine.

As a monk Caesarius attached great importance to a settled life. Too many monks, after spending some time in a religious community, took to the roads. To some of them this kind of nomadic existence represented a special form of asceticism; as they wandered along, with neither hearth nor home, having literally to beg their way, they could pretend to themselves that they were following in the steps of the Lord, who also had nowhere to lay His head, and that they were at the same time devoting themselves to missionary work. But very often such pilgrimages were without dignity, although not unadventurous. Apart from the fact that to the local populations these itinerant monks appeared too frequently as a disorderly and occasionally scandal-provoking rabble, the abbots, whose institutions might lose all their inmates from one day to the next, too often found themselves without any permanent staff with which to administer them usefully and regularly. Caesarius also enforced the rule of poverty much more strictly and forbade the use of those sealed and locked coffers in which the more miserly ascetics hoarded their few humble treasures. In order to put an end to this practice he had all the cell doors removed.

He imposed even stricter vigilance on the women in the convent of St John, directed by the Abbess Caesaria, his sister, and drew up a detailed rule for them. All intercourse with the outside world, which those who declared their hatred of it sought more often than might be imagined; all correspondence, of which there was a good deal in female religious society; the exchanging of small gifts or services between inmates of male and female monastic institutions; a slight inclination to indulge in minor luxuries incompatible with the true spirit of poverty (there are so many different ways of arranging a veil); all this was rigorously banished from the holy cloisters. The abbess, who was elected independently, without the intervention of the bishop or the ministering priest, was to have her authority reinforced by the assistance of a council of elder nuns. She was given a dispensation from performing manual labours in order to supervise those of her nuns, who were obliged to spin the white wool for their habits or else to copy out manuscripts. Particular attention was paid to divine service, and at night they were to rise to chant the psalms. Two hours daily were devoted to reading. The rod was only used sparingly. Organized according to this method the monastery presented a very different picture from those in which the laws were merely based on everyday customs. It is not surprising that Caesarius's rule made a great impression on the whole of Gaul before the adoption of the Benedictine rule.

Lérins was not the only monastic centre in Provence. Towards 415, a little after Honoratius had founded his institution, John Cassianus, then in his fifties, settled at Marseilles, near the tomb of St Victor, where he died around 433–34.

Local nationalism claimed that he was a Provençal, but it is more likely that he was a Scythian from the district of Dobrudja. Dedicated to monastic life, he had spent two years at Bethlehem with his friend, his inseparable, indefatigable, and rather simple Abbot Germanus, but from time to time he also visited Palestine, Syria, and Mesopotamia. In the course of these pious journeyings he developed his vocation as an investigating monk. The two friends left Bethlehem for Egypt, where they promised not to linger, but they remained there for twenty years or so, with only one more brief stay at Bethlehem. Sometimes they settled down, sometimes they travelled, becoming acquainted with all the roads and all the huts of the desert, but—an odd detail—contenting themselves with visiting Panephysis, Skete and the Cells, never penetrating further south, towards the Thebaïd. They visited all the famous sages, learning from them the secrets of holy philosophy. They did not leave the desert until towards 399, for great disputes were taking place there over Origen. Cassianus then went on to Constantinople, to John Chrysostom, who ordained him deacon, then to Antioch and to Rome, where he made the acquaintance of the future Pope, Leo, and became a priest. At that moment his friend Germanus, who had never strayed a step from his side, died. Having lost half his motives for travelling Cassianus had nothing left to do but to settle down in some retreat. In Marseilles he founded a monastery for men, St Victor, and one for women, the Holy Saviour. His travels in the Holy Land gave him great prestige. He revealed to the West the treasures of wisdom amassed in the course of his Eastern pilgrimage in two famous works—the *Institutions* and the *Conferences*. Several of the latter were dedicated to Honoratius, to Eucherus, and to four abbots of the islands of Hyères, for there were also monks in the Iles d'Or.

Cassianus, who had also read but did not care for profane literature, was a learned but modest man; he only wished to be the echo of the desert Doctors. He was full of his subject-matter, which he edited slightly, and inexhaustible on it. His sonorous phrases, carefully worked out, unroll in slow periods. He was partial to anecdotes and knew how to give colour to the exploits he described. He admired the anchorites, but preferred cenobitism as being more suitable to the average man and a better safeguard against over-enthusiasm and eccentricities. His writings, inspired by Evagrius the Pontitian, the great religious writer of the East, were to be found in all the monasteries and rapidly became classics, giving the monks more detailed information than the *Life of Anthony* on the techniques for attaining perfection. 'If the life of solitude was tending to disappear in southern Gaul and more or less everywhere in the West, to be replaced by a better disciplined, more cultured, and better balanced type of monk, this was to a large extent due to his work.'[1] Even today, when in the monastery churches the hooded figures gather at twilight before the office of Compline, Cassianus is still the author for whom they have the greatest preference. The monks may possibly smile at his occasionally nonchalant good-humour, and at his simple-minded friend Germanus, and in passing notice the blush-saving cuts in a text that they have known since their novitiate, but we know that they all venerate the teachings of the Egyptian Fathers so well served by Cassianus.

At the period of their most vigorous expansion the monasteries of Lérins and Marseilles were engaged in a lively argument which, as it involved the whole problem of human activities, is of interest from the humanistic point of view. Its subject was Pelagianism, to which there was already a tendency before it was actually formulated.

It is impossible to sum up in a few sentences two theories bristling with difficulties and which conflicted with one another for decades, but we will nevertheless attempt to give a general outline of them.

Pelagius was a Breton monk (we would suggest that he was English). He was highly virtuous, a rigorous ascetic, soundly educated and a good writer, who was greatly esteemed in the Mediterranean world. According to his theory, which was based on solid arguments, man, by his own free will and, as it were, by virtue of a certain stoicism, might attain to a state in which, by constant perseverance on his part, he was beyond sinning. As, originally, human nature was neither impaired nor vitiated, on the moral plane man, therefore, was free to choose between good and evil, and able to attain salvation by his own efforts, grace being additionally vouchsafed him from above, according to his merits. This ethical point of view had a special appeal for ascetics, but the excessive optimism regarding man's nature on which it was based rendered it liable to close scrutiny on the part of the Church. It is interesting to note that this view of man's inherent goodness was later taken up again,

---

[1] D. Cappuyns.

rather confusedly, and from quite a different point of view from the ascetic, at the Renaissance and in the eighteenth century.

St Augustine, however, had had personal experience of human frailty, and of the mysterious power of grace to rescue him—as he in all sanctity hoped—from the 'mass of perdition'. His own experience, allied to his theological investigations and his understanding of doctrinal traditions led him to maintain, in terms that before his time had never been formulated, that man, his nature impaired by original sin, was incapable of working out his own salvation. God alone was the Creator of everything that fell within this order of things, from man's first steps in that direction to the final reward of his perseverance, and those who were chosen were predestined to being so. This was a severe doctrine which at first sight would seem to mean the denial of all free will, and which, when stated unmitigatedly, would present God as the author of damnation. Pelagius, by according too much scope to free will, seemed to set restrictions on God's universal powers. Augustine, by placing the latter at the source of all activity, ran the risk of presenting human beings as being merely blindly and passively involved in the matter of their own salvation or damnation. But Augustine took care to define the term predestination much more precisely. His doctrine of original sin and grace became that of the Church, whilst the more extreme Augustinian theses were maintained with pitiless logic by the Jansenists of the seventeenth century.

Even then the conflict was endless. Pelagius, whom Rome for a time protected, had considerable success in the West and even more so in the East, where metaphysics were a greater preoccupation than morals. Many people, and not the least distinguished, e.g. Paulinus of Nola and Sulpicius Severus, regarded him as a saint. His disciples were very active and, as usual, went further than their master, who, it must be admitted, had a regard for prudence and possibly even for moderation. Whilst Augustine battled unceasingly to destroy this ever-resurging hydra, eighteen Italian bishops sided with Pelagius. It is worth noting the fact, by the way, that Augustine's tone was always courteous and his polemics never insulting. Although his doctrinal attitude was one of iron, he dipped his sword in salute to his opponents. He recognized that they did not deserve contempt, lived chastely and holily, and duly worshipped the Trinity. His attitude was a different one from St Jerome's, for that old battleaxe, when he entered the conflict, intended to resolve it after his own fashion, always a tempestuous one. His paradoxes, his invectives, the clamour he raised (Pelagius, 'the new Catilina', could only be an Origenist) gave no greater weight to his arguments and even caused him some misfortunes, as when his monastery at Bethlehem was burnt down and looted, and one deacon was left for dead.

In 417 Pelagius was condemned, and it was on that occasion that St Augustine spoke the famous words: 'The case is over. May the error also be over.' But the error was long-lived, and for another twenty-three years, until he drew his last breath, St Augustine was to struggle against it. After his time the controversy continued, becoming known as semi-Pelagianism, a term unknown at the earlier date, and stemming from the sixteenth century. This sequel was not eliminated until 529, by only fourteen bishops at the Council of Orange, without reference to the extreme theses of Augustinianism and in spite of the disagreement of the bishops of Burgundy. This date is worth remembering if one wants to be fair to the supporters of semi-Pelagianism, who were at that time all dead and who during their lives, far from being considered heretic were for the greater part regarded as saints.

The Provençal monasteries, whose inmates were intellectually alert, and where asceticism was strictly practised, were strongly influenced by the Augustinian theses. The monks of Marseilles and Lérins, all of them determined anti-Pelagians and as such strongly refuting any idea of man's innate goodness, asked themselves whether Divine grace was as generally effective as Augustine had stated. Filled with respect for the Master, whom they avoided referring to by name, but frightened of the consequences of absolute Augustinianism, they claimed that in taking his first steps towards salvation man might show a slight degree of individual merit. But by doing so they were taking the risk of once again re-opening the whole question. At St Victor Cassianus was this movement's mouthpiece. He was backed by the Lérinians of his own generation, whose conduct was above reproach and who were all of them highly qualified theologians, although little inclined towards polemics. St Lupus, Bishop of Troyes, who was a Lérinian, was an anti-Pelagian but not an Augustinian. St Germanus of Auxerre, his neighbour and friend, was of the same opinion. Faustus of Riez was out-and-out on Cassianus's side, against Fulgencius of Ruspe. Vincent of Lérins, less respectful than his peers, apparently went even further; in his 'Aide-mémoire', in which he so strongly insisted on the role of tradition in the Church, he was thought to be aiming at the new Augustinianisms that he referred to as 'little private opinions' (*privata opiniuncula*). Prospero of Aquitania, 'too utterly docile',[1] and inclined to accuse anyone who disagreed with the Master of Hippo of Pelagianism, was perhaps not wrong in placing Vincent among the 'un-grateful', i.e. those who would have

[1] P. de Labriolle.

nothing to do with grace. The only great Augustinian of Lérins was Caesarius of Arles, but he was more of a man of action than a theologian and was much younger than those who belonged to the great Pleiad.

ST RADEGUNDA, THE JEWEL OF MONASTIC GAUL

One day, about twenty years after Caesarius's death, two modestly attired nuns knocked at the door of the monastery of St Jean aux Alyscamps, which was at that time ruled by the Abbess Liliola. Saint Radegunda and Agnes, her superior, had come there in order to learn the rule of Caesarius at first hand and to study the means of introducing it in their own foundation at Poitiers.

Radegunda was a distinguished person in Gaul, a princess of the Thuringian nation in the district of Tongres, whose ancestors had fought under Attila. Her father, Berthaire, was murdered by his own brother, Hermannfried, who wished to be the sole ruler of the kingdom. A little later Hermannfried was killed by the Franks, in the course of so bloody a battle, according to Gregory of Tours, that one might walk dry-footed across the river, completely choked by the piles of the dead. After this settlement of accounts Radegunda, then ten or twelve years old, became part of the booty that fell to Clotaire, son of Clovis, after the Frankish victory.

Radegunda was an intelligent child who gave promise of becoming a great beauty. Clotaire intended to marry her, and she did in fact become the fifth and last but one spouse of this Frankish king, who apart from marriage had many concubines, and generally led a vicious life. Radegunda, Catholic as she was, soon realized that this royal house, although its members had been baptized according to the orthodox Trinity, had nothing in common with Christianity but the name, and that they behaved more horribly than any Arian heretics. Clotaire, in concert with his brother, Childebert, himself murdered his own nephews, the sons of Clodomir, and their entire household, including their tutors, as well. (The only survivor was Clodoald, the future St Clodius.) That was one of his first crimes. One of the last was just as Shakespearian. Clotaire burned his son Chram alive—who had rebelled against him but was not much better—in a hut, together with his wife and daughters.

One can readily understand that Radegunda, proud of her lineage, a punctilious Christian, civilized, with a pure and gentle heart, felt nothing but disgust for her brute of a husband who shortly after their marriage also had his young bride's brother murdered. She was able to leave him

8. ST HONORATIUS OF LERINS. From Marichal Boucicaut's prayer-book: fourteenth century: Jacquémart André museum.

(Photo: Arthaud)

9. ST RADEGUNDA. From the MS Life of St Radegunda: twelfth
century: Bibl. de Paris.   (*Photo: Archives Phot.*)

for the cloister, and applied for the veil to Bishop Medardus of Noyon. But the man of God hesitated to grant her request; he was not over-anxious to take the wife of such a husband into the cloister, and the werewolves' howlings against her admission did nothing to reassure him. Then Radegunda, revealing another side to her character, herself took the veil, and the bishop was obliged to agree.

She settled at Saix, on the borders of Poitou and Touraine, not far from the spots formerly sanctified by St Martin, where she authoritatively and methodically transformed her villa into a convent-hospice. One day, however, she learned that Clotaire had set out to recapture her. Whilst preparing herself for this trial she also sought to evade it and it was then that, according to a fourteenth century account, the miracle of the oatfield occurred. As, accompanied by two nuns, she was fleeing from her importunate spouse, she met a peasant who was sowing oats on the borders of her land. She ordered him to reply, in case he were questioned, that he had seen no one pass that way. 'And by God's will the said oatfield in that same hour grew to such a height that the saint and her two nuns were enabled to hide in it . . . And when King Clotaire shortly afterwards arrived in the said place and asked the labourer whether he had seen anyone pass by that place, the man replied that as he was sowing the said oats he had not done so. Then the king, hearing the reply of the said labourer and seeing the miracle, turned back.'

Shortly afterwards Radegunda settled at Poitiers, where she founded two monasteries, Notre-Dame for the living nuns and Ste Marie-hors-les-murs for the care of the deceased and which also housed the officiating clergy. The superior was not Radegunda herself but her friend, the nun Agnes, consecrated by Germain, the holy Bishop of Paris. Far from claiming the position of honour the foundress was satisfied with living in a cell fourteen feet long and fifteen feet wide, including her oratory, in which from time to time she was confined, a form of asceticism which was at that period frequently practised. She also chose the meanest tasks; at night she polished the shoes of the sleeping sisters, also cleaning the vegetables as well as emptying the slops and disposing of the community's refuse. But although the rule was austere it was humanitarian—the nuns were allowed to play backgammon.

Towards 567 a strange and attractive character arrived at Poitiers. Venancius Fortunatus was an Italian from the region of Treviso. Like so many others he was drawn to the tomb of St Martin, but it took him two whole years to arrive as far as Tours, 'sometimes sleeping, tired of walking, when he was not heavy-headed from drinking'. From Tours he reached Poitiers, where, after a short trip to the Pyrenees, he settled down. Having reformed he was on familiar, respectful, and devoted terms with the inmates of the monastery. Through grace this odd fellow became a priest and a bishop of Poitiers, of which he in due course became a local saint.

He was cultured and a minor poet and put his gifts to good use, so much so that with his little affectations and occasional clumsiness—for his grammar and prosody were not too sound—he figures as the last of the Latin poets. He felt at ease and happy in the company of Radegunda, 'the most precious pearl of Gaul'. For her part the saint—and this was one of the most feminine qualities of that strong-willed woman—honoured him with her friendship, that was indulgent and almost maternal. Knowing the little weakness of this friend, who was extremely greedy, it amused her to encourage him slightly in it, receiving in thanks a flattering and high-faluting poem. She herself ate no more than one meal of lentils or cabbage, flavoured with a little mead or beet-sugar, but it gave her pleasure to cook him little dishes; vegetables in honey, of which he ate four helpings, or a meat stew. Another time she served him vegetables in a thick sauce, on a silver dish; or on a marble plate with other vegetables done in honey, a glass bowl containing plump chickens, and a black earthenware one filled with milk. They tickled the good man's nose almost as much as his palate: 'I could have satisfied myself with their smell alone.' Agnes, the superior, imitated Radegunda, and sent their greedy friend a kind of pudding covered with fresh cream, ornamented with 'artistic designs drawn by finger'.

In those days, in the West as in the East, relics had as great an attraction as miracles. Constantinople, very rich in holy remains, rivalled Rome in this respect, and in the City itself, the principal store-house of them was in the Sacred Palace of the Emperor. There were some strange ones among them, such as Moses's staff, the trumpets of Jericho, and the well of the Good Samaritan. Others were more authentic. Even if they were open to question it was in accordance with the simple and naïve piety of the period to wish to keep beside one the remains of those venerated as saints. Their physical presence was regarded in the nature of a talisman, this being a slight legacy of paganism. Those who had none either stole them or invented them, and those who had occasionally trafficked in them. Whether genuine or false, the remains of the saints travelled around the world. People throughout the Christian world thought that by possessing some sacred object they would gain all kinds of advantages for themselves, but, lacking those that might be genuine they were quite satisfied, especially the populace, to have at their disposal some piece of material that possessed the miraculous powers of a relic that might be elsewhere. At the end of a pilgrimage that might be a very long one they would take a piece of cloth, weigh it, lay it on the saint's tomb and weigh it again; the extra weight shown by the scales after due and effective prayer was due to the *virtus* or miraculous power it contained, or so, at least, we are informed by the excellent Gregory of Tours.

Radegunda, who had a passion for relics, assembled a considerable collection of them in her sacristy. But she lacked the one she most longed for—a fragment of the True Cross, which would be the object of her own particular devotion, her monastery's greatest treasure, and a unique attraction to the crowds of pilgrims in Gaul. She knew through her informants that there was an important relic of the True Cross in Constantinople. Her cousin Amalafrid had taken refuge there from the descendants of Clovis, and, better still, the Byzantine court was in contact with the Frankish kings. So she sent an official embassy to the Emperor Justinian, who in spite of his avarice granted her request and sent her a fragment of the piece in his possession, first having it mounted in a precious setting. One can imagine the procession that then set out across Europe, by sea and by land, transporting so valuable a treasure to Poitiers. But it was decreed that at that moment, one of the greatest in her lifetime, Radegunda's joy was not to be unalloyed. When the procession arrived at the city gates they were shut. The bishop, Marovius, a good prelate but a disagreeable man, had chosen that moment to mount his horse and ride off to his country house. But Radegunda was resolved that the priceless treasure should be received with full honours, and as Marovius had taken himself off she ordered the procession to return to Tours. She possessed enough prestige and authority to persuade the king, Sigisbut, to appoint another bishop to replace the defaulting prelate. St Euphronius of Tours headed the cortege and installed the precious relic in the monastery of Poitiers.

It was a triumphant moment. Radegunda and her women, in obedience to their vows, did not leave their cloister walls, but awaited the arrival of the clergy who, surrounded by a dense crowd, a forest of candles, and in the incense-laden air, carried the Imperial cross in which the relic was encased. A new chant, composed by Fortunatus, arose from the multitude, in magnificent and regular strophes.

Vexilla Regis
Les étendards du Roi s'avancent,
Le mystère de la croix resplendit,
Sur ce gibet l'auteur de la chair
par sa chair a été suspendu.

In response to these solemn phrases came those of the *Pange lingua*:

> *Chante, langue,*
> *le prix du glorieux combat*
> *et sur le trophée de la croix*
> *entonne un noble triomphe:*
> *comment le Rédempteur du monde*
> *a vaincu par son sacrifice.*

In the thirteenth century St Thomas Aquinas returned to the style of the *Pange lingua* in honour of the Eucharist. His poem, based on the highest theological inspiration, soars into the serene heights of intellect and faith, but whatever may have been said of it, lacks genuine lyricism. But Fortunatus, for once rising above his usual level, was moved by an exceptional occasion to genuinely poetic and emotional poignancy.

> *Fléchis tes rameaux, grand arbre,*
> *relâche la raideur de tes fibres,*
> *puisse s'amollir la dureté*
> *que la nature t'a donnée:*
> *aux membres du Roi suprême*
> *tends un bois de douceur . . .*

The chanting died away but Radegunda was contented. Her monastery, which now enshrined the greatest of treasures, was thenceforward called The Holy Cross. It only now remained to provide it with a foundation which she hoped, although with some foreboding, might safeguard it against internal difficulties, always to be feared, and the proceedings of disobliging bishops. Under her good rule, which was held in universal esteem, and thus secured, her nuns would have the sound direction that Marovius had not given them, and the monastery would be autonomous and so protected from episcopal bad humour. It was then that she made her journey to Arles, returning thence with the rule of Caesarius, which in spite of certain grumblings was then adopted.

She died on August 13, 587, surrounded by her two hundred nuns. On this occasion Marovius was again absent, but with no ill intentions, as he was on a pastoral mission. It was Bishop Gregory of Tours, appointed by the notables to do so, who led her funeral procession through the concourse of weeping people to St Marie hors les murs. The nuns did not leave the cloister. They clustered at the monastery windows and embrasures and as the bier of the first foundress of the French abbeys passed along, wept and clapped their hands to mark their sorrow.

GREGORY OF TOURS, 'FATHER OF OUR HISTORY'

Our most valuable source on Radegunda and her period is not a monastic one. St Gregory, Bishop of Tours, was a devoted friend to the monks, the wise and when necessary reproving counsellor of the Frankish kings, and the faithful chronicler of his time. He died in 594.

He was one of the best educated men in Gaul, but his culture was not on a very high level and proves to what a low degree literary activity had fallen under the Merovingians. His peasant style, which he himself rightly described as rustic, saved him from falling into affectations; his Latin was clear, but also very barbarous. He was aware of it and bemoaned it, honestly; no efforts were made in Gaul to cultivate intellectual ability, and there were none who knew their own language correctly. Admitting his own ignorance, he compared himself to an ox or an ass in a ring of clever players. His morphology was muddled, he was unsure of his masculine, feminine or neuter terminations, and did not know how to use prepositions correctly. However, he made the best of it. Whilst shortly before his time Sidonius Apollinarius or St Avitius were only writing for the literate, Gregory aimed at being understood by all: 'Few people understand the dissertation of an orator, but many understand the words of an uncouth writer.'

We could not expect our ancient historian to have exercised the ruthless degree of criticism to which we ourselves are accustomed. In that respect Gregory also belonged to his period; he was credulous, naïve, and always on the look-out for miracles. But although he examined nothing very closely he did at least honestly report what he had seen or heard said. Clumsy though his style may have been, he was an admirable storyteller. His *Histoire des Francs* consists of a succession of paragraphs each one of which contains a tale, an anecdote, or a 'miracle'. Thus he gave us a series of pictures which are rarely lacking in colour. He was used to horrible sights and described without the slightest tremor scenes which in their savagery equalled anything that the first Barbarians, including the Huns, could have invented. It is to him that we owe the classically horrific story of the murder of Clovis's grandsons by their uncle, Clotaire, as well as others like them.

Lord Raiching was a man 'full of every kind of vanity, swollen with conceit and of arrogant impudence'. His favourite pastime was to torture his serfs. He ordered burning candles to be held against the thighs of the youth who served him at table, until his legs were burned. At the slightest movement of his victim Raiching drew his sword, and whilst the sufferer wept he 'felt great transports of joy'. Two of his other servants went to church and asked the priest to marry them. Their lord went after them, to fetch them back. The priest, knowing his man, only agreed to deliver them to him on condition that he promised not to separate them. Raiching 'swore to it, his hands on the altar', and thereafter took back his property. He then had the trunk of a tree hollowed out, laid the young girl, dressed as for burial, down in it, forced her betrothed to lie on top of her, closed down the lid and ordered them to be buried alive. Thus, he claimed, he had not broken his vow; the lovers would not be separated.

Gontrand, King of Burgundy, was no monster, and was even known as Gontrand the Good. He was honest, for 'he did not sell his bishopric'. He was pious, too, and although he loved luxury, many thought him saintly on the evidence of the numerous churches and chapels he built. But his wife Austragilda, 'before she surrendered her wicked soul', requested that her doctors, to whose remedies she claimed her premature death was due, should be killed 'in order that at her burial there should be others to be mourned for as well'. Her husband duly carried out his wife's last wish, and Gregory observed that 'there are many reasonable people who opine that such cannot be done without sin'.

Dagobert was a clever politician who knew how to combine justice and cruelty to serve his purposes, and was one of the better kings. His friends thought him a saint. But this did not prevent him from keeping a large number of concubines as well as his three queens. 'Yet he gave generous alms to the poor and had he not destroyed the merit he earned by his good works by his extreme rapacity, he would have gone to Heaven'. This was the view of one of his enemies, who was not in the least astonished by this king's strange court.

Such customs, too, were practised by many bishops, who were also men of power. Simony, the traffic in holy things, was common among those prelates who thought more of the Lord's profits than of their own duties. The priest Euphrasius was intriguing to obtain the see of Clermont, in Auvergne. He had made a lot of money in commerce, and was rich, so he sent one of his relatives to the king to obtain by bribery what his merits did not entitle him to. 'He was a man of elegant manners, but in fact not at all chaste. He often made the Barbarians drunk, but seldom fed the starving. In my opinion this is the reason why he did not obtain what he wanted, for he did not seek to gain these honours from God, but from men.'

The prelate whom Euphrasius wanted to oust, Cautinus, was even more horrible. His bouts of drunkenness often led to epileptic fits, in which four of his servants had to carry him to bed. Anastasius, one of his priests, had been given certain title deeds by Queen Clothilde. The bishop constantly harassed him to turn these over to him, but Anastasius, as was still the case of a certain number of priests at that time, was a married man, with children, and wished to provide for his family. In his fury the bishop decided to murder this recalcitrant and disobedient servant. Anastasius was taken down to a crypt and shut up in a sarcophagus containing a decomposing corpse. Men-at-arms guarded the door. In his sarcophagus Anastasius found that he could move his arms, and feeling around, his hands came in contact with the entrails of his companion in misfortune. The smell was suffocating him and the miserable man did not know what to do. If he stuffed the end of his cloak into his nose he would choke, and if he removed it he was still certain to be asphyxiated. Finally, groping along the partition, he discovered a crowbar that had been left between the sarcophagus and its lid. He lifted up the latter, peered out, freed himself and saw that the guards, having been drinking mulled wine, had fallen asleep. Stepping out on tiptoe he found another exit, but this one, too, was locked. But at dawn, fortunately, Anastasius saw a workman passing by, providentially carrying a hatchet, and managed to attract his attention, whereupon the man, understanding his plight, let him out. They had no doubt made little noise, for the guards still slept on. When at last he was free, Anastasius denounced the wicked bishop to King Clotaire, and the court pronounced him worse than Nero or Herod. 'There was nothing either holy or estimable about Cautinus. He was totally lacking in profane or divine knowledge. But the Jews, in whose clutches he was, thought highly of him. This was not on account of matters of salvation, as is the duty of a pastor, but matters of commerce. They flattered him and by openly suborning him, sold him their goods at the highest prices.'

Accounts such as these reveal to us a world mostly of illiterates, brutes, robbers, looters, and murderers. And it is a fact that after Clovis came to power many civilizing influences were destroyed in northern Gaul. The Frankish kings regarded themselves as the absolute owners both of land and men, and dealt with them according to their own fancies or interests. When they lacked money or could no longer loot, they sold their fiefs to the highest bidders and the new overlord soon proved that they were of the same race as their masters. Although they were baptized as Christians both the powerful and the common people had but little understanding of Christianity and in many cases their religion was little more than superstition. In her early childhood France, soon to become known as the elder daughter of the Church, was not particularly pretty. Since Clovis's conversion the bishops, protected by the kings, had forfeited most of their independence. They received less and less democratic support from the people, whose voice was often the instrument of God. At that time they were appointed from above, generally by the rulers, and many times after striking bargains in which the predominating motive was the law of supply and demand. It often happened that against all canonical rules the holders of bishoprics were mere laymen. In these conditions of ignorance and corruption the Church of Merovingian Gaul was spared only one trial; there was no heresy, for in order to become heretical it is necessary to have at least some education and knowledge of theology. And it is noteworthy that the many councils of the period only legislated on matters of morals and discipline.

Nevertheless, besides the unworthy prelates who were mostly men who had been placed in the positions they held by the kings, this condition of barbarian despotism was to some extent mitigated by certain of the bishops and monks. Gregory of Tours, who also depicted good as well as evil, was the chief ornament of the episcopate. And on their part the monasteries offered a refuge to those souls who, horrified by the customs of the period, still retained a sense of eternal values as well as feelings of morality and decency. But in such conditions the monasteries could be no more than refuges, and not centres of civilization.

THE SCHOOLS

It is difficult to discover any form of scholastic activity in Gaul during the sixth and seventh centuries. To a greater degree than anywhere else the school as a State institution had disappeared from the towns after the Barbarians had settled in at the end of the fifth century. The Franks, especially, having no conception either of the State nor of the City, never entertained the idea of supporting schools, and in spite of a few private attempts here and there to preserve some remnants of the old tradition the fall in intellectual values was an almost permanent feature of Gaul from the end of the fifth until the middle of the seventh centuries. During this long stretch of time the Church and the monks only played a very small part in safeguarding traditional culture by means of scholastic institutions.

Until the monasteries became wealthy owing to the considerable donations they received in the seventh century, monastic life in Gaul very closely resembled the ancient ideal of the desert. The monks lived in huts grouped around small churches, similarly to the Eastern Scythians. They prayed and laboured with their hands, and when they were able to read their interests were non-intellectual. At the beginning of the great monastic vogue the work done by St Martin's copyists was chiefly utilitarian. They shared the opinion formerly expressed by Sulpicius Severus that 'the rule of God is not expressed in eloquence but in faith'. Yet as education was a professional necessity to them, they organized what with somewhat far-fetched euphemism have been called the monastic schools. This meant no more than that the better educated among them, who could have learned a certain amount outside the monasteries, helped their illiterate brethren to a better understanding of their prayers by teaching them to read the liturgical books, works of edification, and others of a religious kind. When, for instance, St Ferreol stated that the monks should know their letters (*litteras discant*) this meant no more than that they should learn to read and write. Everywhere knowledge was meagre, and used solely for the purposes of immediate necessity. To engage in learning for pleasure would have been regarded as a form of intellectual indulgence amounting to a kind of disloyalty or at any rate as a blameworthy waste of time. In any case the means were not at hand, nor was any particular form of temptation. In Merovingian Gaul, even after the big properties had come into being, monachism and culture were never synonymous terms. The small amount of literature the monasteries did produce consisted mostly of books of rules or else hagiographical tales written more or less in the vernacular and within the understanding of the simple populace, the style of which their authors would probably have been unable to improve upon.

Although they were unconnected with monachism one must necessarily mention here the episcopal and presbytery schools, which from a comparative point of view complete the contemporary picture. It is not, however, possible to draw any fixed distinction between these two kinds We can only suggest that the presbytery schools were probably parochial schools directly under the control of the bishops, whilst with regard to the episcopal schools we have only certain meagre scraps of information.

At the time of the disappearance of the Imperial schools the educated bishops naturally looked amongst their adherents for those whom they might educate in turn. There followed in certain cases, then, a kind of episcopal preceptorate, which cannot, however, be fully described as a school. Gregory of Tours was trained in this manner by two bishops of Clermont in Auvergne, Gallus and Avitius. Under Gregory the Great, Bishop Didier of Vienne in the same way gave a secular education to certain children, an occupation which was deemed unworthy of a bishop and for which he was sharply rebuked by the Pope. If there were in fact episcopal schools organized as such they were either so few in numbers or of so little distinction that they left no trace of their existence behind. The only one that may possibly have been of some duration was that of Chartres, where seventy-two clerics lived as one community. But even here it would be difficult to determine exactly what they were taught.

Both in the cities and townships the educational level of the presbyteral schools was a very low one. It is difficult to imagine that at a period when it was enough for a priest to be able to read, write, chant a little and preach a very simple sermon, even if their teachers knew a little more, their pupils could in the ordinary way hope to learn anything but the rudiments.

In any case the teachers themselves were so few and often so poor that as long as they agreed at all to carry on their profession, little else was expected of them. In this connection Gregory of Tours tells a significant story. Etherius, Bishop of Lisieux, in search of a teacher, found a certain cleric. Little was known about his knowledge, but his morals were far from perfect. Gregory had no reservations when in Latin he described in very great detail the numerous and various vices of this individual, who indulged in every kind of turpitude (*omnique immunditiae valde deditus*), yet he informs us that in spite of these blemishes in his conduct the bishop bestowed lands and vineyards on his 'doctor'. The latter, however, took advantage of his position to seduce the mother of one of his pupils, and finally, after having attempted to murder the bishop, decamped. There is good reason to assume that this was an exceptional case; but it nevertheless proves that at that period there was so great a lack of teachers that it was necessary to make do with even the least desirable individuals.

Were there, under the Merovingians, any exclusively lay schools at all? The Belgian historian, Henri Pirenne, maintains that there were. According to him, as the Church had not yet acquired a complete monopoly in education, as it was to do under the Carolingians, when 'going to school amounted to joining the clergy', education was 'widespread among the lay population'. According to this eminent historian the reason for this development lay in 'the persistence of the Imperial tradition'. In support of this theory he brought forward a series of facts, some of which were already known, but which he interpreted and elucidated in his own fashion.

The Merovingian kings were not illiterate. Their children were taught their letters, presumably grammar and arithmetic. Those employed in the king's service, who were always laymen, needed a certain degree of knowledge and the means of transmitting it, and in this administration 'the remains of the clerical administration of the Empire' had been preserved. The application of what remained of Roman law required 'the daily practice of writing'. The old senatorial families in which the classical traditions were still preserved, and who were mostly settled south of the Loire, thanks, no doubt, to private tutors, still retained elements of Roman culture 'as proof of their social status', and some of the women belonging to this aristocratic society wrote better Latin than Gregory of Tours. Illiterate merchants employed clerks who kept their books (*mercenarii litterati*). There exist documents, letters, and inscriptions that we have been able to relate to the tradition of classical Latin literature. Judging by the quantity of papyrus that until the end of the seventh century was brought to Marseilles from Egypt by Syrian navigators, a good deal of writing must have been done. The general prevalence of cursive Roman script, although in a very debased form, does seem to prove that it was used hurriedly and not painstakingly, 'because writing is a daily necessity of social life'. There were, therefore, a number of laymen with enough education to cope with everyday affairs as well as an élite who still possessed the necessary means and sufficient interest to keep up certain cultural standards. And without forgetting to give credit to the part played by individual tutors in all this M. Pirenne concluded: 'Where would such education have been acquired except in schools attended by a fairly large number of laymen?'[1]

But the facts lead us to hesitate to agree with this author when, as regards the Merovingians, he concludes on this point that there was 'a survival of the civilization of the Empire in the West'. What was evidently the case in Italy, and to a lesser degree in North Africa and Spain, was very much less so in Gaul. It is incontestable that the priests did admit some laymen to their schools, but so long as we know nothing about either the statutes or curricula of these schools, it would

[1] H. Pirenne, *De l'état de l'instruction des laïques à l'époque mérovingienne*, in *Histoire économique de l'Occident médiéval*, Paris, 1951.

seem wiser not to generalize as regards the survival in Gaul of the scholastic institutions of the Roman Empire, especially as, judging by results, the knowledge at that time both of grammar and of law was of a very low order. If it be admitted that the Visigoths, the Ostrogoths and the Vandals were influenced by Roman culture, the same cannot be maintained of the Franks, and there was nothing in Gaul under the Merovingians that could in the remotest degree be compared to the education available in Theodoric's Ravenna.

Finally we must point out that Pirenne's interpretation of the known facts supported a pet theory of his, namely that the spread of Islam, by closing the Mediterranean and breaking off all communication between the Eastern and Western worlds, completely destroyed the Mediterranean characteristics that Western Europe had until then preserved, thanks to the survival of Roman civilization.[1]

However that may be, it did not very much improve the situation in Gaul at that time. Victims, as they were, of the barbarianism of their period, the Merovingian Churchmen and monks were only able to

---

[1] If historical prejudice were not tenacious to the point of dogmatism there would be no question of recalling the famous 'palace school' under the Merovingians.

Owing to the fact that he failed to understand the exact meaning of the word *schola*, the Benedictine, D. Pitra (who after becoming a Cardinal died in 1889) claimed that the Merovingian palace school was 'a high school where the learning of the day was taught on a superior level' and to which the young noblemen came to perfect the education they had received at home. D. Pitra gratuitously attributed to the Merovingian palace a strictly Carolingian institution. This lapse, coming from such a scholar, gave D. Leclercq the opportunity to triumph over his most eminent colleague and to call him, with no excessive reverence, 'a romantic provincial', as well as to handle equally roughly those distinguished perpetuators of the same error, Ozanam and Fustel de Coulanges.

And there is in fact no reason to assume that at the Merovingian court there was a scholastic institution with teachers who provided a superior education. The Merovingian *schola* was no more than a replica of the Byzantine *schola*, a special corps that, in the East, had the duty of protecting the Emperor (*protectores*) and similarly, in Gaul, to protect the king. The young men who joined this *schola* did so after having received their early education, intellectual or otherwise, at home. Scions of the nobility, they were 'nourished' and 'vowed themselves' to the king, to whom they swore loyalty and protection (*trustem*). They were the 'trusties' or king's men. Their corps, under the master (or mayor) of the palace, formed the *truste*. The term *schola* was widened to include all the officials of the royal household, including the body of scribes and notaries. Such was the 'palace school' under the Merovingians. At most one might grant that certain teachers may have attempted to educate the more ignorant members of the *truste*.

In another sense the term *schola* was applied to that quarter of a city in which foreigners lived in homogenous groups and often in corporations. In Rome, in the seventh and eighth centuries, there was a *schola Graecorum* around Santa Maria in Cosmedin, and in the eighth and ninth, *scholae* of Franks, Lombards, Anglo-Saxons and Jews. In Gaul there were also *scholae* of Syrians and Jews.

maintain an inferior educational standard on the lower rungs of the ladder. As regards monastic life in general, Gregory of Tours, who until the end of the seventh century remains our chief source of information, approved of the monks, but as he was too much interested in details he was unable to make the necessary effort to present us with a coherent picture of the monastic institutions as such, apart from the blemishes by which he was in certain instances saddened. The father of our history was no model historian.

When he died in 594, St Benedict had already been dead for forty-seven years, leaving behind him at Monte Cassino the charter for the complete reorganization of the monastic state. In the same year another Gregory, Pope and monk, was preparing to send a Benedictine mission to the British Isles. There they were to find among the Celts a monastic body strongly established on the traditional basis of holiness and, already, of culture.

CHAPTER V

MONASTICISM AND THE
CELTIC CLANS

All the regions in which the monks made their appearance and which we
have dealt with up to this point bore the imprint of the Roman occupation. But both before and after the conversion of the Irish Ireland
differed from those countries in that it always remained entirely outside
the Imperial orbit.[1]

Throughout Antiquity that cold and green island had a bad reputation. Under the Emperor Augustus the geographer Strabo reported
that the Irish were even greater savages than the Britons; they were both
vegetarians and cannibals, who ate their own kin, whilst their morality
was of so low an order that they respected neither their mothers nor
their sisters. St Jerome, who had his malevolent moments, declared that
this swinish race, with beastly habits, practised copulation in ignorance
of the meaning of marriage. He even stated in detail, in quite unequi-
vocal Latin, that in that country cannibalism provided certain culinary
specialities, and that the choicest and tenderest dishes were provided
by the unfortunate Irish ladies.[2]

But leaving aside such absurd details, Ireland at that period was a land
of shepherds. There were no towns. Its social organization was based on

[1] Let us once and for all clarify these points: (a) Ireland (*Eriu*, dative *Erin*)
did not become *Eireland* or *Ireland* until the Anglo-Saxon period, and late at
that, in the eleventh century. In Latin it was called *Hibernia* or *Scottia*. At the
period with which we are dealing the present-day Irish were known as the Scots.
(b) The name *Scottia* did not refer to Scotland until in the course of the eleventh
century. (c) Great Britain was originally called *Alba* by the Scots or Irish and
Albion by the Romans. Some *Brythons* settled there in the second century BC
and gradually gave their name to that part of the island, which as the result
became known as Britain. We therefore use the term *Bretagne* to denote the
present Great Britain. The word *Anglia*, whence Angleterre (England) dates
from the Anglo-Saxon occupation. (d) Our French Bretagne (Brittany) was then
called *Armorique* (Armorica).
[2] *Adversus Jovinianum*, Vol. II, Chap. VII.

174

the family, and the families in turn belonged to one or another clan, forming a closed community. Each clan had its chieftain, each tribe and province their king. One supreme king reigned over the whole island, but even when he was feared, did not cut any great figure. He travelled in a chariot, exacted tribute, enjoyed certain privileges in the way of hospitality and carried off hostages, for 'he who has no hostages in chains is no king'.

These people lived in log cabins and their customs were those of a shepherd race. A bride was worth three horned beasts, plus an indemnity for her 'honour'. But legitimate unions might be merely temporary and concubinage also existed. War was always a thrilling business, in which the women also took part, and when great orgies were held the bravest warrior, i.e. he who had cut off the biggest number of heads, had the privilege of carving up the venison. As still happens today, the hunters boasted of their exploits, but at that time such bragging frequently led to bloodshed. Poems, tales, legends and music provided the entertainment at their banquets, based on patriotic or religious themes or inspired by natural sources such as streams and trees, as well as sacred stones or idols standing in the open fields. The bards chanted these old legends in verse, to a harp accompaniment. Together with the *filid* (poets or masters) they were greatly honoured, nor did the missionaries of the future, a certain number of whom themselves came from bardic families, regard them as enemies. The situation was a very different one, however, with regard to the druids, magicians, and prophets, who formed a separate priesthood, supervising the sacrificial rituals, practising sorcery, and eating acorns, which bestowed the gift of prophecy on them. They knew how to conjure up mists and fogs, fire and bloodshed, and to enclose people in magic circles. They believed in an after-life; when they died the brave were wafted to a paradise of gods and fairies, where they enjoyed sweet music and lovely surroundings.

The situation in Britain, across the water, was a somewhat different one, for that country had been Romanized. Caesar had only raided it once, for a year, in 55 B.C., but a hundred years later, from 43 to 85, the island was conquered by Claudius and Agricola. Yet the Romans never penetrated as far as the Caledonia of the Picts. In order to defend themselves against their raids, Hadrian, and later Antoninus, built a double *limes*, roughly along the present boundary between Scotland and England. Thanks to the Romans the Britons were familiarized with cities, mostly garrison towns, the baths and gateways of which they were enabled to admire; such as York, Gloucester, Lincoln, Verulam,

Chester and London, and they also travelled along the Roman roads. But not being very adaptable they were only very superficially influenced by civilization. They, also, were a nation of shepherds and clung to their own social organization, based on the family, with their herds of cattle and pigs, their wooden huts, their druids (of whom there were still a certain number in Britain) and their own language.

The missionaries, as they always did, followed the legions, attached themselves to the merchants' caravans and laid the foundations of churches in certain localities. Having come from Gaul they were not received with enthusiasm. Nevertheless, Christian settlements were organized from the beginning of the fourth century. They were hardly at all affected by Arianism, but later on they were contaminated by Pelagianism, for as we have seen, its originator was a Briton. Germanus of Auxerre and Lupus of Troyes collaborated in introducing the monastic system to these distant shores. It was Germanus who ordained Iltut, known as 'the grand master of the Britons' on account of his knowledge both of profane and Christian literature. On Caldy Island (South Wales) Iltut's disciples became famous—Samson, Paul Aurelius, and possibly also Gildas and David.

There were regular encounters with the Scots clans in Ireland, mostly inimical and consisting of piracy on both sides. But by one of history's paradoxes it was a Briton who converted the whole of Ireland, which until then had hardly been evangelized, if at all.

ST PATRICK, THE BARD OF GOD

St Patrick was born towards 389 at Daventry. He was the son of a deacon, who was also a farmer and a decurion; his grandfather was a presbyter. During his youth it never occurred to him to follow his family tradition and enter into holy orders, but, as the result of an unfortunate experience, he began to think the matter over. During a raid by Irish pirates he was captured and sold into slavery to a Druid. Young Patrick was put in charge of a herd of pigs, and thanks to his care they became exceptionally good breeders. Whilst he watched over them in the countryside he learned Erse and his mind also turned towards God. He managed to say one hundred prayers, both by day and by night. The bad weather—frost, ice, and snow—far from impeding his asceticism, strengthened it.

According to custom, he, like all slaves, should have been freed in the seventh year of his servitude, but the Druid did not want to lose his swineherd. Patrick learned in a vision that his ship was about to sail and ran away. But he had to find his ship. After trudging along for 200,000 feet Patrick embarked with some sailors who were taking off a cargo of Irish wolfhounds. After spending three days and nights at sea they landed in Britain, at the edge of a desert which appeared to have no end, and which they spent the next twenty-eight days in crossing. The hungry seamen cursed Patrick's God, but on suddenly meeting a herd of swine they rejoiced. 'And they remained there two nights and were well fed. Their dogs, also, were well fed.' And in addition to this good meat they also providentially discovered some honeycombs. According to one version they then all gave thanks to God; according to another, a later and more detailed one, as the sailors reserved part of their share to offer to their idols, Patrick refused to touch any of the food. He was obliged to prolong his fast for another twenty days, but as the narrator took care to point out, with no ill-effects.

He was reunited with his parents, who wanted him to remain with them. But St Patrick had heard 'the call of Ireland'. His mission was clear to him and in order to prepare himself for it he travelled to Gaul. If he went to Lérins he may possibly have met Lupus there, who at that time was still a monk, as well as his compatriot, Faustus, who was to become Bishop of Riez. He does not appear to have travelled as far as Rome. He spent fifteen years with Germanus at Auxerre, during which he studied the holy books and to a very limited extent profane literature, for his Latin always remained bad. When he left Auxerre he was a bishop. His first Irish see was Leinster and although he was not a monk his field of activity was nevertheless as much a monastic as a missionary one.

The Druids had predicted his arrival:

> A man with a shaven head will come
> Over the madcap waves of the sea
> His habit will have a hole for his head
> His staff will have a crooked handle
> His table is at the east of his house
> And all will answer him: Amen, amen.

In these lines we can identify his cloak, with a hole in it for his head to pass through; his pastoral staff, bent like a crutch, called a crook, and the altar in the church.

The Druids, who maintained their hold over the people by their magical arts, immediately evinced the most implacable hostility towards this new apostle, whom they challenged to a contest in magical feats. They preferred, however, not to challenge him to the water test, of which they noted that Patrick frequently made use, for, they declared, 'his water contained God'. With confidence in his own Druid, the missionary accepted every challenge, and from time to time had certain adventures, but although he was invariably the victor the people still clung to their magicians.

According to the accounts, heavily legendary, and written two, three or even four centuries after the events, the most extraordinary occurrences then took place. Their authors borrowed as much from their own imaginations as from history, or when they were at a loss, from the Bible; failing which the apocryphal gospels provided them with plenty of material. In his encounters with the Druids Patrick was a second Moses vying with the Egyptian magicians. He, too, had his fiery bush, and on the day of his death the sun stood still. Among so many episodes some are dramatic, some amusing, some charming, and some, we must admit, are absurd.

One day an infuriated band, riding on chariots, launched themselves against the saint. Thereupon Patrick raised black clouds and an earthquake; in the darkness his enemies killed one another. Of seven times seven warriors only four remained alive—the king, his wife, and two Scots.

Another day, when Patrick was dining with the king, a magician poured 'something' into his drinking-cup. The saint tipped the cup forward and the contents flowed out in a kind of jelly, from which he took out one drop—the one the magician had poured into it.

An ordeal by fire was more spectacular. It was agreed that a famous Druid should compete with a disciple of Patrick's called Benineus, and a wattle hut was built, in two separate halves. The saint sportingly agreed that the magician's half should be of green wood, whilst the other half, his disciple's, should be of dried wood. In addition, the magician was to wear Patrick's mantle, and Benineus, the magician's. When everything was ready they each took up their places in their respective compartments and the hut was set on fire. In the section built of green wood, the Druid burned like a torch; only Patrick's mantle remained intact. In his section, of dry wood, Benineus was quite comfortable, whilst only the wizard's mantle was burnt. All that happened to the devoted disciple was that he was obliged to emerge from the hut stark naked. The king, who was present at this scene, was, however, not amused, for Patrick had caused his Druid to die. His first reaction was to punish the saint, but then, fearing retribution, he said to himself 'that it would be better for me to believe than to die'. He nevertheless remained unconverted.

This king, whose name was Loigaire, had two daughters. One of them, a blonde, was called Ethne; the other, a red-head, Fedeln. One day, as was the women's custom, they went to a stream in which to wash themselves with soap (soap, *sapo*, was allegedly a Celtic invention), when they saw there some men dressed entirely in white. As they believed in ghosts they were at first scared by them, but were quickly reassured and began to converse with the saint, who spoke to them of God. They then plied him with questions. Was He rich? Did He have sons and daughters? Were His daughters beautiful, and loved by men? Was He young or old? Was He on earth, in the sky, in the rivers and the mountains? Patrick answered all their questions and explained the *Credo* to them. The sisters were quite satisfied with his replies and 'having received God's eucharist sank into the sleep of death'. They were placed on a bed and covered with their clothes. Their friends and the Druids came to mourn over them and when the saint began to preach they were all converted to God. When the period of mourning was over the two sisters were buried in a circular grave next to the stream.

When preaching Patrick particularly aimed at the conversion of the king or head of the clan, because if they were won over the whole 'family' would follow them into the Christian fold. He asked a king called Daire for a site on a hill, but Daire allotted him one in the plain. A short time afterwards one of the king's horsemen put his mount out to graze in Patrick's meadow. The latter was displeased, and told the horseman that 'it was stupid of Daire with no reason to send animals to ruin the poor strip of ground he gave to God'. The horseman made no reply and went away, leaving his steed in the meadow. On returning next morning he found the animal dead. 'It was the Christian who slew my steed,' he told the king, who, furious with Patrick, replied, 'Let him also be killed'. But now Daire himself was at the point of death, and his wife advised him, 'This is to do with the Christian; do not kill him, but let him bring us his favours'. Then Patrick sent them some holy water. First the horse was sprinkled with it and was brought back to life; then the king was also cured in the same manner. As a mark of his gratitude he sent the saint a fine brass bowl containing three measures; and Patrick said '*Grazacham*', meaning, thanks. Daire found this acceptance somewhat curt and sent his men to fetch back the bowl. Once again Patrick said '*Grazacham*', meaning, thanks. Daire could make nothing of it, and finally himself carried the bowl to Patrick and also gave him the meadow on the hill for which he had asked him. Patrick and all his people went out to it and found there a doe lying beside her fawn. The monks wished to kill the fawn, but Patrick picked it up, laid it across his shoulders and went off, followed by the doe, as docile and affectionate as a ewe. This is the legend of the two monasteries of Armagh, founded by Patrick towards the year 444, and later the see of the primates of Ireland.

Like all those of his race Patrick was an ardent ascetic. He had made a vow never to eat meat, but we know that temptation is not removed by a mere vow. Thus it was that during one of those periods of weakness when time hangs particularly heavily on one's hands he felt an irresistible longing to eat some pork. He cut off a slice, and in order not to shock his followers, hid it under a barrel. As he went away he met a man with eyes in his face and, as well, eyes in the back of his head. Patrick looked at him in surprise. 'I am a servant of God,' said the man. 'With the eyes in my face I see what men generally do. With the eyes in the back of my head I see a monk who has hidden some meat under a barrel.' Patrick immediately threw the slice of pork into the sea, and was at once forgiven. The piece of pork was changed into fish, which it was quite permissible for him to eat.

Such stories abound in the accounts written to praise their master by his more or less immediate disciples. In Ireland as elsewhere at the time those were the only accounts that today we would regard as evidence of a spiritual vocation. In accepting them as such we must take into consideration, apart from their miraculous content, the Irish saint's actual achievements. There is little doubt that both within his own lifetime and afterwards as well, true religious faith was unable completely to eliminate all the superstitions which were merely ridiculous caricatures of it, in spite of the fact that he took care to provide every head of his foundations with alphabetical summaries (*abgitoria*). And at that time, too, the soil of Ireland proliferated miracles. In a country where a man, it was claimed, could live seven years after having been beheaded, where werewolves abounded, where a ship had been seen to fly into the air, it was not exactly surprising that infants at their mothers' breasts invoked Saint Patrick's name. But it was he who founded monasteries throughout the length and breadth of Ireland. In that country, where towns were non-existent, the monks and bishops, like the Druids, wandered around more or less everywhere amongst the clans. And it may perhaps not be too rash to suggest that the monasteries, as Christian schools and mission bases, were especially suitable for counteracting the influence of the Druidical schools, to which they might have appeared to provide an answer. In Patrick's time Ireland was not yet the Isle of Saints. It became so because it was he who saved it from heathenism, unaware of the fact that he was proving that Christianity was not dependent on any temporal civilization, not even Roman civilization.

According to legend, as usual generous in its estimates, Patrick lived for 120 years. More simply, he died towards 461, aged about seventy. After having worked so hard, the old bishop was obliged to suffer the opposition of his earliest companions, the elders, amongst whom was his best friend. It was to this trial that we owe the *Confession* he wrote in order to justify himself. It only covers a mere fifteen pages in laborious Latin, badly expressing his ideas, but its sincerity and sober humility place this document well above the mass of those which claim to describe his activities with so many absurd embellishments.

THE ASCETICS AND THE SEA

In 407 the Roman garrisons, led into Gaul by the usurper Constantine III, evacuated Britain, leaving the country open to the Barbarians. The Picts thereupon surged down from the north and the mountains of Scotland, waded through the swamps and crossed the dismantled *limes*, spreading out towards the south. They ran alongside their war chariots carrying hunting-poles, their swords dangling round their necks, and their naked, tattooed bodies protected by narrow shields. The Scots of Ireland also again attacked the larger island, increasing the hatred of the Britons towards them. But those whom the British most detested were the Saxons, Angles and Jutes, who came from Schleswig-Holstein; odious in the sight of God and men, they were like wolves descending on the fold. Rendered homeless by the Danes, held back with considerable difficulty by the Romans hitherto, piracy was now no longer their aim, and they were determined to settle on British soil.

Although divided amongst themselves, the islanders resisted heroically. According to legend, in 429 Saint Germanus of Auxerre, who had arrived on a mission aiming to root out Pelagianism, distinguished himself by an unusual feat of arms. The Britons, faced by a coalition of Picts and Saxons, remembering that he had once been a military commander, managed to persuade him that his mere presence on the battlefield would be worth a whole army, for if he were there 'Christ in person would be fighting in their camp'. It was Eastertide. Under Germanus's orders the Britons, 'still wet from baptism', planned an ambush. When they were engaged by the enemy, at a given signal all the Britons yelled 'Halleluia!' Their shouts were re-echoed by the mountain gorges, and as the great clamour rose into the air the opposing army trembled with fear under the avalanche of rocks descending on them and the thunder of the heavens. Thus, without having to strike a blow the army of the righteous were the witnesses of their own victory. Such was the story of the famous 'Halleluia' battle, more precisely, the battle of Verulam.

But Germanus's exploits were no greater than those of King Arthur, handed down to us in a document of the ninth century and which in the Middle Ages provided the material for the Tales of the Round Table. At the head of his Britons Arthur won twelve successive victories, and during the last of these with his own hand slew 960 warriors, which, however, did not in the end prevent his defeat.

The truth is, in fact, that apart from a few dates and names of battle-fields we know next to nothing regarding the earliest centuries in British history. Under ever-increasing pressure by the invaders in ever larger numbers the islanders were pushed back towards the west, into an area roughly consisting of the Cornish hills, the Welsh mountains, and the Pennine chain, and three-fifths of the country thus fell into enemy hands. In consequence Britain endured a long period of regression and barbarism. The Church alone survived, especially in its monastic institutions. In spite of ancient enmities their frequent tribulations brought them into closer contact with the Irish church, so that at a not much later date it was possible to refer to the Celtic church. Latin, which had never completely taken root in the country, was preserved by the Churchmen as an almost dead language, and this was to be of great future importance.

One of the most famous Britons was the monk Gildas. He had worked in Ireland as a missionary, made a journey to Italy, and was ship-wrecked in Armorica (Brittany), where he founded the monastery of Rhuis, which bears his name. It was in Armorica that, in 540, he wrote his little book entitled *Gildae Sapientis de excidio et conquestu Britanniae*. This work, which the author wished to be indulgent although lacking in good style (*vili licet stylo tamen benigno*), is in fact one of the most violent diatribes ever written by an exile against the invaders of his country and those of his countrymen who remained there. 'Britain has kings, but they are tyrants. She has judges, but they are impious.' The clergy were not dealt with more kindly. 'Britain has priests, but they are madmen ... She has pastors, but they are raging wolves, seeking to kill souls ... They are more anxious to rise up in the hierarchy than they are to gain the kingdom of Heaven.' Carried away by his own vehemence, Gildas declared that they stuffed themselves like pigs (*porcorum more volu-tantes*). Needless to say that as a monk Gildas particularly had the secular clergy in mind, but one cannot help wondering what else he would have written, had he not been in a benevolent mood. Nor should we take him too literally. However disastrous the state of Britain at that time may have been, it is certain that Gildas was expressing himself more like a prophet than an historian.

On the point of death he felt again the longing—if indeed he had ever lost it—all Britons had for the sea. He stated his final wishes quite definitely: 'You will place my body in a boat, and under my head, the stone on which I habitually lay it. No one shall remain in the boat. You are to push it out to sea and let it float wherever God may wish.' Two brethren had come from Cornwall to fetch the body back. They discussed the matter at length and whilst they did so the boat, containing the saint's corpse, went to the bottom, leaving not a trace.

Gildas was one of the many emigrants who, after the Anglo-Saxon invasion, landed on the shores of Armorica, Galicia, in the Iberian peninsula, and Ireland. At that moment the monks led their followers away on epic sea-voyages that inevitably produced their legends. This was known as the *navalis emigratio*. Their boats were constructed of wattle lined with oxskins, or at best, careened with wood. Using sail and oars, the emigrants made for the south, taking their own customs with them, and determined to remain faithful to them. Thus Brieuc landed at the mouth of the Gouet, with a company of men who wore reddish goatskin cloaks. They cleared the forest, built a church of wood, and a village of 200 huts, laying the first foundations of the town that later was to be known as St Brieuc.

If a legend of the ninth century is to be believed, St Guénolé was born of a strange family of emigrants. His father, Fracan, had two sons, Guénoc and Jacut. Fracan's mother, Blanche (Alba), was nicknamed the women with three breasts, 'because she had as many breasts as sons, the sister not being included in the number of her breasts, since it is not customary to write down the genealogy of women'. When he disembarked at Bréhec, Fracan found affluence there, as well as the joy of having a third son, 'which symbolized the face of the Trinity'. This son, Guénolé, decided to become a monk. In order the more completely to eschew the world, with eleven companions he settled on a small island, and then on another one, which was so barren that the little colony would have died of hunger had it not been for the fish he caught. Finally, having discovered a wooded shore, Guénolé built his huts there, and remained for good. This was the origin of Tevennoc or Landévennec, the monastery of Guénolé in the Crozon peninsula.

At that period numbers of British monks settled in Armorica. The Welshman, Pol-Aurelian, Bishop of Léon, founded Lampaul, and also the see of Castel-Pol, later Saint-Pol-de-Léon. Tutwal was the Bishopmonk of Trécor, whilst Samson was at Dol. The parish, of which the monastery was the centre, contained only Britons. This was the *plou* (from the Latin, *plebem*, people), whence are derived Plouha, Plouescat, and Plouvénez. When the faithful were scattered at a distance the missionaries would go to them, gathering them around a portable altar; at the services they were assisted by women, who distributed the sacrament from the chalice. Such customs were, of course, in complete contradiction to those of Gaul, but our British emigrants, although territorially they were attached to the diocese of Tours, retained their own customs and organization. They took no notice whatever of the recommendations or the orders they received from the metropolis, even in spite of a decree of excommunication already fulminated in 567 against any bishop who, without express permission, conferred the episcopal consecration on any Britons.

But this maritime migration was not solely due to the invaders who had arrived from the east. The British and the Irish all loved the sea, responded to its call, and knew how to turn it to ascetic uses. They were more completely cut off from the world in their northern isles, lost in fog, and far from any known shores, than were the solitaries of Egypt by their deserts. Towards the south there were also souls remaining to be converted, and monasteries to be founded. As God had commanded Abraham to leave his own land and his clan to wander into the country He would point out to him (Genesis xii.1), the Celtic monks, who for lack of persecution were unable to achieve the 'red martyrdom', determined to do so by way of maritime adventure and voluntary exile. And although these migrations did partly spring from a certain innate restlessness in the British race, they were not, on the whole, due to a kind of saintly travel mania, or, as has been said, a form of cheap tourism. In this respect our seafaring monks had nothing in common with the holy vagabonds who were tramping all over the continent. Rome was not yet attracting the crowds of forerunners of the heroic Age. In the eyes of many of them Tours was merely an interfering and annoying metropolis, which they did not bear with easily. Even St Martin's fame would have seemed a very different matter to some of them if he had not been charged with an additional portion of original sin, as he was born neither in Ireland nor in Britain. This maritime asceticism was a very different matter from the pilgrimages to the tombs of the saints, for it consisted first and foremost in an act of blind faith, which all those who undertook it knew to be fraught with uncertainty and danger. The seas were a vast desert, and even when the navigators were not captured by pirates and by them sold into slavery, their unknown destination might often prove to be only another desert. Thus Iceland was occupied by Celtic monks even before the Scandinavians arrived there. The odd thing is that, having made so great a renunciation, to the point of no return, it never occurred to them to accept the final sacrifice involved in their self-imposed exile; for only very late in the day did they fully and of their own free will agree to adapt themselves—or submit to—the customs and laws, even the ecclesiastical ones, of their adopted countries. On this point, as in other respects, they remained ferociously insular.

This asceticism of the sea gave rise to a new kind of literary cycle, the *Imrama*, or *Voyages*, of which the best-known was St Brendan the Navigator.

Brendan, who died either in 577 or 583, was an Irishman. He founded among others the monastery of Clonfert in Galway, and entrusted himself to the waves to carry him to Scotland. He must have had some adventures, for 300 years after his death his Odyssey became the subject of a legend, which, with successive additions, was turned into such an extraordinary story, so farcical in parts, that we are tempted to ask ourselves whether Rabelais had not read the *Navigatio Brendani*. At any rate its success was so great that it was translated into Norman, French, German, Provençal, Italian and Norwegian. Brendan embarked with fourteen disciples, and as they allowed their boat to drift with the currents (*per devia maris*), they were carried along in search of an unknown island. They touched at various shores, some of which were a terrestrial paradise, whilst others were guarded by bare and dangerous rocks. Whenever they landed near a settlement of their brethren they were received with transports of joy. They discovered strange beasts— sheep as large as oxen, because they were never milked and spent night and day at pasture. One day a 'gryphon' flew over their boat. We thus learn that a 'gryphon' was a beast as large as an ox, with the beak and claws of an eagle. Another day their ship was followed by a huge marine monster, which 'blew out the water through its nose'. The sailor-monks were all the more terrified by it because as it neared them in order to devour them, the swell it threw up left them no hope of escape. Only Brendan showed no fear. He lifted his hands up to Heaven and said a short prayer, when, behold, another monster, spewing fire from its nostrils, attacked the first one in horrible combat. 'The monster pursuing the monks was thereupon torn into three parts, and after his victory the other one returned to the place whence he had come.'

At Eastertide they found themselves on the high seas, but as they did not wish to sing their Halleluiah on board ship the brethren discovered an island, on which there was neither sand nor a blade of grass, and which appeared to be roughly covered with a kind of skin. They installed themselves upon it for the night, which they spent in vigil and prayer, and next morning sang Mass. Brendan, however, had preferred to stay on board ship. Having finished their devotions, the brethren returned to it in order to fetch meat and fish, lit a fire on the island and placed their conventual cooking-pot upon it. But when their soup began to boil the island began to move. Terrified, they all hurled themselves aboard ship, leaving both pot and victuals behind them. Yet the island continued to float on the waves, and at a distance of two miles they could still see the fire which was continuing to cook their meal. Only then did Brendan—who from the very beginning knew what was going on— reveal the answer to the mystery to them: 'You did not land on an island, but on a fish, the hugest of all sea animals. He is forever trying to join his head to his tail. His name is Casconius.' Although they did not land on the back of a whale every day, for seven years Brendan and his followers voyaged from one marvel to another.

THE LOST ISLE OF IONA

In Ireland, as the result of the impetus given to it by Patrick, monasticism went from strength to strength. Its Golden Age was towards the middle of the sixth century, that of the great foundations which in their turn created many lesser ones. Killeany, in the Arran Islands, thanks to Enna or Enda became the nursery of the Irish saints. Among dozens of others, the most renowned on account of the holiness of their abbots, the number of their adherents, and their high standard of asceticism, were Clonard, under Finian; Moville, under another Finian; Clonmacnois, under Ciaran; Clonfert, under our Brendan; and Bangor, under Comgall. Bangor was not far from Belfast, in Ulster. This monastery had a famous rule:

> *Benchuir, bona regula,*
> *Recta atque divina,*
> *Stricta, sancta, sedula,*
> *Summa, justa et mira.*

But the most famous monastery of them all was that of St Columba in Iona. A member of the O'Donnell clan, both on his mother's and his father's side, Columba was of royal descent. Niall, one of his ancestors, was the supreme king of Ireland in the fourth century. Like three of his cousins he could have been king had he not chosen to become a monk. His real name is said to have been 'Fox' (Crimthann). Columcille or dove of the church was apparently merely a nickname.

He studied at the monastic schools of Cill-Enna, Moville and Clonard. Legend reports that when at Clonard the holy Bishop Finian had sent him to be consecrated as a bishop he returned a mere priest; probably because during the ceremony his consecrator had used the wrong formula. He himself, deprived in this manner of an episcopate, decided like a true saint to remain satisfied with belonging to the priesthood, for according to report he declared that the mistake that had been made was according to God's will.

Having reached the age of action Columba, like all those of his ilk, began to create foundations; at first at Derry, which he loved, and the praises of which he sang like a true bard.

After a pilgrimage to the tomb of St Martin of Tours he founded in succession the monasteries of Durrow, Kells, and certainly many others, since in Ireland alone forty-one monasteries or churches claimed him as their patron. At last he, too, decided to set out on 'pilgrimage for the sake of Christ'.

His departure was described in an episode which, although its embellishments if not the remainder of it were untrue, does hand down to us the impression his personality made on posterity. As a lover of fine manuscripts he knew that at Moville (and not at Clonard as has been stated), his former teacher, Finian, possessed a psalter of great price, which the Father Abbot had brought back from Rome. No doubt under the influence of the devils of bibliophily, the young monk therefore paid a visit to Finian and arranged matters so that he was shut up alone at night in the church where the precious book was kept. He had no candle, but the five fingers on his left hand shone like so many torches, whilst those on his right hand lovingly and carefully followed the lettering. He thought himself alone, but a monk sent there by Finian and 'more inquisitive than was necessary' glued his eye to a crack in the doorway and discovered his offence. It was the other monk, who, apparently, was in the wrong, 'and so that this tale-bearer should learn from personal experience not impudently to spy on the secret consolations that God bestows on his servants', a magpie with one stroke of its beak tore out the unfortunate man's eye. Finian was extremely annoyed by this, and truth to tell, the loss of an eye is no trivial matter. According to the documentary account of this business, which we may suppose did not report the Abbot's reactions very exactly, the tale-bearer received no more than his deserts, and by a sign of the Cross 'the eye, which was hanging down over his cheek, was restored to its socket'. One miracle more or less made little difference to Finian. On the other hand he made a great to-do over the matter of the manuscript. As a book-lover the

Father Abbot felt his position endangered by such a famous copyist, for he was already aware that a manuscript thought to be unique might lose much of its value if a duplicate were in existence; he therefore insisted that the clandestine editor should deliver his work up to him. Little did he know his man. Columba, even more indignant when this was asked of him, bluntly refused to do anything of the kind, and their quarrel became so embittered that the case was referred to King Diarmait for decision. The latter gave his ruling in verses which apparently have ever since remained famous in Ireland: 'The calf belongs to the cow.' Beaten and disgruntled, Columba resolved not to accept his defeat.

Some time later, on King Diarmait's orders, one of Columba's friends was killed. Still very angry, the monk decided to take advantage of this incident. He intended to avenge his friend but neither had he forgotten his manuscript. He announced that an offence had been committed against God, mobilized his forces, and the clans were now on the war-path. Their meeting took place and the occasion was an extremely embittered one, each of the two parties being headed by its Moses; Finian on Diarmait's side, and Columba on God's. The weight of the prayers on both being exactly equal, it appeared that the tussle would have no end. So Columba sent Finian a messenger to inform him that it was useless to continue the contest, since he, Columba, knew that his own clan was bound in the end to triumph. And as Finian knew that his former pupil was incapable of telling a lie, he ceased to pray. On Diarmait's side the dead numbered three thousand; on God's there was only one casualty, 'who had been rash enough to go beyond the limits laid down for the fight'. Such was said to have been the battle of Coll-Dreverny. Needless to say that the copy of the psalter was handed over to Columba. This was the famous *Cathach*, i.e. the 'Combatant' (*proeliator*)[1].

It is not surprising that after such an event Columba's popularity was considerable, although by no means general. He was excommunicated, but pardoned. Probably in agreement with a certain section of public opinion, an angel informed him that he must leave Ireland. The holy monk Molaise also held the same view, and gave very personal

---

[1] It still exists, in the Royal Academy of Ireland, in Dublin. Certain authors consider that it is by Columba's own hand; others refer more prudently to a sixth century manuscript, and still others give it a later date (seventh century). It consists of fifty-eight pages, contained in a silver case of the eleventh century and very much mutilated. When in 1824 the 'Combatant' was removed from this case it was a compact mass, which had to be soaked in water in order to detach the separate pages from one another. Cf. J. Anderson, *Scotland in Early Christian Times*, 2 Vol. Edinburgh, 1881, Vol. I, p. 147, *et seq.*

reasons for doing so. Although the offence committed by Columba was in fact a mere peccadillo, and possibly even no offence at all, Molaise, 'in order to fulfil the will of God' ordered Columba 'to leave his land and his people'. He was to save as many souls as the number of the slain in the battle of Coll-Dreverny. Having provided himself with twelve valorous disciples, Columba knelt to receive the blessing prior to his departure and set out on his pilgrimage.

He sailed northwards and landed on an island where he climbed a hill, gazed out towards the horizon and beheld beyond the sea a dark strip, his native land. He was still not far enough away and must proceed further. At a great distance from Ireland, hard by the cliffs of the Isle of Mull, to the west of Scotland, in a tiny archipelago he landed in the isle of Y, or Hy, which since has been known as Iova or Iona. There he was certain not to be tempted by the sight of his homeland, and the austerity of the landscape was in accordance with his plans. The little island was only three miles long, and only one and a half wide, windswept, treeless, low and flat, with rocky soil, a few strips of white sand, a small amount of pasturage, peatbogs, a pond, hills and a little harbour. This was the desert in which Columba decided to erect his huts. In order to take possession of it in perpetuity it was according to custom necessary for a corpse to be buried there. In consequence the Abbot, anxious for the future, prayed the monk Odran kindly to render this service to the budding community. The holy man offered himself to God, who immediately took his soul, leaving his body to the foundation. The monastery church was built over his tomb.

The mainland was chiefly peopled by Picts, who had formerly been converted by St Ninian, but who had since relapsed into heathenism. Their neighbours were Scots who had come there from Ireland. With the latter the Abbot felt at home, but he immediately undertook the conversion of the Picts, beginning with their king, Bruda, who as the result of his baptism would give his tribes the necessary orders to follow suit.

Columba was to spend thirty-four years in Iona. The first twelve pioneers were quickly outnumbered. Many of the new monks came from Columba's own clan, but the local Scots and converted Picts also contributed their contingents. Thus, all around the island, which remained the mission centre, a kind of monastic federation came into being, which was known as Columba's 'family'. In the country and vicinity of the Picts the foundations of nearly sixty churches or monasteries were attributed to the saint. Including the foundations on Irish soil as well, there were probably around one hundred such establishments, although, no doubt, we must discount a certain number which were merely called after him. It was from Iona that Christianity, a little later, reached the Angles of Northumbria. And on the east coast, opposite Bamborough, in the islet of Lindisfarne (today Holy Island), in 635, the monk Aidan laid the foundations of a monastery that was to become famous.

This enormous task was carried out by a man of iron. We may note a few other conflicts of this period, which, with such a man in charge, and on the basis of his call to the clan or monastic 'family', infallibly led to armed warfare. In 579, at Dal-Araidhe, Columba's party came face to face with the monks of Bangor. A little later more fighting took place near the monastery of Clonard.

Columba, however, was not merely a warrior or conquering monk. In his monastery he organized a school on the model of those of Ireland in which he had received his own training. The chief subject taught there was Holy Writ, and in this respect also Iona was in no way inferior to Bangor. Even the poem *Altus Prosator*, famous as the oldest literary composition in Scotland, was attributed to the Father Abbot. This *Altus Prosator*, which sings of creation, sin and judgment, is an alphabetical piece, in which each strophe begins with a letter of the alphabet. Each one contains six verses, which gives it a certain degree of amplitude. Its vocabulary is not altogether accurate. For instance, the first two words, which give the poem its title, *Altus Prosator* ('The Great Creator'), are far-fetched, although not unknown in classical Latin. The verses do not follow the rules of metrical quantities but scan according to the tonic iambic (a weak beat followed by a strong beat). Each verse is divided in the centre by an assonance repeated at the end of the line:

> *Christo de coelis Domino descendente celsissimo,*
> *Perfulgebit clarissimum signum crucis et vexillum*
> *Tectisque luminaribus duobus principalibus,*
> *Cadent in terra sidera, ut fructus de ficulnea,*
> *Eritque mundi spatium ut fornacis incendium:*
> *Tunc in montium specubus abscondent se exercitus.*

This passage has an undeniable epic quality, but all the Scots authors were not of so high a standard.

The *Life* of Columba, written by Adamnan, ninth abbot of Iona (d. 704) at a period when history had not yet been entirely submerged by legend, tells us of the founder's activities whilst he was the abbot of the 'Holy Isle'.

Like Patrick in Ireland, he at first came into conflict with the Druids. One of them, the personal magician of King Bruda, was extremely annoyed by the conversion of his sovereign, and played the worst kind of tricks on the monks. No quarter was given in the struggle between these two adversaries, both in their respective ways equally implacable. Ever watchful of one another, they never missed an opportunity for coming to grips.

Broichan owned a female Irish slave. Columba, for obvious reasons, had sworn to force him to part with her. Broichan refused to do anything of the kind, whereupon Columba threatened him with death if he persisted in his refusal. And in fact Broichan fell ill. Columba then picked up a piece of shingle on the seashore, blessed it and dipped it in water which he ordered the dying man to drink; if he agreed to release his slave this water would cure him. Everything happened according to plan, and the shingle was held in such veneration that King Bruda, when in his turn he was at death's door, asked to drink of the water contained in the miraculous stone. In spite of hunting for it everywhere, however, the relic could not be found, and Bruda had to resign himself to giving up the ghost like everyone else.

On being present during an argument between some peasants Columba ordered one of them, who was a sorcerer, to milk a bull. Somehow, though we are not told how, the fellow managed to do it and handed the saint a jar full of milk. Columba then said a blessing and the milk turned from white to red—it was blood.

Adamnan's story is a fine example of what might be described as temperate hagiography. He presents his hero, 'the soldier of the isle', as one who fasted constantly, watched indefatigably, was loved by all, and was endlessly praying, reading, or writing. Even the idealized account he gave of the Father Abbot's death, is one of the finest pages of his book. 'Then, when the bell began to toll at midnight, rising in haste he goes to the church, and running faster than the others he enters it alone, and on bended knees falls down in prayer at the altar. At the same moment Diormit, his attendant, who followed more slowly, sees from a distance the whole church filled within with Angelic light round about the Saint. And as he drew near to the door, the same light which he had seen suddenly withdrew, and this light a few others of the Brethren who stood afar off also saw. Diormit, therefore, entering the church, moans out with mournful voice: "Where art thou, Father?" And as the lights of the Brethren had not yet been brought in, groping his way in the dark he finds the saint lying before the altar, and raising him up a little and sitting down by him he lays the holy head on his bosom. And meanwhile the community of monks, running up with lights, began to weep at the sight of their dying Father. And as we have learned from some who were there present, the Saint, his soul not yet departing, with open eyes upturned, looked round about on either side with wonderful cheerfulness and joy of countenance on seeing the holy Angels coming to meet him. Diormit then lifts up the holy right hand of the Saint that he may bless the choir of monks. . . .'

ST COLUMBAN, CHRIST'S PILGRIM

One spring or summer's day in 575 a shipload of monks landed in Armorica, at a spot where a cross still stands today, near the village of St Coulomb between St Malo and the Mont St Michel. For a long time those who dwelt on those shores had been accustomed to seeing pilgrims from across the sea land there. These were like the others. Their heads were shaven in the Celtic fashion; they wore white habits, badly stained by the seaspray, and carried long curved staffs, with their liturgical books in leather bags, water-bottles bound in leather straps hanging around their necks by cords, and capsules containing their holy relics and consecrated wafers. There were twelve of them, led by a gigantic fellow. There was no lack of Celtic colonies throughout the region and they could have settled down there; but for that very reason Armorica was at that time no longer a land of exile and their vows of pilgrimage urged them further afield.

Their leader was called Columban. Born towards 540, he was a scion of a noble family of Leinster and as a youth had been so handsome that he drew the admiring glances of all the colleens. In spite of his monk's frock his appearance was still highly impressive. He was well-read, a good bard, conversant with the arts, poetry, history, philosophy and rhythm. Although he only knew a few words of Greek he had closely read Virgil, the elder Pliny, Sallust, and even such unchaste authors as Horace, Ovid, and Juvenal. His interest in poetry remained unabated throughout his life and he was able on occasion to turn out in a style that was not too far fetched a set of verses in the manner of Horace. He had great determination and people said that in order to become a monk he did not hesitate to pass over his mother's dead body, but they took good care not to mention this in his presence, for they were afraid of his temper. After having first spent some time at Claun-Innis he was trained in spiritual matters and the study of the Scriptures by a learned monk called Sinnell; then, at Bangor, in 'the vale of the angels', the austere Abbot Comgall by means of a ruthless rule prepared him for

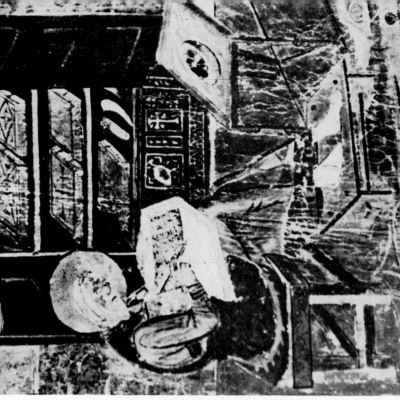

CASSIODORUS IN HIS LIBRARY. Laurentian Lib., Florence.

(Photo: J. Décarreaux)

10. MONTE CASSINO. Entirely reconstructed in accordance
with old plans.

(Photo: J. Décarreaux)

11. ST GREGORY THE GREAT. From the Hartker antiphonary:
tenth century.

(*Staatsbib., St Gall*)

Christ's militia. Yet this self-confident and strong-minded monk had a
secret restlessness. One day, when he was looking out to sea, he remembered that a holy woman he had met by accident had told him that
if she were a man she would become one of God's pilgrims. And
Columban, filled in his turn with Celtic missionary zeal, set out over
the waters in the direction of Britain and Armorica.

He went thence to Gaul and eastward, on foot, like the apostles.
On his way through Rouen, Noyon and Rheims, he observed that
'virtue is more or less non-existent'. As he travelled along the roads he
noted that the country, devastated by the scourge of the Frankish
occupation, had lost the last vestiges of its ancient civilization. When he
made contact with the mighty it was in order to learn whether they were
mutually exterminating one another owing to avarice, cruelty, or
ambition. When he met the bishops he was frequently scandalized, for
men of God were few among the heads of the churches, whilst many
were the princes of that century whose prestige was due to their
temporal powers rather than to knowledge or virtue. Looking for
monks, he found only a few insignificant groups or else a small number
of hermits and recluses, lost in the enormous forests of Gaul. Wherever
he passed by he saw that although there might be some degree of
religious observance in the cities in which the bishops resided there was
far less in the countryside, where the people were still enslaved by the
old Latin or Germanic superstitions. His lively intelligence and
resolute character then showed him what he had to do; the monasteries
he proposed to found, like the Celtic ones, were to be devoted both to
prayer and to missionary work among the peasant populations. In order
to provide a living it would be necessary to clear and drain the ground
before sowing the seed, but new agricultural settlements would bring
great additional benefits to the district.

It is remarkable that in spite of his own knowledge and intellectual
ability Columban did not attempt to create centres of culture in his
monasteries in Gaul. Although his rule provided for a daily period of
reading he did not provide his monks with any actual scholastic preparation for it. Having settled down amongst populations who, whilst
professing the true faith, lived in a state of utter moral corruption,
he determined above all to confront these people, even were they
Churchmen, with the example of a degree of asceticism carried to the
very limits of the most perfect purity. As M. Roger put it so well,
'St Columban taught discipline, not grammar; he fought against loose
morals, not against ignorance.' And no doubt his was the only possible
attitude in the circumstances. 'The very severity of the Irish rule

Iona

Lindisfarne

Derry

Jarrow
Wearmouth

Bangor

Whitby

Armagh

Ripon

York

Kells

Clonard

Clonmacnois

Kildare

Bangor

Clonfert

Durrow

Glendalough

Skellig
Michael

Lancarvan

Malmesbury

Canterbury

Crediton

Sherborne

Dol

Celts

Anglo-Saxons

St.-Gildas

3. The British Isles in the seventh and eighth centuries

appeared as a guarantee against the disorder that at that time was prevalent in the Church of Gaul.'

When Columban arrived in Burgundy the king, Gontran, proposed that he should settle down at Annegray, in the Vosges. The site suited him, for it was 'a vast desert, a harsh solitude, a rocky land', as was noted by his hagiographer, the monk Jonas of Bobbio, who wrote towards 640. They settled in the forest, cut down the trees, made contact with the natives by means of little books containing simple sentences, possibly modelled on the famous 'A.B.C.'s' of St Patrick, and the fame of the saints spread so rapidly that soon one establishment was no longer sufficient. Luxeuil, where Columban spent most of his time, was founded nearby, as well as Fontaine, which like Annegray was placed under a provost towards 590.

These were all strictly Celtic foundations. It would be an under-statement to say that Columban ruled his world with the rod; he also used the big stick and the number of blows dealt out for each offence was laid down in advance. His contacts with the bishops were few and mostly carried on at a distance. Those prelates who had had some experience of his outspokenness felt a kind of reverential fear of him, and preferred to keep him out of their concerns. Nevertheless, although Columban forgot to ask the Bishop of Besançon's permission to settle in his diocese they remained on friendly terms. This was not the only such instance but it is worthy of remembrance. When dealing with the mighty the Father Abbot spoke firmly and adopted a high moral tone. Rejecting all diplomatic calculations he preferred to adopt the attitude of a prophet, and this was to have certain consequences. It was as if his outbursts were a part of his characteristic asceticism, and not only accepted but almost deliberately provoked.

At the time when the new foundations in Burgundy were blossoming forth Brunhild, who according to G. Kurth and F. Lot did not deserve to be described as 'the new Jezebel,' was ruling the country in the name of her favourite grandson, Theuderich II. According to the monk Jonas, one of those who allegedly gave this queen her bad reputation, the old woman preferred to see the king surrounded by a harem—a usual institution at the Merovingian courts—rather than a properly married man, for in her opinion a young queen might have deprived her of her honours, her status and the opportunities for carrying out her ambitions. For his part Theuderich was quite happy to remain a bachelor with no restraint on his vices. He feared God not at all, St Martin a little, but was much more afraid of Columban, who had no hesitation whatever in lecturing him. One day, when the monk was attending the court,

Brunhild asked him to bless her grandson's bastards. The man of God refused to do so, giving her his reasons in perfectly clear terms. 'These children,' he told her, 'come from a bad background, and in any case,' he added, 'they will never reign.' With these amiable words he went off, and as he stepped across the palace threshold an appalling noise shook the city. Brunhild was not to forget it.

Some time later a messenger arrived at Luxeuil with a royal command. The monks were no longer to leave the monastery boundaries and were to have no further contact with the outside world, not even for the purpose of acquiring their foodstuffs. Columban did not hesitate for an instant. Knowing that the king was staying at his country seat at Epoisses (on the Côte d'Or), in spite of the interdict he seized his staff and was off there. When he arrived at the gate Theuderich, who did not wish to have any trouble with such a difficult character, ordered that he be invited to enter. Columban, however, declared that he would not do so, and was thereupon sent victuals, dishes and goblets, as was customary. But he retorted that God did not accept gifts from the impious and the dishes, wine and beer, were immediately thrown down. So Theuderich withdrew the interdict, but Brunhild was not discouraged. Direct action having failed, she possessed other, subtler and more efficacious means, with which the monk himself had provided her. At least, this is what Jonas seemed to convey, when he wrote that the queen-mother spurred on the bishops and the courtiers against him, and that Theuderich accused the Luxovians of holding 'the customs of the country' in contempt. This expression gives us the clue to the whole matter, in which Columban was not entirely beyond reproach. Apart altogether from the annoyance of the courtiers at being refused entry to the cloisters, and at being received at the hostelry like the common people, the affair raised the whole question of Celtic implantation in foreign soil, for like all his compatriots Columban was determined without giving an inch to uphold all the practices of Ireland.

First of all there was the matter of the tonsure. Such a detail appears trivial to us, nowadays, accustomed as we are to seeing the odd head-gear of so many devout individuals. But at that time such matters were of tremendous importance. The Celts were tonsured, for in their country it was a mark of their servitude. For Christ's sake they did not in the least object to looking like slaves, but they intended to do so after their own fashion. Their heads were neither totally shaven, in the so-called manner of St Paul, nor just the crown of them, attributed to St Peter. They wore their hair long at the back and on the shaven frontal part of their heads a half-circle of hair from one ear to the other, leaving a band of hair across the forehead. Although Patrick himself had been completely tonsured in the Roman fashion, the half-crescent of hair from ear to ear had become the mark of Celtic monachism and as such was the cause of a tenacious struggle, worthy of a better one. They were accused of having borrowed it from Simon the Magician, for as everyone knew, the said Simon was the head of the Druids, who also wore this suspect kind of tonsure. Others, equally malevolent, asserted that it had been imported into Ireland by King Loegaire's swineherd. Needless to say, these arguments made not the slightest impression on our hardheaded Celts. At Landévennec in Armorica the tonsorial half-crescent was still worn at the beginning of the ninth century.

The matter of the relations between the episcopal sees and the monastic foundations was, however, of much greater importance. In Gaul it was the rule that every monastery, like every rural parish, was under the jurisdiction of the local bishop. But following the customs of his own country, where there were no territorial limitations to the dioceses, Columban founded his monasteries, organized his mission centres, proselytized, preached, and dispensed the sacraments, as if the bishops were non-existent. This supererogation was not without its drawbacks, and the bishops were not wholly in the wrong to be uneasy about and to take a severe view of the Luxovian missionaries, who behaved on foreign soil as if it were their own, and whose successes in many cases appeared as veiled criticisms. The bishops found the redoubtable holiness of their head difficult to tolerate and were not going to miss any occasion to rid themselves of so tiresome an apostle.

The date on which Easter was celebrated was another source of conflict. There were in the Church at that time three different computations regarding this; one in Rome, another in Gaul, and another in Ireland and Britain, as the result of which this very same Easter feast was celebrated on three different dates of each year. When one of these computations had been generally accepted in one region the lack of concordance between the Roman and local calendars might be regrettable, but did not cause any practical difficulties. But when, on the contrary, two different computations were competing in any given region, paradoxical complications were bound to ensue. As at that period the whole liturgical calendar was based on the date of Easter, the movable feasts were not in consequence celebrated at the same time in the same places, and at an interval of a few days the faithful were taking part in two Easter celebrations, two of the Ascension and of Whitsuntide, not to mention the differing periods of Lent.

Now Luxeuil, together with its foundations and missions, followed the Irish computation in competition with the Gaulish one. It even happened, although Christians always tried very hard to avoid it doing so, that the Irish Easter coincided with the Jewish Passover, which resulted in a general outburst of indignation. Columban, convinced that his own computation was the better one, although in fact it was the least exact, was also indignant, but the outrage from his point of view was that neither Rome nor Gaul had aligned themselves alongside Ireland, as Ireland, naturally, could never be in the wrong. We have two letters from him on the subject, addressed to two different Popes, one of whom was St Gregory the Great, written in his grandest manner. Its general tone is respectful, flattering even. In this he referred to the Pope as the Church's finest ornament, the very august flower of a wavering Europe, and far from presenting himself as the Pope's adversary, the author requests his counsel and enlightenment. He even went so far as to describe himself as timid (*mihi timido*), which is not a little surprising. But when he came to the point regarding the Easter controversy he once more returned to his usual form, affirming unequivocally that whosoever, were it the Pope himself, did not follow the Irish computation, was no better than a heretic to be thrown out (*hereticus vel respuendus*).

On their part the bishops of Burgundy, sitting in council at Châlon in 603, summoned Columban to appear before them. They wished to clear up with him this question of Easter, which interested—and embarrassed—them to the highest degree. Columban took a lofty tone with them and refused to go. He was astonished that so great a number of prelates should have met together to concern themselves with him, observing that they would do better to meet one another periodically, as the canons required, in order to study more urgent matters, and that for the rest they should more closely imitate Christ, particularly as regarded humility. After this he ended in peaceable and charitable terms. He was possibly not altogether wrong in reprimanding these bishops, but this was not what they had requested of him. Although he refrained from giving his reasons for refusing to appear before them his attitude was a logical one. An out-and-out Celt, and considering himself as such to be independent of all episcopal jurisdiction, he could not agree to take orders from them. In these circumstances, had he accepted their summons, this would have meant not only that his own computation was a permissible subject for discussion but also recognizing by implication a jurisdiction that would have brought him into line with the general laws of Gaul. He simply asked them to leave him in peace to his own devices. The council, clearly aware of the fact that in dealing with such a man prudence was the mother of peace, took good care to press the matter no further.

These quarrels, during the course of which Columban never missed an opportunity to make himself unpopular, played into the hands of Brunhild. She might have made a martyr of him, and according to the moral outlook of the time one murder more or less was no great matter. But it was against her policy to take such a step in the case of a man who, already enjoying a halo of sanctity, would not have hesitated to accept 'red martyrdom'. An order of exile would rid the country of him at lesser expense.

Apprehensively and with all possible prudence, Theuderich informed the monk that he was to leave Luxeuil. Columban was escorted to Besançon, but escaped and returned to the monastery. He was re-arrested and once more banished, together with all those Celts who were refractory to Gaulish customs. As he left his brethren he bade them take care to resume the office at the point at which he had been interrupted by the King's emissaries. He was taken westward, where, on the Atlantic coast, a ship would be found to return him to his home-land. So now Columban was once again on the road, guarded by a not unduly severe escort. Via Autun, Auxerre, Nevers, Orleans and Tours—where he prayed at the tomb of St Martin, who had his stolen baggage returned to him—he arrived at Nantes, forcibly expressing himself when opportunity arose, against 'that dog, Theuderich', who, he added, would not be on the throne much longer. On his point of departure from Gaul he wrote a letter to his successor, Athala, which would prove, if that were necessary, his greatness of soul, and which gives us a glimpse into this tough monk's gentle affection for his old companions at Luxeuil.

He went aboard ship, but his vessel appeared to be in no hurry to sail. There arose a strong swell and a powerful wave threw sailors and passengers back on shore. As they all realized what was happening, they left Columban there and the sea having calmed down again they were soon well afloat. In fact he had once more escaped, for having volun-tarily gone into exile for Christ's sake 'and the healing of his soul' he was spared the humiliation of a forcible return to his own country. Although he was now in his sixties he picked up his pilgrim's staff and once more fearlessly took to the road, again travelling eastward and only avoiding passing through Theuderich's domains.

He went by way of Rouen, Soissons, Paris, Metz, Coblenz and Mainz, following the course of the Rhine towards Lake Constance. In

all the settlements along the river banks the missionaries were attempting to break down the local paganism, but with little success. After
remaining for two or three years at Bregenz, where they had thought of
taking up residence, they were obliged to move on again in order to
escape from Theuderich's clutches. It was then that Gall, Columban's
old companion, who ever since they had been at Bangor together had
not left his chief's side, and whose perseverance in overthrowing the
idols had quite recently made a stir, admitted that he was able to go
no further. Columban, whose standards were implacable, unfairly
declared that he would not hear of any such weakness on the part of his
companion. In spite of his fever, he suspected Gall of being only a
lukewarm pilgrim, and although he reluctantly agreed to tolerate such
alleged weakness, he forbade Gall to celebrate Mass until he heard of
Columban's own death. And the rest of the pilgrims once more set out
in the wake of their leader. But when they had left him behind, Gall
wasted no time. The hermitage he chose as his retreat became the
monastery which later bore his name. And when Columban died he
learned in a dream that now he might once more celebrate Mass,
which he immediately did, for the soul of his old master. A few days
later a friar brought him the news he had been expecting, and in
sending him absolution the Abbot sent him also the staff he had used
during their long years of pilgrimage together.

Still travelling southward the little troop, now exhausted and thinned
out, passed into Italy, and crossed the river Po, finally coming to a halt
beyond Pavia, at the foot of Mount Penici. The spot seemed suitable for
the foundation of a monastery, as it was agreeable and fertile, whilst at
the junction of the rivers Bobbio and Trebia both water and fish were
abundant. It was there, the historian Jonas noted, that one winter
Hannibal had lost a number of men, horses, and elephants, forgetting,
however, to add that it was there as well that he had won a memorable
victory over the Romans. They found a church already built, and
decided to settle down there. Dense firwoods covered the ground and
would provide an ample supply of logs for their huts, giving the Father
Abbot occasion to stretch his arms; for he was a lusty woodcutter, and
knew better than anyone how to fell a tree at one blow of the axe, and
when it was necessary to clear away the undergrowth at a spot which no
carts could reach, he would gaily lift the branches on to his shoulders
and bear them off. Perhaps he learned on such occasions that it was
easier to break wood than to bend souls.

His own, apparently, was beginning to relax a little. At Luxeuil, as
at Bobbio, he had always shown an almost Franciscan love of animals.

Like the rest of the monks of his country who were also priests he always wore gloves when working, out of respect for the unction by which his hands were consecrated. When a crow stole one of his gloves he waited patiently until the bird brought it back to him. One day he came across a bear whilst it was devouring a stag it had killed; when he ordered it to desist the huge beast quietly gave up its meal, leaving the brethren with a nice new skin which would provide them with excellent shoes. Jonas took care to point out that the bear did so without a growl, gently, lowering its head and trying to cut a friendly caper. When for a time Columban retreated into a hermitage he delighted in the visits of the forest animals. The squirrels were his friends and the birds would perch on his hood. From time to time he also scolded them. One day when a bear had killed one of the two oxen harnessed to the cart that was clearing away the undergrowth, Columban gave the culprit such a sermon that he repentantly took his victim's place.

Yet he had not altogether given up his former belligerence. Columban owed his last foundation to the benevolence of the Lombard King Agilulf, anxious to be on good terms with such an important personality. His relations with that monarch, in his palace at Milan, were all the more cordial as the Queen, Theodolinda, was a Catholic. It was through her and the local bishops that he learned that northern Italy was no longer in communion with the see of Rome, and that the Pope was alleged to have prevaricated over the question of the Three Chapters, a sequel to the Christological discussions which had been the subject of the Council of Chalcedony in 451. It would have been a great asset to them to have been able to include such a champion as Columban in their ranks. But on the contrary, the monk immediately took the part of the Pope, Boniface IV, and in case the pontiff might have weakened sent him an epistle to refresh his orthodoxy. With all due respect to Rome, in passing he made a dig at Vigilius, one of Boniface's predecessors. Punning somewhat heavily on Vigilius's name, and having come to the conclusion that the Church's vessel was shipping water, he wrote: 'Watch, I beg thee, Pope, watch. I repeat, watch, for Vigil did not keep his vigil too well.' Truth to tell, Columban, who was no theologian, only knew the gist of the matter vaguely and incorrectly, but it was a good opportunity for him to prove to a pope who might be suspected of heresy the dogmatic purity of the Church of Ireland. Although simply an abbot, he expressed himself in the somewhat obsolete language of a prophet: 'We Irish,' he stated, in accordance with the leitmotif which since then has become well-known, 'have never included either heretics, Jews, or schismatics . . . Ever since Christ, the supreme Lord of chariots came to us, borne by the sea gales on the backs of dolphins, Rome became for us noble and famous above all others.' And using the plural form he addressed himself not only to the ruling Pope but to all the popes: 'If you are held in high honour through the honour of your see, you should beware of losing such honour by any lapse whatever. Your power will last as long as your discernment. For the heavenly porter is he who opens the gates to the worthy and closes them to the unworthy . . . If he act otherwise he will be unable either to open or to close them.' It is interesting that in the course of this broadside Columban again felt it necessary to state that he was 'in some ways a timid man and a warrior of little valour'.

At Bobbio this eternal pilgrim at last found his haven. When on November 23, 615, he surrendered to death he had accomplished a task worthy of his mettle. He dealt roughly with his fellow-men, intractably when he thought that the truth was imperilled, remaining obstinately faithful to his Celtic vocation and heroic in his asceticism. Columban, who might easily have turned everything upside down, in fact valiantly sowed the good seed and was even beginning to reap his crop in the virgin lands he tilled. It has been reckoned that he and his immediate disciples, or those directly influenced by him, founded around forty monasteries. Luxeuil, Bobbio, and even St Gall were the flower of his achievement. But to mention only a few of the great French monasteries, these included Rebais, Jumièges, Fontenelle (St Wandrille), Chelles, Faremoutier, Corbie, St Omer, St Bertin, Remiremont, Hautvillers, Montiérender, St Valéry sur Somme and Solignac; the fruits of what was rightly described as the Irish miracle. On the right bank of the Rhine the Alemanni, the Bavarians, and the Thuringians had already been contacted.

For the Germanic tribes on that bank were less hostile to the Irish monks than they were to the Frankish missionaries. The conquered tribes did not willingly accept baptism from priests who appeared to be sheltering behind their warriors' shields. To refuse to do so might have dire consequences, for the battle-axe could add its powerful weight to the argument, but to accept under such conditions was part of the humiliation of defeat. The Celts, however, came to them with no protection save that of their holy relics. When they proclaimed that they did so neither in the interests of a prince nor of a policy, their deeds confirmed it. They were totally disinterested and there were no strings attached to their sermons. It was to this law of all missionary conquest that they owed their obvious successes, although these were limited by other considerations.

For in spite of the great monuments their endeavours left behind them their activities suffered from certain weaknesses. Stability was not characteristic of the Celtic monks, and although some of their foundations rested on solid ground, owing to their innate wanderlust others were less firmly rooted. Their rule was so harsh that at Bobbio later on there were defections, and at Luxeuil, serious internal difficulties. Their ways were so peculiar and their characters so obstinate that these gave rise to perpetual contradictions. At Luxeuil itself, which was the Gaulish citadel of Celtic conservatism, as well as the foundations mentioned above, Columban's rule had to be mitigated at a very early date by the more humane Benedictine rule. These various adaptations became known under the general heading of *Regula beati Benedicti ad modum Luxoviensis monasterii.*

IRELAND, THE ISLE OF SAINTS AND SCHOLARS

It would be an error to see in the Celtic monks no more than a set of original characters, for these men, with their brand-new resolution and thirst for the absolute themselves emerged from a very particular kind of environment.

Whilst on the Continent the churches were organized in dioceses within the framework of what remained of the administrative cadres of the Empire, in Ireland the monastic centres were formed on the basis of the 'family' (*muintir*), the clan or the tribe, the only groupings known there. The monastery therefore was itself a 'family', recruited at all events in the early days from those who came of the same stock. A centre for prayer and asceticism, it was also a base for departure to the mission field. When a monastery was flourishing and lasting it served as the kernel of an extensive agglomeration.

The abbot, head of a monastic clan, had an important part to play. His religious authority still stemmed from the importance of the 'family' of which he was a member. It was not merely confined to his own foundation but was exercised over all its dependencies. It was not exceptional there to come across whole dynasties of abbots. Among the first twelve abbots of Iona ten belonged to the same clan as their founder. And this practice, although it was neither customary nor obligatory, was yet a frequent one until the beginning of the eighth century. The abbot was thus both a spiritual and temporal head, especially if the monastic properties were many. His name, incidentally, had wider connotations—the Pope was referred to as the Abbot of Rome, and Christ was sometimes called the Great Abbot.

The prestige of the abbot's position was so great that it was often considered to be superior to a bishopric. If one dare say so, some abbots even refused a bishopric with a kind of coquettish humility. Even when he was not himself a bishop the head of the monastic 'family' might suggest that certain of his monks be given bishoprics, but it was understood that whatever outward honours might be paid to such a monastic bishop over and above the respect shown to an ordinary priest, the same obedience to the rule was expected from him as from all the other monks and he had no especial powers whatever within the community. His duties were merely professional ones, consisting in bestowing ordination on those whom the abbot might recommend to him for it. But at the coronation of the first king of the Scots of Dalriada it was the abbot-priest Columba, and no bishop, even selected by him, who took charge of the ceremony. Elsewhere, as dioceses did not exist, there were no exact jurisdictionary boundaries either. The abbot, or if he had passed on a mandate to him to this effect the bishop, visited the missionary fields scattered around the foundations, or among the tribes, each tribe generally possessing a bishop-monk. Columba of Iona, whose case is the best-known, although not unique, ruled over a number of monasteries in the Big Island, the isles of the north, and the land of the Picts. If necessary, he sent his bishops on missions.

Thus the clergy and bishoprics of Ireland were almost exclusively monastic. There were more ordinary monks than ordained monks, but the latter so far outnumbered and outweighed the parish priests that historians might well have asked themselves if there had ever, indeed, been a secular clergy in Ireland. In Britain, where after the Anglo-Saxon invasions the monastic institutions tended to draw more and more closely towards those of Ireland, bishops and secular priests were slightly more numerous but there, also, the monks predominated. Nor did the latter have a very high opinion of their secular brethren, readily declaring that whilst a monk would give one hundred fold, a simple priest would give no more than sixty (although with perhaps a higher percentage as regarded humility).

Among the innumerable Celtic foundations there were some that only housed a small family whereas others sheltered a whole population. Clonard, under St Finian, was said to have trained 3,000 students and provided 100 bishops. There were 3,000 monks at Clonfert and 2,000 at the Irish Bangor. At St Asaph in Wales there were 965 monks, of whom 300 were illiterate and employed in agriculture; 300 worked indoors, whilst 365 were responsible for maintaining in the church the office of perpetual praise, without interruption day or night. It is possible that these admirably exact figures may have been exaggerated, but there is no doubt that these monasteries did house a very large number of cenobites.

In nearly all of them there were various different categories—elders, worker-monks, children or young people, scholars, students or novices. Pilgrims were numerous and frequent in that itinerant world, and were received with discrimination, sometimes with particular attentions, as when the abbot himself would ceremoniously go forth to receive a pilgrim.

There were also monasteries for women, although it was less easy to recruit them than the men. It was often necessary to tear away a slave from a master who possessed various rights over her, or to safeguard a young Christian girl from the hostility of her still heathen family. The great Irish nun was St Bridget of Kildare (second half of the fifth century). It appears that her foundation was devoted to supporting the missions of the monks, but it is uncertain whether this abbess ruled over a double monastery for men and women (as happened elsewhere). Her reputation was so great that by some she was called 'the mother of Jesus', a theological enormity the ineptitude of which was not justified by the incontestable fervour that gave rise to it.

The outward aspect of the Celtic monasteries resembled that of the Palestinian laure, consisting of a number of huts grouped around a church, either inside or close to the stronghold of a clan. Such huts were built either of wooden laths, clay, or wattle reinforced by it. The churches, also wooden, had thatched roofs; the largest of them might be about thirty-five yards long. The refectory, library, and forge stood on a square around the abbot's hut. The community was enclosed within and protected by a wooden fence and a ditch, like a fortified *vallum*; at Clonmacnois this ran to nearly 500 yards. The ovens, barns, stables, hangars and farms lay beyond it. There was also a water-mill, which removed the need for a treadmill. All these buildings were made of wood, to which the Celts gave preference, for according to them man's ephemeral dwelling-places should not claim to be as durable as stone, as was wrongly held in Gaul. It was therefore easy for them to move into their settlements, and, when necessary, to abandon them without foreseeing that they would leave next to nothing of value behind them for the archaeologist.[1] There were, nevertheless, a few stone buildings, although these were the exception, such as that of St Ninian

---

[1] The stone watch towers which are still to be found on numerous monastic sites in Ireland are of much later date; from the tenth, eleventh and twelfth centuries.

among the Picts of Galloway, which was called the 'White House' (*Candida Casa*), the name given it on account of its colour. It appears that such stone buildings were put up when wood was not available in sufficient quantity. From this point of view the remains of the small monastery of Skellig Michael or Great Skellig (off the coast of Kerry, at the south-west corner of Ireland), is a small-scale example of an Irish monastery during the fifth or sixth centuries.

The islet of Skellig Michael is a circular rock, arid and bare of all vegetation. The monastery stands on a flattened space of about sixty yards by thirty-five, and is reached by a flight of 670 steps. It consists of only eight cells and a church, the whole built of untreated stone with no cement. The diameter of the largest circular cells varies from just over fourteen feet to about twenty-four feet. The rest, which are square, are fourteen feet by ten. The sloping walls meet at the top in the shape of a cone or a keel in reverse; they are of a thickness of from four to four and a half feet, pierced by a door and a window. The oratory is nine feet nine inches by six feet. The whole edifice is enclosed by a wall.

Another similar set of buildings, founded in England in the seventh century by Irish monks, provides the kernel of the great abbey of Abingdon, near Oxford. The primitive monastery was 120 feet in diameter. It comprised twelve cells and as many churches, and was also surrounded by a high circular wall. In such buildings, if there was any attempt at art at all, it was altogether rudimentary, consisting of a few lintels, columns, crosses or inscriptions, all of them of a primitive kind.

The Celtic monks also lived as solitaries when their abbot, on their conventual behaviour, judged them to be worthy of this higher level of existence, either for a time or until they died. In these cases the anchorites would leave the monastic enclosure for huts at a shorter or longer distance from it, 'the hard prison of stone', or else a grotto or an islet. These were known as the *disert*, in breton, *peniti*. But even there the hermits were still under supervision, and a *disertach* or hermitage superior was in charge of them. If pirates passed close by the islets it happened that they were never heard of again.

The regime of the Irish monasteries was extremely hard. The life of the monks was a completely conventual one, nor did the abbots allow the individualistic idiosyncrasies characteristic of certain Egyptian or Syrian monasteries. The ordinance of the Celtic monasteries was closely regulated and the day was divided into three parts, one each for prayer, manual labour, and study.

If the monks were numerous an agricultural community was organized solely in order to provide them with food. They always had flocks to tend and harvests to sow, glean, thresh, and store. Inside the walls the foundations possessed their own blacksmiths, artisans, and if necessary, goldsmiths, who were all monks. At Iona they built boats from wood that the abbot imported from across the sea. Their work was at the same time both utilitarian and penitential. At St Asaph in Wales the monks drew the ploughs.

The recitation of the psalms provided the basic essentials of prayer both in the churches and at work, but a rigorous form of asceticism was additional to it. As is still the case today in the Eastern Christian world, the daily prostrations were numbered by hundreds. They often prayed standing upright, their arms crossed. A virtuoso at this exercise, St Kevin of Glendalough, is said to have remained in this position uninterruptedly, day and night, for seven years, although it is true that he leant against a board. The birds responded to his asceticism by building their nests in the holy man's hands, and perching on his head and in his cowl. A prolonged bath in a pond or a river, whilst reciting the psalms, was recommended as a cure for the temptations of the flesh, as a form of voluntary asceticism, or as a punishment for certain faults. There was much fasting; meals were light and taken late; their diet vegetarian, consisting of eggs, vegetables, bread, milk and water, a little fish, and sometimes, sea-calf. On special occasions, or to honour a guest, the abbot would grant an alimentary consolation (*consolatio cibi*), which was generally beef or mutton. The monks wore an undergarment, the tunic, and an overgarment, the scapulary, made of rough wool, and when possible, bleached white. At Iona the brethren wore shoes for working and travelling, but discarded them on entering the refectory. They slept fully clothed, on cots provided with a straw mattress and a pillow. Their slumbers were only brief. The rule of Luxeuil, which was not one of the easiest, recommended to the brethren not to go to bed unless they were tired, and if necessary to sleep whilst walking. It is remarkable that the Celtic monks did not regard dirt, even monastic dirt, as a mark of sanctity, but washed themselves.

The rules, which were numerous and all differed from one another, drawn up either in prose or verse, are less representative of a complete set of observances than of an ideal to be attained and general directives for doing so. For everyday purposes the abbot was the living embodiment of them. Absolute and immediate obedience to him was expected. The monks went down on their knees to receive his orders and reprimands. And in order that none should remain in ignorance of the punishments that might be meted out to them, very numerous and minutely detailed penances, appropriate to each and every misdemean-

our, were inflicted on them. Like Gildas, Columba of Iona and Columban of Luxeuil, each abbot of high repute had his own list of penances.
One need only dip into them haphazardly in order by such indirect
means to discover certain customs and details of Celtic life, given the
fact that the examples quoted did not apply to all the monasteries
indiscriminately. Anyone who laughed, yawned, coughed, spat,
sneezed, or sang out of tune during the services was given six strokes of
the stick. The same applied to any deacon who served at the altar without first having shaved. Six strokes were also given to any monk who
was in too great a hurry to sit down to table, without awaiting the
abbot's blessing or taking his time to respond *Amen*. Another six
strokes were awarded to him who 'licked' his spoon without first having
sanctified it by making the sign of the cross over it. A monk who spoke
to a woman, except in the presence of witnesses, received 200 strokes
unless he opted instead to fast on bread-and-water for two days. If in the
course of a scuffle or brawl one monk was hurt by another, the aggressor
did penance for three years. According to Gildas' penance list a monk
who had committed fornication was sentenced to three years' ex-
piation and was not allowed to sing the psalms with the rest of the
community until he had served eighteen months of them. Other
penances might last for seven or twelve years. Enforced exile from their
native soil was a particularly disgraceful sentence and a murderer was
condemned to ten years' banishment. Certain penances might be
exchanged for others, shorter but more severe, as for instance sleeping (?)
on a bed of nettles or in a tomb, together with a corpse. During his
period of penance a brother, even when doing dirty work, was only
allowed to wash his head once a week, on Sundays. Gildas, who had
worked in Ireland, paid particular attention to drunkenness. A monk
who through drink was unable to take part in the chanting was excommunicated. The priest, i.e. the monk-priest, if he had become
intoxicated owing to ignorance, did penance for thirteen days, and forty
days if it were due to carelessness; whilst if he did so in contempt of
discipline he was given three times forty days. At Iona and also
elsewhere in general, the abbot had recourse to public confession. Daily
confession was widespread. The confessor, the friend of the soul, was
held in especial veneration. 'A man without an *anmchara* is a body
without a head.'

St Columban of Luxeuil, to whom we owe two very detailed
penitentials, which he never failed to put into practice, was so convinced
of the usefulness of confession, which before his time was much less
current, that he applied it on a considerable scale even to his common

flocks. He literally made all the laymen whom he proposed to convert go down on their knees. Nor did he forget his penitential scales. The penitent knew in advance what to expect; if he had eaten himself sick, one week's fast on bread-and-water, whilst for the same sin a monk received forty days. For certain carnal sins the layman might receive punishments lasting as long as seven years; three years on bread, water, and vegetables; four years abstinence from wine and meat, after which the sinner might again be admitted to communion. Three Lents on bread and water, apart from restitution, were inflicted for the theft of an ox, a horse, or a sheep. If they had often gone to confession the more powerful Franks would have had to diet on numerous occasions. It is even less probable that Brunhild, whose name stood highest in the table of absolutions, would have bent over the hand of the terrible Abbot whilst he inflicted the most thumping of all penances on her. But those who did submit to this discipline, which in our eyes seems merely mechanical and rudimentary from a psychological point of view, did find it a means of emerging from their barbarism, of refining their characters and raising them above it. Columban's successes incline us to the view that his methods were well adapted to the environment in which he applied them.

It is in fact undeniable that these usages, as they spread beyond the monasteries, conformed to a general longing, in this barbarian environment, for education. At first sight we are inclined to equate the penitential scales with the scales of compensation (*wergeld*) which in the Germanic world regulated offences against the common law; as the owner of a mutilated horse or a bereaved family was paid an indemnity, penances regulated all offences towards one's neighbour or God. But a closer examination reveals that those who laid down these penitential scales in general did so, even if it was not a deliberate tactic on their part, in order to eliminate all desire for revenge by the injured party and to underline the explicit hope of finally redeeming the sinner. And, in fact, in spite of the payment of *wergeld*, which in principle should have settled every quarrel, the primitive urge to the vendetta, with its endless repetition of hatred and crime, did constantly and cruelly re-emerge among the Germans. In those circumstances, when the guilty party had paid the monetary compensation demanded by the law, the Church, by obliging him to make public confession, and enforcing the appropriate penance, raised the significance of his amends on to the moral and religious plane, thereby attenuating the lust for revenge to the advantage of the social order, and protecting from it the human being to whom her shelter was given. And in addition she made it clear to the culprit that in order to cleanse his conscience it was not enough merely to pay an indemnity, but that it was necessary as well to purify his soul by prophylaxis. In spite of the scales automatically laid down by it, the Bobbio penitential showed a certain understanding of the necessity for the psychological rehabilitation of these barbarians.

In the case of certain categories of monks, apart from prayer, asceticism, and manual labour, study was one of the essential laws of their lives. It was not esteemed particularly highly in Egypt and Syria. When the ascetic retired to the desert he left everything behind him, even learning. If he had some, it might be of use to him. If, like St Anthony, he had none, this lack of it did not in the least prevent him from achieving a career as a great abbot. Virtue sufficed without knowledge and the experimental teaching of the elders was enough to provide the edification of holiness. Augustine, in Africa, insisted on learning because he needed priests. But in Gaul, Martin, the proselytizer of the countryside, although he had manuscripts copied out for the pious reading of the brethren, never thought of becoming a schoolmaster. Only in the south, i.e. in that part of Gaul which had retained something of Latin influence, were the isles of Lérins a centre of Christian intellectualism. The Celts agreed with the Lérinians that the monastic state should be enhanced by the benefits of education. They went even further and did not overlook profane literature either.

The Scot, i.e. the Irish monk, was well versed in Holy Scripture. Although his intellectual knowledge of theology was at first somewhat slight, by his persevering study of Holy Writ he acquired that general understanding of theology which nourishes the life spiritual. He knew that in order to improve his status a knowledge of Latin was indispensable. He therefore, naturally, learned Church Latin, but as a logical consequence of doing so went to the sources themselves, to profane Latin, and in this respect had no prejudices at all. He was uninterested in the morality of paganism and the civilization in which it had developed. The local heathenism he met up with in the course of his duties as a missionary did not remind him of the scabrous stories of the Graeco-Roman Pantheon. The fables of Antiquity concerned a foreign world which had no relevance for him, and in placing this heritage at the service of divine literature he never experienced the dramas of a Jerome or the scruples of a Basil.

It is certain that Patrick, who knew Latin badly, was far too preoccupied by his apostolic mission to have thought of bringing culture to Ireland. But after his time the great centres of monastic education quite naturally became intellectual ones. At Moville, Clonard, Clonfert,

Clonmacnois, and Bangor the students were numerous and varied. If necessary they would proceed in stages from one monastery to another, to which they might be attracted by the fame of a specialist in divinity or asceticism. Thanks to them the great Irish monasteries were extremely lively. If the figures that have been produced are correct, it seems that there were no buildings large enough to house them all, and we are told that lessons were given out of doors, where the pupils sat around on the grassy banks. In each foundation there was a library where waxen tablets, awls, pens and inkwells were supplied to the monks. The calligrapher was a person of importance. As much 'blood money' was demanded for the murder of a scribe as for that of an abbot or a bishop.

We do not know by what means classical literature reached Ireland. All we do know is that in Patrick's time this country, completely isolated from all Roman influence, knew it not at all, or very little. But on the other hand it was definitely being studied in the middle of the sixth century. Irishmen could go and study in Gaul, whilst Gauls were able to go to Ireland and the Britons certainly went there from England.

When the Romans finally left England at the beginning of the fifth century Latin literature was known there by other means than by the purely utilitarian contact of the natives with merchants, soldiers and civil servants. According to one tradition St Iltut taught both sacred and profane literature. It is in any case a fact that Gildas, who could scan a Latin sentence, went to Ireland between 565 and 568, nor, probably, was he the only one. At the time when the Britons, thrown back towards the west by the Anglo-Saxon invasions, were coming closer to the Irish, intellectual contacts must have been as active as the rest. In any case Latin literature was given a sufficient impetus among the Irish to outdistance in a very short time the teaching of their first masters. People went eagerly to learn Latin from the Scots, but as regards Greek it has not in any way been proved that the monks had a greater knowledge of it than that of the glossaries. Yet it could nevertheless be said that the Irish, or the more learned among them at any rate, from the sixth to the first half of the seventh centuries, were 'the most active upholders of classical culture in Western Europe'.[1]

By reference to what was happening in Gaul during this same period we can measure the intellectual abyss that separated Ireland from a large part of the Continent. On their arrival in the West, the Barbarians, or at least those in positions of responsibility or exchange, in view of the fact that they employed Gallo-Romans in their service, were obliged to

[1] M. Roger.

learn Latin. In Burgundy the *Loi Gambette*, the Visigoth *Breviary* of Alaric, the Salic and Ripuarian laws, were drawn up in Latin. Conversions led to a knowledge of Church Latin. The Merovingian king, Chilperic, prided himself on knowing the poets, and was not in fact ignorant of them. Queen Brunhild was relatively cultured. Yet we must not be deluded by such instances. Classical Latin was a nostalgic memory; ecclesiastical and scholastic Latin had a precarious existence, and the spoken language progressed slowly from the vulgate towards Romance. This was a natural phenomenon which, however, unfortunately occurred at a time of deepest ignorance.

In Britain and Ireland Latin was, on the contrary, an imported language. The Celts, who throughout remained faithful to their native tongue, learned it only as a foreign language, which from the beginning was explained in Celtic terms. Whilst in Gaul Latin became progressively debased; it was preserved by them as a completely separate language, and was never threatened by vulgarization, because concurrently with their study of Latin the educated groups continued to speak their own language and to develop its literature. Thus Ireland and the last British refuges in the West helped both to maintain the language of the Church and also, in part, to save the tradition of profane literature.

As regards the teaching and usage of classical Latin by the Scots, we are not in a position to draw any generally valid conclusions and can only assess these according to their results in the cases of a certain number of individuals. The fact that in the sixth century they produced a Columba of Iona and a Columban of Luxeuil proves that in certain centres there must have been both teachers and pupils of a high order; many instances prove that their Church Latin arose from a sound classical basis. During that same sixth century St Gildas also learned profane literature, although this was not always apparent in his own writings. We know that in the first part of the seventh century there existed at Tuam Drecan a triple school of Latin and Christian literature, Irish national law, and Irish literature, but we do not know what their curricula were. Tírechán, the author of a *Life* of St Patrick and an accurate writer, did not reveal to us how much exactly he knew of the profane authors, whilst at the end of the century, Muirchu Maccu Machtheni, who also wrote a *Life* of Patrick, was a friend of the poets and knew verses by Virgil from memory. At the same period Adamnan of Iona, who wrote a biography of his Father, Columba, in sound ecclesiastical Latin, studied Virgil carefully, although it is impossible to state exactly whether he owed his knowledge of him to Celtic teachers or to Roman missionaries. Whilst it is therefore clear that some of the Scots monks had read the profane authors, even by drawing on a certain number of facts we are not in a position to quote exactly a list of the authors taught in the schools. The same applies to their school textbooks; we only know that the Scots did work at grammar, spelling, scansion and the rules of pronunciation, but with differing results, and without enabling us to learn more exactly the degree of their knowledge of the liberal arts.

To whatever degree of proficiency it was learned, however, classical Latin was held in general esteem, whilst Church Latin was the usual means of conversing of those monks who had assiduously studied the holy texts. Many of them used it with great ease, whilst others give us the measure of the distance that separates an idiomatic language from a foreign one that has been acquired. As good pupils who had pored over their exercises the latter patently enjoyed showing off their knowledge even to the point of absurdity. The *Hisperica famina*, the title of which is in itself a pun, were a model for this kind of thing. It would be an exaggeration to declare, with D. Leclercq, that their authors deserved to have been shut up in a lunatic asylum, yet one must admit that they are only very slightly intelligible, even to those Latinists who have won their spurs. They abound in bad taste, to the detriment of good sense and sometimes of any sense at all, but as such they are still witness to a certain degree of knowledge and preservation. At a time of general debasement on the Continent, in spite of certain havens of learning in Spain and Italy, at this period and until the middle of the seventh century it was very largely among the Celtic monks that good literature was most highly cherished. Possibly the extent and quality of a culture that was still on too small a scale to earn the name of humanism has been exaggerated and it is true that humanism was possessed only by the privileged few. But it is indubitable that the Britons and especially the Scots did provide it with a refuge and safeguarded it for future centres of enlightenment.

CHAPTER VI

MONTE CASSINO
BEACON OF THE WEST

About midway between Rome and Naples, on the ancient Via Latina (today Casilina), the little town of Cassino lies alongside the river Rapido, which joins the Liri a little lower down, the conjunction of the two rivers forming the Garigliano. A very fertile plain stretches to the east and south, the fine fruits of which can be found on the market stalls. A line of steep hills to the north and west quickly becomes mountainous as they rise to the spine of the Appenines. One of these hills, which forms a spur at the western end of the chain, towers so closely over Cassino that its massive cone seems to be pressing down on the last houses. At its summit (1,700 feet above sea-level and about 1,150 feet above the plain) long white walls appear like those of an elongated, squat citadel, lacking only a keep to look completely like a fortress. The Abbey of Monte Cassino towers over the countryside.

We know that during the last world war, on February 15, 1944, during the week of the Octave of St Scholastica, the sister of St Benedict, the allies, having given up hope of capturing this stronghold, destroyed the monastery by raining down on it 576 tons of bombs from 142 Flying Fortresses and 112 medium bombers. Since then, however, the monastery has been restored stone by stone, to its former sumptuous splendour, even down to its most controversial details. (We refer to the frescoes in the Beuronian style as well as the interior decoration of the church.)

Monte Cassino is reached by a five-mile road of hairpin bends. On arriving at the summit, the platform on which the monastery stands, we are struck by the almost completely square aspect of the four façades forming the architectural whole, an enormous trapeze of masonry, over

200 yards long and 130 feet high. Having passed through the gate, the visitor is dazzled by the sparkling marbles. The interior is vast. On one side there is a gallery, the *Loggia del Paradiso*, which opens on to a magnificent view, and where five cloisters meet. The cloister of the Renaissance, the pride of the monastery, contains a charming well, and leads to a monumental stairway, 18 metres in width. There are also among others the cloisters of the Benefactors and of the Priors. The church, as large as a cathedral, is decorated with glittering marbles. The rich and imposing library alone takes up one whole side of the building. The monks' cells, on four separate storeys, are aligned along corridors 180 metres long. This grand and glorious, shiningly white edifice lacks nothing to restore it to its pre-war appearance except a thick coating of patina.

When untidy hordes of tourists are not noisily surging around in them these holy places still give the impression of peace and silence we would expect from them. Yet in 1961 the community had not yet recovered from the disaster of 1944. There were still only a mere thirty monks there, whereas there should be two hundred. The library was difficult of approach, and only in recent times have the monks no longer been its sole custodians.

Sheltered beneath all this massive splendour, the low and humble cell of St Benedict did not have to be reconstructed; a heavy calibre bomb, which fell quite close to it and would have pulverized it, failed to explode. It was here that the Patriarch of the Western monks died after 547.[1]

---

[1] At the moment when St Benedict's appearance marked an epoch in the monastic world, this should be placed in the chronological succession:

Martin of Tours	died in	397
Jerome	„ „	419
Honoratius of Lérins	„ „	429
Augustine	„ „	430
Paulinus of Nola	„ „	431
Cassenius	„ „	435
Hilarius of Arles	„ „	449
Patrick	„ „	461
Caesarius of Arles	„ „	543
Benedict of Nursia	„ „	547
Martin of Braga	„ „	580
Radegunda	„ „	587
Columba of Iona	„ „	597
Leander of Seville	„ „	601
Columban of Luxeuil	„ „	615
Isidore of Seville	„ „	636

ST BENEDICT, FATHER OF EUROPE

In dealing with St Benedict, whom Dante celebrated as 'the greatest and most brilliant of precious stones', we would like to write what is usually called a fine piece. But unfortunately for us his own humility, which formed the cornerstone of his edifice, so completely enshrouds his personality that the most precious details of his biography, after having whetted our appetite to know more about him, leave us unsatisfied on that score.

Not that he lacked an historian worthy of the name. St Gregory the Great, who had been a monk before becoming Pope, and who on succeeding to the papacy became the untiring promotor of the Benedictine institution, was a serious author, well-documented and close to the events he described, since he wrote only forty-five years more or less after his hero's death. But being a man of his own day, as regards the subject in which we are interested, he could only produce a work of edification. Although in the matter of *miracula* he was more cautious than others, it is wiser to admit that a number of instances reported by him—and incidentally indiscernible to the critical view—are more akin to hagiography than to history. Nevertheless Volume II of the *Dialogues* remains of inestimable value.

The historical background shows us Italy going through a period of trial. At the time of Benedict's birth, around 480, 'the Western Roman Empire, that Octavius Augustus, the first Emperor, had begun to rule over in the year 709 of the Roman calendar, ended with the little Emperor' (Ammianus Marcellinus). We understand that this 'little Emperor' was none other than Romulus Augustulus, who was deposed in 476 by the Barbarian, Odoacer, who under the pretence of serving the Empire was furthering his own ends. In 493 the Ostrogoth Theodoric slew him with his own hands and in his stead installed himself for thirty-three years. We know that his reign although severe was intelligent, and provided the peninsula with a period of relief and recovery which after the troubles of the preceding period seemed all the more extraordinary as being due to a Barbarian. Benedict, then, was the Ostrogoth's contemporary, lived through the years of bloodshed at the end of his reign and the no less savage episodes after it. He witnessed the beginning of the new trials, disasters and bloodshed inflicted during nearly twenty years on Italy by the Barbarian mercenaries of the Emperor Justinian in order to restore in the West the former unity of the Empire under the aegis of Constantinople: (535-553). Benedict did not live to witness the end of the Byzantine reconquest.

At the same period Rome, capital of the popes but no longer of the Empire, was just as badly ruled. At the time when Theodoric was striving to give his subjects a little prosperity, Rome was degraded by eight long years of corruption: from 498 to 507. One section of the clergy preferred the tolerance of the Arian king to the protection of the Catholic Emperor, whilst another was serving the interests of Byzantium, and among other less apostolic activities was endeavouring to resolve the schism that already separated the Church of Rome from that of Constantinople (484-518). Pope Symmachus, who was against Byzantium, was faced with a rival pope, the archpriest Laurentius, who had the support of the Byzantine faction. Symmachus was accused of having used the money of the poor as a bribe to secure his own election, to have wasted it in keeping his see, and whilst in that see, having entertained reprehensible friendships with women. Whether he was guilty or not, his reputation was seriously impaired and he defended himself so clumsily and incoherently that at one time he lost the protection of Theodoric. He finally won his cause only because of the general lassitude and by being reinstated in the Ostrogoth king's favour. Rome, meanwhile, delivered over to the factions, was the scene of popular uprisings, looting, and murder. At the beginning of this business Benedict was probably twenty years old.

He was over forty when the Emperor Justinian ordered the closing of the Arian churches of Constantinople and forbade the Arians to all civilian and military employment. Theodoric was personally inviolable, but was humiliated and annoyed by the ending of a schism that had served his purpose; late in life he reverted to sudden outbursts of savagery, and he took this matter very badly. John I was ordered to go in person to Constantinople and as the Catholic Pope, to have the anti-Arian edict withdrawn. Having only partly succeeded in this task he was thrown into jail in Ravenna, where he died three months before his persecutor in 526.

The conflict between Pope Vigilius and the Emperor Justinian was even more deplorable. This autocratic Emperor, who always saw everything larger than life, was ambitious in his undertakings and often fortunate in their results, intended not only to bend the bodies of his subjects to his will but also to control their souls. He fancied himself as a theologian and anxious to win over the monophysites, he decided to add a chapter to the Council of Chalcedon (451), by the posthumous condemnation of three theologians whom the Fathers had not thought it appropriate to attack, but by doing so he merely succeeded in reviving the old quarrel dividing the Empire. Vigilius, the Pope of Rome, was no

217

match for him. He owed too much to Byzantium, which had enabled him to succeed to the throne by deposing, not without a certain amount of trouble, his predecessor, Silverius. His theology was only inter- mittently orthodox, his character unsteady; at times he was firm, even when he felt himself isolated, but he was alternately torn between his responsibilities and his awareness of the precariousness of his position. When he was carried off from the Lateran by Imperial messengers and put on the road to Constantinople Vigilius was so clumsy in his efforts to serve, restrain, or put a break on the Emperor's theological claims that as a result of cruel ill-treatment during ten years he died in 555 before he could return to Rome. Others might have left Constantinople with the halo of a confessor. All Vigilius took away with him was humiliation and occasion for a new schism. Benedict died during the early years of this scandal.

Although St Gregory mentions nothing of the above facts it is impossible that Benedict should not have known of them. They possibly enhanced his disgust with so depressing a world and strength- ened his desire to fly to that solitude where one is certain to find God.

He was born at Nursia, about thirty miles east of Spoleta, in the Sabine mountains, of a race that was still as virile as in the days when the poet Horace sang of it. When he was old enough his family, either a noble or at any rate a very wealthy one, sent him to Rome, to study rhetoric and law, and thus make sure of an honourable and successful future. There, at a very early stage, it would appear, he was tempted both by women and by spiritual pride. Benedict then followed the classical behaviour of all future monks: 'He withdrew the foot he had placed on the doorstep of the world' (St Gregory), i.e. he fled from Rome and its dangerous charms. According to most authors he was then about twenty, but this seems rather old for a boy whom Gregory called *puer* and who still had his nurse with him. It would perhaps be better to assume that he was somewhat younger.

Benedict, still accompanied by his nurse, found a refuge thirty miles from Rome in a community of ascetics near the village of Enfida (Afila). But there an awkward, so to speak, involuntary miracle made him fear the loss of his humility. He parted from his nurse and retreated a little further towards the north, along the river. The austere place he chose, known by the great villa that Nero had once built there on the borders of three lakes, was called Sublaqueum (Subiaco). There he found an elder, Romanus, who became his spiritual father and invested him in the monastic goatskin. Following the example of Anthony during three years Benedict lived a hermit's life in a grotto. But like his model he was begged to leave it in order to become head of the monks against his will. He took the leadership of a group established at Vicovaro, further north. He was young and inexperienced, very hard on himself, and he imposed so harsh a discipline on his followers that they would have poisoned him had a miracle not intervened in time.

He had returned to his grotto in order to 'live by himself' when a new set of visitors arrived. They were better disposed and he was unable to evade them. There were enough of them to form a colony of twelve monasteries, each containing twelve monks, around the centre from which Benedict directed them. This foundation has been regarded as a kind of laura or even an organization of the Pachomian type. The superior was at most twenty-five years of age, and his reputation was so high that rich Romans sent their children to him in order that he might educate them according to the rule of the monks. But once again his holiness and his miracles drew evil down upon him. A neighbouring priest, a nasty character called Florentius, tried to poison him, when a crow—which became his iconographical emblem—flew down and stole the poisoned bread destined for Benedict. Finally Florentius, after having sent seven whores into the monks' garden, attained his aim, for Benedict in disgust handed over his community at Subiaco to a disciple and set out for the south at the head of a little group of brethren. But the long years he spent at Subiaco were not wasted.

When he arrived at Cassino he climbed the steep hill. At the summit, where once had stood a temple of Jupiter, he built a monastery, which was no doubt quite a small one, and two oratories, one of which was dedicated to St Martin. There he tried out a new system. After having successively been first a hermit and then head of a community living in huts, he essayed a form of the strictest cenobitism, partly based on St Basil's, among others. This happened around 529.

In this final stage of his life his age—he was nearing fifty—his experience, his holiness and his prestige seem to have given him the serenity of a man who little by little and without realizing it was becoming a patriarch. He knew very well how he wished to lead his monks and did so with a firm hand. And thenceforward, apparently, his life was only very occasionally affected by outward events.

Following his example his sister Scholastica had also entered a monastery. Once a year she paid her brother a visit, when he received her outside the cloisters. On a certain evening, during the course of one of these meetings, at the moment when Benedict was about to part from her, he was surprised to find her insisting on his remaining with her, although his rule forbade him to spend a night out-of-doors. But a sudden thunderstorm compelled him to stay with her. Brother and sister spent the night in prayer and only parted on the following morning. Three days later, as he sat in his cell, his eyes raised to heaven, Benedict was surprised to see a dove rising straight into the blue. It was the soul of his sister Scholastica, 'soaring to discover the secrets of heaven'.

As Martin had before him, at the end of the day Benedict enjoyed the peace of the evening, when the sun slowly sank beneath the hill. Down below the peasants worked in the fields around Cassino and sometimes armed bands swept through the valley, going down towards Naples or up in the direction of Rome.

One day it was rumoured that Totila's men were in the district. The Ostrogoth Totila, or more exactly, Badwila, had succeeded Theodoric. Although warfare left him little time to spare, he was intelligent and a good administrator. He was the leader of the Gothic resistance in Italy to Justinian, and little by little, at the head of his troops he more or less permanently succeeded in defeating the Byzantine troops aiming to reconquer the country. This lasted for ten years until he was finally killed in combat, in 552. In the year 542 Totila was only at the beginning of his power but he was already feared. As he was passing along at the foot of Monte Cassino, Totila wished to meet the holy man of whom the entire countryside was talking. The Father Abbot agreed to receive him but took advantage of the occasion to give the cruel warrior a stern warning. Totila, intimidated as had surely never happened in his life before, withdrew.

On March 21, 547, or a few years later, Benedict, having received communion, died very quietly, standing in his oratory, supported by his brethren, his arms outstretched to heaven. He left behind him only three foundations, those of Subiaco, Monte Cassino and Terracino, as well as a testament, *The Rule of Monks*, which was written at Monte Cassino after 534.

On first reading through this booklet, the reader's first impression is one of surprise, for Benedict wrote with a total disregard for the rules of composition. Apart from a certain number of principal connecting chapters, he wrote with no preconceived plan, as the ideas came to him, and adding certain pieces here and there. Nor does anything in his rule show the results of his schooling, which we know he gave up at an early date. But this, no doubt, was the last thing he troubled about. Even his language was the vulgate, and in spite of what has been suggested, it is not at all certain that he was still familiar with the literary language, especially considering that whilst he was studying in Rome when still in his nurse's care he had only gone very slightly beyond the stage of learning grammar and a first reading of the poets, historians and orators.

There has recently been a great deal of discussion in the Benedictine monasteries centred on a *Master's Rule*, by an unknown author, and the *Rule of Monks*, which until then tradition had ascribed to Benedict. Basing themselves as a starting-point on the fact that in many important passages the two texts are identical, the critics have tried to define their respective origins. It often happens that research does not provide the solution to the problems it raises, but among the tangled skein from which each inquirer selects the threads that suit him, we may discern four hypotheses. According to one view, Benedict was the author of *The Rule of Monks* and Cassiodorus, who died in 580, allegedly the author of *The Master's Rule*, plagiarized him. According to another, Benedict wrote *The Master's Rule* and not *The Rule of Monks*. Still others believe that Benedict drew on *The Master's Rule* when writing his *Rule of Monks*, whilst a fourth suggestion is that Benedict wrote out his Rule in a first draft, which allegedly was *The Master's Rule*, and when re-written at a later date, either by himself or another, became *The Rule of Monks*.

Until some further hypotheses are produced the critics (who are nearly all Benedictines) take up a filial and cautiously respectful attitude, agreeing that St Benedict does at least count for something in the matter. As the debate is not yet concluded there is no reason from our own point of view for us to differ from the traditional opinion that Benedict was the teacher, if not the author, of *The Rule of Monks*.

There is no doubt that when meditating on his subject Benedict did, as D. Delatte, a distinguished commentator, has said, intend to put a nebulous situation in order. He knew Eastern monachism well enough not to imagine that the institutions of the desert could be transplanted to the Western world without some inconvenience. He venerated St Martin but knew that his extraordinary success did not survive him, no doubt because his methods had not been codified. As for the rest, his own intentions were modest ones. He only meant to suggest 'a beginning to monastic life' in which 'nothing too arduous or disagreeable' would be demanded, in short, as he stated elsewhere, 'a tiny little rule for beginners'. And in fact what he called the instruments of good works was only a summary of the simplest precepts of the Christian life, lived with full understanding in surroundings in which it could expand in all security.

But let us make no mistake about it; in order to gain his ends Benedict did not require miserable creatures worn out by apathy or parasites wishing to hide their own cowardice beneath an appearance of moderate comfort. What he was looking for was a race of strong men capable of hope (*fortissimum genus*). His institution was to be a *schola dominici servitii*. The current translation 'school in the service of Our Lord' is weaker than the original. The *schola* was less of a school than a corporation. It also formed a militant unity like, for instance, the Emperor's personal guard and the soldier who served in it voluntarily was called *scholaris*. Benedict, we see, willingly used military terminology. Although it was not part of his plan to drive his troop along with the stick, he did expect from his flock instant and absolute obedience.

Having had some experience of anchoretic life he considered it to be so difficult and its achievement such a hard one that he regarded it as the final stage of self-perfection. He had also experienced the cenobitic life of the hut-dwellers but this had not entirely satisfied him. He was searching for something more complete, a cenobitic life in one dwelling for all, where they might live together day by day. Unlike the Egyptian cenobites he did not attempt to found large collectives, but aiming to know all those around him intimately he organized their lives like that of a family, in the very wide meaning the Latins attached to this term. Those individuals who belonged to it were of no importance except as members of it, but enjoyed one another's mutual aid. Needless to say that all exaggerated individualism, temperamental idiosyncrasies and rivalry in asceticism were excluded or if they did survive were reduced to a minimum by the daily intercourse of well-behaved people. Strong personalities might bring some distinction to their house but the majority, if they were only commonplace, might also lower its tone. And clearly, an undistinguished monastery where nevertheless good discipline prevailed was of more real and enduring value than one with a great reputation which was marred by collective pride. Benedict was, literally, trying to create a family inspired by one communal ideal, all brought up according to the same precepts and living in such a manner as to perpetuate its spiritual line down the ages.

In order that it should cohere such a family must above all things enjoy stability. Benedict had no sympathy at all for the spirit of pious restlessness that flung so many undisciplined characters on to the roads. He therefore decided that his monks should make a vow to remain throughout their lives within the walls of the community of which they had chosen to become members. Thence it followed that each monastery acquired its own characteristics, living in isolation, by its own efforts, having no ties with other similar houses except those of mutual esteem, a fraternal ideal, charity and prayer. Materially and spiritually each monastery was to be as autonomous as a given family. Benedict never had any idea of any order in the modern sense of the term. It was not in the least understood that the head of such a family should be an intellectual, a man of affairs, a great administrator, a distinguished political counsellor, or a prelate in the grand manner, reigning over an aristocracy of archmonks, but simply an abbot, i.e. etymologically, a father. Above all he should possess the simple virtues—which although rare were not non-existent—of good judgment, prudence, a sense of justice, and affectionate care of his own. His community would elect him for 'the merits of his way of life and his doctrine of wisdom', his awareness of his responsibilities, and his mercifulness. He would never forget that he was in the service of his flock and not chosen for the purpose of his own advancement or the satisfaction of ruling them (*magis prodesse quam praeesse*) and he would be more anxious to be loved than feared (*potius amari quam timeri*). On this point an observation by D. Butler tells us more than any long commentaries: 'St Benedict seems not particularly to have wanted the abbot to be a strong disciplinarian or even a saint, but above all gifted with good sense and wise discretion.' Nor was he, contrary to what has often been stated, altogether the Roman type of *paterfamilias*, who regarded all power as the prerogative of his position, but in the full sense of the term he was the administrator of the family that had been entrusted to him and the most solicitous guide of those whom it was his mission to lead and help along the road to salvation.

His powers were discretionary and it was his duty not to abuse them. When important decisions had to be taken he was helped in doing so by a council. In order to assist him in carrying out the various duties the good running of his house required he appointed 'officers' eager to carry out their work satisfactorily, for they knew that the abbot was not supposed to have any suspicious or nagging afterthoughts with regard to the meticulousness they showed at it. The organization of a Benedictine monastery should rest on commonsense and mutual trust.

We cannot say with any certainty how many monks Benedict gathered around him. Accepting the figure of 150 for the colony of Subiaco it is reasonable to assume that the foundation of Monte Cassino, which Benedict undertook at a time when he had gained both experience and fame, was at least as important but in any case remained sufficiently small in numbers to preserve its organization as a *familia*. These monks included men of all kinds—some of high birth like Maurus and Placidus at Subiaco, poor folk from whom nothing was expected, Barbarians who had come over from Arianism, and children sent by their parents to become monks.

It would be interesting to know more about them. Those who were good and well-behaved, who made no noise, passed unnoticed, but we have a chance to know something about a few of the others. Thanks to them we learn that even under Benedict, both at Subiaco and Monte Cassino, the holy Rule suffered occasional strains. These lapses, which were reported by the hagiographer as having been the occasions for miracles, are useful in allowing us to enter into the daily life of the community. A child monk who was bored escaped from the monastery in order to rejoin his family. There he died and the earth threw back his corpse. The Father Abbot was obliged to go and put things in order again. It happened that although strictly forbidden to do so some of the brethren would call on a pious woman for a bite of food. But this did not escape Benedict's notice. A young monk, having been given two *fiaschi* of wine for his superior, only gave him one and would have kept the other for himself if the Abbot had not guessed at his theft. Another tried in vain to hide two handkerchiefs, the clandestine present of some nuns he had visited. A restless monk, unable to sit still during the service, would vanish as soon as the brethren bent down in prayer, and frittered away his time outside. Benedict took a high hand with that one, whipping him until 'a little black child' who was pulling the monk by his cowl, vanished for good and enabled the monk to remain motionless at prayer again. Another so frequently gave way to the demon of wanderlust that the Father Abbot threw him out. He soon returned, for a dragon having made him turn tail had taught him that fear was the basis of stability.

For such simple folk Benedict devised a rule that they could all keep. The Easterners treated their bodies like enemies that had to be exhausted by fasting, vigils, hairshirts, chains or stones, throwing themselves into amazing feats of asceticism. But Benedict's view was that the body should receive sufficiently humane treatment so as to be at all times the good servant of the soul. He did not think of the soul dwelling within the body as in a prison, but as part of a whole of which each component should be treated so that the entire system developed harmoniously. The Eastern monasteries would have been scandalized by such a view of man. Without making any concessions to laxity Benedict wished his monks to have a standard of living more or less similar to that enjoyed by the peasants who dwelt close by him at Cassino. This was definitely an innovation.

He thought, firstly, that people who slept well were better balanced and more easily manageable than those nervous ones who suffered from insomnia, and the number of hours he allocated to sleeping would

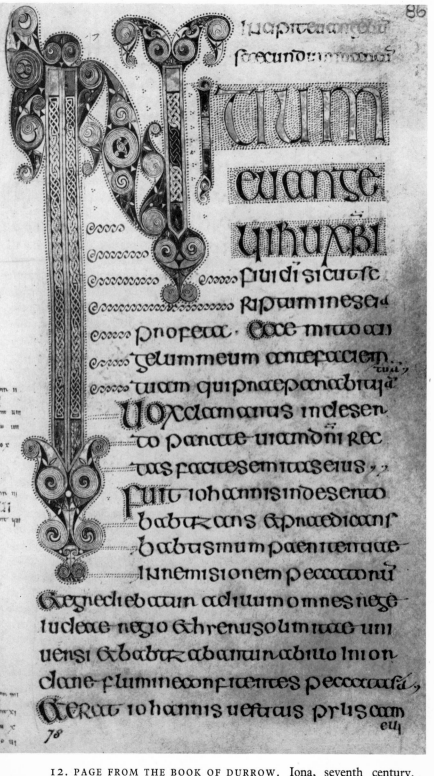

12. PAGE FROM THE BOOK OF DURROW. Iona, seventh century.
Trinity Coll. Lib., Dublin. (*Photo: Green Studio*)

13. ST MATTHEW. From the book of Durrow; seventh century.
Trinity Coll. Lib., Dublin.
(Photo: Green Studio)

astound us did we not know the customs of his day. This point requires explanation.

We know that the Romans divided the day into twelve equal parts, from sunrise to sunset, and the night in the same way, from sunset to sunrise. Consequently it was only at the time of the equinoxes (March 25th and September 24th) that both day and night contained respectively twelve hours of sixty minutes each. The result was that from March 25th to September 25th each of the twelve 'hours' of the day contained more than sixty minutes, whilst the twelve 'hours' of the night contained less. Conversely, during the following six months the twelve 'hours' of the night lasted for more than sixty minutes, and those of the daytime, less. In the latitude of Monte Cassino the longest hour of summertime lasted for seventy-five minutes and the shortest forty-five; and the converse was true for the shortest day and longest night of winter. There was, therefore, a considerable discrepancy in the timetable.

Taking into account the almost unavoidable approximations in his reckoning, Benedict allowed his monks nine good hours of sleep during the longest winter nights, but only five during the shortest summer nights, in addition, it is true, to the siesta, which was customary in Italy in the hot weather. This was obviously a very big allowance of sleep for monks, but there is no doubt that the Cassinians, like the local peasantry, lived by the sun.

According to D. Schmitz, historian of the Order, their timetable was as follows:

Rising: Mid-June, 1 a.m.

End-December, 2.30 a.m.

April, 3 a.m.

Office of Vigils or Matins, lasting around 1½ hours.

Reading until Lauds at Christmas, 5.45 a.m.

Mid-March, 4.30 a.m.

June 21st, 2.15 a.m.

Working time, divided by communal recitation of short prayers, (small hours) from the end of Lauds until 2.30 p.m.

Meals: One only during the winter semester at 2.40 p.m.

In Lent at 5 p.m.

Two during the summer semester, the first towards noon, the second towards 5.30 p.m. in April and 7 p.m. from June 21st.

Vespers: Towards 4 p.m. in winter.

Before the second meal in summer.

Compline: At end of day.

Sleeping: (always uninterrupted), immediately after Compline either at 5 p.m. at the end of December or 6.30 p.m. in April or before 8 p.m. in summer.

According to this timetable the monks spent three and a half to four hours daily at services, more or less the same amount of time in private prayer or reading, and according to the season, six to eight hours daily at manual labour.

When writing the other articles of their daily Rule Benedict gave as much thought to a balanced programme. Complete poverty was obligatory, but the monks should have available two cloaks (the cowl), of which the warmer was kept for winter use; two tunics, one for night-wear; a scapulary, or working apron; a belt, socks, strong shoes, a stylo and tablets, a needle and a handkerchief. They were not to look shabby and old clothes were put aside for the poor. If it was necessary for a monk to travel he was given such clothing from the stockroom as would not dishonour his calling, and, as well, pants or under-pants that he had to return in clean condition. As we have seen, there was plenty of time for sleeping. They slept in common dormitories, where silence reigned. Each monk had a rush or straw mattress, a rough sheet, a bedspread or a rug and a pillow. Meals were taken in common, during which there was invariably reading aloud. Their food, although always vegetarian, was plentiful, consisting of one full pound of bread, two cooked dishes, both of which they might eat or else choose the one they preferred, and, as well, vegetables and fruit. They even drank wine. As regards this, Benedict, whilst firmly stating that it was absolutely unsuitable for monks, recognized that it was impossible to persuade those of his own day to dispense with it. Those who were in good health seldom washed. Baths were considered as a debilitating luxury and were rarely granted to the young although those who were ill were given them.

Going even further, to all accounts Benedict thought that a certain mental outlook was preferable to blind mechanical obedience. Instead of absolute silence he asked for the spirit of silence (*taciturnitas*), and instead of absolute poverty an economical attitude (*parcitas*). He even made allowances for those who were a little late at Matins. Knowing that heavy sleepers could always find a good pretext for a last stretch (*somnolentorum excusationes*), he laid it down that the first psalms of the matutinal service should be recited sufficiently slowly to make it possible for the laggards to arrive at the very last moment permitted. But having done so Benedict would allow of no dodging this service altogether; strict sanctions were laid down for latecomers who made a habit of it, and he preferred to see them taking their places as penitents but participating in the service, even when it had already begun, rather than to send them away, when they might either return to their beds, go out for a breath of air, or stay indoors gossiping. The same held good for meals; a monk who arrived late for them was punished, and if he did so again was deprived of his mug of wine and made to eat by himself. Several chapters of his Rule deal with punishments, but far from being regulated according to a set of standards as was the case with the Celts, penitences were to be allocated with a view to effecting a cure, as a doctor would prescribe for a patient.

If it were objected that this was a relatively soft monastic life, especially at that period, it would be easy to reply that Benedict had his reasons for wanting it thus and that his success was the proof of the excellence of his method. The old Abbot held the view that the more humanely he treated his brethren the more he could require from them. He knew that the pursuit of perfection consisted less in rigorous observances than in spiritual devotions. And his scale of perfectibility, which comprised twelve degrees of humility, went very far in the direction of self-abnegation. He did not seek to exhaust the human element in us, but to exploit, purify, and ennoble it, preparing it to receive the crowning rewards as well as the demands made on it by grace. Such an ideal was not in any way meant to appeal to the Epicurians of a life of devotion.

The most important task with which the day began, and which controlled all its activities at regular intervals, was the joint recitation of the office. Benedict considered it of such importance that it took precedence over all other activities. He called it *Opus Dei*, God's work, and *servitutis officium*, the prime duty imposed on all those who had placed themselves in the service of God and were his servants. This daily service was no novelty; all the cenobites practised collective prayers. But Benedict, in placing it at the pinnacle of all the duties of a monk, worked out the order and composition of the psalms which formed its main substance down to the last detail. Oddly enough, Mass was not celebrated nor was Communion given out every day. This function was performed by the priests whom the Abbot either admitted —but with great caution—into his monastery, or else by a neighbouring minister. All the authorities agree in admitting that Benedict was merely a pious layman.

The *lectio divina*, or as it is translated for better or worse, the reading of works of piety, by providing spiritual nourishment, aimed solely at providing food for prayer. Without it the recital of the psalms in common might have degenerated into mere gabbling. This activity leads us to conclude that all the monks could read and write. But as all were not equally competent at that particular form of reading it was arranged that during the time set aside for it they might follow some other occupation. The works read consisted, naturally, of the Bible, the books written by the great monks, either translated from the Greek, like those of St Basil, or written in Latin, like those of Cassianus. In Lent each monk was given a book, the whole of which he was expected to read during that period. There must, therefore, have been a fairly large library or number of bookcases at Monte Cassino.

The *lectio divina* was not synonymous with intellectual culture in the modern sense of the term, with its apparatus of research, reading, and knowledge. Such matters never preoccupied Benedict. Like all spiritual beings he considered that the reading of works of piety served to nourish not only the mind, but the whole soul as well, leading it gradually towards the mystical realms of contemplation. His method was a simple one—reading, re-reading, becoming familiar with and gradually assimilating texts which, at first merely part of the monks' mental equipment, finally became a very part of themselves. Thus, as in Benedict's own case in his search for God (*quaerere Deum*), doctrine could be acquired in spite of a lack of knowledge and the illiterate could achieve wisdom (*scienter nescius et sapienter indoctus*).

We should point out that in Benedict's day reading and meditation were analogous terms. In Antiquity and the Middle Ages people did not read with their eyes alone but also with their lips and their ears; in fact they read aloud to themselves. Reading also meant speaking and hearing. It was done more or less half-aloud but the sounds invariably followed the text as the eyes discovered it and the ears took it in. In the same way, when they wrote they, as it were, followed their own dictation. On the other hand, meditation was not a matter of reflection, examination, or mental analysis, but the repetition of what had been read, spoken aloud and retained by ear. Such repetition, which was really a form of memorization, was a form of mental training and preparing the will to action. Thus the Christian writers wove a kind of thread of Scriptural texts which formed the very stuff of their own style. To read and meditate on a book was, literally, to chew on it, digest it, and assimilate it as one might in the case of actual nourishment. The Ancients were not scared by the word but called this activity *ruminatio*. Needless to say, such 'rumination' also had its place in prayer.

In the intervals between these exercises—communal prayers, private prayers, and private reading—Benedict found a place for manual labour. Of course the anchorites, and the Pachomian and Basilian cenobites also practised manual labour, but now it was to be rehabilitated by being given a definite institutional value, for we know the contempt in which servile labour, almost entirely performed by slaves, was held throughout Antiquity and the scant respect paid to it by those Easterners who were purely contemplatives. The Father Abbot detested all forms of parasitism, even when it was devotional, and did not intend that his monastery should become a house in which his monks would be completely idle between services and meals. He spoke up firmly in praise of the dignity of labour; not only was 'idleness the enemy of the soul', but 'he is not a true monk who does not live by the work of his own hands'. Under the direction of 'officers' detailed to supervise them, or if necessary with the aid of workmen attached to the *familia*, the monks worked either within the walls, or in the vicinity of them in such a way as would enable the community to live by its own labour. It is, however, necessary to clarify this matter on one important point, namely, that the prime objective of this kind of labour was wholly spiritual insofar as it required asceticism, obedience, and action. The second aim was to earn a profit, in order to provide the monastic family with its necessities, but always taking care that this did not engender a love of money. If a surplus was produced it was to be disposed of below current prices.

A united family, Benedict's monastery formed a completely self-sufficient organization. The body of the *familia*, autonomous on the institutional level, became an autarchy on the economic level. The monastery included a church, a refectory, a dormitory, a certain number of places which were regularly at the monks' disposal, certain quarters reserved for children and novices, a school, or what then passed for one, a lodging for guests, workshops where everyone worked according to his abilities, a mill, a garden, lands and woods. We do not know the exact extent of Monte Cassino, but from what we know, for instance, about the foundation of Bobbio under Columban, we may reasonably assume that the land was either freely given as a pious foundation or else reclaimed from the state of abandonment which at that time was the lot of many Italian properties. If it was a donation its extent was possibly delimited, as was frequently then done, by the circle which a donkey or a mule could circumscribe in the course of one day. If on the other hand we reckon that around fifty monks were regularly employed on manual labour and that each of these worked at least six hours daily, this would give us a considerable figure in the course of a year. From this we might reasonably conclude that the domain of Monte Cassino, although on a somewhat smaller scale, might have approximated in size to the classical type of the large Roman estates, (*latifundia*). It may partly have included hunting-grounds to be cleared and there were in any case fallow lands to be brought into cultivation. The monks of Monte Cassino had wood for their fires, corn for their bread, acorns if they bred pigs, which they did not eat but which they could sell, bees for their tapers, and vines for their comfort. Even if the various buildings were only humble ones there was a sufficiently large number of them to provide all the elements required to form a centre of agricultural economy. Thus in its general outlines Benedict's monastery corresponded to the definition of the villa given by Marc Bloch: 'A property organized so that a large part of the products of the soil belonged either directly or indirectly to only one master.' The difference lay in the fact that this colonial type was not a secular but a monastic one, that the unskilled labour was for the most part provided by the monks, and that the master in question was at one and the same time the Abbot and his family.

From the text of St Gregory and even more so from the Rule the Patriarch's personality stands out as an example of most lofty humanity and superhuman greatness. A very beautiful vision reported in the *Dialogues* makes it clear that Benedict had reached the heights of mysticism. As a man of experience he possessed to a far greater degree than most the gift of discerning men, i.e. that faculty of intuition, developed by studying souls and purified by asceticism, which instantly saw through to the most hidden of their recesses and could guess quite infallibly a human being's spiritual qualities. The numerous *miracula* reported by Gregory to a large extent are illustrations of this particular gift of his. A man of doctrine, Benedict accepted his monks on an ordinary human level and raised them, in both senses of the term, less by leading them along the dark paths of the fear of hell than along the bright ways of charity. As an optimist, instead of putting too great a strain on human nature he had faith in it, knowing that the better a man became the less opportunity there would be for his capacity for evil to develop. Such optimism would alone entitle him to be regarded as one of the fathers of humanism, were such an appellation sufficiently worthy of him. As an organizer he ruled his community harmoniously for its collective development, whilst at the same time giving each individual in it due attention. He did owe nearly all his ideas to his predecessors and in that sense he did not innovate so much as sift, modify, define what he had taken over and in doing so worked out an entirely new code of living. In order to apply it and if necessary explain it he brought to this task (and demanded from his successors) those qualities of common sense, balanced judgment and 'discretion', i.e. tactfulness and respect for human nature when dealing with others. To these he added the reserve of a well-educated person (*pudor*) and the quiet sincerity of his own asceticism.

His work at Monte Cassino can only be correctly judged in the light of his own day. As we have seen, it was a dark one. The documents have provided us with a picture of it which from any point of view is an appalling one. Many a province was reduced to desolation by the movements of troops at war, all of them Barbarians, even although not in very large numbers. Those who were for the Goths were pursued by Byzantium, whilst those who were with the Byzantines in their turn paid dearly for it. During such times of catastrophe, worse even than what have been called the great invasions, the links that hold a society together get broken. Families were torn apart; cities, even Rome, ruined, looted, abandoned. Weeds invaded the untilled soil. Peasants from Emilia and the Roman Campagna, bereft of everything, came to die in the Picenum where they had hoped to survive. Many also died in Tuscany. In the Appenines the mountaineers made their bread from acorns and fell victims to scurvy. People ate nettle-pies, dogs, rats, excrement. In Rome the too-numerous dead lay around unburied. Even the vultures found nothing to eat, for the corpses, reduced to skeletons, had no more flesh for them to feed upon (according to Procopius).

In the midst of such desolation Benedict's monasteries offered a refuge where those still able to do so learned anew to become men whilst working to become men of God. There is nothing surprising in the fact that Benedict at the beginning of his Rule stated that he only aimed at introducing a certain degree of honesty into ways of behaviour. He did in fact begin at a rather low level but straightaway and without premeditation he built at one and the same time a house of God and a monument to civilization. A stable environment far away from the cities was likely to attract people who had become uncertain of everything. Poor and rich, Romans and Barbarians, received on a footing of absolute equality, intermingled with one another in the observance of one sole rule. They purified their souls in prayer and study and discovered that labour had its own dignity. On the death of their founder there were only three monasteries at the mercy of looters, but already they were centres of attraction and, multiplying by hundreds, were to regenerate the face of the world.

The trunk of Monte Cassino spread out over Christianity its branches through which ran the Benedictine sap: missionaries throughout the Western world, masters of small schools, choristers of the services, men of learning who applied the working rule to research, pioneers and cultivators of large agricultural enterprises, all of them honourably, rightfully, and faithfully, claimed to be the sons of their Patriarch. Benedict was not only the Patriarch of the Western monks but also, as Pius XII said, the father of Western civilization. And here we cannot forbear to quote Newman. The historian will make the necessary allowances for his very lyrical outlook, slightly tinged with romanticism, yet his intuitive genius gave him a splendid insight into the essence of the achievement that spread out from Monte Cassino:

'He (St Benedict) found the world, physical and social, in ruins, and his mission was to restore it in the way, not of science, but of nature, not as if setting about to do it, not professing to do it by any set time or by any rare specific or by any series of strokes, but so quietly, patiently, gradually, that often, till the work was done, it was not known to be doing. It was a restoration, rather than a visitation, correction, or conversion. The new world which he helped to create was a growth rather than a structure. Silent men were observed about the country, or discovered in the forest, digging, clearing, and building; and other silent men, not seen, were sitting in the cold cloister, tiring their eyes, and keeping their attention on the stretch, while they painfully deciphered and copied and re-copied the manuscripts which they had saved. There was no one that "contended, or cried out", or drew attention to what was going on; but by degrees the woody swamp became a hermitage, a religious house, a farm, an abbey, a village, a seminary, a school of learning, and a city. Roads and bridges connected it with other abbeys and cities, which had similarly grown up; and what the haughty Alaric or fierce Attila had broken to pieces, these patient meditative men had brought together and made to live again.'[1]

At the time of Benedict's death he had not even envisaged the plan of such an achievement. All the future patriarch of the Western monks aimed to do was to introduce some order into the monastic state as he saw it around him. The day was soon to come when, in a curious roundabout manner, a pious layman, a contemporary of Benedict's, was to impose on his own foundation a character which in the course of time was to become definitely Benedictine.

MONASTIC STUDIES: CASSIODORUS

Whilst in Gaul barbarism was progressively ruining the language as well as the people, in Italy Latin, although already evolving along lines on which the spoken tongue was diverging from the written word, was still

[1]*Historical Sketches*, Vol. 2 (Mission of St. Benedict), Cardinal Newman.

more in keeping with tradition, although not entirely free from affectation and preciosity. Vestiges of good literature still survived in Rome.
Theodoric, who reigned in Ravenna from 493 to 526, not only adorned
his capital with monuments and mosaics (the Arian Baptistry, St
Apollinare Nuovo) but also condescended to surround himself with
cultured Romans who were both a credit to his court and the enlightened ministers of his government, and in whose company he took
pleasure. Although he never learned to sign his letters in a firm hand,
in conversation and with a little encouragement he was able to pose as
the Platonic philosopher-king. During thirty years or so Ravenna,
paradoxically, was a centre of civilization under a barbarian king.

The least distinguished man of letters at Theodoric's court was
Ennodius, a salaried deacon in the Church of Milan and above all a
clever talker. As it was to his own interest unabashedly to flatter the
Arian overlord of his day Ennodius, a Catholic cleric, congratulated him
on his 'interest in the divine' and did not hesitate to discover in him—so,
at least, he said—'the gentle qualities of a priest'. He went so far as to
take pleasure in the scabrous myths of which Catullus had sung in the
past, including the adventures of Pasiphaia and her bull. He wrote easily
on any subject with hyperbole and bad taste, embellishing his vacuities
with inept symbolism. Fortunately an illness induced him to return to
interests more in tune with his station; and he actually ended his career
as Bishop of Pavia, more worthy of respect as a person and more
temperate even although not less futile as a writer.

Boethius, who has rightly been accounted the last of the Romans and
first of the Schoolmen, was in an entirely different class. He belonged to
the high Roman aristocracy of the *gens Anicia*, Christians since the fourth
century, which provided Rome with a succession of officials and even
with two Emperors, of whom the second, it is true, was called Olybrius.
He was both by nature and predilection a reserved character, and kept
his distance from anything smelling of barbarism, yet in the circumstances he nevertheless collaborated loyally with the new order. It was
his opinion that if the Roman order could continue to exist under the
Goths it would save Italy from barbarism and gradually raise the
invaders to a higher stage of civilization, until it finally absorbed them
by a fusion of the two races. But in this he was, at least for the time
being, mistaken, for although the Barbarians in power might be
influenced by the fascination of Rome, its attraction for them, however
strong, could not strike any deep roots so long as they remained
entrenched behind the barriers of racial and religious segregation.

Boethius was, however, very learned and deeply depressed by the decadence of Roman literature. He was convinced that it could be regenerated if it could only once again recapture the inspiration of its Greek sources, which were almost wholly unknown in the Western world. He himself was a perfect Hellenist and now undertook to bring the knowledge of Greek literature to the intellectuals in the Peninsula by placing in their hands translations of Plato and Aristotle, with whom as was the case at that time he was mainly familiar through their Alexandrian commentators. He went still further in thinking that he would be able to bring these two philosophers into harmony and even reconcile them with Christian dogma. But however laudable his intentions may have been Boethius was mistaken in thinking that to return to Greek in this fashion would enable him to realize them. It would never be possible to reinvigorate a declining culture by translations and commentaries but only, if it could be done at all, by direct knowledge of the language, the original works, the great exemplars and in fact the entire civilization of Ancient Greece.

And his plan in any case came to nothing owing to a complicated plot, as the result of which Theodoric in his later years was overcome by a renewed access of his innate ferocity, and threw Boethius into prison before ordering his execution in 524. When misfortune overcame him this staunch Roman, who even when holding the highest positions had never indulged in vice or the intrigues of the powerful, died like a great Stoic, philosophically, and very probably an innocent man. His greatest claim to fame was his *Philosophical Consolation*, a meditation on the destiny of mankind and his spiritual testament, written in prison; in addition he left four hundred manuscripts and around twenty commentaries. Both for his *Consolation* and the whole of his works Boethius became one of the most widely read authors in the Middle Ages. His father-in-law, Symmachus, who was also an aristocrat, a Hellenist and philosopher, and a magistrate under Theodoric's rule, shared his ideas and collaborated in his literary work. He was also involved in the same plot, died in the same way and with equal Stoicism, and like his son-in-law, as a Christian.

Next to Symmachus and Boethius, Cassiodorus appears to carry less weight. A Syrian by origin, he was born at Squillace in Bruttium (not far from Catanzaro in Calabria as we know it). A new man, although his ancestors had grown old in high office, he also agreed to serve under the Barbarians, and, a very learned man, shared the ideas of Boethius on the future of civilization. According to the classification of their respective activities which agreed with Theodoric's own views, he wrote: 'Let other people bear arms and let the Romans forever be armed only with eloquence.' He nevertheless did not despair of 'introducing the usages (of Rome) into those savage souls'. He was the perfect civil servant, chancellor and irreplaceable minister, a methodical and intensely industrious worker (*solus ad omnia sufficiens*), belonging to that race of cultured subordinates who, for want of genius, become great office-holders by their steadiness and industrious penmanship. He was undeniably a clever courtier, who knew so well how to use the art of panegyrics that when he was charged with discovering the origins and retelling of the exploits of the Goths, he retouched history so cunningly, with such discreet omissions, that Theodoric himself was astonished to discover what a great man he was (*ut miraretur ipse qui fecit*). For the rest, both loyal and constant, he uninterruptedly stayed the course (*cursus honorum*). Successively as quaestor, chief of the civil service, prefect of the Pretorium, i.e. prime minister, and lastly Patrician, he served continuously for forty years under four Barbarian kings, with only a few intervals of retirement. He never asked himself whether or not his masters might be usurpers, or have murdered their own families. Although he was related to Symmachus and Boethius he had none of their pride and felt no vocation for strangulation. When Boethius was arrested in 523 he remained quietly at his post, more devoted to his career than to his friends, and without showing a trace of emotion, in case the slightest funereal speech on his part might be taken as an admission of complicity. He did not retire from office until 538, at the moment when in the course of the Gothic wars, Vitiges, the last of his overlords, was about to raise the siege of Rome. He himself informed us that even at Ravenna he always endeavoured to avoid equally honours and responsibilities which might have a dangerous flavour (*noxio sapore conditis*). Having passed over to Byzantium, he reappeared at Constantinople in 550, and was favourably received there by the Emperor Justinian.

The reconquest of Italy, the hardwon but stubborn advance of the Byzantine armies, put an end to Cassiodorus's political dreams. It had been possible for him to collaborate with Theodoric so long as the latter, broadminded and with no intention of germanizing Italy, had succeeded in prolonging the life of Roman civilization, all the more so when a glance beyond the Alps revealed how under the Franks Gaul was being delivered over to the excesses of barbarism. But the victory of Byzantium, the new Rome, destroyed this aftermath of the civiliza-tion of the old Rome, and when Theodoric's order was abolished the future looked dangerous indeed. After their great defeat in 553 the Goths were finally crushed in 555 and it was natural that at that moment Cassiodorus, who was nearly seventy, should be thinking of retiring. In fact his real career had not yet begun, and his new life did not end until he was on the threshold of his hundredth year, dying in 580. This new career, which he was also to spend at his desk, was to be of more lasting service to civilization than his earlier one.

Because of this new life we are inclined to view Cassiodorus's earlier activities with some embarrassment. It makes us uncomfortable to have to admit that this honest civil servant was not always a brave man as well, and rather vaguely, for want of a better excuse, we shelter behind the usual one advanced in similar cases, I mean the customs of the period. It is perhaps not sacrilegious to admit quite simply that Cassiodorus's piety and love of letters were made of better stuff than his character. Enjoying the highest honours at a court that was for the largest part Arian—and incidentally, tolerant—he not merely preserved that piety intact, but when one might have expected of so prudent an official that he would keep it within the bound of reassuring conformism, he on the contrary deepened and developed it and in a direction to be of benefit to others. In 535 when he felt that his star was rising, in agreement with Pope Agapetus he planned to found in Rome a school and theological library modelled on that of Origen in Alexandria. This could have been of much service to Western Christianity, which was then badly in need of theology. Only the war put an end to this scheme. In Constantinople he finished a monumental commentary on the psalms which he had already begun in Ravenna, and when he heard of the school of Nisibis in Persia, which at that time was far-famed, he returned to the plan he had been developing under Pope Agapetus. He left the city on the Bosphorus a little before 555, with his scheme in mind and in his coffers the means of carrying it out. On his estates in Calabria he would build a monastic foundation devoted to prayer and study.

He installed himself a few miles south of Squillace, 'clinging to the mountainside like a bunch of grapes'. According to the founder, Squillace then offered certain advantages which nowadays make little impression on travellers—easy of access (?), a temperate climate (?), sunny winters and cool summers (?), a clear light, supposedly free from heat-mists and which enabled one 'delightedly to contemplate the green plains and dark blue sea'. The rivers that bordered the property were so full of fish that when he was still at Ravenna the owner had them brought there in 'Neptunian containers' in which 'shoals of fish, playing freely in captivity, filled the eyes with pleasure and the spirit with admiration, greedily running towards the hand of man to seek their food before themselves becoming alimentation'. This jargon, hammered out according to the fashion of the day, simply meant that certain fish-tanks were arranged in such a way among the rock-pools that by means of sluices they could be opened or shut at will. The spot gave its name to the foundation, which was called the *Vivarium*, or Fishpond.

It was there, at the foot of Mount Moscius, that Cassiodorus built his monastery around a chapel dedicated to St Martin. He organized it according to the cenobitic rule, but once they had proved themselves worthy of it, he allowed the cenobites to enjoy the delights of anchoritism (*secreta suavia*) on the slopes of Mount Castellum, not far from the walls. Realizing that intellectual activity requires a certain amount of physical ease and wishing to 'spare the monks the temptation of seeking elsewhere what they might reasonably wish for', he decided that the Vivarium should be comfortable. In addition to the constant supply of fresh fish there were sundials, a water-clock (*aquatile*), oil-lamps of the latest model, kept constantly burning by mechanical means (*mechanicae lucernae conservatrices illuminantium flammarum*), a kitchen-garden irrigated by the river Pellena, and baths for those who were sick. Outside the walls the fields, tilled mostly by peasants, provided sustenance for the community. The founder, however, was not the superior; Cassiodorus decided to live there simply as a *conversus*, i.e. at home, without becoming a monk, merely as a pious layman who had renounced all mundane activities. Needless to say that as the founder and land-owner, an intellectual and former great man of affairs, he did have a very distinct influence on affairs within the cloisters and we may also suppose that his piety led him to take an honoured part in the devotions of his monks. Nevertheless, the community as such was ruled by an abbot who perhaps was not too prominent to eclipse such an important lay monk. At the end of the short history of the Vivarium there were even two superiors, the Abbot Calchedonius and his coadjutor, Gerontius.

It is certain that Cassiodorus did not impose on his monastery the rule of St Benedict, of whose reputation he must however have heard, since Benedict died in 547, i.e. eight years before the Vivarium was founded. Unless he was the author of *The Master's Rule*, which expert opinion is very far from attributing to him, we do not exactly know what body of ascetic doctrines he gave his monks. But like the Patriarch of Monte Cassino he intended his foundation to be first and foremost a house of prayer, a city, as he said, that belonged to its inhabitants, and in which, if they lived there in concord, 'they would so to speak enjoy in advance the image of their heavenly home'. The liturgy was an institution in the life of the Vivarium. As in Benedict's case, the *lectio divina* was designed to pave the way for, sustain, and prolong the services of praise. From this point of view the master's commentary on the psalms, which fills more than a thousand columns of our Latin Patrology, gave them plenty of food for meditation on the substance of conventual prayer. But in addition, those who were capable of more than well-digested reading—and Cassiodorus wished them to be many—were directed beyond the *lectio divina*, to actual intellectual activities which Benedict had overlooked, or waved aside. Whereas at Monte Cassino the *lectio divina* was primarily a diffuse form of contemplation, with Cassiodorus it became a subject of study in the precise meaning of the term. 'The monks will meditate on the sacred texts with application enhanced by curiosity' (*curiosa intentione*). Such curiosity, which, without any doubt refers to an inclination for studying as well as the fact of doing so, was to be temperate according to Cassiodorus himself, when he remarked that it would be tempting God to endeavour boldly to seek what is beyond our understanding, but it was altogether alien to Benedict's thought. Benedict would only have regarded it as a superfluous encumbrance to prayer, leading in the direction of spiritual pride, i.e. a disturbance to the service of God and a threat to the Golden Rule of humility. If he had had to express himself on the subject he would more likely have written *pia intentione* and not *curiosa intentione*. These shades of meaning both have their programmatic values. Cassiodorus permitted the satisfying of intellectual interests of the most varied kinds, whilst, by the way, grading them according to an hierarchy. Both by its quality and by its subject sacred literature held absolute pre-eminence, but in order to be thoroughly understood it had to be subjected to the methods and read in the light of the general information to be gathered from the study of profane literature. The Vivarian monks, therefore, had a dual aim— both to save their souls and at the same time to keep pace with the knowledge of their century (*salus animae et eruditio saeculi*). Whilst Benedict desired his monastery to be only a 'school of the Lord' strictly in accordance with spiritual tradition, Cassiodorus did not, as has been claimed, wish to found a learned society but in building a house of God he also aimed at founding a house of learning.

The master of the Vivarium drew up for the usage of his monks (most of whom were not intellectuals) a manual which was intended at one and the same time to be a working programme, a guide to reading, and a bibliography, the *Institutiones divinarum et saecularium litterarum*, a title which in view of its contents might be translated as *A directory to the reading and study of sacred and profane literature*. This booklet comprised two parts of unequal length. The first, dealing with sacred literature, aimed at preparing the reader for an intelligent perusal of the Bible by clarifying its meaning through the commentaries of the Fathers and other ecclesiastical authors, in addition to history, geography and the natural sciences. Cassiodorus foresaw the publication of a Biblical text which he wished to be as good as possible, both literally, in its immediate context, as well as its general context.

But—and this was the original thing about it, especially in a monastic environment—profane literature and the methods of teaching it were to be called into collaboration for the acquisition of wisdom. Cassiodorus thought that a learned and intelligent understanding of the Bible should not despise the assistance of a technique which during centuries had proved its usefulness to all intelligent people. This was why the second part of his *Institutions* explained the theory of the liberal arts, a pedagogical method which was universally accepted, which had been taught in Rome since the time of Varro (d. 27 B.C.), was re-edited by the pagan grammarian Martianus Capella and adopted by his contemporary, St Augustine. Thus, in order to understand the Bible, the monks of the Vivarium would have at their disposal the technical resources available to the pagan for the understanding of Homer or Virgil. The *Trivium* would teach them grammar, 'the use of a beautiful style according to the poets and good writers'; rhetoric, which deals more with practical matters, would train them in dialectics, which control a discourse, exposing and upholding its arguments. The *quadrivium*, or mathematics, would teach them the principles of arithmetic, music, geometry, and astronomy. In the *Institutions* a small treatise, with definitions, explanations, and references, is devoted to each of these disciplines. It seems a great deal of preparation for the reading of Holy Writ, and one might well wonder whether having remained for so long on the porch the monk would ever enter the building itself, but it should not be overlooked that this was meant as a form of preliminary schooling spread over several years as a prelude to specialization later. Thus equipped with such preliminary instruction the monk would become a Biblical authority as he might have become a lawyer had he remained in the world.

We must also bear in mind that this programme was presumably only meant for a small élite. It is probable that apart from the specialists and their students the general community of the Vivarium, of whom no more was required than to provide accurate copyists, may not have been initiated into the secrets of the *trivium* and the *quadrivium*.

Needless to say that those Vivarians who were capable of doing so were not plunged headlong into profane literature as was later the case of the humanists of the Renaissance. Their master had no prejudices against those works and that was already a great deal (*non debent respui*). And it is also remarkable that he was more in favour of using the methods than of the actual perusal of the works in question; whilst prescribing the study of Donatus and the grammarians he insisted much less on direct reading, which in any case was merely assumed, of Virgil, the most widely read profane author at that time. And in giving their due to the great classical Christian authors of the fourth century, notably Ambrosius, Jerome, Augustine, and John Chrysostom, he considered that if they did become learned men this was partly due to the early training they had sought to acquire from the rhetoricians of profane teaching.

Cassiodorus helped to modify the attitude of Christians in this respect. We know that the best of them only read profane books with a guilty conscience and that they sometimes fell into temptation as a result of doing so, even when they did not, as St Jerome did in the desert of Chalcis, loudly proclaim the fact. But Cassiodorus simply put in the forefront of preliminary instruction those profane authors whom others, filled with fanaticism, denounced as 'authors of stupidity and perdition'. Although he did not positively recommend it neither did he forbid an acquaintance the attraction of which was not, after all, without danger, and of which his passion for study had possibly not allowed him to envisage the full consequences. And in spite of what may have been said on the subject, the danger was not an imaginary one. In allowing himself to become fascinated by the charms of the means, a Christian, and more especially a monk, ran the risk of forgetting the end to which it was supposed to be leading him, apart from the fact that having been seduced by the beauty of pure literary style, he might run the risk of being no longer able to endure the rough simplicity of Scripture. When reading a particularly fine page it is difficult to remember only the form whilst forgetting the content, and to apply a strictly scholastic dichotomy as to such form and content in the case of a master whose thought and style were inextricably and indissolubly united. However good a monk he might be, and however unresponsive to beauty, the reader could hardly fail to be enchanted by the discovery of a masterpiece. To attempt only to remember the recipe and the method, as if they alone would suffice to produce a work of beauty, would mean no understanding of it at all. We can readily understand, therefore, that even after the disappearance of paganism in a religious sense, and taking into account the fact that remnants of it still lingered on in the minds and morals of the people, from that period onwards, especially in the monasteries, an acquaintance with profane literature justified their possession of a 'hell' to which curious readers were only admitted with due precaution. Certain particularly lofty minds, well above the average, having duly assimilated and outgrown everything available in profane literature, might attain a height at which their serenity would be undisturbed by contamination, but such cases only result from long experience, when having accepted all the implications of the situation, sifted and weighed them up, a man of learning has acquired an unshakeable sense of values. It is not at all certain that Cassiodorus himself had done so.

His monks were Latins. Whilst his own views on the necessity of turning back to the study of Greek were not as definite as those of Boethius, he nevertheless considered that a certain degree of knowledge of it was indispensable to those whom he was training to understand the Bible. At that period little was known in the West of Greek literature, which had been ruined by the invasions. In the fifth century Pope Celestine did not understand the correspondence he received from Nestorius, which was not very helpful in dealing with a heresy. When St Leo was obliged to examine the Acts of the Council of Chalcedony he was handicapped by a lack of translators. At the court of Theodoric aristocrats like Symmachus and Boethius were almost the only persons who understood Greek perfectly. In Rome the leading Hellenist was a monk, Denys, who was the official translator between 497 and 540. Like Jerome and Rufinus, Symmachus and Boethius, he took on the task of familiarizing the Western world with the best documents of the Eastern. His ability astonished Cassiodorus: 'He translated any book he had in hand without hesitation, and in the same way transposed Latin works so well into Attic that from his quick and unimpeded speech one would have thought him to be reading an untranslated text.' This translator was also intelligent; he was not merely satisfied with finding the right words but took care to correlate them with their context. Cassiodorus was not so learned; Greek to him was an instrument rather than an element of culture. At the Vivarium he did not attempt to promote a methodical study of it but only used it when the Latin authors failed him: 'Everyone finds it pleasanter to acquire what is said in his native language.' In Italy the Latin authors were their own recommendation (*commodissime*). With regard to the voluminous commentary by St John Chrysostom on St Paul, he recommended that it should not be translated from the Greek unless it were impossible to acquire Latin texts of the same importance. It is remarkable that he did

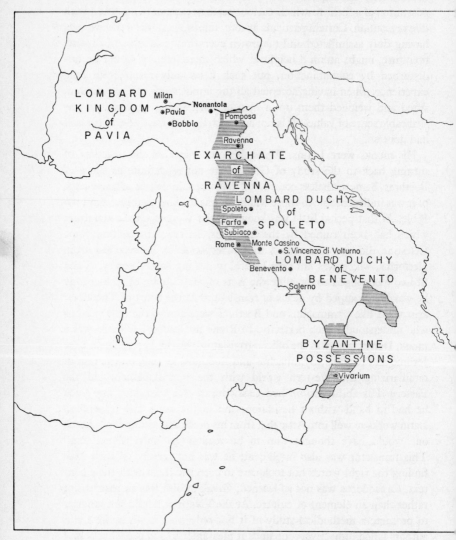

4. Monastic Italy in the sixth to eighth centuries

not translate such works himself, but employed three experts for the purpose, who no doubt had returned with him from Constantinople: Mutatius, Bellatorus, and Epiphanus. But at that period it was already a great deal to regard Greek as a necessary instrument.

At Monte Cassino, as we have noted, the rule prescribed a period of manual labour for the monks, either in the monastery or in the fields. In Cassiodorus's case manual labour consisted chiefly in copying manuscripts. This occupation, which both for St Benedict and St Martin was merely incidental, was for him a regular and methodical one, employing specialists who were not all monks but *notarii*, professional copyists, employed either privately or in licensed offices, and also bookbinders and translators. From this point of view Cassiodorus's workroom (*scriptorium*), one of the very first of note in the Western world, was a model of its kind. The master, who had equipped it perfectly, was demanding. The work had to be carried out in such a way that not only did the texts have to be correctly and clearly transcribed, but also critically, with corrections where they were faulty, and re-edited in full. This was particularly so in the case of the Bible, for one could not be too careful regarding the Word of God. And Cassiodorus himself revised it. In order to educate his monks and, as well, to provide them with standards of exactitude and uniformity, at the end of his life he wrote a treatise on orthography. He liked a manuscript to look well, for in his eyes it was a kind of sermon 'not given by voice but by hand', since 'every word transcribed was a wound inflicted on Satan'. The sheets were bound in a manner worthy of their contents by competent binders, according to models chosen for their elegance (*ut litterarum sacrarum pulchritudinem facies semper decora vestiret*). For the Vivarians the *scriptorium* was a second sanctuary. The master recognized that all the brethren were not worthy of being employed there, and those who were not so he sent to cultivate the kitchen-garden, taking care to recommend them to read, in order that they should do so according to the right methods, Virgil's *Georgics* and the horticultural experts of Antiquity: Gargilius, Columellus, Emilian. In this he revealed the simplemindedness of a learned man who could not enjoy an onion unless it were grown according to the most erudite precepts of Antiquity. One may be allowed to assume that the gardener-brethren had enough sense to take his advice in their stride.

The greatest treasure of a well-organized *scriptorium* was the library. Cassiodorus, who was always a bookman, had one in Ravenna. In Rome, apart from the one he had begun to found for the school of theology of Agapetus, he had another of his own, which, however, did not survive the looting of the Gothic war. At the Vivarium he had his private one, containing, notably, a collection of medical works. The monks also had theirs, not as large as we might imagine according to our own present needs for research. D. Cappuyns suggested that according to the *Institutions* it was classified as follows: (1) Holy Writ; (2) Scriptural introductions and interpretations; (3) Historians; (4) Christian authors (Hilary, Augustine, etc.); (5) Practical works for manual workers; (6) Liberal arts; (7) Dialectics; (8) Greek literature. These eight sections were contained in eight bookcases (*armaria*) and not on open shelves, as has been stated, in which the *codices* were kept. These cases, which were not very large, might contain around twenty bound volumes, but not more. On the other hand it is certain that the librarians (*armarii*) were constantly asking for loans of manuscripts to supplement the gaps in their collections, as was usually done.

In one of the rarest manuscripts of the Latin Bible, the *Amiatinus*, dating from the end of the seventh century and now in the Laurentian Library in Florence, there is an illuminated miniature of a *scriptorium* at the time of Cassiodorus. Esdras, a famous scribe of the Old Testament, so runs the superscription, is 'repairing' a work 'after the burning of the *codices* in the disaster of war'. Esdras, to whom the miniaturist appears to have given Cassiodorus's features, is seated, with his feet on a stool, and is writing in a codex with a long pen. There is a desk in front of him and around him lie the copyist's tools, an inkwell, a knife, an awl for ruling his lines; on his left and forming the background of the illumination, is an open bookcase. This piece of furniture, the proportions of which resemble those of our own bookcases with two doors, contains four shelves, as well as the flat base which provides another. It contains nine *codices* laid down flat, in bindings decorated with geometrical patterns in punchwork. The books are heavy ones and we know that each of them sometimes contained more than one work. An identically similar bookcase is depicted on a mosaic in the mausoleum of Galla Placida at Ravenna (around 450); it is only slightly smaller and contains nothing but the four Gospels, lying flat on two shelves.

The library did not survive its founder any more than the Vivarium itself. It is possible that the monks were obliged to leave owing to the return of Byzantine influences in southern Italy. At one time it was thought that all Cassiodorus's books had been taken to Bobbio, but M. Courcelle has proved that most of them went to the Lateran Library, a collecting-centre for transcriptions and the sale of manuscripts, where the Western world came to acquire them, notably in the seventh and eighth centuries. It was at the Lateran that the Anglo-Saxon monk

Benedict Biscop, on a pilgrimage to Rome between 671 and 684, acquired the Latin text of the Vulgate established by Cassiodorus. It was later transcribed at Jarrow in Northumberland on the orders of Abbot Ceolfrid, who also procured for us the famous *Amiatinus*, which was first offered to the Pope, later taken to the Cistercian monastery of Monte Amiata south of Siena, and again later to the Medician in Florence. In similar fashion other manuscripts went to Bobbio, to Cologne, Bamberg, and Verona, from the end of the seventh until the end of the ninth centuries.

The Father of Librarians, in spite of this honorific title, Cassiodorus was only of second-rate intelligence. An excellent bureaucratic director under Theodoric, he ruled equally well over the intellectual activities of his monks at the Vivarium. He was a sensible pedagogue, a methodical worker, a precise grammarian, a well-informed bibliographer, who demanded a high standard of work, which he endeavoured both to inspire, lead, and control; but in his monastery he does not seem to have been a very different person from the civil servant of Ravenna. He was neither a thinker nor a theologian and instead of genius he had perseverance. He was merely an episode in monastic history. He was not the first to have manuscripts transcribed, but by organizing this profession according to scientific criteria and on a suitable basis he proved how perfectly this kind of work accorded with the conditions of monastic life. Its steadiness, the patience needed for it in the course of a life untouched by outward events, and regulated daily in exactly the same manner, made it an occupation which could easily be resumed in the intervals between the hours devoted to prayer, and as a secondary form of intellectual activity it left the mind free from all active speculation, putting it wholly at the disposal of the *opus Dei*. For all this the monastic routine made an ideal setting, in which spiritual and intellectual activities might be combined in perfect harmony.

It was a more daring matter to import into the cloisters of the Vivarium the educational methods of the century, but nevertheless perfectly logical to do so, since it was after all a sign of respect for the Bible to approach it only after due preparation. The master's deliberate broadmindedness regarding profane literature permitted it to be discreetly tolerated in the monastic *scriptorium*. It is interesting to note that his medical books, which were taken over by Monte Cassino, played their part in the medical science of the day until the emergence of the school of Salerno. His *Variae*, a collection of twelve volumes of official documents written at Ravenna, and addressed in the name of the Emperor Theodoric to all kinds of personages, were used as models by the chancelleries of the Middle Ages. And Cassiodorus contributed even more to the preservation of the Christian texts than he did for the profane. We have noted that the *Amiatinus* was directly based on an original work at the Vivarium, and this is of importance in view of the fact that the text in question forms the basis of our Latin Vulgate. And especially through his *Institutions* Cassiodorus became 'the literary and religious guide to learning in the Middle Ages'.[1] In matters of learning St Benedict allowed no more than what was required for the *opus Dei* and the *lectio divina*. His sons, who repeated the experience of the Vivarium without infringing the spirit of their Rule, both as copyists and men of learning acquired for themselves a strong claim to be regarded as the creators of Western civilization.

ST GREGORY, 'CONSUL OF GOD', MONK AND POPE

In the first weeks of the year 590 the warm-hearted people of Rome unanimously acclaimed the monk Gregory as successor to Pope Pelagius II, who had recently died in an epidemic of plague. After he had honestly and steadfastly refused it the newly elected Pope was obliged to succeed to the throne of St Peter. Gregory was the most popular man in Rome. There is no evidence that he belonged to the famous *gens Anicia*, but he did come of a Patrician family. Whilst he had previously been Prefect of the City he had governed, defended, and fed it. He had then withdrawn to the *Clivus Scauri* (today the church of St Gregory in Monte Celio), his paternal mansion, where he founded a monastery in the name of St Andrew and under the Rule of St Benedict. He might have been the abbot, but preferred to remain there as a simple monk. His wealth also enabled him to build six other monasteries on his lands in Sicily, which was better sheltered from the raids of the Barbarians than the Peninsula itself. But then he was obliged to emerge from his retreat, when Pope Pelagius II ordained him as deacon and sent him as ambassador to Constantinople. Deacon Gregory was the first monk to be raised to the Papal throne; he died in 604.

We do not know what his physical appearance was like, but he himself has informed us that his health was precarious. He found the Italian summers trying and he suffered from his liver. He was not strong enough to be able to fast without fainting, which, at a time when the faithful were in the habit of subjecting their bodies as well as their minds to the imitation of Christ, he found deeply humiliating. He was seldom free of a low fever. Four years before his death he was so crippled by

[1] J. de Ghellinck.

gout that he could hardly stand to perform his office. In view of his physical ill-health he thought that he was ready for the tomb, but this invalid, who would have preferred to remain in his cloisters and in all circumstances lived like a monk, at the time of his elevation to the Pontificate still had fourteen years ahead of him. And those few years sufficed him to work as no man of action has ever done.

As a child he had lived through the final stages of the Gothic war; as a young man he had known those brief twelve years or so of respite during which, according to the *Liber Pontificalis*, 'Italy was happy', by which the author apparently meant that not to be bowed down under tribulations was a state of happiness.

But in fact this was only to be an interval between two catastrophes. In 568, when Gregory was not yet thirty, a new wave of Barbarian tribes, arriving by way of Aquileia, invaded the Peninsula, over which they were to dominate for a little more than 200 years.

They also were Germans. They came from the mouth of the Elbe, and at first few in numbers, in the sixth century were settled in Pannonia. They were joined by contingents from Saxony, and at that moment they were fleeing from the Avars. According to their national *saga*, retold by the historian Paul Diacre, they were known as Long Beards. These Lombards were physically repulsive. Their heads were shaven from their foreheads down to the base of their necks, and the remaining hair, on either side of this broad parting, fell down on either side of their faces, framing them with a hirsute fringe. The tribes (*farae*) were led by dukes (*duces, ducere*). The chiefs were indisciplined and in times of peace, autonomous. In wartime they obeyed a king, providing that they were not powerful enough to stand up to him. Before they settled in Italy the *farae* were semi-nomads, mostly cattle-breeders, of horses for warfare and pigs for food. Only a certain number of them were converted to Arian Christianity; the remainder were heathens. They were much feared, 'a race more savage than the usual savagery of the Germans' (Velleius Paterculus) and 'whose friendship is a punishment from God' (St Gregory). They were cruel by nature and murdered just to keep their hands in, were looters and incendiaries, 'killing men who had grown up on this earth, close-packed as ears of corn'. The consequences of this new tribulation were as might have been expected—'cities destroyed, fortifications torn down, countrysides depopulated, the land laid bare as the desert. Not a day passed but the little that was left of the human race was stricken down.' Rome herself, although remaining unsoiled by the presence of mercenaries, was bled white: 'She, who had seemed like the mistress of the world, this is what she has become—broken again and again by the enormity of her trials, the desolation of her inhabitants, hard-pressed by her enemies; ruins upon ruins.' When writing those lines St Gregory may have given way a little to rhetoric, but disaster can also be eloquent.

In general Pavia was the capital of the invaders, but each powerful tribe had its own headquarters in one city or another. As they needed oil they occupied Friuli, and moving southwards they gathered around Spoleto and Benevento, where, after having to a large extent dispossessed the inhabitants, they created two important dukedoms. Rome was now within their reach.

On arriving in Italy they found it still occupied by the Byzantine administrators, together with some remnants of those Roman cadres which had survived the Gothic war. As they gradually extended their conquests, kings and dukes threw out the Byzantine officials from their posts and instead installed there intendants or governors of their own (*gasindi*, later *gestaldi*). Only at a very late stage did they amalgamate with the more numerous local provincials. Their ambition was to recapture the entire Peninsula from Constantinople, but this they never completely succeeded in doing. They were finally converted to Catholicism between 652 and 661 and restored Monte Cassino, which they had destroyed towards 577, but although they founded, among others, the famous monasteries of Bobbio and Farfa they nevertheless continued to remain a constant threat to Rome, which legally if not in fact still depended on Constantinople, together with the Italian Byzantine provinces to the north-east, the Exarchate of Ravenna and Pentopolis. Surrounded by the pincers of the occupying forces both north and southwards, Rome was both an obstacle to the unification of the Lombard kingdom and a tempting prey to the conquerors. The stubbornness of the Barbarians was only matched by the clever tactics of the Popes until Charlemagne, victorious, assumed the Lombard crown in 774.

At the moment when Gregory took in hand the Church's destinies Italy was passing through her greatest trials, the settling-in of the victors. Byzantium, to whom she had appealed for aid, was helpless to prevent it. In order to restrict the damage the Pope had no alternative but to treat with the hated race. Sacks of gold also did their work, and a little later, the friendship of Queen Theodelinda, a Bavarian Catholic and wife of King Agilulf. Owing to this policy, for which the Exarchus of Ravenna denounced him to the Emperor, it was possible for Gregory to preserve Italy from a further series of disasters and to pave the way for the conversion of the Lombards to orthodox Catholicism. In Rome itself the Pontiff had to provide the population, which although sparse was miserable, restless, and enfeebled by idleness and suffering, with the weekly ration of bread, wine, oil, or soup. The Church was rich enough in fertile land to provide it, but in those troublous times the transport of these victuals provided an additional problem.

Byzantium presented a further anxiety. It was a long way off; the material aid sent from there was invariably inadequate and made little impression on the situation. The corrupt Byzantine officials in Italy had a greater interest in embezzling the funds at their disposal than in their efficient administration. Byzantium nevertheless insisted on maintaining its political jurisdiction over Rome. And in addition its patriarchs, who were both powerful and secure, had an annoying tendency to regard the Roman Pontiff as the bishop of a diocese which formerly had been a glorious one but which had lost its prestige. In these circumstances Gregory had to weigh up the dual risks of refusing to protect the Lombards and thereby coming to some arrangement with them, and of no longer accepting from Byzantium an inadequate form of political tutelage which in certain respects was also humiliating. And he chose boldly to provide his city of Rome with a degree of independence which in due course re-established the prerogatives of the Apostolic See.

He did not lack the means of doing so. In Italy, Gaul, Dalmatia, Sardinia, Corsica, Sicily and Africa the patrimony of St Peter was a rich one. Even although at such a distance from Rome these possessions were too dispersed to be recognized as those of a State, founded on public ownership instead of remaining in private hands, they still enabled the Church of Rome to appear before the world as an independent Power on the temporal plane, thus assuring the free exercise of its spiritual powers. Gregory's genius, although still with a certain lack of clarity and hesitatingly, nevertheless sketched the outlines of what a little later, on the ruins of the old Imperial Rome, was to become the pontifical State of the new Rome of the Popes. He could not foresee the implications inherent in this coexistence of the spiritual and the temporal and in any case at that moment he had no other choice.

Yet these political activities did not distract him from the leadership of the Church. Apart from the schism of Aquileia, as the result of the matter of the Three Chapters, which was not disposed of until the end of the seventh century, important questions of dogma were at that time settled by the Councils. In that respect the Church was at peace, and in any case the Western Church still knew too little to indulge in speculations which might have led to consistent heresy. Yet the Western Church did require firm government. All the bishops were not by a long way obedient, and a good many of them were liable to corruption. Gregory courageously denounced those candidates for the episcopate who 'aspiring to power enjoyed in advance in secret the thought of subjecting others (and) sought worldly advantages in an honour which itself should condemn them'. He reminded such clerics that the bishop's throne should be the seat of 'humility' and not that of 'proud domination'; even less a means of 'selling grace'. They would do better to endeavour to 'dominate their own vices instead of their brethren'. And thenceforward episcopal elections were put under control. Prelates who invested the revenues of their sees in businesses were sharply admonished, like a certain Paschasius, Bishop of Naples, who was involved in ship-freighting. They were ordered to devote one-third or at least a quarter of their revenues to the poor. This was the obligatory meaning of alms-giving: 'When we give to the poor what they need for subsistence, we are not giving away our own goods but returning their own to them. It is altogether just that those who have received what has been given to us by our common Master should share it with others.' In order to cleanse the morals of the clergy he decided that no presents should be given at ordinations and that the charges for private tombs in the churches should be abolished. The bishops were to be in charge of the monasteries and with certain exceptions the monks were not to become priests and therefore would not preach.

Although Gregory did not rule with an iron hand he had not forgotten his own precept that 'the art of all arts is the governing of souls'. To Cononius, Abbot of Lérins, to whom his predecessor had left some difficult problems, including a handful of undisciplined monks, he wrote: 'Tackle them boldly, but taking care not to inflict hurt where healing is required. In using greater severity than is necessary you run the risk of harming him to whom you wish to be of service. Be gentle and vigilant, but not too good-natured, and punish when necessary, but without harshness. One must complement the other.'

These activities of his are substantiated by his correspondence, consisting of 848 letters. The name Gregory, incidentally, means alert, and no detail escaped him. Glancing through the reports of the administrator of the patrimony of Campania, he noticed that the Church properties in that district possessed too many sterile cows, too many useless oxen, too many fillies, and that it would be sufficient to retain 400 broodmares. From Sicily he received a consignment of mounts but on looking them over was dissatisfied with them and wrote to the responsible official, telling him so: 'You have sent us a bad horse and five good donkeys. I cannot ride the horse because he is no good, nor the donkeys, because they are donkeys. If you wish to contribute to my upkeep, send us something decent (*aliquid noblis condignum*).'[1] Whilst keeping such a close watch on things Gregory did not forget that he was the Pope.

But he thought above all that as Bishop of Rome his first duty was the education of his people. And to this we owe a series of homilies which raised him, as a doctor of the Church, into the same rank as St Jerome, St Ambrosius, and St Augustine. Whether oral or in writing, his preaching was simple, homely, but weighty. Allusions to the disasters of the day were not lacking in it. It contained a great deal of moral teaching and in many cases, when writing for those who could follow him, the line he took was far above the common level. We have already noted, in connection with St Benedict, the importance and tone of his *Dialogues*. He sometimes went even further in his commentaries; when he felt that he could really speak his mind his experience of living theology reached mystical heights: 'We hear the voice of the Lord when the higher part of our mind (*mens*) is touched by the breath of grace, when the insensitivity of our inner deafness is broken, when our hearts, awakened to the longing (*studium*, which also means passion), for supreme love, are filled with the clamouring of this innate power' (*virtute*). Even when Pope, Gregory remained a contemplative monk.

Needless to say that he did not express himself with the exactitude of classical Latin, but it is enough to compare his style to that of Gregory of Tours to know that in quality they were worlds apart. Although he was less picturesque, Gregory of Rome was never at fault in the usages of grammar. Generally his meaning is clear and except when he indulges in too many allegories, nearly always vividly expressed. Culturally he owed no more to profane literature than any other well-educated Roman of his day. But having to this extent benefited by it he had neither the time nor the interest to explore it further: to write well according to the precepts of the School held no importance for him. With sound professionalism and abundant talent he was satisfied to be able to say what he wanted. Although he spent six years in Constantinople he never took advantage of the opportunity this gave him to learn Greek. This diplomat, in fact, did not know the language of the country to which he had been sent on a mission, and without doubt this was a drawback.

This indifference to good literature has contributed to the view that Gregory was inimical to culture, and two documents might lead one to think that this was the case. When addressing his *Moralium on Job* to his friend Leander of Seville, he remarked to him that he cared nothing for either morphology or syntax: 'I opine that it is unworthy to submit the words of the divine oracle to the rules of Donatus,' and on another

[1] According to P. Battifol.

occasion, having learned from a report that Didier, Bishop of Vienne, was teaching grammar, the Pope sharply reproached him for so doing. He held that it was not permissible for the same voice to praise both God and Jupiter, nor for a bishop to allow himself to indulge in an activity that would even be unsuitable to a pious layman. It is not impossible that Didier's accuser blackened him to excess, and that in the course of its travels from Gaulish Vienne to papal Rome his sin, venal on departure, had become mortal on arrival. Gregory, who took justice to heart, ordered a second inquiry, but this very fact taken in conjunction with his letter proves the importance he attached to the matter.

In order to understand this attitude on Gregory's part it is necessary to remember that the teaching of grammar included that of mythology, and that in the Church at that time there were no Fénelons to dress up the pagan divinities in chaste costumes. And here was a bishop, occupying one of the most prominent sees in Gaul, placing young men in danger of immorality owing to his own exaggerated liking for profane literature, when very different works should have been claiming his whole attention. In the Pope's view such preoccupation appeared as 'execrable'. Yet in recalling a bishop to his duties Gregory did not for this reason despise belle-lettres. As was observed by Father P. de Lubac, he admired the prophet Isaiah as a cultured and well-educated man (*nobiliter instructus et urbanus*) and held that St Paul's superiority over the other apostles was due to a sound early education. For all the more reason, whatever he may have said about him, Gregory was not the enemy of Donatus. Like everyone else he had benefited by him, but he was no longer interested in him save as an instrument which on occasion might be misused. In his view the only worthwhile studies, even as regarded pedagogy, were of the words of God: 'Holy Writ surpasses all the sciences and all the disciplines (*doctrinae*), even as regards means of expression.'

Two manuscripts, amongst several others, represent St Gregory the Great; one in the Bibliothèque Nationale of Paris (second half of the ninth century) and that of St Gall (end of the tenth century). In the latter Gregory is shown in the course of receiving inspiration. The Pope is heavily tonsured, like a monk; his face is rounded off by a short beard, and he wears the insignia of his office, the planet and the pallium. He is seated in a room of his palace, of which the architecture, the roofs covered with broad tiles, the curtains looped back, recalls the mosaic of the *palatium* of Theodoric at St Apollinaris the New in Ravenna. Next to him a beardless monk is writing at an enormous desk. A white dove is sitting on the Pope's right shoulder, stretching out its neck and cooing into his ear—this obliging bird has brought him messages from Heaven which he need only transmit to his secretary, the deacon Peter. This was alleged to have been the case with regard to his homilies on the prophet Ezekiel, and, in a wider sense, of Gregorian plainsong.

This legend, dating from the beginning of the eighth century, was confirmed, in particular, by Deacon John[1] in a biography of Gregory dating from the last quarter of the ninth century, i.e. more than 250 years after the death of the Pontiff. According to this author Gregory was usually (*consuetudionaliter*) represented with his dove, and in another passage he states that Deacon Peter declared that he had many times (*frequentissime*) seen the dove inspiring Pope Gregory. He also wrote that Gregory compiled melodies for his choristers and organized a *schola cantorum* in which bad pupils were given the cane. This tardy evidence of Deacon John's is embarrassing, for its profusion of detail gives the impression that in the manner of the period its author had done some serious research work. But on the other hand we have reason to be suspicious of his book, on account of the unlikelihood of many of its passages, and the late date of its appearance. And we have all the more reason to withhold our assent to it in view of the fact that there is no known copy in existence of the original *antiphonale missarum* by Gregory of which Deacon John makes much. The most ancient manuscripts, whilst they do represent an anterior tradition, only date from the ninth century as regards those possessing a musical notation, whilst those that do not have this date from the eighth. It is not, in fact, until the end of the eighth century that the Prologue in hexameters to the so-called Gregorian antiphonary, which was attributed to Pope Hadrian I (d. 795), gave Gregory as the author of a treatise on music (*libellum musicae artis*) that was used in a *schola cantorum* or precentorship. The same document, re-edited later by Hadrian II (d. 872), is similar in content.

It is therefore by no means certain that Gregory, who died in 604, in fact, 'in his triple activity as pope, executant, and professor, gave a strong impetus to ecclesiastical plainsong' as is claimed by D. Leclercq. The only indubitable fact regarding Gregory and this matter of plainsong is his vehement protest against an abuse which in his time was cropping up among the Roman choristers; the deacons who filled these posts were wasting time in training their voices and practising that in

---

[1] The three following deacons were concerned with Gregory: Peter, the Pope's pupil (d. 605); Paul (Warnefrid) monk of Monte Cassino (d. 797), author of a biography of Gregory consisting of only a few pages inspired by Bede's text; John, monk of Monte Cassino, who wrote after 872, under Pope John VIII, and whose biography of Gregory fills 180 columns of the Latin Patrology.

view of their duties they would have done better to devote to preaching and almsgiving. It even happened that certain choirmasters were more interested in discovering fine voices and training them than in controlling the morals of their choristers. And in such cases the Pope dipped his pen in the same ink which he used when admonishing Didier of Vienne: 'Whilst his singing pleases the people the chorister's morals are an offence towards God.' This text is the only definite evidence of Gregory's intervention in matters pertaining to singing.

Prudence therefore suggests that we should go no further. According to D. Froger the so-called Gregorian repertoire should not be attributed to St Gregory the Great. It was not laid down and did not attain to its highest degree of perfection until the eighth century, under another Pope Gregory, the third of that name, who died in 741, roughly 137 years after the death of the first one. Needless to say this peak was the result of a long period of development, the beginnings of which may reasonably be supposed to date from the beginning of the fifth century. During this period of three centuries the 'musical mould', as D. Froger calls it, was composed of very varied elements. Nor was the *schola* created by Gregory; it was natural that it should have come into being as soon as singing became an important part of the liturgy, i.e. at a fairly early date. By contributing more than anyone else to the organizing of the liturgy of the Mass on the grand scale as we know it today Gregory certainly did encourage Church music, which is so intimately linked both with words and action, but in the present state of our knowledge it is difficult to know exactly what he did contribute to it.

At that period, in Rome for instance, the liturgy played a very considerable part in the lives of the Christian people. Preaching, which was introduced into it particularly as a form of commentary was not, at its best, a mere form of exhortation without substance or an exercise in ostentatious exhibitionism, but a continuous endeavour to teach and train them. The active part taken by the people in the liturgical drama, as well as the processions that took place before and during the ceremony, the singing in which they joined as best they could, certainly with no thought of its aesthetic effects, all this, taking place below the holy images painted on the walls to remind them of the uplifting powers of salvation, produced an atmosphere in which even the most ignorant developed quite naturally. This was the function of the liturgy, a ritual performed by men to the glory of God, which entirely swept them up— their minds, feelings, words, gestures and physical movements—and by including them in a synthesis of the highest values bestowed on them a positive share in religious culture, or better still, a whole way of life. In this connection it is impossible to underrate the part played by Gregory in Rome, nor the influence he exercised beyond it, taking into account that the quality, both of the liturgy and the sermon, their excellence or mediocrity, depended on the quality of the clergy and the attitude of the faithful, all of which elements make it impossible to generalize further on the subject.

With all his precise genius Pope Gregory did not lack imagination. He regarded the ancient Roman order that had ruled over the Western Mediterranean countries as outdated, and felt, although possibly rather vaguely, that Eastern Christianity was tending to elude the influence of Rome; he therefore endeavoured, whilst living in the present, to prepare for the future. Thus he looked northwards, towards the foggy and insular land of Britain, where the Anglo-Saxon conquerors had by then settled down. He was partly unaware of the missionary adventures of the Celts, and of their deep-seated hatred of the invaders. But he did know that in the larger island dwelt heathen peoples awaiting conversion. He thought that the Franks, who lived nearer to them, should take charge of the business, but he was soon convinced that Brunhild's bishops had no missionary zeal, and so he decided to take this matter in hand himself.

This was an old idea of his. Some time before his election to the Pontificate, when one day he was strolling alongside the slave market, he had noticed certain handsome young fellows with blue eyes and fair hair and had asked their nationality. We know that story and the bad puns on the Angles, who were to be transformed into angels, and on their country, Deira (south of Northumberland) which had to be rescued from the wrath of God (*de ira*), and also on their king, Aelli, who would learn to sing the Halleluia. He was said already to have set out there, to the great distress of the people of Rome, who searched the countryside in order to bring him back, first having charged the reigning Pope with offending St Peter and destroying the Church by letting Gregory go, or rather, 'by driving him away'. He himself, allegedly, at three days' march from Rome, had sat down to rest and read, when a grasshopper landed on his book, and from its name (*locusta*) he deduced that he was to go no further (*loco sta*).

Having become Pope he ordered his administrator in Gaul, the priest Candidus, to buy on the market of Marseilles, the great emporium of human beings in the Western Mediterranean, young Angles who after a training in a monastic community were to be sent back as native missionaries. But he changed his mind and in 595 appointed Augustine, prior of the monastery of St Andrew in Rome, a second-rate cleric but reliable, to head a monastic missionary colony in Britain.

On arrival in Provence these travellers went to Lérins, where they received some information on the island of the Angles according to which it only very faintly resembled the land of Cockaigne described later on by Bede, who was born there and became the historian of this mission. The stories told of the ferocity of their future flock were such that, seized with panic, Augustine turned back, arrived in Rome, was reassured by the Pope, and on his orders once again set out. With him he took a fine letter to the brethren explaining to them that it was better to undertake nothing than to do so with the intention of giving up. Augustine was also given recommendations to the Frankish bishops and to Queen Brunhild, whom the Pontiff reminded that she was 'naturally given to good works'. The missionaries then travelled through Gaul in good order and escorted by Frank interpreters disembarked at the end of April 597 at the mouth of the Thames in the Isle of Thanet (now part of the mainland) with no other weapons than their faith.

Augustine was aware of the fact that the king of that country of Kent was married to Bertha, daughter of Caribert, King of Paris. With her husband's consent she had remained a Catholic. He informed Ethelbert of his arrival and within a few days the king sent for Augustine and his companions. He decided to receive the mission in the open, according to the old German custom, for the powers of evil were not as potent there as indoors. Augustine arrived, preceded by a Cross and a picture of the Saviour and followed by his companions chanting litanies. The monk preached a sermon setting forth his doctrine and his mission, but Ethelbert was not immediately converted. 'Those are fine words,' he said, 'and fine promises, but they are quite new and uncertain. I cannot agree with them and put behind me everything that I have believed in for so long, together with the whole Anglian nation.' As, however, the missionaries had come so far and had made an excellent impression, he agreed to give them house-room and food according to the German laws of hospitality. Those who wished to do so might become converts. But Augustine did not have to wait long; Ethelbert was baptized a few weeks after their first meeting. At Christmastide 10,000 heathens followed his example. Bertha, the 'new Helena', like her ancestress Clotilda, could claim some part in this success.

Apart from Scotland, at that time the island of the Angles was divided into kingdoms forming a confederation known as the Heptarchy, although the numbers belonging to it varied from time to time. At the time of Augustine's arrival Ethelbert, King of Kent, presided over seven kingdoms, but it did not necessarily follow that the Anglo-Saxon masses would be converted according to his example. In fact it happened that these kings and their nations exterminated one another and in some cases the conversion of certain of them provided a reason for others to remain heathens.

When Gregory received the good tidings from England he replied to it by sending reinforcements and charging Augustine, head of the new Church, to organize his conquest, whilst the missionaries were to conform to strict instructions regarding the methods they should use. The missionary-monks were to live in a community. And in fact, between 600 and 601 the first monastery, St Peter and St Paul of Canterbury, was founded under the rule of St Benedict. The Roman liturgy was used, but adapted, as regarded exterior practices, to local customs. As it spread bishoprics were gradually established. Together with the earlier Celtic foundations they were placed under the Latin Primacy of Canterbury. The natives were dealt with intelligently; the heathen temples were not destroyed but taken over into Christian service, especially if they were built of stone. Heathen festivals became Christian festivals. Thus, at the winter solstice, the festival known as Yule would retain its name, but be replaced by the real festival of Noel. Even the animal sacrifices and the huge feasts which followed it were not forbidden, but now took place 'in praise of God'. Thus by avoiding any violent changes in local customs it would gradually be possible to modify them in the long run (601).

And these methods were successful, the missionaries gradually spreading out over almost the whole island. In 617 they had progressed northwards as far as Northumbria, where the dramatic conversion of Coïfi, the high priest of Woden (Wotan) brought about that of the king. According to Bede, who reported this incident, this Coïfi was dissatisfied with his gods. He had served them better than anyone else, but unlike many others he had received neither great benefits nor honours for doing so. If these gods had been any good at all they would have shown him greater favours, and therefore the religion he had hitherto followed was worth nothing at all (*nihil omnino virtutis*). If, therefore, the religion the missionaries had brought with them was a better and more efficient one he would accept it without hesitation. But a local chief then spoke up more poetically: 'When, on a winter's night when the tempest is raging without, many men are seated in company at a meal in the well-heated great hall, a sparrow may fly through it on rushing wings. None knows whence he came nor where he goes. Such is the life of men, who know not what came before nor what will come after them. If, therefore, this

new religion brings us some assurance, it seems that we should accept it.'
Having received instruction from the missionaries, Coïfi declared that
his former religion was naught, and offered to be the first to destroy
'with wisdom' the temples that he venerated 'through stupidity'. He, the
high-priest, asked the king for arms, which he had no right to bear, and
for a stallion, which he had no right to ride, for mares were the only
mounts allowed to priests. The stallion reared and the people thought
Coïfi mad. But after having shot an arrow at the temple and ordered all
his followers to destroy it, burning it to the ground, 'he rejoiced greatly
that he had found the faith of the true God'.

The work of the missionaries was not, however, without setbacks and
trials. Sometimes a kingdom that had been converted relapsed into
heathenism, as happened in Kent after Ethelbert's death, in East Anglia
and the wide lands of Northumbria. The monks would then withdraw,
some of them even taking refuge in Gaul, awaiting the moment of
return. One hundred years were to elapse before the last strongholds
were overcome. Native monks and priests fairly quickly filled the
breaches; the first indigenous bishop was consecrated in 644. As the
native clergy had received a monastic and Roman training their missionary work had a dual aspect. Augustine, who died in 605, could only
dimly foresee the fruits of the seed he had sown.

ANGLO-SAXONS, CELTS AND LATINS: ST WILFRID

When he arrived in the country of the Angles, Augustine had definite
orders from Gregory to bring the Celtic bishops he would find there
under his own jurisdiction. Viewed at a distance from Rome this
seemed a matter of course, but on the spot it appeared to be far less
simple.

Living as they did in their foggy islands at the edge of the then known
world the Celts were naturally inclined to cultivate the virtues of
insularity. Their character, tending to extremes, increased this inclination to a point at which they were led to condemn everything that
differed from their own idea of the world. In these conditions any
contact with foreigners, which was bound to lead to a comparison
between their mutual values, was regarded as an adventure which they
viewed with mistrust, since in their own opinion they had more to lose
than to gain by it. Their links with Rome, to which after all the Celts
owed everything, had formerly been strong but had slackened with
time; distance, the lack of regular communications, the rigorous
asceticism of their faith, their attachment to what had become custom-

ary, gradually hardened the attitude of the Celtic Christians. The same beliefs, although firmly held on both sides, but in widely differing climates, had in fact developed in mutual ignorance.

Geographical factors were as well complicated by historical events. When the Anglo-Saxon invaders pushed back a number of clans to the furthest limits of their own country, compelled others to emigrate, whilst subjecting those who remained, they not only increased the isolation of the islanders, who more than ever were determined to remain true to themselves, but created enmities which were to last for centuries, traces of which still remain to this very day as between the Irish and the English. Thus the Celtic bishops and monks felt not the slightest inclination to lead along the path to Paradise heathen nations who in their eyes were not worth converting and with whom, hating them as they did in this world, they had no wish to mingle in charity in the next. Beaten and humbled by them they wished to keep intact their revenge in Heaven. The Anglo-Saxons, on their side, either from instinctive hostility to them or fear of being assimilated, felt that if converted they must be they would prefer to receive the Gospel from missionaries who were not their enemies.

And now here were these strangers who had come to save the Anglo-Saxons' souls. The Celts naturally considered that this was none of their own business, and with some apprehension they hoped that the newcomers would kindly stick to theirs. Nevertheless the arrival of the missionaries brought with it certain unpleasant problems concerning their closeness and other implications for those Celts who had remained under the domination of the heathens. Indignation followed close upon their first instinctive mistrust. The 'Romans' did in fact demand the submission of old Christian communities which until then had flourished far from any foreign jurisdiction. They did not conceal the fact that they had been charged with organizing the dioceses according to the Continental rule. And finally they condemned the good old Celtic traditions concerning the Pascal calendar, the form the tonsure should take, the liturgy of baptism, the consecration of bishops, and declared that on all these points they intended to impose the Roman discipline. This was a matter of importance, for a nation that was renowned for the integrity of its faith and still paid the highest deference to the Pope, but which, all the same, was firmly attached to its own customs that, owing to its entire ignorance of those of others, it was convinced were the best in all Christendom. On this last point in particular the missionaries were in danger of being opposed by a national intransigence that was all the greater owing to the obstinacy of the monks, who were the guardians of the country's religion and generally referred to as the saints. St Columban's difficulties with the bishops of Gaul regarding the preservation on the Continent of his insular traditions were only a later development of this opposition, for the quarrel had begun with Augustine's arrival in England.

When he first arrived in England Augustine was unaware of this thorny problem awaiting him in the country of his mission, but he found there a certain number of Celtic bishops who were hardly more willing to come to terms with the Latins than with the Anglo-Saxons, and in any case determined not to make an act of obedience towards him. In 602 or 603, having progressed quite a long way in his apostolic mission, he met in a certain spot called 'Augustine's Oak' (probably on the north-eastern shore of the Bristol Channel) a certain number of priests whom he requested both to help him in converting the Anglo-Saxons and to align their practices according to Roman usage. The priests refused to do so on behalf of their bishops, who had abstained from attending this meeting. Then, according to Bede, Augustine suggested referring their dispute to God. A sick man was to be brought, and which ever side cured him would prevail over the other. The Celts accepted this trial reluctantly (*inviti*). As a man of good breeding Augustine invited them to be the first to try their powers on a blind man who had been brought to the spot agreed upon. They did so and failed, whereas Augustine subsequently succeeded in restoring his sight. Although this shook them they would still not give way, for, they stated, 'they could not renounce their customs without the consent of their own people' and they demanded a second conference.

Meanwhile seven bishops, including the wise Dinooth, Abbot of Bangor Iscoed, went to consult a highly respected anchorite. 'Should they submit to Augustine?' 'Yes, if he be a man of God.' 'How may we discern it?' 'If he be gentle and humble of heart.' 'How to make certain of it?' 'Arrange matters,' answered the anchorite, 'so that he and his followers arrive first at your meeting-place. If he stands up when you arrive this will prove that he is a servant of Christ. You will in that case do as he bids you.' When on the appointed day the bishops arrived Augustine remained seated; Heaven had given a sign. They were furiously angry with him and taxed him with pride, contradicting every word he uttered. Although Augustine endeavoured to come to terms with them regarding the customs, providing that they would accept the Roman dating of Easter and undertake to collaborate in converting the heathens, the Celts announced that 'they would do nothing of the kind and would not accept him as their archbishop. And they pointed out to one another that as he had failed to rise to greet them he would despise them even more if in spite of it they agreed to submit to him.' Annoyed in his turn, Augustine prophesied that they would be destroyed by the Angles. And in fact a little later, in 613, Bangor Iscoed was overwhelmed, and 1,200 monks were murdered. Nevertheless, the fifty who escaped were still not moved to change their minds, any more than the 'Romans' were by pity. For another 150 years the two Churches continued to exist side by side, in a state of vigilant hostility, reciprocally denouncing one another as schismatics and heretics. Instances of their mutual discourtesies abounded. In 609 Bishop Lawrence, Augustine's successor, complained that Bishop Dagan refused to sit at his table or to sleep under his roof. Lawrence himself did not conceal his bitterness: 'The small number of Celts, living at the world's ends, cannot claim to know better than all the Churches of Christendom.' A century later the Welsh Christians still refused to pray in the same churches as the Latins, or to share their meals. They refused to greet a 'Roman' and if they had anything to do with one they ran the risk of having to do penance for it. Anything that he might have touched or handled—food, utensils or bottles—was thrown away, burnt, or buried. They had not become any more charitable, but at an early stage, helped by time, necessity and commonsense, certain cracks did appear in their armour. Owing to a lucky accident a part of the Celtic church emerged from its self-sufficiency to gain fame in the North, among the abhorred Anglo-Saxons. In 633 Northumbria, which in 627 had been converted by the monks of Rome, but had subsequently relapsed into heathenism, was taken in hand by the Celtic missionaries. The king, Oswald, who during his childhood had taken refuge at Iona, had there found monks sufficiently broadminded to give him baptism. Needless to say that the new convert, who later became St Oswald, was under obedience to the Celtic rule and, as well, very pious. As soon as he ascended the throne he asked the Abbot of Iona for missionaries, and these were sent to him. Missionary zeal was now stronger than racial prejudice, and possibly also another kind of zeal, aiming at taking over their former missions from the Romans, and miracles soon began to occur. The first bishop sent there, however, offended everyone owing to his ill-humour; but his successor, Aidan, who was of a very different mould, became St Aidan.

A Celt and monk of Iona, he was neither bad-tempered nor fanatical. He arrived in Bernicia (in the northern part of that vast Northumbria) towards the end of 635, and decided to make his headquarters in the tiny island of Lindisfarne, which reminded him of Iona, opposite to Bamborough, the fortress of the king on the mainland. He first founded a monastery there as a base of departure for his missions. He could not speak the tongue of the Anglo-Saxons, but the king himself, who was his friend, became his well-qualified and efficient interpreter. And Lindisfarne was already on the way to becoming, as it was soon called, Holy Island. Like all the Scots, Aidan went about the countryside on foot, building wooden churches in the Celtic style, monasteries and schools. He was immensely active and enjoyed considerable prestige, even among the Roman missionaries. Bede described him as a model of forbearance, deliberation, and zeal. He only deplored that Aidan did not understand all that he should have known (*non habentem plene sapientiam*), i.e. he should have given up the Celtic customs to which, however, he was ardently devoted. The achievements of the Latins might induce us to underestimate those of Aidan, but he undeniably advanced very quickly and to such effect that historians like Lightfoot, possibly with somewhat exaggerated admiration, considered his achievements superior to those of Augustine: 'If Augustine was the apostle of Kent, Aidan was the apostle of England.'

By the time of his death in 651 the whole country had been converted, by the Celts in the north and the Latins in the south. True, the Anglo-Saxons were not as yet very sound Christians, still with barbarian customs and liable to relapse into their ancestral heathenism. This was a major reason in the decision of the Benedictine missionaries to organize their conquest with increasing firmness, by unifying the two Churches, rivals and opponents, under the effective jurisdiction of Rome. On the Celtic side the urgency of such unity was not felt so strongly, but gradually their prejudices were broken down. Pope Honorius I (d. 638) formally made his decision in the matter known to them. Owing to more and more detailed information that arrived both from Rome and from Gaul their minds began to waver regarding the perfection of their old traditions. The moment seemed to have come when the Romans were to prevail. In 664 a synod took place at the monastery of Whitby on the Northumbrian coast.

The conference took place under the presidency of King Oswio, who belonged to the Celtic obedience, and his natural son Alchfrid (Alfred) on the Roman side. Two protagonists faced one another; Abbot Colman, Aidan's successor in the see of Lindisfarne and a man of great reputation, defended the Celtic traditions and was opposed by a young Northumbrian, about thirty years old, Wilfrid, Abbot of Ripon, who had already become famous owing to his strong character, knowledge, pilgrimages and enthusiasm for the Roman usages. Having listened to both of them the king was to decide the matter. It was his view that if a king could decide on the conversion of his people, in the same way he had the right to arbitrate regarding the religious practices of those same people. Once the most important question, that of the Pascal calendar, was settled, all the rest would follow and there would be agreement between the two clerical bodies.

As the first speaker Colman claimed in favour of the Celtic Church a tradition that according to him went back to the apostle St John and which the great abbots, St Columba of Iona in particular, had carefully preserved. Wilfrid countered him with the Roman usages which, he said, were introduced by SS Peter and Paul and were practised in the Church universal, with the exception, he added with an obvious allusion, 'of a hidden corner at the ends of an island'. He admitted Columba's good faith, but did not refrain from criticising it: 'As for your Father Columba, in whose holy footsteps you claim to follow, I might make reply that many who at the Last Judgment may claim to have prophesied, driven out devils, and accomplished many miracles in His name, will hear the Lord Himself tell them that He knoweth them not. I would not speak thus of your fathers, for regarding those whom one does not know (*de incognitis*) it is far more righteous to believe good than evil . . . and whilst admitting that your Columba may have been a saint and worked many miracles . . . might he yet be preferred to the blessed Prince of the Apostles to whom the Lord said "Thou art Peter and I will give thee the keys of Heaven"?' His argument was certainly devoid of deference towards St Columba, nor was it altogether sound in dialectics. Such as it was, however, it made a great impression on the king, whose ignorance appears to have been stupendous. 'Is it true, Colman, that God spake thus to Peter?' 'It is true, O king.' 'Can you claim that such powers were also conferred on Columba?' 'No.' 'If, therefore, you admit this point as being beyond further discussion, if Peter did receive the keys of Heaven from our Lord, he is a porter with whom I wish to have no trouble. As regards myself I intend to conform to his precepts, for if he does not agree, none will open them to me when I arrive at the gates of Heaven.' (Bede.) This royal argument, even weaker than those that had preceded it, carried the day. Then Colman, 'finding his doctrine despised', asked the king in a dignified manner to appoint a successor to himself at Lindisfarne, and departed with a handful of his companions to finish his days in holy silence on the coast of Ireland, faithful to the end to the traditions of his father Columba. All he wished to do first was to return to Lindisfarne in order for the last time to venerate the relics of St Aidan and to take a part of them with him. He died in 675.

Whitby sounded the funeral knell of Celtism as a whole. There were still one or two centres of resistance, but this was chiefly merely a point of honour. Iona, the citadel of the old tradition, surrendered in 716, and the Welsh did likewise in the middle of the eighth century. Thus ended a quarrel which from our point of view was puerile, but significant and important in its own place and time and had it lasted, in its consequences. It is all the same remarkable that in spite of everything it neither harmed the doctrine nor even set back the missionary work to any marked extent, so firm was the faith of those old Christian communities. Neither were the Roman customs indiscriminately imposed on all the monasteries. In most cases there was a transitional compromise between the Rule of St Columba and the Rule of St Benedict.

The victory of the Roman Church at Whitby was a triumph for Wilfrid, whom we know chiefly through his *Life* written by one of his companions, Eddius. Eddius was a good hagiographer but a bad historian. Like all his colleagues he sinned both by exaggeration and omission. His account, permeated by devotion to his subject and malevolence towards his enemies, whom he leaves us in no doubt were also the enemies of God, still does not succeed in presenting to us the edifying portrait that we usually find in books of this kind. The mass of trials and tribulations that overwhelmed Wilfrid seem to the reader occasionally touched up; no man, be he ever so saintly, can accumulate so many misadventures without in some way being responsible for them. And as a matter of fact Wilfrid's natural bellicosity has much more in common with our own, today, than his endurance in suffering or his speed of reaction.

He was handsome, well-built and strong (*corpore strenuus*), intelligent as well, and good-tempered. He had memorized the 150 psalms of the Bible, but for the monks of that period this was not an incredible performance. Although he was not exactly an intellectual he knew everything that the Celts were capable of knowing and daily longed to learn more. He prayed a great deal, but above all he was so anxious to achieve results that those he did obtain invariably spurred him on to others rather than satisfied him. His natural generosity often caused him to act on impulse, which he would do with enthusiasm but not always wisely. He had a vivid imagination and often lived in the future as much as in the present, and he had so much energy that when it was not impeded, or frittered away in different directions, he felt himself capable of meeting every demand on it and sometimes even of more. With all the obstinacy of his race he was determined always to be in the right; always at fever heat he sometimes rambled, but would never accept a rebuff.

When he came up against insuperable obstacles in one direction he turned in another; the world was wide and there were many souls in it to be gathered in. And he did everything in his own grand manner. Whilst in private he mortified himself, in public he was ostentatious, nor did he disdain spectacular deeds and settings which today one would say smacked of publicity seeking. He felt that it was justifiable to exploit all one's abilities for the greater glory of God, since He had been graciously inclined to bestow them on some of his creatures.

At the age of thirteen, when he quarrelled with his step-mother, a disagreeable and hardhearted person (*molesta et immitis*), he decided to become a monk, and had the odd notion, in order to do so, of dressing up as a soldier and followed by a train of companions to arrive on horseback for an audience with the queen. He entered Lindisfarne 'untonsured', i.e. as a layman. Here the pure Celtism of its founder, Aidan, was still the rule. This did not satisfy him and he was anxious to learn more at first hand of the Roman usages, which there were only referred to in hushed tones. In order to study them he did not go to Canterbury, where he would have found all that he was seeking, but to Rome itself. No monk filled with the spirit of pilgrimage was ever put off by great distances. And Wilfrid was so used to walking (*pedibus velox*) that he made the journey from Northumbria to Rome on several occasions, without deviating or lengthy rests, always on foot, as the apostles had gone. He made his last great expedition to Rome when he was seventy; only once, in Gaul, on his way home, did illness and exhaustion oblige him to accept a mount and even a litter to carry him on his way, but this only for a short distance, as far as Meaux, where thanks to St Michael a miracle put him back on his feet.

He spent a long time in Rome visiting the holy places; learned the Four Gospels 'to perfection', as well as the Pascal computation 'of which the schismatics of Britain and Ireland were wholly ignorant'. Having been converted to the Roman discipline he brought to its adoption in his homeland a neophyte's enthusiasm combined with his own extraordinary powers of persuasion. But he was in no hurry to return to Northumbria and spent three years at Lyons, where he rejoined his old friend Archbishop Dolfinus, who having met him on his way out and already thinking highly of him, had wanted him to marry his niece. On Wilfrid's way home Dolfinus gave him the final instructions and then tonsured him according to the Roman discipline. On finally reaching home Wilfrid obtained the king's consent to his introducing the Roman discipline in Ripon monastery, which had a short time previously been founded by the Celts of Melrose. Their feelings, when now he ousted them, can easily be imagined. At Ripon his monks militantly followed the Rule of St Benedict, wore the crown-shaped Roman tonsure, celebrated Easter according to the Roman calendar and observed all the customs that their Father Abbot had brought back from Rome. The Council of Whitby, having set the seal on the defeat of the Celts, blessed his undertaking and encouraged Wilfrid to consolidate his success.

And at that moment he was chosen by the king and chiefs of Northumbria to succeed the short-lived successor of Colman, who had been defeated at Whitby, in the bishopric of Lindisfarne. But Wilfrid had no trust in the validity of consecrations conferred by the Celtic bishops and decided to have his own conferred upon him by a Roman bishop, Agilbert, the former bishop of Dorchester, who had formerly ordained him as a priest and now held the see of Paris. Gaul was not so far away and the journey was hardly worthy of being called a pilgrimage. So Wilfrid rejoined Agilbert at Compiègne. Even before the ceremony he enjoyed the bishop's grace to the full and he entered the Church in a manner worthy of a king or a pope, perched on a throne of gold carried on the shoulders of the twelve consecrating bishops, to the music of hymns and canticles. As the see of Lindisfarne was now regarded as unworthy of the new prelate it was agreed that he should reside at York, capital of Northumbria, which was more convenient as well as worthier of him than a mere islet in the North Sea, and also a former bishopric. But his journey home was impeded by many delays, including scuffles with pirates, and storms which swept him out of his course, in spite of the holy relics which he had crammed into his baggage. So that when he finally arrived back he learned that his throne was already occupied. King Oswio, ill-advised by Wilfrid's detractors according to Eddius, but more likely annoyed by the procrastinations of this clergyman who was so long in turning up, had nominated to this see a bishop who belonged to the Celtic discipline, Ceadda (St Chad). Wilfrid found himself obliged without a word to return to his abbey at Ripon, possibly too, with a slightly guilty conscience. But he was not to behave so virtuously and quietly again. Meanwhile, at Ripon, the Bishop-Abbot built a church entirely of stone, with columns and porticos, where the monks chanted in the Roman fashion. In the monastery itself a school was founded and a *scriptorium* was organized in order to produce a codex on purple vellum with characters of gold, contained in a case of pure gold encrusted with precious stones.[1] In the meantime also, to satisfy

[1] This Gospel is not, as was believed, the famous Hamilton 251 manuscript, purple, with gold uncials, which is Carolingian. (Cf. S. Berger, *Histoire de la*

his own need for action, the Father Abbot decided to convert Mercia.

At Canterbury the Primate of England was an Eastern monk, born at Tarsus in Cilicia, who late in life, when he was sixty-eight, had been consecrated a bishop by Pope Vitalian, who had then sent him out as a missionary, in 668.

Theodore was a man of experience, culture, and authority, whose task it was to reform the Celtic clergy, to ensure that the decisions of the Council of Whitby were implemented, and to organize the dioceses throughout England. He even went so far as to confirm in the Roman manner certain episcopal consecrations which had wrongly been judged invalid on account of having been conferred according to the Celtic rites. His intellectual achievements will be discussed separately, but even leaving them out of account, he succeeded so perfectly in his tasks that he has been called the Father of the Church of England (he died in 690). Meanwhile, owing to his unyielding nature he was, somewhat unjustly, unable to come to terms with Wilfrid's explosive virtues. He began, however, by recalling him from Ripon and installing him in the see of York. Wilfrid took advantage of this move to restore the cathedral, which had become a ruin, open to all weathers and a nesting-place for the birds. He roofed it over with lead and also sent specially for workmen to come from Gaul to provide it with (stained?) glass windows (*vitro per quod intro lucem radiabat*), a great novelty at that time.

But there was not peace for long between Wilfrid and his Primate. At York the bishop began by falling out with King Egfrith whom he annoyed by his indiscreet interference between the king and his two successive wives. The second of these queens disliked him and criticized his love of luxury, his architectural activities, and his too many rich and flourishing monasteries. And Theodore himself considered that the huge diocese of Northumbria was too much for one bishop, even a Wilfrid, to handle, and decided to divide it into four. Eddius bluntly accused Theodore of having allowed himself to be corrupted (*cum muneribus*), and to have gone 'against God's will' which, obviously, could only be the same as Wilfrid's. Frustrated, the latter protested against having only been subsequently informed of the *fait accompli*. He was told, however, that there was nothing against him personally, but that the Primate's decision was irrevocable. Thereupon Wilfrid once

Vulgate pendant les premiers siècles du Moyen Age, Paris, 1893, p. 36, 259–62, and E. M. Thompson, *Handbook of Greek and Latin Palaeography*, London, 1873, p. 41, note.) According to M. Nordenfalk (*Le haut Moyen Age, l'Enluminure*, Geneva, 1957, p. 121, *et seq.*), the only known illuminated manuscript that might be attributed to the School of York and Ripon in Wilfrid's time is the fragment of the Gospel of Maeseyck, St Catherine's church.

again took the road to Rome. He avoided Gaul—for there, as well, he had enemies as well as friends—and a tempest threw him on to the Frisian coast. Those who dwelt there were heathens, and he stayed in order to convert them. Then he proceeded up the Rhine, in due course arriving at the tombs of the Apostles, but meanwhile Theodore had had plenty of time to inform Pope Agathon of the situation. Whilst refraining from taking the Primate's side the Pope recommended him to appoint new bishops, and advised Wilfrid to endeavour to come to terms with them.

On returning to Northumbria, Wilfrid was not welcomed by the king, whose authority this recourse to Rome might have undermined. The documents with which he returned were declared to be falsified, and Wilfrid was finally thrown into a dreadful cell, where, for once having nothing else to do, he passed his time singing the psalms; incidentally a heavenly light shone in the darkness of his prison. At the end of nine months he was set free, but as he was forbidden to reside in Mercia and Wessex he converted Sussex and the Isle of Wight.

Theodore then made his peace with Wilfrid, whose good qualities, in spite of his stormy character, had finally overcome that perfect organizer's prejudices. Wilfrid was reinstated at York, although his diocese remained divided and the bishops who had already been appointed were to be his suffragans. Nevertheless they were no friends of their new Archbishop's. Matters went even worse with Alfrid, the new King of Northumbria. Imprisoned, banished, unwelcome wherever he endeavoured to establish himself, Wilfrid decided once again to appeal to the Pope, now John VI. He was seventy years old by then, but still a lusty walker. He paid a second visit to Friesland and in Rome, according to Eddius, it took four months and seventy sessions before justice was done him; according to Bede there were only forty, but even this is a respectable figure. Yet Wilfrid was still dissatisfied and did not want to return home; the Pope, however, commanded him to do so. Knowing his duty (*sciens obodire*), the eternal pilgrim once more set out, taking with him a goodly load of ornaments and relics. He made his peace with Bertwald, Theodore's successor in the Primacy of Canterbury, but not with the king, who refused to allow him to return to York. He had to be satisfied with the bishoprics of Ripon and Hexham, and having at last accepted the situation he spent the last years of his life peacefully, dying in 709.

In describing his death Eddius, in spite of his stumbling Latin, found words of moving simplicity: 'Bacula, one of the abbots, spread a sheet upon the ground. On this the brethren laid his holy body and after having washed it with their own hands and dressed it in his church vestments, in fear of God carried it to its appointed place to the singing of chants and canticles. And several times they heard above the house the sound of birds, as if they were nesting there, and several times a soft rustling of wings as of beings flying up to Heaven. The wise men present declared with certainty that choirs of angels had concerted with St Michael to carry the soul of the holy pontiff to Heaven. Then, having set up a tent outside, they bathed his holy corpse and afterwards emptied the bath-water on the ground. The inhabitants of a cell at this spot later built a cross of wood there, and the Lord was in the habit of (*consuevit*) performing various miracles there. Our own people, having wrapped the holy corpse in grave-clothes and placed it on a bier, set out to the chanting of the psalms for Ripon monastery, where the whole (monastic) family came to meet him, bearing the holy relics. Barely anyone there could withhold his tears. Raising their voices (the monks) received him chanting hymns and canticles and with great honour laid the body of this very holy man in the cathedral that our holy pontiff had in the past built and dedicated to the honour of St Paul the Apostle. He was seventy-five years old. May his glory endure eternally.'

By the very abundance of his gifts Wilfrid was a turbulent and tiresome apostle, yet on balance his achievements to a great extent compensated for his impetuosity. His missionary work, though often disconnected and interrupted, was nevertheless considerable. Yet he alone did not do everything. St Cuthbert, his contemporary, who died in 687, a member of the Benedictine Order, did just as much, although more quietly. Even more than a missionary, Wilfrid was the man of Whitby. He had understood that unless they emerged from their obstinate isolation, the conservatism of the Celts was doomed to sterility. In pursuing them he helped to correct it and to re-direct their splendid energies in the direction of the Church Universal, infinitely more important than either Iona or Lindisfarne. His success in this was far greater than that of St Augustine, without whom it would not have been possible, and St Theodore, without whom it would have remained incomplete. Standing midway between the two hostile parties, and himself a violent partisan, this Northumbrian was still better able than anyone else to affirm the union of both Celts and Anglo-Saxons under the unchallenged aegis of Rome. However injudicious or picturesque, his constant recourse to Rome was the result of deep thinking and showed an entirely new orientation. He it was who led a new form of pilgrimage for Christ's sake, which in future was to lead to Rome rather than to haphazard wanderings at the mercy of wind and waves; an ever-growing and in due course overwhelming number of pilgrims in search of faith,

piety, relics or books. Nor was this all. By bursting open the too carefully guarded doors of the Celtic monasteries and introducing into them
the Rule of St Benedict he made it possible for the spirit of Monte
Cassino to reach out to remote places, the very existence of which the
Patriarch had never suspected. After the work of preparing the ground
and missionary efforts was over, those monasteries were to become,
even more gloriously than they had been under the Celts, centres of
culture, as well as prayer and praise, where literature, singing, the
illumination of fine manuscripts and schools were to develop during
centuries as the endowments of the Benedictines. Historians, dazzled by
the personalities of Augustine and Theodore, have not always accorded
his rightful place to Wilfrid. Yet to a large extent it was thanks to him
that the Church of England became a melting-pot in which Celts and
Anglo-Saxons gradually co-mingled, and which bore the triple stamp
of Rome, St Benedict, and a civilizing mission. After Wilfrid it was
prepared to develop in its island home and spill over on to the Continent
the benefits of its activities, henceforward finally unified.

CHAPTER VII

THE ANGLO-SAXON BENEDICTINES:
THE ITALIAN REVIVAL

When St Augustine of Canterbury began his missionary work in Kent he followed the traditional method; he knew that by converting the king his baptism would be followed by those of his subjects. At the beginning, as always, the results were impermanent, and so long as the missionaries were uncertain of being able to remain indefinitely there would have been no point in creating cultural centres without a reasonable chance of endurance. It has not been proven that Augustine did in fact found the school of Canterbury. The first 'Roman' school that was definitely established dates from the reign of King Sigisbert of East Anglia, who died in 637. As far as we know, prior to this date the teaching of the Benedictines consisted chiefly of the rudiments of religion, the liturgy, and singing.

As we have already seen, the Celts began at a very early stage to take an interest in learning: the Scots of Ireland enjoyed it, and their monastic schools had a very high reputation. They studied the Bible and also, to a degree that it is difficult to estimate exactly, learned the essentials of grammar and pronunciation, as well as studying a limited number of profane works. Although they did not give up their native language Latin was beginning to be generally used in their schools. This was also the case in the Celtic monasteries of Britain itself; long before the foundation of Lindisfarne by St Aidan many monasteries there were educational centres. From this point of view the Celts held a very definite position in their own country.

Their capitulation to the Roman discipline and their missions among the Anglo-Saxons only strengthened, had this been necessary, their own desire for learning as a means towards worshipping God more effectively, and the propagation of the Gospel. And the Benedictines in their turn, as soon as they felt themselves established sufficiently solidly, were able to found flourishing schools. But whilst the Celts had been satisfied with a less highly organized regime, and if one may say so, a less thorough degree of humanism, the Benedictines introduced a greater and more methodical degree of discipline. Thenceforward the Anglo-Saxons, keen and intelligent neophytes, whether converted by one side or the other, were able to acquire both faith and education before they themselves very soon became masters as well as scholars.

Let us not, nevertheless, think of those monastic centres merely as so many academies in which the pupils were imbibing general knowledge, even when in addition to the schools they contained a library and a workshop for copyists and illuminators. First of all it was a matter of teaching Latin to children destined to be monks, who, when they arrived there from their clans or tribes knew only Celtic or Germanic, and through constant practice to give them some knowledge of the written or spoken forms of an unknown tongue in order that they might be able to acquire their spiritual nourishment through the Latin texts. Such a curriculum alone was probably not available to all. It would, for instance, be extraordinary if the 600 monks of Wearmouth–Jarrow had all been through the usual cycle of Latin and Scriptural studies, especially bearing in mind the difference between lay monks and choir-monks which at that period did not exist. Only the foremost of them were chosen as teachers, and we must also point out that the Doctorate of the Church conferred on St Bede was a very minor one compared to those of St Jerome or St Augustine of Hippo. There are only ten names known to us over a period of a century and this elite suggests that there were many other masters, for there were masses of students. Yet this small number set its seal on the entire period.

A CENTURY OF MONASTIC CULTURE IN BRITAIN

As we have seen, Theodore of Tarsus, who died in 690, was a great organizer, but he was also one of the most learned men of his day. A doctor of sacred and profane knowledge, he naturally spoke Greek, which was his native language, and also knew Latin perfectly. Pope Agathon, successor to Vitalian, had a high regard for this distinguished monk, whom he called *archiepiscopum et philosophum*, i.e. an archbishop learned in profane and sacred literature, and not, as translated by Montalembert, 'a mitred philosopher'. Theodore, who when leaving Rome had certainly some cultural plans in mind, was accompanied by another monk, Hadrian, born in Africa and abbot of a monastery near Naples. Like the head of his mission, Hadrian was also a man of learning, and Theodore put him in charge of Canterbury monastery, and the school attached to it. From that moment onwards both of them 'cultivated the spirit of science' in their listeners' minds.

The general educational plan followed as preparation for the study of the Gospel seems to have been more or less the same in all the schools. Apart from the ecclesiastical disciplines the masters dealt *ex professo* with a limited number of profane authors along lines following those of the *trivium* and *quadrivium*—grammar, in the wider sense, dealing with the spoken language and the authors in question; prosody, i.e. reading and the proper usage of accents and pauses; versification, or the techniques of verse founded on syllabic quantities. Another basic subject was orthography, which, as under Cassiodorus, corresponded more or less to grammar as we know it, and, of course, writing. These subjects were taught more or less everywhere, occasionally with appreciable differences, according to the relatively greater importance attached to one subject or the other by the teachers, but in every case these techniques were regarded as more important than the books themselves. To these subjects were added, in particular at Canterbury, astronomy, computation (indispensable in dealing with the controversies centred around the date of Easter), Gregorian chanting, known simply as Church music, and Greek. Bede went so far as to claim that at Canterbury the scholars spoke Greek as if it were their native tongue. As he himself only knew it very slightly Bede was going somewhat far in making this claim; if Greek was ever spoken there it was only by the elite of the pupils under Hadrian himself. Bede was closer to the truth when he wrote with understandable admiration of the enthusiasm of all the pupils for learning and for saintliness at a time when peace had been restored: 'Never since the arrival of the Angles in Britain had there been happier times. All the kings whose subjects were particularly valorous Christians were the terror of the Barbarian nations. The hopes of them all were centred on the joys of the Kingdom of Heaven, which they had only recently discovered, and all those who wished to learn sacred literature found masters to teach it to them.'

The monk Benedict Baducing or Biscop was a contemporary of Theodore's. He was a scion of one of the greatest Northumbrian families and an officer at the court of king Oswin. At the age of twenty-five he laid down his arms in order to seek Christ, Whom he found everywhere. Benedict, known also in English as Bennet, became one of the most famous foot-pilgrims of the day, making no fewer than five journeys to Rome. As an indefatigable walker he rivalled Wilfrid, with whom he went on his first pilgrimage to Rome, but owing to their mutual incompatibility the two travellers parted at Lyons. He took advantage of his second pilgrimage to make a detour to Lérins, where the abbot Aygulf, from whom he received the tonsure, had installed the Rule of St Benedict. In Rome Pope Vitalian, who at that moment was engaged in arranging the mission of Theodore of Tarsus, found that this pious Northumbrian monk of noble lineage also possessed commonsense and resourcefulness (*sapientem et industrium*). He asked him to renounce the asceticism of pilgrimage in order to serve as Theodore's interpreter, and at Canterbury the Primate made him director of the establishment. But being, as described by E. Gilson, one of those 'whose ardour in founding monasteries prevented them from remaining there', Benedict could not for long resist the demon of pilgrimage. He became the best-known traveller along the stages leading to Rome, and each time he would return loaded with relics, 'images', which perhaps were paintings on parchment or on wood, sacred vases, ornaments, and particularly books, which he had either bought or had given to him, for books were his second passion. Unlike many other pilgrims Benedict Biscop arranged his journeys in such a way that they were always of use to the monks in his own country. When he returned from his last visit to Rome he brought with him the precentor of St Peter, John, abbot of the monastery of St Martin, who was very successfully to teach the choir-masters of Northumbria to sing the litany, as well as the liturgy. Benedict himself had become an abbot. Egfrith, who had succeeded King Oswio, allotted him land at the mouth of the river Wear, where he built the monastery of Wearmouth in honour of St Peter, and a little later, on another adjacent piece of land, a second monastery, at Jarrow, on honour of St Paul; two great names in the history of monachism. In order that these buildings should be worthy of them Benedict sent to Gaul for masons who worked according to plans based on Roman architecture and who, according to Bede for the first time introduced to Britain stained glass windows bound together by leads. His monks were under the Rule of St Benedict adapted, as was then the custom, to the Northumbrian disciplines. There were also a school and a library, richly endowed by the Father Abbot. He died as the result of a long illness, during which paralysis condemned him to virtual immobility which, if he had not wished for it he had certainly earned, and which, according to Bede, only allowed him to use 'the upper part of his body, indispensable to living'. But before dying he particularly recommended the care of this library to the brethren; it was to be carefully cherished, and not dispersed. Having given this direction he applied himself to departing from 'the dirty furnace of the flesh' (*luteam carnis fornacem*) with due holiness, and when death finally came for him in 690 the brethren chanted over his corpse in alternate choruses.

Although Benedict spent a good deal of time on the roads, he must not be included amongst those wandering monks whose bad behaviour to a large extent discredited ascetic pilgrimages in the eyes of a certain number of the virtuous. It is true that in comparison with the voluntary exile chosen by the Celts and Anglo-Saxons in order to convert the heathen, his kind of pilgrimage seems a pretty easy one. It was nevertheless quite justifiable within the limits that had inspired it, namely a form of devotion that involved a self-inflicted trudging in imitation of Christ's wanderings through Galilee. There is no doubt that Benedict Biscop was one of the best of the itinerant ascetics. Bede, who knew him, and who himself was inclined to be sedentary, spoke of him as a saint in tones of warm deference that were not misleading.

Together with Wilfrid, Benedict was the forerunner of the great Anglo-Saxon pilgrimages to the tombs of the Apostles. There is nothing more touching than the devotion to Rome of this newly converted nation, of which it was an original characteristic. Even kings tended to partake in these pilgrimages. Caedwallader, who was converted by Wilfrid, died in the city of the Popes. His successor, King Ine of Wessex, who settled in Rome after having abdicated, founded a kind of seminary close to St Peter's for the education of young Anglo-Saxons, as well as a hostel for pilgrims, where St Boniface was to find great encouragement for his missions. Nor was this the only Anglo-Saxon foundation. To a large extent such devotion must be placed to the credit of Benedict Biscop, who was a kind of liaison officer between Rome and Northumbria. Even more than the precious manuscripts with which he returned from the Continent, his real claim to fame lies in the propaganda he made in this way for the Roman cult; to quote only the obvious example, after him all the great Anglo-Saxon missions were undertaken on the directions of the pope. In this way Rome was able to recapture in the West the influence that she was already losing in the East.

Although he was less popular than Benedict Biscop, Ceolfrith was also one of the great abbots of Anglo-Saxon monachism. Bede, who knew him personally and owed him a lot, praised his lively, active, ingenious and sober mind, apart from his great religious zeal. As a monk under Wilfrid at Ripon, where he was in turn baker and master of the novices, Benedict Biscop sent for him to direct Wearmouth. In view of his own predilection for pilgrimage Benedict rightly considered that monastery to be in need of continuity in its government whilst he himself was taking to the road and vaunted the steadiness of his monks. But whether or not this was a difficult community to control or whether the travelling abbot, each time he returned, wanted more or less subconsciously to make his weight felt during his intermittent stays there and enjoy the exercise of power, Ceolfrith did not remain at Wearmouth for very long. He returned to Ripon, but was once again brought back and re-installed. When the founder died Ceolfrith was in charge of 600 monks at Wearmouth and Jarrow.

As a follower of the Roman discipline, Ceolfrith undertook to break down Celtic separatism in Scotland and even to win over the Abbot of Iona himself; Adamnan, the eighth successor and hagiographer of St Columba. It would be a fine victory to reduce the very stronghold of Celtism. But Adamnan, who had allowed himself to be won over with regard to the date of Easter, remained adamant with regard to the tonsure; he was determined to keep his half-circle. Then Ceolfrith, who was a fervent supporter of the full crown in the Roman fashion, used one of those fantastic arguments which the monks of the seventh century regarded as dialectically sound: 'If you cling to the crown of life, why are you so obstinately bent on a shortened form of tonsure (*decurtatam*)?' This was certainly an argument that must be taken into account, and Adamnan did so, but was nevertheless unable to carry his monastic family with him in the matter. So for some while still Iona persisted in its separatism.

We know that this same Ceolfrith had copies made of the text of the Cassiodorian Bible which had been brought back from Rome. There were three copies of it—one for Wearmouth and one for Jarrow, both of which are lost, and the third is the *Amiatinus* in Florence.[1]

This manuscript was so beautiful that the Father Abbot decided to present it himself to Pope Gregory II, which would also give him the chance to see Rome again before he died. As he was old he first resigned his post. On the appointed day the pilgrimage set out. After celebrating Mass before the assembled convent Ceolfrith, a golden censer in hand, prayed before the altar and embraced his brethren. The procession then began, pausing at the votive chapels on its way. When it reached the banks of the Wear there were final farewells, genuflexions and tears. The deacons, carrying a golden cross and candles, boarded the barges with the pilgrims. On the further bank the latter worshipped the cross, then mounted their steeds and turned southwards. More than eighty

---

[1] There has been a great deal of discussion with regard to the origin of this document. In the present state of our knowledge it is accepted that the manuscript transcribed at Jarrow on the orders of Ceolfrid is 'a true and direct copy of the Cassiodorian Vulgate' (D. Cappuyns). Cf. the paragraph on Cassiodorus.

monks accompanied Ceolfrith, but not all of them were to reach Rome. When in 716 Ceolfrith died of fatigue at Langres the troop split up, a certain number, discouraged, turned towards home; others, more faithful, remained beside his tomb, 'among peoples whose language they did not even understand' (Bede). And the more determined continued on their pilgrimage.

Among this series of masters St Bede, Doctor of the Church, has not yet completely lost the title by which he is still best known—the Venerable Bede. This description, without in the least detracting either from his greatness or his wisdom, has the advantage of lowering the barriers between ourselves and him of his doctorate and his sainthood, which in all cases are slightly awe-inspiring. Thus we may feel more at ease at entering, without apprehension, his monk's cell.

We have two relevant documents dealing with his life. The first of these is from his own hand. At the end of his *Ecclesiastical History of the British Nation* he wrote, as might any humble scribe, the following postscript: 'Bede, servant of Christ and priest of the monastery of the blessed Peter and Paul of Wearmouth and Jarrow. Born on the land of this monastery, at the age of seven I was entrusted by my parents to the Very Reverend Abbot Benedict (Biscop) and to Ceolfrith for my education. Since then, throughout my life, in this monastery, I have spent all my care in meditation on the Gospels. Observing the discipline of the Rule, chanting each day in church, I have always taken pleasure (*dulce habui*) in learning, teaching, or writing.'

The second document is by Abbot Cuthbert, who was his pupil and witnessed his final moments: 'On the Tuesday before the Ascension of Our Lord he felt more violent spasms and his feet were slightly swollen. He nevertheless survived the day and dictated with good humour. He also said, among other things: "Be you in haste to learn, for I know not how much time still remains to me, and whether my Creator will not soon take me to Him." To us it was clear that he was perfectly well aware of his last moment. And thus he spent the night without sleeping, in acts of grace. At dawn next day, the Wednesday, he pressed us to finish that which we had begun to write. This being done, at the third hour (nine o'clock) we went to the procession of the relics of the saints, according to the custom of that day. One of us, who remained with him, said to him: "Very dear Master, there remains one chapter. Are you still strong enough that we may question you on it?" "It is easily done," he replied, "take up your pen, hurry, and write quickly." Which the other did. At the ninth hour (three o'clock) he said to me: "Run quickly, and fetch the monastery priests; I wish to give them the little presents that I hold from the Lord" . . . And he spoke to each one of them, insisting that they should take care to celebrate Mass and to recite fervent prayers for him, which they gladly undertook with all their hearts to do. All were sorrowful and weeping because they would no longer see his face in this world. But they were also joyful because he said: "The time has come for me to return to my Creator." . . . Thus he spent the day until eventide. Then the pupil who has been mentioned said to him: "Master, there is still a sentence to be transcribed." "Hurry," he answered him. A little later the pupil said: "There, the sentence is finished." "Good, thou are right, it is finished. Take my head in thy hands, for it is very agreeable to me to sit opposite the spot where I was used to pray, so that, being seated, I may still invoke my Father." And thus, (seated) on the paving -stones of his cell he sang "Glory unto the Father, the Son, and the Holy Ghost." At the moment when he mentioned the Holy Ghost the last breath left his body and he departed to the Kingdom of Heaven.'

The master's dictation ceased, apparently, at Verse 9 of Chapter iii of the Gospel of St John.

Bede, born in 673, a deacon at seventeen, a priest at thirty, dying when he was sixty-two, led a completely cloistral life, untouched by events in the outside world, nor did he even make any pilgrimages in the course of it, excepting for one or two journeys connected with his studies. Whether as pupil or teacher he lived in and only for his monastery, knowing that on every day at such and such a time he would have before him the same task as ten or fifteen years earlier, and the same ten or fifteen years later. Those who can physically and psychologically bear such an uninterruptedly regular life, with its repetitous monotony hour by hour, must in the course of a year produce a considerable amount of work, even when their daily timetable is not a particularly full one. Bede followed this regime for fifty-five years, and in consequence produced forty-five works contained in 9,000 columns of the Latin Patrology. Others have done better; others have done more; but all did not labour so usefully. He died in 735.

A sedentary monk with no ambitions to high honour, Bede lived the life of a great scholar. His encyclopaedic knowledge, derived partly from that of Isidore of Seville, partly from the Fathers, and in general from any and every source he could discover, was daily put at the disposal of the pupils of Wearmouth and Jarrow. He was a master of Latin and trained the more gifted among them to use it easily. He was a practical man, and wrote a treatise on orthography, in the definition of the term we have already given. In order that the choir-monks should sing better he wrote a treatise on metrical values, accentuation and sound for them. To help them in their meditations on the Gospel he put his immense commentaries at their disposal. He neglected neither computation nor martyrology, for the composition of the calendar was of importance for the ordering of the monastic and ecclesiastical year. And to these works he added a voluminous correspondence, some of his epistles also being veritable treatises. He was of simple piety and wrote hagiographical works on the holy monks of his monastery. He even occasionally relaxed by teasing the Muses, although in very Christian fashion. We are particularly indebted to him for his *Ecclesiastical History of the British Nation*, the first great national history of a Barbarian people led to civilization by the Roman Church. Since St Augustine of Hippo Western Christianity had not known so learned a man.

It is difficult to judge exactly how well he knew Hebrew and Greek, although it is certain that he did not know those languages perfectly. But his Latin, especially if one compares it to that of Gregory of Tours, was well-grounded; Bede could write limpid pages and his syntax was uncomplicated, his words simple and free of all common debasement. This high quality of his style was to a large degree due to his long and assiduous study of a certain number of Christian and profane authors.

He had read Virgil, Ovid, Persius, Lucan, and with more favour Paulinus of Nola, Sedulius, Fortunatus; minor but Christian poets. Yet he did occasionally condemn the profane poets. Writing of the plagues of Egypt he condemned them indiscriminately for quite other reasons than morality: 'In my view the second plague, that of the frogs, represents the songs of those poets who, by their puffed-up emptiness, exactly like that of frogs, produced deceptive fables (*fabulae deceptionis*).' He went even further when he dared write of the Prodigal Son: 'The acorns on which he fed his swine were the profane disciplines (*disciplinae seculares*) . . . at which the demons rejoice.' Being no philosopher he was suspicious of philosophy and in connection with it quoted Tertullian's epigram that 'The philosophers are the patriarchs of the heretics'.

Dialectics was another plague of Egypt, and one of the most unpleasant was that of the mosquitos: 'Thanks to its wings this animal remains suspended in the air, but it is so light and slender that unless one has perfect sight it is invisible. When it pounces on the body its sting is so sharp that one feels it before having seen the creature. In my opinion this beast can be exactly compared to dialectics, which penetrate our souls with such tiny and subtle needlets, and so cleverly elude us that, although startled and misled, we do not perceive or understand the cause either of our surprise or our deception.'

It did not occur to the author of this passage that a certain class of dialecticians would not be at all displeased by such a comparison, for they frequently pride themselves on being able to prove anything whatever, by means of no matter what arguments, to the very limits of foolishness. Nevertheless, Bede owed much more to the classics than he was willing to admit. His observations on metrical theory reveal an intimate study both of the theoreticians and also of the classical texts, and when he amused himself by rhyming—although in a very pedestrian and colourless fashion—he very easily produced hexameters and pentameters according to the good old examples of Virgil and Ovid. He even occasionally went so far as to describe God in the terminology of the profane writers.

As a Churchman first and last, he held the study of Holy Writ to be the queen of sciences. He was taught by a master of high repute, Trumberct, and he spent the greater part of his time in examining 'with delight the marvels of the Scriptures'. His commentaries amount to a vast compilation, unblemished by any particular sign of originality, and the reader of which finds himself astray in a world of allegory; nevertheless they do reveal his theology and spiritual quality. As they stand, his commentaries were perfectly adapted to the use of the monastic centres of his day. On occasion the master did not fail to benefit others by his own commonsense. Quite often we find remarks like the following: 'There are two kinds of useless individuals; those who do harm and those who refuse to do good.' In the same way, in the first quarter of the twentieth century, a Father Abbot who was a man of great prestige, convinced that the best of all theological knowledge was to be found in the Scriptures, and that all that was needed for the sustenance of our minds and souls was to know how to extract it from them, for many years gave a daily commentary on important Biblical passages without ever wearying his audience.

As the historian of Christian Britain, Bede was a landmark in historical method. Next to him Gregory of Tours, although so indispensable and valuable, appears like a pedlar of old wives' tales. Bede was as keen a hunter of information as his colleague in Gaul, but he scored over the latter by giving due weight to its value instead of accepting everything indiscriminately, and only retaining what seemed to him worth while. Although he was still somewhat inclined to accept miracles on the cheap, yet without any precise method and as if instinctively he seemed to recognize the authentic. D. Cabrol, a good judge, placed him 'in the first rank of the historians and recorders of the Middle Ages'. And Bede distinguished quite clearly between hagiography and history; apart from his historical work he gave free rein to his piety in singing the praises of the five great monks of Wearmouth. The result was a charming booklet of filial devotion, containing also plenty of historical facts.

From a merely superficial point of view Bede does perhaps at first glance appear as an example of the learned, anachronistic, and rather dusty Benedictine, as he might seem to the unlearned and prejudiced. He was certainly of an inquiring and open-minded disposition, a patient, methodical, conscientious, and somewhat heavy-going worker. But above all he appears to have been a marvellous teacher, one of those who are not only learned themselves but know even better how to communicate their knowledge and organize their teaching; a more experienced friend, who whilst he aroused their admiration also aroused in his pupils' minds the desire to learn, digest, and gain even more knowledge than their teacher imparted to them. 'The Venerable Bede' was the name his best pupils gave him. Yet this wealth of talent only stemmed from the superabundance of his mind, and oddly, soul. The true Bede was the pious monk, who regularly attended service, pursued the *lectio divina*, and who, at the moment of dying, insisted on taking up an attitude of prayer.

A Saxon like Bede, St Aldhelm did not belong to the school of Jarrow. There is no need to dwell on the nonsense written on his name in the eleventh century by Fabricius, Abbot of Abingdon. If one were to believe him, the German word *ald* would in Latin translation become *senex*, and *helmus* equivalent to *almus*, which would give us *senex almus* or 'grand old man', a pedant's silly invention which would appear as an odd name to give a new-born babe.

The monk Aldhelm was born of a royal Wessex family, became a pupil at the Celtic foundation of Malmesbury, then at Canterbury, and after having ruled at Malmesbury he died as Bishop of Sherborne. It was at Malmesbury that an Irish monk, Maïdulf, introduced him to study and saintliness, and his education in both directions was completed at Canterbury, at the school of Hadrian. Aldhelm was, literally, a product of two influences which not so long previously had been in opposition to one another and at his time were in the process of converging. Although he did not omit to work for the conversion to the Roman discipline of the Britons of Devon and Cornwall, he appears to us here as the first great intellectual of Anglo-Saxon monachism as it developed from the agreement between the Celts and the Romans. He died in 709.

Although he owed his early education to a Celt, on reaching maturity he no longer deemed it necessary to send out expeditions of students to study in Ireland; Britain was now just as well provided with 'Roman and Argive teachers'. When writing those words Aldhelm was possibly slightly forgetful of his own early training under Maïdulf, and perhaps somewhat pleased to observe that the Anglo-Saxons had succeeded in destroying the monopoly of intellectualism that the Celts had until then enjoyed. But it is true that under such teachers as himself the monasteries of the converted British were well launched on the road of learning.

Their main subject being theology based on the Bible, Aldhelm took care that before this was undertaken their preparation should be based on a knowledge of grammar, and the liberal arts in general: 'As grammar is the only basis on which words can be joined together, the more of the multiple rules of this discipline you have learned, the better will you understand the profound and holy meaning of the divine Word.' Aldhelm had read Virgil, Horace, Ovid, Lucian, and even Terence, Persius and Juvenal. Among the prose writers he seems to have preferred the second-rate authors to the classics. He had a genuine liking for classical literature and gladly went further in search of intellectual pleasures for their own sake than reading those works which were strictly necessary. He also occasionally wrote verse himself. Those around him were equally pleased that a poet of their own could still enshrine their local legends in classical style: but let us make no mistake about it. As a poet Aldhelm was in the position of a man who, not being of good breeding himself, has had to acquire it, and who in conceitedly showing it off, falls into the trap that should always be avoided, exaggeration. Having been introduced to the Latin world and a few corners of the Greek, Aldhelm still felt something of a stranger there. This was another reason why, knowing as much as he did, he felt an urge to trick out his style still more, by the use of either far-fetched, superfluous, or often ambiguous words, so that too often he produced, as E. Curtius called it, an incomprehensible jargon.

Strangely enough, he admitted to possessing two different styles—one for the man in a hurry, and the other for the man of leisure. The first is fluent and clear; but when he had the time and wanted to show the reader what he could do, he overwhelmed him with exoticisms that sometimes remind one of the worst passages in the Irish *Hisperica famina*. In his sober moments it is a pleasure to read him, for he was a good observer and not without critical sense; but his grand manner is simply untranslatable.

When writing verse he was much preoccupied with matters of prosody, and in this, more than anything else, he had everything to learn. The current rhythmical poetry of the Anglo-Saxons had neither content nor manner in common with classical Latin poetry, for an understanding of which it could be no preparation, since Latin poetry was a highly skilled form, imitated from the Greek, divided into very clearly separate compartments and with an inflexible metrical system. It is odd that he should have claimed to restore the conventions of Latin poetry at a time when tonic accentuation had eliminated the former metrical rules from it. He would have been interested to better purpose in Christian poetry, founded on the rhythm of the accents rather than on the length of syllables, and freer in its literary styles than classical poetry. But to this intermediate method Aldhelm preferred to produce complete imitations of the classics, with all their conventions and artifices. And on the subjects of prosody, accentuation and scansion he wrote treatises that were all the more complicated because, he said, 'There are fewer teachers of them'. But the restraint imposed on him by his preoccupation with these rules was beneficial, for when he was obliged to concentrate within these narrow confines he sometimes wrote better verse than some of his prose. Having written in praise of virginity both in prose and in verse (and in entirely different styles), he did so better in hexameters although not more interestingly, for he required no less than two thousand five hundred verses, which leave the reader somewhat breathless, to deal with this rather tenuous subject.

But he was really formidable when, after having mastered prosody, he amused himself by indulging in verbal acrobatics. As we know, the acrostic is a poem in which the first letters of each verse, read vertically, give us a word or a sentence. Aldhelm could perform this trick in masterly fashion, but even this did not always satisfy him, for in the prologue to his poem on *Virginity*, he used double acrostics. The phrase *Metrica tirones nunc promam carmina castos* (Let now our measured songs inspire chaste novices) is to be read not only at the beginning of each verse *descending* on the left of the line, but also on the right, at the end of the verse, from the *bottom upwards*. The miracle is that after such capers the poem still makes sense.

Enigmas are little poems solely invented for amusement on unimportant subjects having nothing whatever to do with Christian literature, such as the hornet, the owl, the mosquito, the salamander, the minotaur, and Aldhelm left us a hundred examples of them written in hexameters, the tone of which is reminiscent of the Odes of Horace, and which occasionally show a pretty turn of wit: *The Scales*, for instance: 'In the past nature made us twins, we who are always ruled by the laws of justice. It is our habit to despise masks (*personsa*) and to follow the right. Man's span on earth would be a happy one, if, like these two sisters he were to remain well-balanced.' Or *The Bee:* 'By my art I ripen the golden fruits of kings. Ever cruel, I carry the sharp darts of war, and without hands I am stronger than the blacksmith's metals.'

Admitting that these are merely the futilities of a minor poet and of little literary merit, this kind of literature is nevertheless significant, less on account of its intrinsic value than for its appearance in a Barbarian nation only recently brought into contact with civilization. Thenceforward profane literature took its place, although not the first one, among cultured Churchmen, who accepted it without feeling a sense of guilt or the need of repentance for so doing. Before Aldhelm the Scots and some of the Latins had already lost their prejudice against the classical legacy of Antiquity; after him, they were definitely won over to it. Aldhelm, the first Anglo-Saxon to leave behind him literary works of his own, became a classic of the School that flourished in Britain. It was a modest beginning but nevertheless the basis of a characteristic culture that in due course was to develop further.

During the first years of his career St Boniface also belonged to the world of the monastic schools. Before he adopted the name of the Roman martyr by which he is universally known, he was called Wynfrith (around 675 to 754). He was born in Sussex, and after having been entrusted to the Benedictines of Exeter, went on to Nurstling, a monastery midway between Winchester and Southampton. Having become a priest at thirty, and a very successful teacher as well, when he was nearing forty he was filled with the spirit of pilgrimage and decided to become a missionary. His evangelical work is worthy of separate consideration; for the moment we will only deal with him as a scholar.

His written works include an important number of letters among the hundred and fifty in the collection bearing his name, the remainder of them being from his correspondents. He also left a grammatical treatise, one on scansion, and poems.

His nephew, disciple, and historian, Willibald, assures us that his uncle was 'an extraordinarily powerful man of learning' and as such he appears to us, also; a man who had perfectly mastered his intellectual material. Trained in the techniques of profane literature, which enabled him to acquire a proficiency in thinking and writing that earned him the title of *grammaticus germanicus*, he successfully studied sacred literature in search of divine knowledge, 'the charm and brilliance (*venustas*) of true and radiant beauty'. Wynfrith's conception of the order of intellectual disciplines was a perfectly accurate one. In his treatise on grammar he placed each of them in a kind of design which took the place of a synthesis—a circle, in the centre of which was a cross and the name of the Lord, contained the two Testaments, the first and foremost subjects of study, as well as grammar, scansion, and history, the instruments of such knowledge.

His Latin, which was more complex than Bede's, was influenced by the models provided by Aldhelm, and his classical training is most apparent in his verses. He was fully conversant with Virgil and Ovid, and handled hexameters, distichs and iambics with equal ease, to the extent of referring to the Almighty as *Regnator Olympi*, in the pagan fashion, following the culture of Antiquity with no afterthoughts, although with a certain degree of affectation. He also occasionally rhymed on trivial subjects such as ink, becoming to an intellectual; wine, which would have horrified the ascetics of the desert, and ignorance, to which he attributed all misfortunes: 'For a long time I have been called folly and the wet-nurse of error. Throughout the vastness of the world my seed has borne the pernicious wages of sin. That is why the land of Germany and the coarse (rustica) race of the Slavs and rude Scythia have always loved me. The father of the child to whose help I come will have no joy of him. When I contemplate sky and earth, the sun and moon that cross over the salt wastes of the sea, and the fiery stars above, I do not ask myself who created them. No nurse ever taught me wisdom. Nowhere, at no time, has a more repulsive female existed than I. That is why wise Greece detested me, severely, for I never longed to avoid sin'. One might already be reading a humanist of the Renaissance.

The school of York was both episcopal and monastic. Its cathedral arose from a monastery, its rule did not differ from that of a monastic school, and all its teachers were followers of Bede. York, an ancient city dating from the Roman colonization, occupied in the middle of the fifth century by the Saxons, under them became the capital of Northumbria. Its first archbishop was Paulinus, companion of St Augustine of Canterbury. As the result of the reorganization of the dioceses under Theodore of Tarsus it regained its title of metropolitan, which at one time had passed to Lindisfarne under St. Aidan. At the time of which we are writing its school rivalled Wearmouth-Jarrow and had a higher reputation than Canterbury; during half a century it was to be 'the core of intellectual Europe',[1] a kind of Christian Oxford in Northumbria.

Although it had already existed as a centre of learning before his time, Egbert, an Anglo-Saxon of Royal lineage, gave it its full lustre. According to the author of the *Life of Alcuin* he was a born teacher.

[1] Gaskoin.

'From dawn onwards, unless inevitably prevented, until midday and often three o'clock, he was seated on his bed, explaining to his disciples the secrets of the Scriptures for the good of each of them. . . . At night-fall, in winter as in summer, apart from Lent, he would take dinner with his pupils, little but well arranged, but without interrupting his teaching in order to do so, in order that they might be nourished with bread of both kinds. One might then see the young pupils bring out before their teacher the points they had previously prepared in private discussions and which they now produced in public.' We observe in passing that Egbert required no cumbersome scholastic apparatus in order to acquire a great reputation.

On his promotion to the bishopric in 732, Egbert passed on his teaching post to his relative Aelbert, who was also a first-class master. His pupil Alcuin praised him as a wise man, who spoke little, but with authority. Loving the poets for their own sake Aelbert played 'the flute of Castalia' and pursued lyricism 'on the heights of Parnassus'. He taught the liberal arts, with the exception of dialectics, for which it seems that our Anglo-Saxons had no great passion, and also fostered music which was, apparently, the subject of special study for the perfect mastery of Church singing. He also gave great attention to the library in which according to Alcuin, he had collected 'the flowers of Britain'. 'It contained the works of the ancient Fathers, all that the Romans claimed as their own in the world, all that luminous Greece transmitted to the Latins, all the divine rain that quenched the thirst of the Hebrews, all the works on which Africa shed her radiant light.'

With such a cultural background Alcuin (730 or 735 to 804) was to become the shining light of the school of York. It is questionable whether, although he was well endowed with abbeys, he was, in fact, ever a monk. But although this is a matter of importance as regards his salvation, for us it is a secondary problem. If Alcuin did not actually make his profession he did, in spite of it, belong to the establishment; he was educated either by monks or else by clerics trained by monks, and he spent a great part of his life in monastic circles.

In his own Germanic tongue he was called Alhwin, but all his life he preferred to be known by his surname or nickname, Albinus. He also belonged to Northumbria, that produced so many great men. His family, which was both pious and rich, already included various saints; Willibrord, the apostle of the Frisians (d. 739), was his cousin once removed. As a small child (*parvulus*) 'he was taken from his mother's breast and entrusted to the Church to be nourished at her mystical breast', i.e.—whatever may have been the custom with regard to breastfeeding in Northumbria—when he was seven or eight years old. The 'Church' in question was the school of York, then in all its glory. Of his two masters, Egbert and Aelbert, the latter appears to have thought particularly highly of him. And already young Albinus enjoyed Virgil whom he even preferred to the psalms. Nor did he like getting up before dawn in order to sing in Church with his brethren. One night when he was asleep in the cell he was sharing with a somewhat uncouth brother (*tonsuratus rusticus*) the latter turned over on the other side when the 'arouser' came by.[1] Albinus thought that he heard some 'dark spirits' speaking roughly to the drowsing brother: 'Are you sleeping well, my brother?'—and they began to beat him up. Half-dead with fright, Alcuin feared the same chastisement, but the 'dark spirits' having taken counsel together, decided on a form of penitence for him that was, to say the least, comical—they decided to cut his corns (*callosas tondere plantas*) which relieved both his mind and body'. And the half-dead 'rustic' brother followed the child as he ran at top speed before him, until both of them found refuge in the church under the protection of the saints.

The course of the master's pet at school does not always run smooth. Some of the pupils, jealous of Alcuin's success, did not regard him with 'a clear eye' but they were disarmed by the charity of their intended victim. Alcuin was ordained a deacon in 776, and was to remain one throughout his life. Two years later he succeeded Aelbert, who gave up teaching and his bishopric to devote himself solely to contemplation. Having been for several years assistant to his master Alcuin was the obvious choice as his successor as rector of the school and administrator of the library.

It was around this period that he wrote the praise of the great men of the Church of York in hexameters. This poem, which has been compared to Virgil, is in fact superficial, flat, colourless, and its prosody occasionally stumbling. It lacks everything that Virgil has, both inspiration as well as the enchantment of words that by their unexpected juxtaposition irradiate one another by mutual refraction and produce an inimitably poetic *aura*. Alcuin's verses, nevertheless, show the aptitude of an excellent pupil and are valuable in spite of their deficiencies for the information they give us on the great men of York. They were also a witness to genuine culture there, for in very few places in the world at that time could anyone have done as well.

[1] This was the name given to the unlucky monk who was obliged to get up before all the rest and to have the disagreeable task of making a great deal of noise to awaken the community before the first choral office.

Although he was less erudite than Bede, who knew everything, Alcuin was an excellent teacher. When he was nearing fifty it seemed as if he were destined to remain until he died rector of a school which was his very reason for existence and his real family. But an accidental journey was to change his fate.

He knew the road to Rome, where in the past he had gone with Aelbert, to acquire piety, relics and books. On a second journey he had the opportunity of being presented to King Charlemagne at Aix-la-Chappelle. A third led him to Rome in 781, when he went there in order to request the pallium for his archbishop, Eanbald, from Pope Hadrian I He was on his way home with this decoration in his baggage when he learned that Charlemagne, on his way to Rome, was staying at Parma. This was an occasion for Alcuin, who was in no particular hurry, to meet the king again. Now it happened that at that very moment Charlemagne was planning to restore instruction in his kingdom, and told him so. Why, after having accomplished his mission on behalf of the Archbishop of York, should Alcuin not return to the Continent to carry out the royal plans? Alcuin hesitated; he was no longer young and he loved his own school. But he finally gave way to the king's insistence, accompanied by enticing promises, for he remembered the words of his old master, Aelbert, who before dying in the previous year had ordered him to take this journey to Rome. Aelbert's command and Charlemagne's offer together appeared to him to prophesy his future road. He left England in 782 in order, in the palace of Aix-la-Chapelle, to become the minister for national education in the kingdom of the Franks. Parma was the beginning of a second career for Alcuin, even more illustrious than the first: 'A new Athens would arise in Francia, and still more beautiful, since ennobled by the teaching of Christ it would surpass the wisdom and teaching of the Academy. The school where Plato had taught shone by the seven liberal arts, but this one, additionally enriched by the wealth of the seven gifts of the Spirit, would in excellence surpass all the dignity of profane science.'

Having sprung from the twofold stock of the Irish monks, who by then were given more and more to contemplation, and the Roman monks, who had prepared the ground for it, the tree of Anglo-Saxon holiness and culture had borne fair fruits: Theodore, *qui genuit* Benedict Biscop, *qui genuit* Ceolfrith, *qui genuit* Bede, Aldhelm, Boniface, Egbert, Aelbert, Alcuin, *qui genuit*. . . . And these names, which we may note all stemmed from Northumbria, ruled over whole companies of clerics and of even more monks. Thenceforward, largely thanks to the Anglo-Saxons, a tradition was established—every Churchman worthy of

14. PAGE FROM A
MANUSCRIPT
ON THE
PENTATEUCH
Middle seventh
century.
(*Bibl. Nat., Paris*)

PAGE FROM
THE
ECHTERNACH
GOSPEL.
End seventh
century.
(*Bibl. Nat., Paris*)

15. ST CUTHBERT AND HIS HORSE. From a MS in University Coll. Lib., Dublin.

the name must, according to his abilities, be a man of learning. If, in loyalty to the ideals of the desert, it was not exactly disgraceful to be both a monk and ignorant, the Benedictines of the Isles of Britain, more than any others, contributed towards the development of monachism in the direction of intellectual activities which, although the germ of them already lay within their rule, had not been furthered by their father, St Benedict. But thenceforward in every monastery the school had its appointed place as an institution devoted to culture and holiness.

The women's monasteries also played their part in this advance. They had had their place in the past, among the Celts; notably under St Bridget of Kildare. In Anglo-Saxon circles the great abbesses became one of the ornaments of Benedictine monachism and they were almost as highly thought of as the most famous abbots. We can see the proof of this in the dual monasteries, which included two communities, one of men and the other of women, under the sole leadership of one superior, who might be an abbess. The two communities lived adjacent or at any rate very near to one another, very often sharing a church at which the services for their inmates took place at different times. When the superior was an abbess it was she who received the vows of the monks, appointed the officers, administering and directing the two establishments. This institution was not confined to insular monachism but also flourished on the Continent, notably in Gaul where St Radegunda governed the house of the monks who were in the service of her two monasteries, but it was most popular in the Anglo-Saxon countries.

These abbesses were all ladies of high degree and foundresses of their own monasteries. Ely was governed by Ethelreda, who was first a queen and later became a nun; Princess Ebba of Northumbria ruled at Coldingham. The most famous of them was St Hilda, granddaughter of Edwin, King of Northumbria, and the spiritual daughter of St Aidan.

Hilda, whose name was Walkyra, was a lady of rank, both in the temporal and in the spiritual worlds. Her piety, virtue, culture, and judgment were such that she was obliged to spend a good deal of her time receiving kings, princes, and abbots in search of advice. She was a member of the presidency of the Council of Whitby. Her nuns were exemplary and her monks amongst those held in highest regard. She caused the women as well as the men to learn the Scriptures, and a number of her pupils were appointed to some of the most important ecclesiastical posts.

The most numerous establishments for women[1] were of course simple monasteries, and there, also, the nuns, many of whom were themselves well-born, were governed by abbesses of royal or princely descent. This female aristocracy studied the Scriptures, the Fathers of the Church, read the classics of Antiquity with no thought of evil, occasionally composed Latin hexameters, practised fine handwriting; their embroideries became famous under the name of *opus anglicum*. An Anglo-Saxon monastery founded in 737 by St Frideswida was the origin of Christ Church, Oxford.

But along with their piety and culture these ladies also possessed certain weaknesses. Their distinguished backgrounds were not inevitably advantageous. Those families whose largesse had given them certain rights often transformed these 'parthenons' into hostelries, where they lived on the cheap at the expense of the daughters of God. Many of the nuns were attracted by pilgrimage, from which, as St Boniface observed, they did not always return in a condition of immaculate purity. Sometimes they were only cloistered in a moral sense, which was not invariably without danger to their morals. Even when under vows of poverty the eternal feminine did not lack resources when it came to matters of coquetry. In order to denounce its abuses St Aldhelm had recourse to the florid style he reserved for his days of leisure. These ladies had a liking for fine linen robes dyed violet colour, for purple cloaks, coifs which trailed to the ground, and ribands. They waved their hair with curling-tongs, their hands were well cared for, and their nails so highly sharpened that they were 'like the claws of falcons or hawks'. Others at certain times underwent attacks of grave indiscipline and even savagery.

At Wimborne a rather stern mistress of the novices died, leaving behind her mixed feelings of resentment and relief, whereupon her exultant spiritual daughters, determined to repay themselves with what they considered a reasonable sum of *wergeld* for her injustices, performed certain compensatory rites of a peculiar kind on her tomb. This is Aldhelm's account of the matter: 'The feelings of these young persons, who detested her, were not appeased until, having marked the place of her burial, they could at last reproach her for all her cruelty. More, they mounted the grave-mound, stamping, so to speak, on the unfortunate corpse (*nefastum*), leaping upon it to avenge themselves (*amarissimis*

---

[1] In this and the following paragraph I have followed the plan and directions of D. Cabrol, *L'Angleterre chrétienne avant les Normands*, Paris, 1909, pp. 201–6. Cf. D. Ph. Schmitz, *Histoire de l'Ordre de saint Benoît*, Maredsous, 1956, Vol. VII, pp. 24–9.

insultationibus), relieving their own suffering by insulting the dead. After reprimanding them the Mother Abbess went to inspect the damage and saw that the soil had sunk down half a foot. This subsidence of the soil led her to conclude that the late mistress had been punished, and the ruin of her tomb appeared to indicate that God's judgment had been exercised with severity and justice. She thereupon ordered three days of fasting and psalm-singing, after which, on returning to the cemetery, she saw that the grave, which had been almost empty of earth, had been more or less re-filled by a rising of the soil.' But fortunately such instances to break the monotony of their days were exceptional. There was good discipline in the women's monasteries and the institution of dual monasteries does not seem to have given rise to any inordinate abuses of such close proximity.

In the case of the men their faults were of a less picturesque kind. As everywhere else, there were certain slack communities where the monks, according to Bede, were of use neither to men nor to God. Some of them only had themselves tonsured in order to take advantage of the privilege this gave them to be exempt from compulsory military service. Certain laymen had monastic titles conferred on them, and installed false abbots in their monasteries, charged with collecting together false monks or those who were unfrocked for breaking their vows and drawing fat revenues from these frauds. As in the case of the women, powerful relatives installed themselves in the monasteries, where they disturbed the observances and emptied the communities' coffers. And the national habit of going on pilgrimage to the glory of God also had its adventurers.

These blemishes, however, are barely noticeable on a picture that in so many other respects was so admirable. The great Celtic monasteries, such as Glastonbury (founded apparently by Joseph of Arimathea), Menevia, Llandaff, Bangor, St Asaph, Iona, were complemented by the great Anglo-Saxon monasteries, either of mixed observance or strictly Benedictine, which henceforward came to the forefront—Canterbury, Westminster, Malmesbury, Lindisfarne, Ripon, Peterborough, Melrose, Wearmouth, Jarrow, Croyland, and the school of York. The formerly inimical Celtic and Roman brethren, now completely reconciled, were only rivals in holiness and knowledge.

Yet the influence of Rome, the orientation of culture, the ever more widespread use of Latin as the scholastic and literary language did not, in spite of everything, apply to more than the elite. Side by side with this imported foreign language, and in the very circles where it was most in fashion, the language of the country, in common usage, was also developing its own literature. The story of Caedmon, reported by Bede, although to a large extent legendary, was a proof that among the people the love of their own poetry was as strongly rooted as ever and that even in monastic circles Latin was unlikely to displace it.

Caedmon was a poor cowherd, who worked for a small farmer. He was old and whenever he was junketing with his companions, as the harp passed from hand to hand, he dreaded the moment when it would come to his turn to sing, for he had no voice and rather than face it he preferred to quit them and return to his herd. But one night as he lay sleeping in his stable a man came to him in his dreams and bade him sing. 'I cannot,' he answered him, 'and that is why I left the feast.' But his visitor pressed him, saying, 'Yet there is something that you can sing for me.' 'What should I sing?' 'Sing,' was the reply, 'of the birth of the world.' And the poor old man began to sing of the beginning of the world. The farmer heard of it and took him to see Abbess Hilda of Whitby. The cowherd appeared 'in the presence of learned men'. Certain passages of the Bible were explained to him and he was asked to set them to a chant (*in modulatione carminis*). Next day Caedmon returned with an excellent poem and Hilda immediately took him into her men's monastery where he was set to work seriously on poetic composition, the method being as simple as the man himself. Although he could not read 'he remembered all he had learned by listening and ruminating over it like a very holy animal, and then transposed it into a very agreeable poem. And as they listened to his gentle singing his teachers became his audience.' (Bede.) And Caedmon continued, sometimes to translate, sometimes to paraphrase or to extemporize on passages from the Bible. The name of the great poet Milton has been mentioned in connection with his, but such a comparison, whilst flattering to Caedmon, would be very derogatory to Milton. Caedmon was possibly also the author of a hymn to the Cross of entirely Germanic inspiration, in which certain noblemen made high lamentation over the body of Christ, their leader, and the warriors who died with Him. Among the numerous stone crosses erected by the Anglo-Saxons, the most famous, that of Ruthwell, built towards 665, bears a passage from this poem engraved in runic characters.[1]

Beowulf, the great epic poem written in Anglo-Saxon dialect, was set

---

[1] Runes are a form of alphabetic writing, the precise origin of which is still uncertain, but which the Germans of Scandinavia appear to have used from the third century onwards. The characters are engraved vertically or obliquely on boards of ash or beechwood, on sticks, stones, horns and even metals. There are old runes in Danish, German, English, Gothic, Burgundian, etc. Some of them were of magical significance.

down in Mercia from oral recitation towards the end of the seventh or beginning of the eighth centuries. It recounts the liberation of Denmark by the hero who gave the poem its name. This epic in forty-three stanzas, the oldest in Germanic literature, in many places bears the imprint of Christian influences which attenuate its roughnesses.

The Anglo-Saxon monks, whilst they preserved and propagated Latin culture, also to a very large extent contributed to raise their own language to the literary plane, developing it side by side with the learned Latin they used in the schools. When in the ninth century King Alfred the Great—whose influence on civilization was according to some opinions not at all inferior to that of Charlemagne—wanted to impose at least some degree of culture on his noblemen, he found nothing better to offer them than Latin works which on his orders were translated into Anglo-Saxon; the *Pastoral Rule* of St Gregory the Great; the *Ecclesiastical History of the British Nation* by Bede; with the *Universal History* of Orosius and the *Consolations* of Boethius. These translations, made from original manuscripts written or preserved by monks, are the first examples of Anglo-Saxon literature.

'It is a small number of men with sublime minds who save the world for centuries to come.' This reflection, which Newman applied to St Benedict, also holds good with regard to his Anglo-Saxon successors. It is paradoxical to note that it was in these distant lands, apart from the Roman world, which had not penetrated very far into them at the time of the conquest, at the very moment when the Continent was not yet freed from the barbarism of the Franks, and Italy was the prey of the Lombard occupation—that it was here that Churchmen, the indigenous Celts and the Romans who had been brought there, together with the Germans who had settled in them, turned insular Britain into the refuge of a civilization which elsewhere was going through hard times, and also into a base of departure for new conquests.

THE ANGLO-SAXON MISSIONARIES TO THE GERMANS: ST BONIFACE

The Anglo-Saxons, invaders of insular Britain, converted to Christianity and the guardians of Western culture, were now to undertake the conquest of the German populations whom their tribes had left in the past in order to sail westward. Their invasion this time was a completely peaceful one, taking the form of voluntary exile, pilgrimage for Christ's sake and missionary work. The new missionaries, backed by the Celts

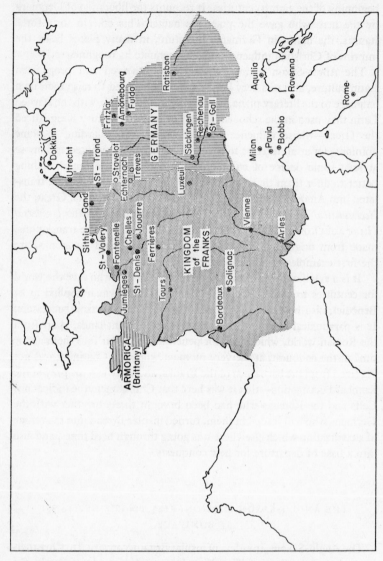

5. Monastic Gaul in the seventh to eighth centuries

and the Franks, were to win by the Cross nearly as much land and as many people as their ancestors had conquered by force of arms. And the new Christians would in their turn become civilized.

By extending the kingdom of God eastwards the missionaries in part made up for the appalling catastrophe that Christianity had suffered in the south. Since the death of Mahomet in 632 only eighty years had passed before the horsemen of Allah, as the Tharaud brothers called them, were able to water their horses in the Indus in the East, and in the West, set up their tents behind the Pyrenees. The green standard of Islam flew over two-thirds of the then known world, and over half of Christendom; Syria, Egypt, North Africa, and Spain paid tribute to Islam. In the Christian East, Arab squadrons on several occasions attempted the capture of Constantinople. In Gaul, where they had obtained a foothold in the district of Narbonne, they travelled up the Rhône and the Saône, ravaged Burgundy, and threatened the tomb of St Martin in the west. When he defeated them at Poitiers in 732, exactly one hundred years after the death of the Prophet, Charles Martel, although he did not completely free the country of them and without foreseeing the full consequences of his victory, saved Western Christendom. And at that moment the Anglo-Saxon Benedictines were already at work in the north-east of the kingdom of the Franks.

We do not know how the Rule of St Benedict was introduced into Gaul. D. Schmitz makes the reasonable supposition that the comings and goings of the Benedictines between England and Rome helped it to become known there. In any case, as we saw with St Columban, at a very early date the code of Monte Cassino tempered and rounded out that of Luxeuil. Thus it happened in Gaul as with the Scots, that the amalgamation of the two forms of observance was only a stepping-stone until the time when the Benedictine Rule eliminated all the others, estimated by D. Schmitz as in the region of twenty.

Thanks to St Columban, and after him to his semi-Benedictine followers, monachism in Gaul took rapid steps forward. The bishops were all the more favourably inclined towards this innovation because it placed the monasteries under their jurisdiction, a detail that Columban systematically overlooked. Those in power, even when not themselves leading very Christian lives, were often generous towards the monks, and lesser folk also contributed their mite. Monastic properties, although encumbered by certain definite commitments, notably that of charity, were in some cases of vast proportions. St Benedict's influence became even greater towards the end of the century when his relics, which had been abandoned after the burning down of Monte Cassino by the

Lombards in 577, were secretly brought to Fleury-sur-Loire (today St Benoît sur Loire) in about 673.

In the north of Gaul, in the Rhinelands, and further east, however, the situation was a very different one from the remainder of the country. In spite of all their faults and their anarchism the Merovingians revealed a sense of continuity in endeavouring to establish themselves more and more securely beyond the Rhine. Governors such as Pippin of Herstal, Charles Martel, and Pippin the Short, strengthened this political line. They either dominated or in any case made their military power and influence felt in the geographical region which to a great extent became Charlemagne's own—Friesland, a long coastal strip extending from the island of Walcheren to the mouth of the Weser, Saxony, through which this river ran, Thuringia, stretching from the Saale to the Danube, Alemania, the country of the upper Rhine and upper Danube, and Bavaria, to the south of the Danube. All these regions were almost entirely heathen, and there was little doubt that they would become much more manageable once they were converted to Christianity.

During one hundred years, from the middle of the seventh to the middle of the eighth century, they became the field of intense activities by the missionary monks. We have described those of St Columban and St Gall on the road along the Rhine. In Alemania, St Fridolin founded the dual monastery of Säckingen. In the same region St Pirmin, who came from the Narbonne district, after having founded Reichenau on Lake Constance, organized his foundations into a kind of Benedictine congregation. He died in 753. In Bavaria St Rupert (d. 715) settled in a place known for its salt mines, which was to become Salzburg. St Emmeran and St Corbinian also worked in Bavaria. Towards 689 the Irish St Kilian was murdered in his chosen apostolic field in Thuringia. But all those names are slightly overshadowed by those of the three great pioneers—St Amand around the Scheldt, St Willibrord in Friesland, and St Boniface in the heart of Germany.

Although he was born in Aquitania, Amand was not for that reason a southerner, since in the seventh century Aquitania stretched from the Loire to the Pyrenees. A native of the region of Herbange, and in fact of the Vendée, he received his monastic training at the Ile d'Yeu, going from there to Tours, where he was tonsured, and after fifteen years of voluntary seclusion at Bourges, according to his hagiographer went on pilgrimage to Rome. 'There he kissed with enthusiasm the thresholds of the churches of the holy apostles' and as the consequence of a pious misadventure received his mission from St Peter in person. Having succeeded in having himself shut into a church that he might spend the night in prayer there, Amand was discovered and thrown out by the sacristan. He obstinately decided to remain and await the dawn on the church steps. It was there that St Peter appeared to him and ordered him to Gaul. The idea on which he had been for a long time brooding, of becoming a pilgrim exile, definitely took shape at the very tomb of the apostle, with the Roman Pontiff's blessing.

Fortified by the Pope's instructions he also took care to win over King Dagobert, asking him for letters in which it should be stipulated that those who refused baptism would be constrained to accept it by the secular powers, which, however, does not appear to have happened. Dagobert was not so pleased when the saint dared to reproach him for the scandal of his royal harem, but he was intelligent enough to realize that in working for God the missionary was also working for the king of the Franks and continued faithfully to support him.

The area of Amand's activities lay around the Scheldt and the Lys, as well as Tongres to the east of the Black Forest, and at Antwerp. Towards 636 he founded in the middle of the swamps a monastery as a base for his missions—Elnone, from the name of the river Elnon (St Amand les Eaux). Jonas of Bobbio, St Columban's hagiographer, worked under him for three years, and to him we also owe a *Life* of St Amand: 'Either because of the fierceness of the people or on account of the sterility of the land,' he wrote, 'no monk until then had undertaken to convert that country.' Amand, who had been consecrated as bishop, worked unremittingly in the midst of a population under the control of charlatans, fortune-tellers and sorcerers. They were heathens who worshipped sacred trees, interpreted the song of the birds, planned their activities according to the phases of the moon, dressed up as calves or deer on the first day of the year, celebrated the solstices with dances and ceremonies, invoked demons and local deities, and on Thursdays and holy days ate caterpillars and rats. The apostle sought the collaboration of the local landed proprietors, slowly felt his way, took soundings, occasionally losing patience, but where he felt some hope of success he built a church and a monastery, leaving a few brethren in charge of the mission, and proceeding on his way. Sometimes he was driven off, molested, and even thrown into the water, but he held good, from time to time with the help of some impressive miracle.

The most famous of these, at least according to his hagiographer, was the resurrection of a man who had been hanged. Some poor devil, a victim of the vindictive populace and the brutality of the Frankish Count Dotton, was dragged to the gibbet after what was politely called an interrogation. Amand unsuccessfully tried to intervene on his behalf, and after having established the unfortunate man's death, took him down and carried him to his own cell. He prayed all night and at dawn asked the brethren to bring him water. 'The latter thought that this was in order to prepare the body, as was customary, for burial, but when they entered the cell they suddenly saw this man, whom they had left for dead, sitting beside the man of God, hale and hearty, and talking to him . . . He washed his body and dressed his wounds, so well that no trace remained of the beating he had received before he was strung up . . . The news of this miracle spread far and wide through the land and the inhabitants rushed in crowds to the saint, humbly begging him to make Christians of them.'

In addition to his difficulties with the heathens, Amand had others with the local clergy. When he was raised to the see of Malines, in order to obtain obedience he had recourse to the Holy See. A letter from Pope Martin I recommended him to prevent the promotion to higher orders and if necessary to depose from them 'priests, deacons, and other persons in the priesthood who sully their station after ordination'. It was the bad faith of these clerics that in a moment of discouragement persuaded him to undertake at the end of his life, and without much success, two missionary expeditions; one to the Slavs of Carinthia, 'captives in the devil's net' and the other beyond the Pyrenees, to the Vascons (Basques) 'misled into grave error'.

But in fact his vocation was only really successful in Flanders. Amand was the prototype of the wandering bishop of the countryside. Although his achievement was not among the greatest, in spite of certain improvisations it remained firm and lasting. Among others we owe him the foundations of the monasteries of St Peter and St Bavon in Ghent. The apostle of Belgium died towards 676.

Further north, that part of Friesland that stretched from Toxandria southwards to the present Zuyder Zee, was the field of St Willibrord, an Anglo-Saxon from Northumbria. When he was very young he entered Ripon as a lay monk, where his teachers were the famous Abbot Wilfrid, a missionary in his day, and the monk Ceolfrith. But he did not remain at Ripon. When he was twenty—apparently at the time when Wilfrid, dissatisfied with the organization of the Northumbrian dioceses, left for Rome—Willibrord took ship for Ireland, which had a high reputation for learning. He was received there at the monastery of Rathmelsigi, of the Benedictine obedience, under the direction of Abbot Egbert.[1] There he remained twelve years.

[1] We must distinguish between this Egbert of Ireland, who died in 729 or 730, and Egbert of Northumbria, Archbishop of York, previously mentioned, who died in 766.

At Rathmelsigi there was much talk of pilgrimage to the land of the Frisians, virgin territory which, when Bishop Wilfrid, Bishop Eloi, and Bishop Amand had set foot there, had refused to embrace the religion of the Frankish bishops, who were suspected of being the agents of the invaders. At Rathmelsigi it was thought that where the Franks had not succeeded Anglo-Saxons might do so. The Father Abbot enthusiastically encouraged the future pilgrims of Christ in his monastery and before the winter of 690 Willibrord, with eleven monks, arrived at Katwijk, at the mouth of the Rhine.

Pippin of Herstal, 'a powerful man, famous for his triumphs and his good morals [sic]'—according to Alcuin, ruled the country. He accepted the missionary because 'he did not wish to deprive his nation of so learned a doctor', whom, clearly, he knew little enough about but whom he intended to make use of in order to spread the Gospel and at the same time strengthen his own influence. Willibrord on the other hand thought that his Anglo-Saxon origin would enable him to make contact with the heathens in spite of the protection extended to him by the all-powerful governor. He installed himself temporarily at Antwerp and then proceeded to Rome, where Pope Sergius I having bestowed the name of Clement on him, he was consecrated bishop-delegate to Friesland. He then established his see and missionary base at Utrecht, a former Roman camp, which on its islet was still a stronghold in this Barbarian country. Then, further to the south, in a villa which had been given him by Irmina, Pippin of Herstal's mother-in-law, he founded a monastery as his second base and also, if necessary, a refuge. Meanwhile he incessantly travelled through those parts of the country that were beyond the reach of the Franks, even as far as Denmark, where, however he was unsuccessful in spite of having worsted the sacred animals on the island of Heligoland, to the annoyance of King Radbod.

In 714, on the death of Pippin of Herstal, this Radbod, who had only been awaiting this opportunity, invaded the country. The mission of Utrecht, regarded as one of the enterprises of the hated overlord, was destroyed. Willibrord barely had time to retreat to Echternach, which had become the chief monastic centre for the whole country, and did not return to Friesland until four years later, behind the chariots of Charles Martel. Whilst he had still been at Echternach the Anglo-Saxon monk Wynfrith arrived in his turn in Friesland but then went away again. Now, however, after a journey to Rome and a sojourn in Thuringia he reappeared at Utrecht. The future Boniface remained for two years at the mission school of Willibrord, who wanted to appoint him as his successor, but returned to the south-east to follow his own vocation.

Willibrord's methods were simple. Like all the Anglo-Saxons he worked together with Rome. In order to reach the heathen people he tried first to win over the chiefs in the hope that their subjects would follow them, and tried to impress them by spectacular acts, sometimes, however, at his own expense. He was supported by the temporal power with help, protection, and donations, but this was at the risk of finding himself embroiled in the fortunes of politics and war. The heathens undoubtedly did regard the missionaries as the agents of the Franks, but it is equally certain that without the latter's protection the missionaries' advances were always precarious. Willibrord was only able to work with the means at his disposal, yet it is noteworthy that that same heathen king, Radbod, who destroyed the mission at Utrecht, did not throw out the future St Boniface when he first made contact with the Frisians.

Willibrord died at Echternach in 739, leaving behind him a legacy of richly endowed and well administered foundations, whilst his spiritual conquests in the Antwerp region, to the south of the present-day Netherlands and the Duchy of Luxemburg, were destined to prosper.

We have told how in his monastery at Nurstling the monk Wynfrith, a famous teacher, resolved to sacrifice the pleasures of study to heroic pilgrimage. After the failure of his efforts to convert King Radbod he returned to England. Nurstling wished to appoint him abbot, but he refused and once again set out. He decided to make a detour via Rome, where Pope Gregory II changed his name to that of Boniface, and after his sojourn with Willibrord he plunged into the forests of Germany.

Boniface, in full mastery of his apostolate, knew no rest during thirty years, from 722–54, consolidating the existing Christian foundations and creating new ones. He spent two missionary years in Hesse, ten in Thuringia, six in Bavaria and central Germany, six more in reforming the Frankish Church. He left behind him more than sixty monasteries in Germany. Some of them were already in existence before his arrival there, but we owe the most famous of them to him.

Consecrated bishop in 722, archbishop in 732, he would only work on the closest terms with the see of Peter. He went to Rome on three occasions and throughout his life was faithful in word and deed to the Roman faith of his episcopal consecration. He lived under four Popes— Gregory II, Gregory III, Zacharias, and Stephen II, all of whom thought highly of him, and with whom he kept up so regular and detailed a correspondence that although he was outspoken and very active in his own domains one might be inclined to think that when it came to Rome he lacked all initiative. Many of the Celts were inclined to wander about aimlessly among the Barbarian tribes, starting up projects that did not endure, whereas Boniface, although he also for long years had been an itinerant bishop, always made sure of the approval of his plans by the popes, and there is little doubt that this was one of the reasons for his success.

Like Willibrord and almost all of the missionaries at that period, he thought it necessary to rely on the temporal powers; but, luckier in his missions than his old master, he was not compelled to quit his foundations. He wrote that without the protection of the Franks he would have been unable to control the peoples he converted, to protect his clergy, or to attack superstition. He even declared that failing the prince's mandate and the fear he inspired (*sine mandato et timore*), his efforts would have been in vain. In spite of this, nothing leads us to conclude that he was a political time-server and propagandist, yet it is a fact that his missionary work did help to strengthen the hegemony of the Franks deep into the heart of Germany and make the Rhine no longer a frontier but an axis.

His old friend Daniel, Bishop of Winchester, advised him to base his evangelical work on the methods that Gregory the Great had recommended to his Roman missionaries to the Anglo-Saxons. Calm and moderation were preferable to vexatious and irritating practices (*non quasi insultando vel irritando*). Should the heathens cling to their former gods it were easy to prove to them the silliness of doing so; those whom they took to be gods were only men without power over all things and their cult was mere superstition. They did not punish the Christians who were attacking them—a very sound argument—and—a more questionable argument—the Christians lived in lands that produced wine and oil in plenty, whilst the heathens only possessed lands that were poor, foggy, and cold. By means of these dialectics Boniface was to convert thousands.

He did not hesitate on occasion to give them demonstrations which immediately proved the man's mettle to these simple folk. At Geismar, not far from Fritzlar, in the depths of the forest was an oak tree famous for its beauty and venerated as part of the local cult. Boniface decided to hew it down, not in order to defy the heathens, who knew him to be under protection and were even well disposed towards him (*intra se devotissime devotabant*), but in order to prove to them that by cutting down a sacred tree with impunity the Christian God was the only powerful and therefore the only true one. On the appointed day Boniface and his followers appeared on the spot, surrounded by a huge concourse of people who had come to watch the judgment of God. No sooner was the oak-tree struck than it crashed to the ground with a thunderous noise, 'as if blown down by a divine breath of wind' and split into four equal parts. This demonstration was a striking success; the wood, no longer sacred, was used to build an oratory in honour of St Peter.

Although he had become an exile in order to serve God Boniface still remained in very close contact with his friends in Britain, whence he drew reinforcements. His assistants were nearly all Anglo-Saxons and he was sent books as well as subsidies, for in spite of his missionary work he had not lost his love of reading. Thanks to the help of those left behind he was able to found, in well-chosen spots, monasteries which were at the same time houses of prayer, teaching centres for his catachumens, schools for his monks, and where he himself might rest in between campaigns. They included Amoeneburg, Fritzlar, Ohrdruff, Benediktbeuren, and especially Fulda. The site for Fulda was discovered by one of his disciples who came from Norica, the monk Sturm. Little Sturm, as he was familiarly called, was the perfect monk. He loved the Scriptures, had commonsense, spoke in measured tones and led a blameless life. He was young and handsome, but so dignified in manner that he seemed like a middle-aged man (*gressu composito*). Above all he loved solitude, and his biographer several times called him 'Boniface's hermit'.

One day the bishop, having blessed him, sent him out with two companions to discover a suitable spot for founding a monastery in the forest of Buchenwald. This Buchenwald, or Beech Forest, which at that time covered a part of central Germany, had a sinister reputation; it was a desert, where one glimpsed only earth and sky, and its enormous trees, with their thickset branches, grew so closely together that the squirrels could cover miles simply by hopping from branch to branch. It was even more fearsome on account of the wild animals that roamed about in it. Two rivers ran through it, the Fulda and the Werra, and at their point of confluence, where Münden lies today, became the Weser.

On leaving Fritzlar the three monks penetrated into the fastnesses of this solitude. After marching on for a couple of days they thought that they had found the desirable spot and there proceeded to build cabins of tree-bark. Sturm returned to give a description of it to Boniface, who, however, thought his choice injudicious on account of its proximity to the Saxons, who were reputed to be cruel. Sturm went back and this time turned directly southwards, remounting the course of the Fulda. But having explored this region without finding a suitable place, he returned to the cabins of his first encampment. Boniface, having sent for him to Fritzlar, ordered him to pursue his explorations.

Indefatigably obedient, Sturm saddled a donkey, took a few provisions with him, and departed alone. It was a difficult and dangerous journey, during which he had to be constantly on his guard. At night, in order to secure his donkey against the wild beasts, he was obliged with his axe to cut down bushes and brushwood out of which to make some kind of shelter in which the animal might rest in safety. Only twice did he meet with human beings. The first time it was a band of Slavs, who were swimming in the river and frightened his mount, unused to the sight of naked men in the monachal stables of Fritzlar, and whose stench repelled the monk in spite of the fresh air and water. His second encounter was more satisfactory. One evening, as he was preparing for nightfall, Sturm heard, apparently, the sound of water. Not daring to raise his voice, he struck a tree-trunk with his axe. A man then appeared, with a horse on a leading-rein. He knew the place perfectly and described it exactly; they were in the heart of the Forest of Oaks. Having slept side by side they parted next morning with a mutual benediction. Sturm, who until then had noticed nothing in particular, now saw that he had discovered the ideal spot 'And the further he went, round and about (*gradiebatur*), the happier he became (*gratulabatur*).'

When Boniface was informed of Sturm's discovery, he asked the governor, Carloman, to grant him the land; and Carloman not only did so but imperatively ordered the local landowners, who did not look too kindly on the establishment of a colony of monks in their midst, to treat them amiably and generously, which was done. In the depths of winter Sturm settled down there with seven monks. In the spring, two months later, Boniface arrived with crews of workers. This is the story of Fulda, the glory of monastic Germany, founded in 741 or 744. The orders Boniface gave the monks there were as simple as those he had given to the pioneers of Fritzlar when writing to them in 735: 'Tatwin will be abbot. Let the priest Wigbert teach the children their rule, the canonical hours and all the *cursus* (offices) of the Church. Let them preach to the others, be the teachers of children and teach the Word of God to our brethren. Let Hidde be provost and take charge of our serfs, and let Hunfrid assist him according to his needs. Let Sturm be in the kitchen. Let Bernard be mason and construct our little cells when it may be useful. And ask Abbot Tatwin for everything you need, and all that he tells you to do, do it.'

After a training period at Monte Cassino, Sturm became abbot. Boniface came there every year, for it was his favourite resting-place. When Sturm died, Fulda, a monastery of strict observance, where only the lightest of beer was drunk (*tenuis cervisia*), counted 400 monks, some of whom lived within the abbey, the remainder on the outskirts. When he considered that his creation was sufficiently consolidated, Boniface decided to bring over nuns from England. This was no novelty, for Anglo-Saxon Benedictine nuns were already established in Bavaria and along the Rhine, notably at the place which was soon to be named after St Odile, who died in 720. But by the choice of his first abbess and the services he expected from his nuns St Boniface's female foundations were to acquire a reputation unequalled until then. He had left at the monastery of Wimborne one of his cousins, Lioba, of whom he was very fond, and who herself was pleased to correspond with him. Lioba, like many nuns, was a fluent writer, and from time to time she would send Boniface a little poem, which she asked him to correct for her, obviously enjoying this intellectual relaxation. Lioba was a perfect nun, pious, learned, and a passionate reader. She was amiable and possessed sound judgment. Boniface persuaded her to take up without hope of return the pilgrimage into a heathen land, 'for the relief of his own pilgrimage and to have a helper in the accomplishment of his mission'. With her first companions he installed her on the Tauber, at Bischofsheim. 'Careful never to teach others anything she had not first done herself,' Lioba, abbess, educationalist and auxiliary of the missions, conducted her monastery in every way as well as Boniface could have wished. Following her example and under her instigation several monasteries for women were founded in Germany; Schornsheim, Kitzingen, Ochsenfurt.

A nun of high quality, Lioba was revered and loved, especially by Boniface's monks. When on arriving one day at Fulda and being invited to be seated amongst them for the choral office, she accepted this incredible invitation with good grace. Boniface cherished her as if she had been his sister or his daughter. When leaving on his last mission he requested that his body might be laid beside that of Lioba, 'in order that side by side they might await the resurrection, since during their lives they served Christ with the same devotion and the same passion' (*pari voto et studio*). But this wish was not to be granted. Boniface was buried at Fulda and Lioba, who died in 782, at Schornsheim.

After 737 the bishop created on the field of his conquests the bishoprics of Bavaria, Hesse, and Franconia. But this was a mere beginning. In 741 he was asked by Carloman and Pippin the Short to restore order in the Frankish Church. His spectacular successes as a missionary have sometimes obscured his ungrateful task as a reformer in the eyes of some historians. Yet this latter activity was the more important of the two, for whilst it is easy to find men good at conversion, efficient and humanitarian disciplinarians are far less easily come by.

The Frankish Church, which under the Merovingians had already fallen very low, had not improved under the Pippinides. Not that at any time had there been a dearth of saints to follow in the footsteps of St Columban and St Benedict: there were the 'great St Eloi', goldsmith, treasurer of King Dagobert, and bishop; a great number of monks whose names may be mentioned at random among so many—Wandrille, Ouen, Philibert; two Scots, Fursy and Fiacre; the bishop St Leger, who was murdered after a horrible 'passion'; the queen, St Bathilda, who made many foundations and ended her days as a nun at Chelle in 680. There were others of lesser degree.

There had never been more monasteries in the West and especially in the land of the Franks than from the end of the seventh century until the middle of the eighth. Nor were they ever put to greater trials, as were also the bishoprics as far as concerned the standards of their vocation. This crisis was due partly to their great wealth, partly to the corruption of certain individuals but even more to the political situation and certain very special practices. The anarchic strife between the Austrian and Neustrian Franks had spread to the Church as a whole; in many cases the victors simply took over as booty of war the ecclesiastical and monastic properties that lay ready to their hands. The incursions of the Saracens, sometimes with the support of Frankish dukes, caused damage for which the victory of Poitiers provided no compensation; they ravaged Gascony and Poitou, ruined monastic Provence, sacked the valleys of the Rhône and the Saône, and devastated the countryside as far as Autun, Dijon, and Troyes. Charles Martel's counter-offensives only increased the general desolation.

Inside the Church the situation had deteriorated even more. A number of bishoprics, endowed by the kings, at their designation were given to individuals, whether clerics or laymen, whose devotion to their princes was more to be admired than their way of life. During long years episcopal sees remained empty in order that their revenues might revert to laymen. Embezzlement, simony, and other unmentionable practices were the general rule, and in this trafficking the monasteries were a choice prey, for most of them owed their very existence to the generosity of the great—kings, princes, or bishops. In theory these grants were supposed to have become Church property and as such inalienable from it, but in fact the donor, under whose protection they were, remained in possession of them. It was no longer the Church as an emblem of morality charged with administering God's patrimony who owned them, but private individuals who held their title deeds. It was they who either chose or caused to be elected abbots whose role was simply that of a docile administrator. Whenever they found it advantageous or convenient they handed over monastic property to some powerful person, most frequently to the king, the all-powerful 'protector'. He in his turn disposed of it as he wished, either to ecclesiastics or laymen, whether worthy or unworthy, whom it was to his own interest to conciliate or else simply as a reward. Hugues, bishop of Rouen, who was considered a saintly prelate, combined among other benefices the abbeys of Fontenelle and Jumièges with the bishoprics of Paris and Bayeux. There were lay 'abbots' or laymen abetted by assistant abbots who were merely their tools. On occasion those who held these foundations would reduce the number of monks in them to the lowest possible number in order to have fewer mouths to feed and thus to increase their own profits. The monks, then, in order to live, became beggars, tramps, or even worse. Thus the monasteries passed from their protectors to their possessors. Although Charles Martel was favourable to the Church it was nevertheless he who, for the sake of his own policies, was more responsible than anyone else for certain unfortunate circumstances that later characterized the feudal regime.

Nor were these the only evils. Boniface's correspondence contains much circumstantial evidence of others. Bishops and priests, unbridled fornicators (*acerrimi*), claimed to have received licence from the pope to practise their ministries, not without considerable profit to themselves. The older ones amongst them claimed (with some slight exaggeration) that no councils had taken place for more than eighty years. The metropolitan organization had been disrupted to the point of non-existence and clerics without morality (*scortatores*) were promoted to bishoprics. Individuals who since childhood had been brought up in vice were appointed to deaconates whilst keeping four or five concubines, succeeded in a similar state to presbyteries, and if they were able to manage it, to bishoprics, without in any way changing their mode of living. Among the bishops some, who were not adulterers, nevertheless spent their time in drinking and hunting and behaved like mercenaries, gaily and indifferently spilling the blood of Christians and heathens. The lower clergy wallowed in ignorance. Boniface described a priest who performed baptism *in nomine patria et filia*. Rural priests believed in the superstitions they were supposed to be fighting. Neglected by their bishops they were little inclined to obedience, but much more interested in arranging their lives according to their own convenience and too often living in vice.

To this general picture may be added several details of a somewhat exceptional nature quoted by Boniface. The priest Aldebert was a false bishop, a strange creature, half hypocrite, half believer, who made a point of saving Christians without recourse to the sacraments and who gave absolution without prior confession. An angel of God had brought him some all-powerful relics (according to Boniface 'of dubious sanctity'). Aldebert built churches in his own honour, erected crosses around the countryside, and distributed his own private relics—his nail-parings and hair-clippings. Claiming that it had come from Christ Himself, he produced a letter which had fallen from the skies at Jerusalem, and reached his own hands. Impudence of this nature had the greatest success. Among other examples of it were the cases of the Scot, Clement, priest and false bishop, who was even more than heretical, a particularly notorious loose-liver. Milon, Bishop of Treves and Rheims, was killed in a boar-hunt, and his colleague of Mayence, Gewiliob, stained his hands with murder.

Among such characters Boniface found no friends. And in addition they charged him with being an Anglo-Saxon and as such unqualified to reform a foreign clergy that, comfortably settled in its vicious ways, proved more difficult to convert than the most inveterate heathens. Nevertheless, strongly supported by Rome and the princes, he went to work, organizing or influencing a series of councils in which laymen of high degree participated by the side of the prelates—the Germanic Council, the site of which, in 742, has not been identified; the Council of Estinnes (Hainaut) in 743 for Austrasia; the Council of Soissons in 744 for Neustia, and Councils for the whole kingdom in 745 and 747.

The ecclesiastical metropoles were reconstituted. The bishops were to make submission to their archbishop, and the priests to their bishop. False priests and deacons, as well as debauched clerics, were deposed, not always without difficulties. All clerics were forbidden to hunt, 'to range the forests with a pack of hounds' and to raise either hawks or falcons. All heathen practices were forbidden to the populace—sacrifices to the dead, prediction, sorcery, charms and auguries. All the monks were to militate under the Rule of St Benedict, which already was becoming more and more widespread. These Councils also provided for the restitution of those ecclesiastical or monastic possessions confiscated by Charles Martel, but this was a delicate matter since the governors could not carry this reform through without weakening or upsetting their benefactors. This was understood and an agreement was arrived at; only part of these possessions were to be restored to their ecclesiastical proprietors; as for the remainder, the beneficiaries were to pay an annual income to the church or monastery which had formerly been despoiled of them; (right of precarium). This system upheld the principle of proprietary rights and in fact, as E. Lesne pointed out, the prince's beneficiaries, who were his supporters, continued to draw substantial advantages from it, whilst on their side certain monasteries still retained considerable, even although less extended properties.

In order to achieve these results Boniface needed all his courage. For a time even Peppin the Short held aloof from him. Although Gewiliob was deposed from his see of Mayence, Aldebert and Clement did not receive the punishment they deserved. Boniface, who until then had been an archbishop without a see in Austrasia, was given the see of Mayence instead of that of Cologne. 'The Franks have not kept their word,' he wrote to Pope Zachary on this subject. At the Council of 747, which convoked the whole Frank kingdom, there were only thirteen bishops; this abstention of his colleagues tells its own story.

Yet in spite of his difficulties Boniface was the first personage in the Church of the Franks. The moment had arrived when he was to come out openly in favour of the Carolingians, his protectors, for the future of the crown and the inclusion of the temporal power within the Church. His policy, a merely preliminary one which, however, was to be followed by more striking results, is worth examining.

In 687 Pippin of Herstal, governor of Austrasia, definitely defeated the Neustrians near Péronne, at Tertry. Since then, in spite of the obstacles which later arose, the governors of Austrasia were in fact the masters of the *Regnum Francorum*. By saving the country from the Moslem threat Charles Martel appeared as the champion of Christianity. One of his sons, Carloman, entered holy orders, and the other, Pippin, known as the Short, worked energetically at unifying the kingdom. The Merovingian kings, more weak-kneed than ever, who until then had been suffered as figureheads, were destined to disappear from the scene.

In 750 Pippin, considering that the powers he held in fact should belong to him by right, decided to make an end of the descendants of Clovis. Burchard, Bishop of Wurzburg and a disciple of Boniface, and Fulrad, Abbot of St Denis, were sent to Rome on a mission to ask Pope Zachary if it were just that there should be kings in France who did not hold royal authority? To which the Pontiff replied that 'it were better that he who held royal authority were called king rather than he who did not hold it, to the end that the order of things should be upheld.' The conclusion to be drawn from these words was an obvious one.

This embassy had, naturally, been carefully prepared for. When planning his coup d'état Pippin was anxious not to appear to be an usurper, and it would indubitably be legalized if his demand were upheld by the formal approval of the papacy. On his side the Roman

Pontiff found it advantageous to meet him in the matter. He was threatened by the Lombards, who were exploiting Italy to their own advantage, and ill-disposed towards the Byzantine emperors, who still obstinately held to their claim of universal imperialism. The only way out he saw was by means of the Franks, whom he thought sufficiently powerful to free him both from the Lombards and from the tutelage of the *basileis*, whose bases in Italy, notably at Ravenna, were still strong ones.

In 751, after having received the Pope's reply, Pippin sent Childeric III, the last Merovingian king, back to his convent of Sithiu (St Bertin), from which he had been brought out nine years previously. He then summoned a general assembly at Soissons where he had himself 'elected by the people' according to the German custom, and rounded off this political move by a ceremony that was quite extraordinary in the country of the Franks. Pippin was anointed with holy oil, as were Saul and David in the past, and from that moment onwards, by virtue of this ceremony, which in those days was regarded as a sacrament, the people's chosen became God's chosen, the anointed of the Lord was king by divine right. The minister who performed this historical ceremony was the monk Boniface, Bishop of Germany and Papal legate.

By this action, the Church of Rome, in freeing itself from Byzantium, turned definitely towards the West. The kings of the Franks, protectors of the Roman pontiffs, had a mission to intervene in Italy against the Lombards. The sacrament of Soissons, apart from its immediate results as concerned Pippin the Short, had others which were very soon revealed. In 754 when Pope Stephen II anointed Pippin again, he extended the sacrament to his two sons, Charles and Carloman. In exchange he demanded the 'restitution' to the Church of the territories of the Exarchate of Ravenna, which had never belonged to him, but which were to form the kernel of the future Pontifical State. This two-fold prelude led to the expected result when at Christmas in the year 800, Charlemagne was anointed 'Emperor of the West'.

Boniface was now eighty years old. He might have prepared himself for death by strengthening his work as an organizer and reformer, but instead he once more heard the call of the heathen forest. As he was unable to reach Saxony he went further north, among the Frisians, where he had won his spurs. He entrusted his cowl to Lioba, bidding her to remain faithful to her vow of voluntary exile. He bade his disciple Lull, when preparing his baggage, not to forget a chest of books and a blanket 'in which to wrap his decrepit body'. Then, sailing all the way up the Frise he arrived, not far from the North Sea, at a region close to the Zuyder Zee. Boniface led a considerable party, consisting of fifty-two followers. A large number of converts were to come to Dockum, the nearest town, in order to receive confirmation there.

Whilst waiting for them near to his ships, Boniface was reading when he heard a sudden tumult close by. Instead of his expected neophytes a troop of heathens appeared, who seemed more bent on looting than in search of possible martyrs. They swooped on the encampment, brandishing javelins and shields against the men of the convoy who were attempting to halt them. In the general confusion the bishop came out of his tent and called to his followers who were fighting the brigands: 'Enough, men! Here at last is the day I have so long awaited!' More than fifty dead lay upon the ground and among them, Bishop Boniface. According to Alcuin 'a very old woman, who had somehow escaped, declared that she had witnessed the murder of the servant of Christ. She said that when he was about to be struck down he had tried to protect his head with a copy of the Holy Gospel, to soften the blow. And thus he was preserved by the book he had been reading throughout his life'. He died on June 5, 754, and until recently there was on view at Fulda a manuscript, the wooden binding of which was criss-crossed with slashes, and which was alleged to have been Boniface's.

His body was placed on a bier and transported by boat from Dockum to Utrecht. The people of Utrecht, praying and fasting, wished to retain his holy remains, but when they attempted to lift up the body those who stretched out their hands to do so were unable to move them. So they resigned themselves to taking it to Mayence, where Bishop Lull wished to have it. But now Sturm intervened, informing them of the Saint's own wishes; he was to rest at Fulda. A convoy of boats was formed on the Main and travelled up it to Hochheim. When they landed Lull headed the procession to Fulda. Thus the old bishop's wish was granted.

The best of his biographers agree that Boniface had more practical commonsense than actual genius, but this does not in the least denigrate him. On the plane of sanctity his unshakeable faith, his energetic pursuit of his mission, his utter constancy, his trials and fatigues—that one day caused him to say that the sun had lost its brightness for him—were crowned by his 'red martyrdom'. He achieved considerable results, for 'the extension of the kingdom of God' amongst the heathens, the saving of so many souls, the care of them undertaken in close accord with Rome, opened up broad new roads for the Gospel and for civilization beyond the Rhine and far towards the east. Apart from its immediate results, his reform of the Frankish clergy prepared the way for Charlemagne's vast readjustments and made the Carolingian revival possible. It was then not yet possible to raise at one sole step the Frankish Church to the level of the Anglo-Saxon Church, but the Councils organized by Boniface, at first concerned with restoring morality, were already working towards the future. After him and thanks to him the Frankish Church was soon to be able to profit splendidly by the culture of the Scots, Anglo-Saxon, and a few Italian monks.

FOUNDATIONS AND RESTORATIONS IN ITALY

In the seventh and eighth centuries the monastic institutions in Italy presented a different picture from that of the remainder of Western Christianity. The first Benedictines had time and again to work at extirpating the last remaining traces of rural paganism. They were established in regions where the ancient civilization, although rudely shaken up by the first Barbarians, had not been fundamentally disturbed and had even retained enough of its former character to charm the invaders. When the monks took up their task they were not compelled to become missionaries but more simply, as it was said in the Peninsula, to 'turn to good account' the situation as they found it.

Even the invasion and occupation by the Lombards did not altogether put an end to everything as regarded the monasteries. In spite of the lamentable destruction of Monte Cassino we cannot conclude that these new masters were systematically hostile to the monastic idea. At the time of its foundation Bobbio was an exceptional case; nevertheless certain rather slight but definite indications lead us to suppose that as far as the monks were concerned, the Lombard rulers followed a policy more concerned with their own interests than with destruction for its own sake. To quote only one example, Zotto, whose bands destroyed Monte Cassino, took an interest in certain churches and monasteries in the duchy of Spoleto.

In those regions which had escaped the occupation, in the Patrimony of St Peter and especially in Rome, the popes were anxious to preserve the works of St Benedict. Monks were installed around the basilicas, and whatever their numbers may have been they formed a reserve drawn on by Britain throughout the seventh century. In the south of Italy, which was unaffected by the invasion, there were numerous monasteries in Calabria and Sicily, especially Byzantine ones. The conquests of Islam at the beginning of the seventh century and the iconoclastic persecutions of Byzantium from 727 onwards, drove whole troops of monks towards those regions. In Rome itself, during the course of one hundred and thirty-five years, thirteen Greek or Syrian popes succeeded one another on the throne of St Peter, and naturally surrounded themselves with a large number of their own countrymen. We may therefore assume, roughly, that among the monasteries those to the north were more accessible to the Frankish world, those of the centre gravitated around Rome, and those in the south were under the influence of Byzantium.

Yet after the conversion of the whole Lombard nation during the course of the second half of the seventh century Italian monasticism was to flourish exceedingly. The influence of the Frankish monks was a very strong one and equally so that of the Italian popes and monks, who even within the monasteries themselves were attempting to control the Frank and Lombard elements. Lacking sufficient evidence to enable us to know all the reasons for so vast and sudden a movement we can only accept the fact that during the whole of the eighth century Italy was covered with monasteries.

At first these were only a number of little centres which without arousing much interest gradually spread out their branches throughout the Peninsula; small and humble groups that were more like 'cells' than regular establishments, working in depth to solidify the bases of religion. There were also others, bigger and equally numerous. Without claiming that this number was complete D. Schmitz gave a list of forty or so, scattered throughout Italy.

A large number of them were royal or princely foundations, well endowed from their beginnings. There were, however, afterthoughts to these undoubtedly pious donations, for it was always advantageous for a State to possess in a well-chosen spot a religious centre which by its temporal power, the extent of its properties and influence could at the same time if desirable or even by accident, become a centre of political influence. On their side the popes, who had some reason not to have a blind trust in their new converts, and without at a first glance seeing the monasteries as instruments of domination, summed up the matter similarly. Thus the monastic foundations were destined to become little States, territorially homogeneous, like other establishments belonging to their protectors. There were four great names (although they were not the only places to leave their mark) in the eighth century; of these Farfa and Nonantola, Lombard foundations, remained in the jurisdiction of the kings, whilst San Vincente di Volturno and Monte Cassino, of the Roman obedience, were under papal influence, which extended to the confines of the Lombard duchy of Benevento, where St Peter's Patrimony was considerable.

After the death of St Columban Bobbio, a Lombard foundation, began to gather the first-fruits of its future Golden Age, from the ninth to the eleventh centuries. The monks had left the wooden huts of their heroic period and now lived in solid stone buildings. The monastery was ruled by three abbots, two Franks and a Burgundian from Luxeuil, and fifty years after its foundation contained five hundred monks. They were mostly Italians and Lombards, but Celtic monks on pilgrimage never failed to visit it and brought with them precious Irish manuscripts for the library, which was beginning to become an important one. During the middle of the seventh century the Rule was still Columban's, but it was beginning to be influenced by St Benedict's. The Lombard rulers, who were always generous, enriched their first monastery and strangely enough did not let their benefactions weigh upon it. Thenceforward, as has been said, Bobbio became the Monte Cassino of northern Italy.

In 752 or 753 another centre was founded at the *locus Nonantulae*, about twelve kilometres from Modena. Nonantola, like Bobbio, owed its foundation to the generosity of a king, whose name was Astolf. Astolf had found a good spot in which to install his monks, close to the strategic road leading to Bologna, Placentia, Verona, and Tuscany. The abbot, Anselm, was a relative of his, who had left his duchy of Friuli in order to wear the Benedictine habit. Anselm was pious and charitable and opened many refuges and hospices for the pilgrims on the roads around his monastery. But Anselm ran into difficulties, for in 758 King Didier removed him from his post. Anselm then remained for twelve years in monastic exile at Monte Cassino. Didier had deduced he had the right to depose him, according to the custom authorizing a protector to appoint an abbot of his own choice, but from the canonical point of view it was a very different matter; Anselm remained the lawful abbot of Nonantola with the right to appoint a vicar to represent him in his community, in competition with the new abbot, who was regarded as an intruder. This internal crisis did not further the growth of the young monastery, but it does not seem to have aroused any great concern in Roman circles and was of no consequence for the future.

The Farfa is an affluent of the Tiber which runs through the Sabine countryside about forty kilometres to the north of Rome. Virgil mentioned it and Ovid praised its shady banks according to the good old poetic conventions. Along it stood, not far from the Via Salaria, a monastery which was founded either in the fourth or sixth centuries, but which in any case was destroyed by the Lombards. In 690, or a little earlier, a Frank camped on its ruins. His name was Thomas; he came from Maurienne and was a pious pilgrim. He was returning from a long journey into the Christian East, where he had prayed on the Tomb of Christ and revered the memory of the Virgin at Ephesus. He was anxious to rebuild the ruined monastery and applied for a donation to this end to Faraold, Duke of Spoleta. The latter gave it to him, not perhaps without having considered that it might be useful to have a good monastery on the confines of Church domains.

At Farfa, which he rebuilt in honour of the Virgin, Thomas lived the angelic life according to St Benedict and in imitation of Christ received his passing guests personally. One day three young men knocked at the monastery gates. Although they were dressed in sordid rags they were unable to hide their fine features and good breeding. Taso and Tatto were brothers, whilst Paldo was their cousin. They were all three Lombards and intending to go to Rome. Abbot Thomas washed their feet, and charmed by their company, endeavoured to retain them as long as possible. When they at last decided to leave, Thomas would not part with them and went with them. When all of them had abundantly wept together over the tombs of the Apostles he succeeded in bringing them back to Farfa. When their families, becoming anxious at the turn their sons' vocation was taking, came to fetch them home, they were obliged to leave without succeeding, for the three young men had decided to go to Gaul to study the monastic way of life. Now Thomas became anxious and told them that he knew of a spot in the Samnium, on the banks of the river Volturno, where nothing was lacking to satisfy the aspirations of men determined to live in nudity for the sake of Christ's nudity. It was almost inaccessible, with high mountains covered with dense forests, where there were wild beasts and brigands in plenty, a scorching sun in summer, wind and snow in winter. So the three youths decided not to go to Gaul.

On arriving at their destination they found that Thomas had indeed not misled them, for it truly was a dreadful desert. But then a shepherd appeared, with gifts of wine and flour, and vanished again. An angel had obviously descended to succour them; their minds were made up to remain. 'Their bodies might lose weight but their souls would fatten.' Between 703 and 708 their first cabins, containing relics of St Vincent, quickly gave way to a properly constituted monastery.

The first abbot was Paldo, 'the gentlest man on earth', who took care himself to do as he would that others did. He was succeeded by Taso, the youngest of the three, who, however, was too severe a disciplinarian, and unable to use his discretion as recommended by St Benedict, and by so doing bend others to his will. As he was intolerable to them the community replaced him by his brother, Tatto, possibly as the result of a rebellion which, however, their biographer did not refer to. And as this appointment was against canonical law, Pope Gregory II re-established Taso and the monks of St Vincent were obliged to suffer their uncompromising abbot for another eight years. Ambrose Autpert, who reported this incident, did so with good sense: 'No one was to blame, for they all made mistakes, the pastor through excess of zeal and his flock through narrow-mindedness.'

When Taso died Tatto was reappointed abbot. He was gentle and tactful in dealing with his people (*discretione cautissimus*) and altogether 'a mother' to them, especially compared to his predecessor. He was kind to others but mortified himself to the last degree. From the day when he became a monk he never took a bath, never cut his hair or his beard. After having sweated all day at manual labour, he made himself spend most of the night in prayer. He wore a coat of mail (*onus loricae*) next to his skin, and when he became too old to bear its weight he secretly had a belt made of it, which he wore until his death. 'There is no point in renouncing everything, one's country, family, and wealth, if one does not mortify oneself as well.'

This foundation requires some comment. Situated at the rather vague frontier between the Lombard duchies of Spoleto and Benevento, it was neither a royal nor a princely foundation. It was started in complete poverty, without any endowments. When interior difficulties arose there no lay 'protector' intervened, as was the case at Nonantola, although in quite a different matter. The pope himself settled the conflict with no other intervention.

The narrator of this story was a Frankish monk, Ambrose Autpert. A native of Provence he had—we know not how—attached himself to the community of Volturno, at a time when this monastery had been in existence for about seventy years. He was elected abbot after the post had been vacant for three months, which suggests that there may have been disputes among the electors due to rivalry between the Lombards and the Franks. Autpert resigned after a little more than a year in office and when his successor died four years later a Lombard, Potho, was next elected. Potho liked neither the Franks nor Charlemagne, the conqueror of his race, and showed it a little too openly. One day, at the canonical hour of the sext, when prayers for the king were said, Potho ostentatiously left the choir. This was a rash display of temper in a man who ruled a monastery in which a part of the monks belonged to the

Frankish nation and a former Father Abbot was living in embarrassing circumstances. And losing all sense of proportion Potho even had three monks arrested for alleged subversion. When Charlemagne was informed of it he was annoyed, but with due respect for custom left it to Pope Hadrian to deal with the matter. Taking into account the fact that the majority of the monks were Lombards, the Pope re-established Potho in office, which he was all the more easily able to do as Autpert had just died on the road to Rome where he was to bear witness—presumably on orders—in this monks' quarrel exacerbated by nationalist rivalries. The date of this incident was 784.

Among the Benedictines of his day this Ambrose Autpert was a leading personality. Although his writings were not very voluminous they had their importance: sermons and treatises on spiritual questions and exegesis that were of so high a standard as to be attributed in turn to St Leo, St Ambrose, St Augustine, and St Isidore of Seville. He was truly humble and regarded himself as a peasant labourer in the Lord's service (*rusticanus Domini servus*), which no doubt is why he had a very precise sense of spiritual values. His culture, his theological exactitude, his fidelity to the Fathers of the Church combined to make him a writer whose knowledge ranged far beyond the walls of his community.

No one has yet been able to explain the emergence of this perfectly trained mind apparently educated by no known masters. D. Winandy, his biographer, writes of him as, literally, a phenomenon.

And in addition, Autpert was a monk whose intellectual attitude is particularly interesting. He claimed to know nothing of classical Antiquity, stating that although most of the great authors, such as Jerome, Ambrose, and Augustine had absorbed profane literature before approaching the divine Word, he, Autpert, had not wished to provide himself with this kind of intellectual equipment (*non oneratus divitiis*), he owed nothing either to Homer, Plato, Cicero or Virgil, nor to the grammarians. He had gathered all his knowledge, not from the treasure store of Egypt, but from the hoard of learning provided by the Lord (*de horreo dominicae praedicationis*), for he found more satisfaction in the words of the humblest of sinners (*humillimi piscatoris*), than in those of the most magnificent orators.

However that may be this confession of faith appears slightly disingenuous as regards profane literature, to which he admitted he had not been denied access (*non quo mihi et eorum scientia fuerit denegata*) and which apparently served him in good stead. His Latin was clear and simple and seemingly based on good models. It is remarkable that in his *Life* of the three founders he summed up each paragraph in a few perfectly correct hexameters, which by their imagery suggest that Virgil was not very far from his mind. We know what to think of these anathemas ever since St Jerome's time and like him, Autpert confessed to his shame if not to his satisfaction also that he had occasionally gone slightly astray in that direction; and that under the pretext of teaching religion (*sub obtentu praedicationis divinae*) he read the authors of the century more frequently than he should have done (*plus quam decet familiaritate conjungor*).

His deep piety did not impede his critical faculties. Regarding his three heroes he could, he said, have reported many miracles, but with little inclination to do so he preferred to stick to facts (*teneamus potius quod certum habemus*). He observed that many miracle-workers did not for that reason have their names inscribed in heaven. Churchmen were not expected to provide prodigies (*virtutes*), but to set the example of perfection, and in any case the greatest miracle consisted in forgetting the world altogether.

He was confident of his doctrines and stood up under attack for them; for he was attacked, and in such a way that he did not regard it as presumptuous to defend himself proudly and independently before Pope Stephen in person. 'So long as one does not preach anything contrary to the faith one has not to fear condemnation. . . . Those who deserve to be condemned are rather those who wish to abolish freedom of thought. . . . Because humble Christians prostrate themselves that is no reason why freedom should be debased (*non ideo libertas succubuit, quia libertas semetipsam prostravit*)'. These were the words of a man of character, a humanist and a Christian, which should be accepted by all of us as being harmful to none in a case when the rightful defence of a man's dignity is accompanied by true piety.

Autpert, like many other monks, transcribed manuscripts, although, anxious as he was to get on with more important intellectual activities, he was sometimes impatient with this kind of work, that Cassiodorus had classed as manual labour. He nevertheless resigned himself to it with a beautiful prayer that should be a consolation to all faithful scribes: 'Since, in this laborious work of copying, O Lord, I can find no consolation, I address this prayer to Thee—may my hand, as it forms the characters, may my eyes, as they follow the shape of the words, not prevent my heart from exploring the secrets of the mysteries; thus let my heart be on active watch internally and let the work of my hand never falter externally'.

St Vincent in Volturno lay about twenty-five miles as the crow flies from the ruins of Monte Cassino, which had been destroyed by Zotto's

Lombards between 577 and 580. The monks, not one of whom was injured, had then taken refuge in Rome, near the Lateran, carrying away with them the text of their Rule, as well as the weights and measures for fixing their rations of bread and wine. They had had to leave the body of the Patriarch behind.

In Gaul, towards 673, some Frankish monks realized that the possession of this unique relic, shamefully buried under a mass of rubbish, would do high honour to those who having discovered it, would be able to preserve it. The Benedictines of Fleury, on the banks of the Loire, were so intent on this idea that their Father Abbot charged one of them, Agilulf, to make the attempt. As Agilulf was packing his bags some brethren from the Mans knocked at the gates of Fleury requesting hospitality there. On being made welcome and asked the purpose of their pilgrimage they replied that they were on the way to Monte Cassino to rescue the remains of the Patriarch. On hearing this Agilulf with great sang-froid dissembled his emotion and formed a very artful plan, ingenuously asking the Mans monks permission to join their party with a few companions. They saw no harm in it and they all set out together, in fraternal consort, until in the course of their journey it was discovered that Agilulf and his companions had decamped. He had carefully bided his time and now continued his pilgrimage by forced marches.

Arrived on the spot, they were discomfited, for they could find nothing that they had expected to discover, nothing but stones, ruins, rubble, brambles and undergrowth. But they had a cook with them, and much is learned round and about monastic ovens. A cowherd whom they met there, after being given a good meal, told them what he knew of the local topography. Brother cook missed not a word of it, and pursuing the trail between two snacks, found the bodies of St Benedict and St Scholastica beneath the rubble. Agilulf was exultant but lost no time, for the monks from Mans might at any moment arrive. The holy bodies were washed quickly but piously, and then strapped on the back of a horse 'which carried them for a long time without wearying'. They set off by round-about ways and needless to say avoiding Rome, where inconvenient questions might have been asked. With Heaven's help they arrived without misadventure at Fleury.

About forty-five years after Agilulf's expedition Pope Gregory II thought of resettling some monks on Monte Cassino. When receiving a citizen of Brescia called Petronax, who was on his way to the Holy Land, Gregory suggested to him that he should visit the *sanctum corpus* (which was no longer there) and rebuild the monastery, which the

Benedictines of Volturno would help him to do. In deference to the pontiff's advice Petronax took the southern road and climbed up the holy mountain. He found it not altogether deserted, for some hermits (*simplices viri*) were living in the grottoes there. The Brescian settled down with them and between 717 and 720 gradually organized them into a community.

So monastic life returned to Monte Cassino, although one may assume that under Petronax, who was no more than a pious layman, it was still only loosely improvised. Then, in 729, a foreign monk arrived there, an Anglo-Saxon called Willibald, thirty years old. He had passed by there but without stopping, nine years ago, and now, returning from a short pilgrimage to the Holy Land, he had come there again for a rest. He was interested in the new foundation, and although he had not made his profession, he had been well trained in the right observances ever since his childhood in the monastery of Waltham in Hampshire, which his pilgrimage had not caused him to forget. So he decided to remain at Monte Cassino, where he became in turn sacristan, dean—i.e. responsible for a certain section of the community—and porter, another responsible post which required experience and discernment. But above all Willibald set a useful example by living strictly according to the Rule and when necessary advising or guiding, firmly when necessary, the well-meaning but ignorant monks (*sedulis disputationibus admonens*). They liked him, feared him a little, and followed his example sedulously, so that when Pope Gregory III sent him to Germany in 739 to rejoin Boniface (whose *Life* he wrote) Monte Cassino was enabled to continue along the right lines, supported by the generosity of Gisulf II, the Lombard Duke of Benevento.

When Petronax died in 747 or 750, Pope Zachary had presented him with the precious codex of the Rule. Monte Cassino was reorganized, free from all episcopal domination, and depending solely on the Holy See, i.e. granted the privilege of exemption (*nullius ditioni vel juri subditum*). Sturm, St Boniface's companion, went there for a time before finally taking over the direction of Fulda, and so did Ludger, future bishop of Munster. Anselm, the unlucky founder of Nonantola, also knew some respite there. The Frankish King Carloman and the Lombard King Ratchis died there cowled and tonsured. Charlemagne stayed there in 787. The monastery was once again destroyed in 883, this time by the Saracens, shortly after the destruction of Nonantola, but by then, for more than 150 years it had resumed its mission in the world of the monks and Christianity.

CHAPTER VIII

THE BARBARIANS ON THE ROAD
TO CIVILIZATION

By the middle of the eighth century the links between the Western world and the Byzantine Empire had worn thin, and even in the Catholic world no longer existed except in a theoretical sense. Thenceforward there were two separate forms of Christian civilization—the Greek, which at an early date discarded Latin as its official language, and the Latin, which hardly knew any Greek at all. But at that moment, nearly four centuries after the Barbarian invasions, largely thanks to the monks there appeared in the Western world certain definite indications of a new kind of Christian civilization.

ECCLESIASTICAL LATIN AND THE LITURGY

The reason why Latin has been so frequently referred to in the preceding pages is that language invariably reflects contemporaneous civilization. And we have now reached the stage when a new form of Latin was born and developed—Ecclesiastical Latin. Whilst within certain ethnical frontiers national and local languages were developing here and there, this form of Latin was more and more firmly becoming a link ensuring the spiritual unity of Western Christianity during centuries and across all boundaries. It remained throughout the Middle Ages and far beyond them—since even in our own times the various theological schools continue to use it—as the universal language of Catholicism and a means of international communication. Even the humanists of the Renaissance, whatever their prejudices, and however much they abhorred scholastic jargon—which was no longer Latin—owed a great deal to ecclesiastical Latin, and only to mention Erasmus, admired the language of St Jerome. As they improved the quality of the Latin in use both within and outside the Church, in the sciences and in diplomacy,

320

they remained indebted to the live use of the language by the clerics and monks at the dawn of the Middle Ages.

The strong predilection for classical Latin of the authors of the fifteenth and sixteenth centuries has tended to give us a false impression of the importance before their time of Latin as an instrument of culture. To them a return to classical literature and the closest possible imitation of it formed part of an ethical and aesthetic system based on one particular theory of nature and mankind. Their philosophy disappeared with them, but the cult of Latin survived. We know the services it has rendered to the French language and that until quite recently every person of culture prided himself, or at least claimed to do so, on knowing it. A sound knowledge of Latin was supposed to be the basis of all higher education and even to add a touch of intellectual epicurianism to it. But matters stood very differently before the Renaissance, and especially during the period with which we are dealing. Then it was less a matter of imparting culture than of finding a practical instrument of communication. In the universal confusion due to languages that were still in the stage of seeking adequate means of expression, all that was required of Latin was that it should serve for the elaboration and communication of ideas that could be expressed or translated by no other means, especially for the understanding and exposition of Biblical texts that could not be otherwise achieved. Knowledge of Latin was then neither a fashion nor an accomplishment, but a necessity. This did presuppose a certain basic acquaintanceship with classical works, but the use made of this was chiefly for practical purposes.

The juxtaposition of a revived profane culture and a Christian form of culture in constant evolution presented a particularly interesting feature of the new civilization. We have witnessed the real or imaginative dramas experienced by many Christian authors in the name of morality, due to their classical training, whilst others, notably the Scots and Anglo-Saxons, regarded profane literature as an inoffensive foreign source. In time the unavoidable compromises were made as it became clear that the study of grammar, i.e. ancient literature, and the seven liberal arts in general, were indispensable as a stepping-stone to Christian wisdom. This change in attitude took place with varying degrees of broadmindedness, but by the middle of the eighth century it was no longer fashionable to vituperate against pagan literature and when it was still done this seemed more or less in order to reassure those suffering from uneasy consciences in the matter. Among many others St Boniface no longer suffered the nightmares that disturbed the sleep of St Jerome: 'Training and proficiency in the use of grammar are very useful to those who would study the sacred works, for thus they will be helped to understand the subtleties they contain.' He took his stand in the matter unrepentantly, thereby raising the whole cultural level, for from that time onwards we notice that those who graduated in it wrote better Latin.

This ecclesiastical Latin, which from that time onwards was firmly established for the future, included several elements, which varied from region to region and from author to author. It included a strain of classical Latin, one of Biblical and patriarchal Latin, and, particularly in Gaul, one, or more exactly several diverse forms of spoken Latin that were more or less in general circulation everywhere. It has been called a dead language, and to some extent this is true as regards those works deriving exclusively from the schools and under the tyranny of strict imitation. These had all the faults of this particular genre; a lack of spontaneity, stilted phraseology, exaggeration, the use of inapposite metaphors dragged up from mythology, in short, lack of taste and pedantry. But the authors indulging in such 'classicisms' were neither the best nor the majority, and whatever their faults they did ensure a degree of continuity, and together with those who had freed themselves from the schools, contributed to the maintenance of a tradition, i.e. a thread of life. Nor was this Church Latin decadent, although certainly very different from that in use in the days of Caesar and Augustus. But if we only regarded Cicero's as 'good' Latin, we would have to condemn Tacitus's, just as Claudel's French might be dismissed for no longer being that of Bossuet. Far from being either a dead or decadent language ecclesiastical Latin was a living and original language when it was handled by authors sufficiently virile to use it continually and fluently in their own way. Their language was easy, clear to follow, and in a word, new. It had its own 'fathers' and classics—Jerome, Ambrose, Augustine, Pope Leo. Above all it had something to say, which is a true sign of life and a prerequisite of originality. It did in fact include both their national languages and Latin Vulgate, but in spite of its traditional usage it was nevertheless a living language. This applies to all the great monastic teachers with whom we have dealt.

But the use of ecclesiastical Latin was by no means confined within such narrow intellectual limits, and had a far wider application outside them. Through the liturgy it served as an instrument of general religious and cultural education, and the monks were the principal artisans and very often artists to whose achievements this was due.

It would, however, be a mistake to assume that even in the monasteries the Latin liturgy was accessible to all. As we have seen, the monks were not by the same token always intellectuals; many of them had so much difficulty in learning Latin that St Benedict was obliged to find special means of occupation for those who were unable profitably to follow the *lectio divina*. Presumably their plight was similar to that of certain monks in the Greek communities of our own time, who are used to a common everyday language (demotic) and can only with difficulty follow the ancient literary language of their own liturgy. This applied even more generally to Christians as a whole, who certainly did not understand everything that was recited or sung in church. And we must also bear in mind that in many places the performance of the liturgy was threadbare, meagre, and often lamentably inadequate.

This liturgy is divided into two parts—the general recitation of the office and the celebration of Mass.

The office was the very particular duty of the monks, their *pensum servitutis*, a term difficult of translation, which referred to the amount of wool (*pensum*) which a housewife apportioned to each of her servants for spinning each day. As praying—and in the case of the cenobites, collective prayer—was their chief duty, the monks engaged in it at fixed times daily.

Public prayer was practised from the very earliest times, even before the monastic institution came into being. As the Jews did in their synagogues, so the Christians practised it at their meetings. Originally the two regular prayer periods were at dawn and dusk, on lines laid down according to the psalms. But gradually, and with certain variations according to times and places, the pastors of the faithful whenever possible on the one hand, and the ascetics and the virgins on the other, worked out a timetable, assiduously and according to rule, during which, as St John Chrysostom said, they sang God's praises with the angels. The general outlines of this activity were laid down and allocated in Rome at the beginning of the sixth century. The longest period of prayer was at night, when evil spirits were most likely to be abroad; the 'hours' were to be observed at the end of day, dawn and cockcrow; (vespers before the evening meal, vigil or nocturnal, lauds). During the daytime, when everyday duties left them less leisure, prayers were shorter. The lazy ones, who after lauds might try to cheat and go to sleep, were awakened one hour before going to work (six o'clock or prime). There were prayers every three hours throughout the day (tierce, sext, and nones). Then after the evening meal, when the day's work was done, there were again prayers before bedtime, at nightfall (*completorium* or compline). Thus, eight times in twenty-four hours in all they performed the 'sacrifice of praise'. The symbolism of the number, seven, was replaced by the number, eight, that of the beatitudes.

In this respect also St Benedict was no innovator. He organized the official times for praying of his monks with meticulous care, although he left the application of his directives to the decision of the superiors, conforming to the usages of the Church of Rome, that by his time had laid down the general lines to be followed, and all he did was to add certain touches to them, based on common sense, in the interests of a balanced schedule. The desert Fathers, for instance, tried to outshine one another by piling psalter on psalter, and St Columban's Celts (of whom he was the elder) at night recited a collection of psalms that, according to holy days, ran from twelve to seventy-five. But anxious to preserve the quality of their praying by not over-taxing the strength of his monks, St Benedict simply recommended that the 150 psalms in the psalter should be spread over the whole week, the longest of them to be recited at night. With very sound judgment he chose those most appropriate to the different 'hours' and thus popularized a schedule of which the wisdom, moderation, and harmony were finally accepted. When, after the destruction of Monte Cassino, the Benedictines took refuge in Rome, they introduced their schedule for reciting the office there. As it was impossible for them to carry on their manual labours in the city they had all the more time to devote to prayer and to taking charge of the choral services in the principal churches. In this connection there is no doubt that their enforced exile from Monte Cassino contributed very largely to the evolution and diffusion of the liturgy. Missionaries being trained in Rome and pilgrims visiting the tombs of the Apostles consulted them and subsequently spread the Roman usages throughout the Christian world, either taking them over integrally or else combining them with their own local customs.

Paradoxical as this may at first sight seem, the celebration of Mass was not, originally, the distinct task of the monks. The hermits did without it and the Mass was not celebrated daily in the earlier monasteries, for the monks, including their superiors, were no more than pious laymen. Among many others this also was true of St Benedict. He admitted priests to monastic life, although with a certain degree of circumspection, when it was only natural for them to be appointed to celebrate the Sacrament, but only on condition, nevertheless, that this right did not fill them with vainglory. When priests were lacking it was necessary to bring them in for the purpose, which was not always convenient. In order to avoid having to do so the abbot might nominate to the bishop those of his monks whom he considered worthy of entering the priesthood in order to perform these duties for their brethren. And thus for the sake of convenience, for the sake of missions and conducting services in the most popular churches, the custom gradually arose of admitting a certain number of monks to the priesthood. It is noteworthy that those in question were always in a minority; a third, perhaps a quarter, of the community and sometimes far fewer. And even then all the Father Abbots were by no means priests. This is why, except among the Celts, where the non-monastic clergy were exceptional, the monks of that period had no direct influence either on the constitution or the ritual of the liturgy of the Mass. Yet, and especially in countries where they had gone as missionaries, they were very much concerned with its propagation.

They quite naturally followed the customs of the countries in which they had been trained. There were a number of different liturgies in the West; in Gaul, from the fifth to the ninth centuries, the Gallican; at Milan and around it, the Ambrosian; in Spain, the Mozarabian, even before the Mussulman conquest, the Celtic, which also contained wide variations in Christian forms; as well as the Lyons and especially the Roman. Although it never ousted all the rest, the latter finally prevailed, especially after the final ruling of St Gregory the Great and the expansion of Benedictinism.

The texts, especially those of the Roman Mass and its office, were often of considerable literary merit. In contrast to the luxuriance of the Eastern liturgies, the anomalous character of the Celtic, which Edmund Bishop described as patchwork, the prolixity of the Mozarabian, and the verbose ramifications of the Gallican, the Roman liturgy, as used by the Benedictines, had a moderation which stemmed from its old classical tradition.

The orisons, for instance, which were then known as collects, expressed the most exact theology in terms of which the precision and amplitude revealed genuine mastery. Those of St Leo consisted of one single sentence only, each word of which, strongly emphasized, with pauses in between, formed a link in the cadence which rhythmically controlled its scansion (*cursus*). The perfection of this form, based on number and density, lies midway between poetry and prose, and exactly corresponded to the square periods of Cicero, or the lapidary formulae of inscriptions. And in order to stress their majestic effect, each cadence was emphasized by a chanted recitative. Thus, in the collect for the Feast of Epiphany, they succeed one another like the final lines of verses: *Deus qui, hodierna die, Unigenitum tuum gentibus stella dúce revelásti | Concéde propítius | ut qui jam te ex fíde cognóvimus | usque ad contemplandam speciem tuae celsitúdinis perducámur.*

The hymns provide us with an equally wide and even more varied choice. In this case the liturgy ranged far and wide. To name only some of their authors, St Ambrose above all the rest, St Hilary of Poitiers, Sedulius in the fourth century, Prudentius in the fifth, Fortunatus in the sixth, were rightly famous. Many of them endeavoured to follow the classical metres, but from the end of the fifth century, with Auspicius of Toul (d. 490), most of them renounced a metrical system which in any case was beyond their capacities, replacing the convention of long and short syllables with a combination of accentuated and atonic ones, thereby satisfying the basic laws of prosodic numbers. Other conventions, such as alliteration, assonance, and rhyme were also widely used. A new poetic art form was originated in the service of a new kind of poetry. Christian lyricism had come into being, developing according to the period; St Ambrose's manner was simple and straightforward; Prudentius's, ingenious, whilst Fortunatus wrote on a larger scale.

One is reluctant to quote examples of their verses in a foreign language and in prose, which, in the absence also of music cannot do them justice. The regular iambics of St Ambrose, sung at lauds (*Aeterne rerum conditor*) were in praise of cockcrow (*praeco diei*), the uncertain moment before the dawn when light begins to emerge from darkness (*nocturna lux*):

> *Hoc excitatus lucifer*
> *Solvit polum caligine,*
> *Hoc omnis errorum cohors*
> *Viam nocendi deserit.*

> By him the sun awakened
> Frees the globe from darkness
> Before him the cohorts of error
> Flee from the path of evil.

> *Hoc nauta vires colligit*
> *Pontique mitescunt freta,*
> *Hoc, ipsa petra Ecclesia,*
> *Canente, culpam diluit.*

> By him the sailor gains strength
> And the waves of the sea are becalmed;
> At his song the rock of the Church
> Itself banishes sin.

> *Surgamus ergo strenue,*
> *Gallus jacentes excitat*
> *Et somnolentos increpat,*
> *Gallus negantes arguit.*

> Let us therefore arise bravely,
> The cock awakes the sleepers,
> He rebukes the sluggards,
> And hurries up the laggards.

It will be observed that these verses contain not a single pious effusion; they simply point out that in responding to cockcrow those who do so make ready to carry on the work of the Church.

Prudentius sang more poetically about the Holy Innocents:

> *Salvete flores martyrum,*
> *Quos lucis ipso in limine*
> *Christi insecutor sustulit*
> *Ceu turbo nascentes rosas.*

> Greetings, ye flowers of martyrdom
> Whom on the very threshold of light
> Christ's persecutor ravished
> Like a whirlwind of rosebuds.

> *Vos, prima Christi victima,*
> *Grex immolatorum tener,*
> *Aram sub ipsam simplices*
> *Palma et coronis luditis.*

> Ye, first victims for Christ's sake,
> Tender flock of the sacrificed,
> Playing at the foot of the altar
> With palms and wreaths.

We are compelled to admit that these little pieces read only like minor verse. But, and this is important, the libretto forms only part of the poetic whole. Christian poetry only found complete expression in conjunction with the music that accompanied it, in contrast to classical Latin poetry that even with Horace, excepting the *Carmen Saeculare*, was only written for recitation. In the former case music and words formed an indissoluble whole, so that verses which often alone seem pedestrian, when modulated acquired all the incantatary magic of true lyricism. And thus the Christian poets, allegedly decadent, recaptured the authentic tradition of Greek poetry.

In this manner singing very quickly became of great importance both in the offices and the Mass. When previously discussing St Gregory, we already made certain reservations with regard to the so-called Gregorian chant. Towards the end of the nineteenth century the French Benedictines undertook the splendid task of restoring these chants, which today, in spite of many expert criticisms of their musical bases and methods, are universally adopted. Owing to all the refinements introduced into them they may not exactly reproduce the Roman style of singing in the seventh and eighth centuries. The choristers, trained in the schools, had their part, the most difficult no doubt, to play in them, and developed this as their own speciality, but as the music was never written down and was only a matter of oral tradition there is every reason to suppose that even if their memories were invariably perfect, their performances might have lacked some degree of exactitude. The celebrant himself was not required to be a musician and might, as indeed happened, stumble in the course of his recitatives. As also still happens, the congregation, in its enthusiasm and the musical repetition of a certain number of lines in the form of refrain might have produced sounds that were more lusty than musical, to the horror of our modern purists, had they heard them. In the ninth century John Deacon stated that the Franks and Germans beyond the Alps sang very badly. It seemed to him that their voices were more suitable to bellowing than modulating the smooth Roman chanting (*corpora vocum suarum tonitruis altisone perstrepentia*), and he satirized it, writing that 'in trying to reproduce a melody noted for the softness of its inflexions and accents, the throats of these uncouth drinkers produce hoarse sounds by a kind of involuntary eructation, like the sounds of chariots bumping their way along the roads'. If this observation held good for the ninth century it is probable that it also did so at an earlier date, and if the writer was exaggerating there is still little doubt that in many other places the performance of Church music left a great deal to be desired. Whether this was the case or not, however, liturgical singing was of considerable value, both from the aesthetic point of view and even more for the quality of prayer and Christian training. Whether it was modulated according to the very simple—and difficult—rules of the recitative, or soared to the rafters in highly ornate musical phrases, it heightened both the expression and transmission of the words; by clothing and enveloping them in music it greatly enriched them. The ideas they expressed might by themselves only have provided mental stimulation, but set to music they became ennobled and more easily remembered. It then mattered little whether the words as such were retained for their own sake; what the mind was unable to assimilate was accepted in its entirety by the imagination and emotions, and embedded in what today is known as the subconscious, so that on this basis those taking part in the services were made wholly receptive to their message. Without doubt Church music contributed to softening the most refractory souls.

And even better, words and music were combined in the ceremonial as a whole. When the liturgy was properly performed it was invested with great majesty. The *Ordo romanus I*, of the eighth century, the original parts of which go back to St Gregory the Great, shows us with what pomp it was celebrated on a certain Easter Mass, sung by the monk-pope in the basilica of Santa Maria Maggiore. We will only describe some excerpts from it.

The faithful, from all quarters of the city, pilgrims and foreign visitors, assembled, men on one side of the nave, women on the other. The seven suburban bishops and all bishops visiting Rome, as well as the twenty-five parish priests, were seated in the choir, on either side of the pontifical throne.

The clergy on duty assembled in the Lateran, the papal residence. At a given signal a procession was formed to escort the Pope from his palace to Santa Maria Maggiore. The acolytes and a group of officials headed it, followed by the seven deacons on horseback and their sub-deacons. Behind them came an acolyte on foot, preceding the Pope, who followed on horseback, with an assistant on either side of him. After him came the high dignitaries of the court, and the procession was closed by servers carrying the liturgical utensils to be used during the ceremony.

On arriving at the basilica the Pope dismounted and was received by the priest, who led him to a private room, the *secretarium* or sacristy, where those taking part in the ceremony donned their vestments and received the appropriate utensils. All was now ready for divine service. The sub-deacon on duty called out: 'The choir!' The choir replied: 'We are here.' 'What,' he then asked them, 'are you singing?' To which the choir-master answered, 'Such and such a piece'. The sub-deacon then approached the Pope, and with a genuflection stated: 'The servant of my Lord, sub-deacon N . . . will read the Epistle and deacon N . . . will sing the Gospel.' At a sign from the Pope the sub-deacon ordered the seven candle-holders to light the candles, and himself placed the fuel in the censer.

Meanwhile the choir, ranged around the altar, had begun the opening chant. The Pope rose from his seat and the procession proceeded along the nave to the altar. On arriving in the choir the Pope bowed to the altar, gave the kiss of peace around him and prayed for a moment. After the opening chant was over, the *Kyrie* followed. This ended at a sign from the Pope, who then intoned the *Gloria in excelsis* and sang the orison of the day, or collect. The ceremony continued with the reading of the Epistle and the chanting of the Gospel, the latter with all the solemnity due to the Word of God.

At the offertory the Pope left the altar and moved over to the *senatorium*, in the front of the nave, where the Roman nobility sat, and passing between their ranks received from each one a piece of bread and a small flask of wine, which he handed to his suite, whilst the bishops did the same amongst the rest of the congregation. The necessary portion for the sacrifice was then taken from the bread and wine deposited on the altar. During this time the choir was singing the offertory psalm.

Earlier on in the ceremony, when the Pope had received the sacrament, and after him the high clergy, the priests and deacons, he left his throne, returned to the *senatorium*, and as the nobility rose to their feet, presented them with the consecrated bread which they had offered him a few moments previously. The wine was later distributed by the archdeacon. And similarly, the whole congregation received the sacraments from the hands of the bishops and deacons. This rite took place to the chanting of the communion psalm.

These ceremonies lasted a long time, as Pope St Gregory informed us when he deplored the fact that ill-health hardly left him three hours' respite in which to perform the liturgy.

By thus assembling the community of the faithful, whether they were Romans or belonged to Barbarian nations, the liturgy was an object-lesson to them all. It was thus that they all learned the fundamentals of their spiritual destiny, from the Creation, the history and gradual education of the Jews with a view to the Incarnation, the fulfilment of the prophecies, the wonderful and tragic story of the Redemption, and the promise of life eternal. The words, images, symbols, chants and processions, the whole production (for this is the right word) of the drama of humanity in terms of the liturgy, as it described and emphasized the different phases of the Christian mystery, held all their attention and invited them to participate in it. During the whole year, regulated by the harmonious sequence of the weeks leading to the great festivals of Christmas and Easter, the Christian peoples were provided with a framework which, even although they may not have been consciously aware of it, surrounded each and all of them with a special atmosphere. The rhythmic regularity of prayer, the re-enactment of the mysteries and their common participation in it, gradually made an impression on their souls, and in spite of their coarseness they were gradually awakened to admiration and veneration, and finally became, one might say, impregnated with a sense of the divine. When they were not in church their innate barbarianism still too often took possession of them. But when they stood around the altar they knew a respite which, even although it might be only temporary, was the cornerstone of their education and already an involvement. 'The liturgy,' wrote Romano Guardini, 'was a school of spiritual training for the believer, and even in the eyes of those who only observed it from without, a cultural activity of the greatest splendour.'

SCHOOLS, SCRIPTORIUMS, BOOKS, ILLUMINATION

The Benedictine observance, by setting aside a daily period for the reading of sacred literature, presupposed a certain degree of education in its adherents. Those who did not already have this received it in the monasteries. They were first of all children whose parents had entrusted them to the abbot in order that they should become monks. The Benedictine monasteries therefore all contained a school in which masters taught the rudiments to the lay monks, but in many instances other pupils, who were not intended to become monks, were also accepted. When there were enough of the latter and the organization of the monastery allowed for it, these secular pupils were taught separately from the lay monks.

As we have seen, it was in England that from the middle of the seventh century the monastic schools attained to cultural heights that culminated in St Bede. Thanks to the missionaries who came from the British Isles, Germany and northern Gaul reaped similar benefits from them. In the rest of Gaul, towards the end of the seventh and in the eighth centuries the schools also began to become important, notably those of Luxeuil, Corbie, Fleury, St Martin de Tours. South of the Loire, in regions where the ancient Roman culture had subsisted longer than in others, monasteries and also schools were fewer than in the north. In Italy, where the ancient cultural traditions had not yet completely disappeared, at the end of the eighth century Charlemagne was to find teachers to further his attempts to restore them, yet there were no such important scholastic centres there as in Britain. Spain, in spite of the Arabs, was able to maintain a certain degree of culture. Yet we are unable to judge the conditions and quality of the Spanish schools according to the personalities of Theodulf and Agobard, who were two of the masters of the Carolingian Renaissance. We know almost nothing of the origins and youth of Theodulf, except that he came of a Visigoth family, but whether he was born in Spain, in the district of Narbonne or in Upper Italy, we do not know. Agobard was born in Spain, but as a small child was taken to the district of Narbonne and there was educated under Leidrade, Archbishop of Lyons.

In our own time the Benedictine monks, or at least their elite, are men of learning. At school they have received at any rate in essentials, instruction in the liberal arts (*de arte*) before specializing in doctrinal studies (*de divinitate*). From this point of view, although it was of short duration, Cassiodorus's influence on the Vivarium was lasting. It was in some degree thanks to him that Benedictine monachism developed in the direction of an intellectual training, the results of which very soon became apparent wherever Benedictine monks appeared.

Having examined the great scholastic achievements in some detail, we may now consider the state of knowledge on a lower level, the everyday one. A document dating either from the end of the seventh or the beginning of the eighth centuries, entitled 'Amusements of the monks' (*Joca monachorum*), gives us a very clear picture of it. D. Schmitz sees in this 'a kind of typical eighth century questionnaire used by the examiners' and pities the pupils who were obliged to submit to it. We are reluctant to disagree with such an authority. The terms in which it is written do not preclude the possibility that it was in fact, as its title stated, a form of scholastic entertainment; gems carefully selected by masters in a lighter vein, when constantly being badgered for the correct replies by pupils who knew the answers in advance, as well as their teachers' little peculiarities, and only waited for the opportunity to make fun of them. Whatever may have been the purpose of such 'games', the ideas reveal an obvious ineptitude, the language—which is not the Vulgate but corrupt ecclesiastical Latin—is appallingly misused, and the grammar worse than would be used today by an elementary school boy.

'Who died but was not born?'—'Adam.'

'Who was born of his sister, and raped his virgin grandmother?'— 'Adam' (who was born of the earth and sowed seed on it). *Quid* (should be *quis*) *sorore natus est et* (*h*) *aviam suam dehivolavet* (for *violavit*)?

'Who was born once and died twice?'—'Lazarus.' (*Qui*, for *quis*) *semul* (*simul*) *natus est et bes* (*bis*) *mortuos* (*mortuus*)?

'Who prayed for three days and nights without setting foot on earth or in heaven?'—'Jonah, in the belly of the whale.'

'Who was buried alive in a living tomb?'—'Jonah.'

'Who neither beheld heaven nor came to earth, and fell into another region?'—'The prophet Habakkuk.' (*Quis ne (nec) coelum vidit nec terram tangit (tetigit) et in alia (aliam) provincia (provinciam) cecidit?— Abaco proveta (propheta).*

'How many languages are there?'—'Seventy-two.' *Quod (quot) linguas (linguae) sunt?*

'Who knew her son before her husband?'—'Mary, who knew Christ'. *Q. prius cognovet (cognovit) filius (filium) quam maritum?—Maria Christum.*

'Who saw a ladder rising to heaven?'—'Jacob.' *Quis videt (vidit) iscalam (scalam) suspionta (susceptam) in coelum?*[1]

Form and content were worthy of one another, yet it is fortunate that such a document came down to us. For it enables us to form an impression of some of the teaching and to note how very rudimentary was the professional training of some of the scribes; many other manuscripts contain masses of similar mistakes.

Teaching was an activity quite distinct from the work of the copyists. All the great monasteries—and every important church as well—by now had a workshop for book production, the scriptorium.

The scriptorium (*sedes scribentium*) also served as an office where letters, charters, and various deeds were drawn up, and was the special preserve of the head copyist, who sought for books, purchased, borrowed or exchanged them, and was generally in charge of the workshop. The copyists (*scribae*) worked under his directions. He taught the younger ones to love books and take pride in fine handwriting, but there were also very old ones, whose fingers trembled as they wrote. These monks as a rule were inmates of the monastery, but others were also welcomed for longer or shorter periods. Some of the latter were possibly attracted to a particular monastery owing to its high reputation and came there for training, whilst others might be sent by their superiors in order to transcribe on the spot a work from which the owner refused to part. Yet others, travellers or pilgrims of established reputation might remain there for a time as teachers. Nuns also worked in the scriptorium, and although there were fewer women copyists than men some of them acquired great distinction. Thus St Boniface asked Eadberga,

[1] Text edited by P. Meyer, n *Romania I.*, 1872, p. 483, after the Ms. L. 13426 in the Bibliothèque Nationale of Paris.

an abbess in the Isle of Thanet, to have transcribed for him 'in gold the letters of my Lord St Peter the Apostle'.

The scribes are represented sitting on a bench or a stool, their feet resting on a footstool. They wrote on their knees. Close at hand was a desk on which lay the book they were copying, or a little table with their tools; quills of swans, geese, or crows, which were first tested on the page before beginning the transcription; containers for ink of various kinds, and an inkpot into which they dipped their quills, a knife for cutting up paper and sharpening quills, an eraser for correcting mistakes, compasses for regulating the spaces between the lines, a bodkin with which to draw the lines and margins regularly. Bookshelves or round or square boxes contained the works to be transcribed.

Until the end of the seventh century papyrus imported from Egypt provided a part of their writing material. In Italy it was still in use at a later date, but in Gaul it became more and more difficult to obtain and also more and more expensive. In any case it was fragile and in Western countries liable to be affected by dampness. Parchment was more generally used there, as it had none of these drawbacks and could be obtained everywhere. Parchment was made either from sheepskin, calf or goatskin, first soaked for a few days in chalky water, then spread on frames, scraped and smoothed out with pumice-stone, pressed with an iron and cut into sheets.[1] When a sheet of parchment was too old,

---

[1] Our word 'paper' stems from 'papyrus' but the former is of very different material. Papyrus was an Egyptian product extracted from a variety of reed (gen. *Cyperaceae*) which in Antiquity grew profusely on the banks of the Nile. The pith of this, after extraction, was cut into very fine strips, which were then pressed together vertically. On this layer a second one was laid, joined together similarly, but horizontally. These two layers were then pressed, dampened and possibly glued together to form one sheet, which was next dried in the sun, polished, and glazed. Several sheets were joined together to form a roll which was unrolled as it was being read, the writing being on one side only, in columns. The oldest known roll dates approximately from 2400 BC. The Egyptians, who had a monopoly of papyrus, exported it to Greece and Rome (where the roll was called *volumen*). The use of papyrus spread from Rome throughout the Western world until the Arab conquest of Egypt in 639–42 virtually ended this trade.

It was the Chinese who invented paper at the beginning of the third century BC. They were then writing on silk with brushes, but as this was a very expensive procedure they decided to manufacture a material from silken rags; this was the earliest silk (or tissue) paper. Later on, at the beginning of the second century AD they manufactured a similar substance from the bark of certain plants and cotton waste; and this is still the basic substance of our own paper today. When the Arabs conquered Transoxiana (Turkistan) they found that paper was being used at Samarkand, the last stage of the caravans that came from China. They immediately took it up, also, and began to manufacture it, notably at Bagdad. In the tenth century it was used in Egypt and in the twelfth at Toledo, an important production centre, and it at this period also appeared in Italy.

damaged, or the text written on it was considered no longer worth preserving, it was washed, scraped, and used for transcribing some other document, as far as possible similarly aligned. It often happened that the original text was not completely obliterated and appeared in filigree next to the later one; this was a palimpsest.[1] The expert and industrious copyists liked to use parchment of good quality and not to be restricted as to the numbers of sheets they used. When the cellarer on the excuse of monastic poverty refused to provide him with enough a monk might bemoan the meanness of his superiors with regard to intellectual requirements, and if he had connections might beg or even buy from them on his own initiative vellum of good quality. Presents of this kind were always highly appreciated. Towards 760 a monk named Winithair, a renowned scribe and apparently head copyist of the monastery of St Gall, complained of having been so badly treated by his own community that he was obliged to have recourse to the miserable means of pious industry to procure material for a manuscript sheet by sheet. From this we may deduce that in certain districts parchment was not cheap.

When the skins had been suitably prepared for writing, the work was organized by the head of the scriptorium. Each scribe received a given number of sheets on which to do his copying. Four sheets folded together, about eight leaves of sixteen pages, recto-verso, formed a copy-book or *quaternio*. The format varied; we have some fine manuscripts of about fourteen inches by ten, and others that only measure eight inches by five. There are also even smaller ones. The Bobbio Missel is a portative book of about seven inches by three-and-a-quarter, in the Bibliothèque Nationale. In order the more easily to keep control of each copyist's work the director sometimes made a mark, a name or a sign,

---

Parchment (*pergamena*) came from Pergamo (in Asia Minor, opposite the island of Lesbos). In the third century BC certain hides there were prepared for the purpose of writing. They were found and worked on the spot and were prized for their quality and, up to a point, their price, since papyrus, imported under monopoly, was neither always nor everywhere cheap. From there parchment spread rapidly into the Roman world, where it was known as *membrana*. Its original form was the roll.

The *codex*, a bound collection of sheets, seldom of papyrus but generally of parchment, appeared at the end of the first century. Stronger and more easily handled, from the third century onwards the *codex* replaced the roll; the latter, however, did not, in spite of this, disappear, as it was regarded as a superior book form, and in the twelfth century it gave its name to the roll or roster, and in the following century to the *rôlet* (*rotulus*).

[1] When such sheets were treated by modern chemical methods the original writing on them reappeared, and thus this text and a subsequent one on one and the same page became legible.

on the sheets he had distributed to each of them. During the hours when copying was being done absolute silence was the rule in the scriptorium, and if a document had to be dictated, which did not usually happen, this was done in another room. Methods varied; one scribe might be allocated to copying out a whole work, or several might follow one another in the transcription of it. Frequently, also, the original sheets were distributed among a number of scribes. Each of them was then charged with transcribing exactly each copybook he had been given; a monk who spaced out his writing too widely at the beginning would have to write more closely, or abridge it, towards the end. The different hands revealed by certain manuscripts enable us to estimate the number of copyists who worked at it and *ipso facto* the importance of the scriptorium employing them. The *Eugyppius* in the Paris Bibliothèque Nationale is the work of twenty different hands.

Copying was at first considered as manual labour but in any case the copyists were always under obedience to the Rule. The copyists were often anonymous and took a humble view of their efforts, which, however, were highly esteemed, and regarded by them as a work of piety. The scribe of the martyrology of St Willibrord prefaced his work with the words, 'Christ, favour my endeavours'. It was a profession demanding above all a long apprenticeship, great ability, patience, and endurance. Many copyists complained of their difficulties, for then, as now, the untutored were quick to accuse of laziness anyone who refused to be hurried or hard-pressed. Some of them, notably the Irish, dared to record their complaints in the margin of their copies. 'Only three fingers are writing, but the whole body is suffering.' One of them had a backache, another stomach cramps, a third crooked ribs, and a fourth was half-blinded. Many of them grumbled at the cold, or that their fingers hurt them, or their parchment was too tough and their ink execrable. Occasionally one was satisfied; on such or such a page work had gone well, whilst others complained that it was slow and difficult. Those who were greedy or ravenous were happy when meal-times came: 'Now it is night, and dinner-time.' There was even one addicted to the bottle: 'The scribe has a right to the best wine.' Those who lacked discipline wrote one another messages in the margins, as boys in the schoolroom pass one another clandestine notes. Although all these sentences do not date from the eighth century there is little doubt that they reflect the mental states of scribes at all times.

The work was hard enough in itself and even more so on account of the long time it took to complete. A manuscript of average size on sheets of the normal format took three or four months, whilst a Bible required a whole year. A luxurious work might take several years to finish. Columba of Iona, who was a famous calligrapher and a keen book collector, is alleged to have copied out the Gospels of Durrow in twelve days, an average of twenty to thirty pages a day, and a good measure. (The awkward thing, as regards Columba, is that this manuscript dates from long after his time, possibly a century later).

Once the copying was completed the head copyist would assemble the various copy-books, put them in their proper order, re-read and collate them, add the punctuation and if necessary correct the scribes' blunders. The *codex* was then finished and nothing more remained to be done except to have it bound in skin. For the sake of economy several works, even by different authors, were frequently bound in one volume.

A workshop that had a high reputation, industrious and well organized, was almost like a publishing house; there was no lack of orders for those who could produce numerous copies. By thus disseminating their works they advertised their methods, their style of writing, systems of punctuation and abbreviation, and ornamental style. But as this method of manual reproduction was inevitably a slow one, especially if it was carefully carried out, the number of such 'published' manuscripts was relatively small, and for that reason *codices* were eagerly exchanged. On occasion it was noticed that certain works were lacking or had disappeared; even holy monks on pilgrimage, in the course of a stage in an hospitable monastery, did not invariably resist the temptation of bookstealing.

Transcription of manuscripts was always the monks' business. It was practised at St Martin of Tours in the second half of the fourth century. Lérins, in the fifth, certainly required copyists. Cassiodorus's model scriptorium was functioning in the middle of the sixth century, and towards the same period the Irish foundations, Iona among many others, had their workshops. But it was more particularly from the middle of the seventh century and throughout the eighth that the scriptoriums reached a high stage of activity. In England the renowned scholastic centres produced excellent copies, chief among them Canterbury, Ripon, Wearmouth, Jarrow, York, and Lindisfarne; and in Ireland, Bangor, Durrow, and Kells. During the sixth century and part of the seventh, Gaul lagged behind, but in the eighth was working hard to catch up. Provence and Aquitania, devastated by internecine wars and the Saracens, produced little, but the northern part of the country, from the Loire to the Rhine, flourished. In the seventh century Autun, Luxeuil, Corbie, a Luxeuil foundation, and St Médard de Soissons all possessed workshops of renown. The native and Anglo-Saxon teams of

Corbie to our certain knowledge produced more than fifty *codices*, and in fact even more. In the eighth century St Amand and especially St Martin de Tours were very productive. Echternach became known through the Martyrology and Calendar of St Willibrord; St Gall made a modest beginning in the seventh century but became famous by the end of the eighth. In Italy Bobbio and Nonantola were gaining lustre and from the end of the eighth century Monte Cassino, after it was restored, once again became the leader.

The libraries were on a similar footing. Whenever possible they were separated from the scriptoriums and their doors were invariably kept locked. The books were stored in coffers or bookcases, under the supervision of the librarian (*armarius*), who often was also the head copyist. Our information regarding their contents in Ireland and Great Britain is incomplete, but there was no lack of reading matter in the monasteries of those countries. In Gaul during the eighth century the libraries were poorly equipped. The close investigations for Gaul of E. Lesne inform us that before the middle of the eighth century there were thirty-three manuscripts at Lyons; at St Gall, eighteen before the seventh century, and nine during the seventh and at the beginning of the eighth centuries. St Pirmin's biographer mentioned that the founder brought fifty volumes to Reichenau, and this information no doubt appeared worth recording. St Boniface, a great reader, took a box of books with him on his pilgrimages. If we take into account the dispersal and pillages from which they suffered the monastic libraries were better equipped than the episcopal, but their total contents would still not have been very great, especially in Gaul. In the ninth century, for instance, St Rémy in Rheims contained about 600 volumes and in the eleventh, Fleury, which was considered a very large one, had only half that number, from which we may deduce that in the eighth century a Frankish library containing one hundred books would have been well equipped.

Even in the darkest Ages classical Ancient literature never ceased to be transcribed. Greek texts were practically non-existent, but Latin ones were certainly in circulation. A fifth century Titus Livius (Livy) was re-copied at St Martin de Tours during the eighth. St Amand possessed an Elder Pliny of the sixth. The famous *Mediceus* of Virgil, dating from the end of the fifth, today in the Laurentinus in Florence, probably belonged to Cassiodorus and found its way to Bobbio. We may assume that with very few exceptions the Latin authors were preserved, although in many cases we do not know exactly how, until the ninth century, during which they were re-copied and definitely saved; and this we owe to the monks. The services they thereby rendered to civilization were such that the seven centuries from the fall of the Roman Empire until the twelfth century are rightly called the monastic period in literary history.

Christian literature owes even more to the monks. Greek, which was pretty generally unknown, was transcribed very little.[1] The Greek Fathers were only studied in their Latin translations. The Latin Fathers are represented in particular by St Ambrose, St Augustine, Jerome, St Gregory the Great, St Bede. There was no lack of Bibles, nor of *Lives* of the saints. There were a great many works of liturgy—sacramental, for the use of celebrants; lectionaries and gospelaries containing passages from the Holy Book to be read in public; missals—the name of which in Gaul and England meant from the eighth century onwards a collection consisting of the sacramentary and the lectionary—antiphonaries or song-books, and also hymnals. Some of these documents are famous, such as the Leonian sacramentary, which in particular contains the fine orisons of Pope Leo (d. 461), the Gelasian sacramentary, attributed to Pope Gelasius (d. 496), which was widespread in Gaul during the eighth century; the Gallican lectionaries of Luxeuil and Bobbio in the seventh century; the Gregorian antiphonary, called after Pope Gregory the Great (d. 604). There were very many psalters in daily usage, as well as the ordines, by which the order of the ceremonies was determined; martyrologies, read daily at the office; pontifications, which dealt with the bishop's functions, and penitentials, for the punishment of delinquents. Thus it is clear that if they were provided with parchment in plenty the scriptoriums were never short of work.

As publishers the monks also carried out the kind of work that is nowadays done by the printer, and many of them brought renown to their trade by turning out masterpieces. The most beautiful books were then not preserved in the libraries but in the Church treasuries, together with the most valuable vessels.

As regards the various types of calligraphy, there is no point in entering on an involved discussion of paleography, a subject on which the experts are not invariably in agreement. But in order more fully to appreciate the work they did we should not, at least in their simpler aspects, overlook the different kinds of calligraphy used by the monks. They did not invent the most ancient of these, but those that they did create should at least be summarily described.

[1] *Codex Bezae*, Greek and Latin versions of the New Testament of the sixth century, at Cambridge.

On examining the diverse texts of these manuscripts we find two separate groups of characters. The first of these, rapidly written and not very deeply, sometimes separate and at others joined together according to rules we ignore, appear to have been written in haste or at any rate fluently. This was the cursive, chiefly used in official documents, notaries' briefs and commercial correspondence. In the Charters of Ravenna of the sixth century we have a famous example of it. Another such document, the diploma of Childebert III, drawn up in 695,[1] is a vertical scrawl, squeezed along the lines like a row of woodshavings, with erratic leaps between them; the writing is trying to appear impressive but in fact is chiefly ugly and over-emphatic. Another hand, slower, more careful and regular, proves that the scribe was exerting himself to produce a lasting document. This is the hand of a professional involved in book production. 'The hand of the copyist differs from the hand of the correspondent. Many scribes, excellent and competent at forming characters in books cannot at all, or barely, write a decent letter-hand.' This thirteenth century distinction perfectly sums up the difference existing then, as nowadays, between daily or cursive handwriting and transcription at that time, corresponding to the printed word today.

The famous Western Latin manuscripts on vellum differ from one another according to time and place and the care lavished on them by their respective copyists. Some of them are works of art, their capitals of precisely the same height, their downstrokes firm and clear, their upstrokes fine and elegant, as if inscribed on stone; they contain the square and fairly rare capital letters, for it was an onerous task to transcribe an entire work as formally as this (fragments of the Virgil of St Gall, fourth to fifth century). The so-called rustic capitals were less impressive, narrower, almost rectangular and therefore closer together, and as they could be written more speedily, less rare (Vatican Virgil, beginning of fifth century).

The uncial was also a capital letter, but unlike the former, which were angular, square, or rectangular, was rounded, flexible, full, and sometimes heavy. Its name, popularized by the French Benedictines in the eighteenth century, derives from 'ounce', one-twelfth of a foot, and the scribe who wrote in uncials was working on the grand scale. St Jerome, who preferred useful books to luxurious ones, disliked uncial writing. 'If one insists on it one may obtain old books written on purple parchment in gold and silver characters, or also, as they are called, in uncials, (which are) burdens of writing rather than books.'[1] And indeed a glance at the palimpsest of the *Republic* of Cicero (fourth century, Vatican Library), confirms that the original text, divided on each page into double columns of fifteen lines, each line containing little more than one word, when completely transcribed must, as St Jerome stated, have been pretty heavy. From the fourth to the eighth centuries there are numerous examples of such luxurious writing, either in the traditional double columns or, possibly for practical reasons, spread across the whole page. The Homilies of St Cesarius[2] in line-by-line, bears the following note: 'This book contains the Lives of the Fathers and homilies of St Cesarius. The Venerable Numidius, Abbot, had it transcribed and presented it as a pious offering to the basilica of St Médard (Soissons). Anyone thinking of stealing it is hereby warned that he will be dealt with by God and St Médard.'

The semi-uncial, small or non-capital letters, was much more widespread and also faster, lighter and more supple, but none the less beautiful. It is exemplified by the so-called national calligraphies. The Lombardic was current in northern Italy during the seventh and eighth centuries, and the Visigothic, in the eighth, was used by monks in Spain and Gaul who had fled from the Arab occupation. There were two famous centres for the Merovingian—Luxeuil in the seventh century, and in the eighth, its daughter foundation, Corbie. Of this there are two different types, that of Luxeuil, rather thick and heavy in outline[3] and that of Corbie, vertical and clear. There is an interesting *codex* consisting of extracts from St Augustine, compiled towards the middle of the sixth century by a certain Eugyppius, abbot of a monastery near Naples, and transcribed during the first half of the eighth, according to some authorities at Tours, and others, in the north-east of Gaul.[4] This contains ninety-three pages, seventeen and a quarter inches by ten, ruled by dry-point. These 186 pages were transcribed simultaneously, the original text being distributed in copy-books among the various scribes. It contains three distinct calligraphical types—the uncial, in eight different hands, the semi-uncial, in three hands, the cursive small lettering in at least ten different hands. Folio 48 v° of this work is unusual. The scribe, having allowed himself too much space at the beginning made a dreadful mess of this page; the copy also contains spelling mistakes, the punctuation is irregular and the editor was obliged to insert

---

[1] Preface to the Book of Job.
[2] End of seventh, beginning of eighth centuries, Brussels.
[3] Gallican Lectionary, seventh century, Paris, Bibliothèque Nationale.
[4] Paris, Bibliothèque Nationale.

in it various corrections, over-writing the mistakes. This work, no doubt, had to be done in a hurry.

There are two main examples of the Irish semi-uncial. The first of these is small, narrow, and pointed, as if deliberately closely written in order to give it height and sharpened points, and this writing was done fairly quickly. It was impossible to produce several copies of so beautiful a document as the Book of Kells (seventh century). This exquisite work, the principal treasure of the library of Trinity College, Dublin, is without a doubt the masterpiece of the art of calligraphy. The semi-uncials are fully rounded, regular and strong, with no breaks, proving the copyist of Kells to have had the ease, mastery, and perfect taste of a very great artist. Nowhere else in the Western world was a document ever so superbly transcribed. A thirteenth century connoisseur, Giraldus Cambrensis, when shown a similar book, expressed his feelings in words worthy of quotation here: 'One would think that this piece had been written by the precise and industrious hand of an angel and not a man. The more closely I examine and scrutinize it the more I am astounded by it as an extraordinary achievement, and the more admiration I feel for it.'

Whatever may have been the relationship, which is uncertain, between the Irish and Anglo-Saxon schools, there were two main great English styles. Canterbury, in the south, used a form of writing of Roman importation, in rustic capitals, of which there remain only a few examples. But the monastery of Lindisfarne in Northumbria, founded by St Aidan in 635, was with justice famed as a school of calligraphy. Its masterpiece, comparable in splendour to the Book of Kells, was the famous text produced in this monastery around the year 700, known as the Lindisfarne Gospels.[1] St Cuthbert, in whose honour this piece of calligraphy was done, must have received Bishop Eadfrith, the author of so monumental a work, with open arms.

The literary Renaissance under Charlemagne at a later period produced new types of writing. At that time scribes and calligraphers alternately used the double capital, both square and rustic, a somewhat heavy uncial, an ample and well-rounded semi-uncial, harmoniously blending full and thin strokes,[2] and especially the so-called Carolingian small lettering, already foreshadowed in the second half of the eighth century at Corbie and St Gall. This Carolingian small lettering, dating from the end of the eighth century, was highly commendable on account

[1] British Museum, London.
[2] Bible of Charles the Bald, middle ninth century, Paris, Bibliothèque Nationale.

of its simplicity, elegance, and ease. In the fifteenth century it was revived by the Italian calligraphers who transferred it to the printing-press with little modification, and our present-day types derive from it.[1] When they preserved the texts the monks at the same time safeguarded the art of book-making. They also illustrated them, and this is one of the most original activities for which we are indebted to them, not only on account of the history of bibliography but also for the history of art. Illumination has too often been denigrated as a minor art-form which has to be searched for in libraries and unlike frescoes or mosaics is not otherwise on view. But although illumination may be a minor art as regards its scale (apart from the fact that it provides us with a considerable amount of invaluable evidence) it often, certainly far more than has been generally conceded, had a great influence on the so-called major art of painting. M. Nordenfalk, an authority on the subject, unequivocally wrote that 'without doubt it represents the richest and possibly purest artistic domain for a thorough study of mediaeval painting'.

Etymologically, illumination means introducing light into a book by means of colour. The original meaning of the word miniature was a slightly different one, describing the red minium used by the artist to embellish certain letters. This designation gradually became applied to any painted picture in a scroll or codex, so that in time illumination and miniature became synonymous terms. The paints were not mixed with oils but either with water or gum.

When the copyist inscribed the word *explicit* on the last page of his work, he then either set himself to decorate the blank spaces he had left in it for the purpose, or, if he himself were not an illuminator, handed it over to the brother who was one. The task of the latter was to decorate as magnificently as possible the sacred words transcribed in the *codex*. Thus the text, already precious and finely copied out, would be still more distinguished by an ornamentation that would further enhance its value. On the opening pages there are very often porticos[2] inviting the reader to enter into the temple of the Word. Elsewhere the text is decorated with scrolls, initial letters and symbolical or historical figures, according to the artist's inspiration.

In this respect also the monks invented nothing new. The Egyptians, Greeks, and Romans also illustrated their most important texts, although this does not then seem to have been the usual practice. It is as a matter of fact remarkable that the *Virgilius Vaticanus* and the *Virgilius*

---

[1] The successive phases in this development can be studied at the Musée Plantin at Antwerp, Belgium.

[2] Canons of Eusebius of Caesaria, d. 340.

Romanus (both in the Vatican Library) date from the end of the fourth or beginning of the fifth centuries, as if the artists of the time had a presentiment of the catastrophe threatening civilization and wished to preserve in beauty the purest of all Latin masterpieces. Once the up-heavals caused by the Barbarian migrations were over the Churchmen who came after them, and almost without exclusion the monks, in the seventh and especially the eighth centuries, developed in their own original manner this art, which until then had only been practised in a limited way.

We cannot here go into all the details of this particularly delicate art-form. But a few examples should be enough to give a general idea of the different types produced by the monastic workshops.[1]

From the end of the sixth century Rome had workshops for illumina-tion. The manuscript known as the Gospel of St Augustine, which is today in Cambridge, England, was probably presented at the time of the English mission to the apostle of the Anglo-Saxons by Pope Gregory the Great. In this St Luke is represented sitting on a large cushion, framed in a portico of double columns; above him, in a kind of tympanum or drum, is the winged bull, the Evangelist's symbol. This painting is not in the manner of a great artist; the drawing is flabby and the colours are very dull, greyish blue, a yellowy purple, indistinct yellows and white suggested by leaving certain spaces on the parchment blank. The twelve scenes from the life of our Lord, set into square compartments between the columns, are without relief. This work, however, imported from Rome to Canterbury, nevertheless had a certain subsequent influence and we have reason to assume that both in choice of subjects and tech-nical execution the decoration of the first churches under the Roman obedience in the south of England was inspired by this iconography.

The Ashburnham Pentateuch is in a completely different style. This work was stolen from the Library of Tours some time in the middle of last century by a book-fancier, oddly enough called Libri, was sold by him to Lord Ashburnham and was finally acquired by the Bibliothèque Nationale of Paris. This seventh century manuscript, which derived either from North Africa or Spain, reproduces the warm colouring of its country of origin. It consists of nineteen illuminated pages telling the story of Exodus from the Old Testament in vivid tones—red, pink, blue,

---

[1] In order that the reader who wishes to pursue this matter shall find it easily accessible, we have in most cases based our comments on the fine reproductions published in the work of M. Nordenfalk, *Le haut Moyen Age, du IVe au XIe siècle. L'enluminure*, Geneva, 1957. See also *Les trésors de la Bibliothèque nationale, Département des manuscrits, Epoque précarolingienne*, Commentaries by M. L. Concasty, Paris, 1957, in the *Editions d'art et d'histoire*.

green, violet—in strong contrast to one another. The painting of the Flood, which by itself takes up an entire page, might arouse the envy of a modern illustrator. The ark is a kind of oval box standing on four feet, its doors and windows bolted, painted in blue and outlined in red. The drowned are floating below it, huge pink human bodies, blue fish, three tiny horses, a white, a blue, and a red one, and a blue duck with a red beak, all surrounded by an olive-green base supposed to represent the waters of the Flood. The general impression it gives is both grotesque and dramatic, and other scenes representing everyday life are more attractive than this representation of the cataclysm. All along the margins, which sometimes are asymmetrical, tiny little scenes follow one another or are encircled in lozenges divided irregularly; representing labour in the fields inspired by Abel guarding his flocks and Cain whipping up the oxen behind his cart, or else indoor scenes in which Jacob and Esau, each of them separately, are preparing the dish which will bring them either blessings or curses. There are also little sketches of cities with their gates and domed churches. Each little picture is attractive, either on account of its liveliness, realism, or picturesqueness.

More numerous examples testify to the great industry of the scriptoriums of Ireland and Northumbria.[1] Owing to the impetus given them by the Celt, St Aidan, the Anglo-Saxon apostle in the north of England, from the middle of the seventh century both the Irish and Northumbrians made varied and original contributions to the art of illumination.

We must admit that a certain number of these productions might mislead us by their very particular iconography. In order to judge them, and even more, to appreciate them, it might be wiser not to accept the view of them of D. Leclercq, who was always inclined to snap-judgments of things he disliked. According to him they reveal no more than a lack of observation and are monotonous and insignificant, '*amour de la torsion jusqu'à la contorsion*'. He claimed that this art-form was even worse than the Byzantine or the Cubist, which according to him were the two most abominable opposites. 'The Byzantines made manikins,the Irish only produced monsters.' 'Cubism is only crazy to a certain degree; Irish art was completely so and this is its sole claim to superiority.' Such statements are unfair, for they admit of only one aesthetic rule, supposedly valid for all times and all periods. It is, for instance, obvious that if one applies the classical Greek canons, which referred everything to the

---

[1] This is a controversial matter which has been raised by M. Masaï, according to whom the style of illumination generally known as Irish was of Northumbrian origin.

measure of man and disposed of a perfect technique, to Irish or North-umbrian art, these illuminations do seem to be monstrously distorted. But if, on the contrary, we take the trouble to realize that this art-form was created in an environment that was still a Barbarian one, in this respect not yet freed from paganism and possibly attributing magical powers to certain images, we will conclude that we are face to face with an art-form that, strange as it may seem, has to be accepted as it is, and should not be condemned in the name of alien criteria. All we need now do is to distinguish a certain number of different types amongst these works.

The artists' endeavours to represent certain human and animal forms are certainly open to severe criticism. The Crucifixion of the Gospel 51 of St Gall (eighth century) shows us a deformed Christ with the body of a giant and the arms and legs of a pigmy, in attitudes that defy the most elementary laws of anatomy. The trunk is enveloped in spirals that look more like the coils of a serpent than the wrappings of a shroud, and the face, far from being that of the Man of Sorrows is a hideous grimace. The Crucifixion of Wurzburg (eighth century) is even worse, so much so that in this case we may quote the fulminations of D. Leclercq: 'Under an arcade, the arms of which rest in water, a crucified being is stretched out. His cross is made of lozenges joined together like marquetry, and on the instruments of torture is a hideous, repulsive form, apparently intended to represent a human being. The head is one-third the size of the whole body, with enormous eyes, a black moustache across the face, which is surrounded by a fringe of black beard, against which a small blonde or white goatee stands out. The arms and entire body are covered in fish-scales. Neither the α nor the ω depend from the lower end of the cross, but, instead, two crossbars from which the thieves are hanging like foetuses in spiritbottles. Within a field are some vague forms, which are possibly angels, or possibly, bats, unless they are cockchafers or insects in chrysalis form. There are two parrots on the arms of the cross. At its foot is the haloed Virgin with eight dolls in a row, and, finally, a man with a lade, angling for three fish in the sea.' We ourselves may less emotionally admit that the meaning of this art-form escapes us, that these illuminators had a point of view of their own, and that although it would be going too far to describe them as sacrilegeous we may as well confess that such works do not in any way correspond to the treatment of the subject one would normally expect.

Animals, also, but in another manner, are represented with un-restrained imagination. In a good many cases their exaggeratedly elongated bodies give them a reptilian appearance. There are lions with only two paws, and triangular calves.[1] They are subject to laws of stylization unfamiliar to us. The same applies to the St Mark of the Gospel of Echternach, decorated for St Willibrord at the end of the seventh century. The Evangelist is represented by his symbol, the lion, which takes up a whole page, in a geometrical framework made by a thin, irregular, red line. The animal's body is covered with scales of a yellowish green flecked with red, the head resembles that of a lion whose ancestor might have been a dragon, the neck and shoulders are four times larger than the belly, but the attitude of this fantastic beast, about to spring with all its claws unsheathed, with its fiery open jaws, is superbly supple, powerful, and majestic.

The Book of Lindisfarne[2] follows entirely different and quieter aesthetic lines. St Matthew the Evangelist is painted in the posture of a working scribe, with the young man who symbolizes him above him, and a curtain in front of him, through which peers the haloed face of a saint. The tones are simple, the predominant reds and greens cleverly heightened by yellow and violet. The Evangelist's name is written partly in Greek and partly in Latin, *o agios Matteus*, but this reference is unnecessary to cause us spontaneously to recall the Byzantine hagiography; like the Byzantines, that had served him as models, the painter of Lindisfarne ignores anatomy, stylizes the garments with amplitude, and describes majesty in repose. Greek books circulated in Northumbria owing to the influence of Theodore of Tarsus, the first master of Canterbury, who was an Easterner and had brought a number of Greek texts along with him, and also thanks to the numerous pilgrims returning from Rome. The fact that the Anglo-Saxons may have known the language of the gods little or not at all is no objection, for an artist may be enchanted by a type of iconography without knowing the language of its origin. We have another similar case in the illustration of the *Amiatinus* (Latin) at Wearmouth–Jarrow, in the early years of the eighth century, in which the scribe Esdras is represented in the attitude given to the Evangelists by the Byzantine illuminators.

This same Book of Lindisfarne contains another type of illumination —the carpet style. This is a whole-page square, composed of very subtle chequerwork, in the centre of which is a Latin cross which again is formed of squares and rectangles. The colours—green, yellow, red, lilac, although flat, are put on with a very sound sense of their relationships. The whole gives more the impression of a complicated paving than a mosaic, but pleases the eye by the harmony of its arrangement and

[1] Book of Durrow, seventh century, Trinity College, Dublin.
[2] End of seventh century, British Museum, London.

its discretion. The carpet-page of the Book of Durrow, which is older, shows an equally able but more restless artistry. In the centre is a circle, enclosing a minute cross, contained in a square, which in turn is surrounded by a rectangular decoration, in which quadrupeds and stylized serpents, interlaced and writhing, pullulate. But the choice of colouring is not subtle, as in the Book of Lindisfarne, and the influence of the goldsmith's art, by means of which arms, shields, and harness were decorated, is obvious. In this same Book of Durrow the tunic of St Matthew the Evangelist is represented as a stiff sack, which looks more like an enamelled plaque than a garment. This plaque is elaborately decorated, in contrast to the subject's head and feet, which the artist was manifestly unable to draw.

The Book of Kells[1] is a triumph of interlacing and fluting. Nearly a whole page is given over to the representation of only three words— *Christi autem generatio*. It is entirely dominated by the monogram XPI (*Christi*) which obliterates the word *generatio*. Although the letters of the monogram can only be made out with difficulty, one is obliged to admire the imagination, subtlety, and robustness that emanate from this work. It is as if the artist, having solidly drawn the upright strokes of the three capital letters, had taken an endless thread in order to compose a tapestry of the greatest subtlety. The pen and ruler certainly played their part in this, but even more so, his firmness of hand. A flat yellow predominates, enhanced by strong red lines and flecked with dark green. Like all the Irish and Saxon illuminators the artist was unaware of the uses of gold, but the general tonality is such that it gives the illusion of a picture decorated in old gold. J. O. Westwood, who drew attention to the importance of this decoration, wrote on the subject.[2]

Northumbria of the Roman obedience was the crucible of Celtic and Anglo-Saxon religious values, and was constantly in touch with Rome owing to the numerous pilgrims who took to the roads in imitation of Wilfrid and Benedict Biscop. Owing to them the Anglo-Irish flow was reciprocated by an Irish–Italian stream, which in turn contained Byzantine elements. The *Amiatinus*, to which we are always obliged to recur, was transcribed and decorated at Wearmouth, after a copy from Cassiodorus's Vivarium, and became the prime witness and symbol of the path of civilization which, starting in the south of Italy, passed through Rome and ended in the north of England. Another witness, but of lesser quality, is the Gospel of Maeseyck. In this the 'portrait' of the Evangelist is in tones dominated by green and grey, very flat, the

[1] Eighth century, Trinity College, Dublin.
[2] Quoted in Gougaud, *Les Chrétientés celtiques*.

drawing elementary, the whole heavy, dull, and without imagination, especially in comparison with the firm drawing and brilliance of the *Amiatinus*.

In the south, at Canterbury, illumination only appeared after the mission was assured that its future was no longer in jeopardy (eighth century). Although it first began at so late a date it produced an exceptional work in the *Codex aureus* (today in Stockholm). In this the St Matthew is painted full-length, in the Byzantine-Roman style, majestic and impassive as a *basileus*. He is framed in a low portico formed by two columns, in which are intertwined the twisted fringes of two half-drawn curtains. The capitals of the columns support a canopy in which appears the youth who symbolizes the Evangelist. The upper part is rather too heavy for the lower, and the latter might preferably have had an upward sweep. Apart from the slight movement suggested by the curtain fringes, the two superposed figures are rigid, but the design is precise, well shaded, and imposingly solid. Pink and blue, the predominating colours, are relieved with gold. On every other page the text itself is also in gold on a purple ground. These are two innovations said to have been introduced into England by St Wilfrid.

There were no such flourishing artistic and intellectual centres in Merovingian Gaul as there were in Northumbria, and it did not produce such rich and varied illuminations. The first Celtic pilgrims on the continent, including St Columban himself, during their lifetimes contributed nothing to the art of illumination. It was not until the foundation of Echternach, under St Willibrord, that insular illuminations were introduced to the Continent.

The Merovingian workshops were not, however, idle, although they preferred decorating liturgical books and theological treatises to gospels. Theirs was a modest effort, which developed without sumptuousness and with a certain degree of hesitation. In their books large full-page compositions were rarer than among the islanders. Human figures were also somewhat infrequent, although there were plenty of designs based on fauna and flora. Gold was not used and the colours—red, blue, green, yellow—were in subdued tones. The outlines, drawn with a pen, showed a less firm hand than those of the Anglo-Saxons, and the ruler and the compasses were much in use.

The Lectionary of Luxeuil[1] is rather crude in design. One illustrated page consists only of a capital letter T, the downstroke of which forms the margin whilst the horizontal stroke across the top is formed by a fish upheld by two peacocks, the triangle thus obtained sketching out a

[1] End of seventh century, Paris, Bibliothèque Nationale.

cornice. The Gelasian Sacramentary is very carefully decorated.[1] The back of one page represents the arcade of a portico, the interior of which is filled by a well-proportioned cross. The other side of the same page is decorated less regularly but more interestingly, with a cross and a text in impressive capitals. The tonalities on both pages are well blended, a reddish yellow and a yellowish red with blue and olive green. Rosettes, leaves, quadrupeds and many kinds of birds, especially ducks and parrots, decorate them profusely, and at the bottom of the page the letters of the text are formed by fish and parrots. The arrangement, handling, and colour scheme are reminiscent of a Byzantine textile design.

The painter of the Sacramentary of Gellone, who according to the latest theory allegedly worked at Meaux, reveals a more vigorous style.[2] Although the treatment differs from the Irish, the human body is not flatteringly portrayed here, for the head is enormous and the very long arms emerge clumsily from a sack-like garment. Certain pages reveal a strange, disorderly but picturesque imagination; the letter D of the word *Deus* is sometimes formed by a red thigh over a yellow fish, and at others a red arm is encircled by a serpent. The same letter is also formed by a rose design. These initials are riddles easier to guess at than to unravel. Yet the fact is that all these examples, whether they be British or Continental, are inferior in quality, mastery and magnificence to the masterpieces of the Byzantine illuminators of the sixth century, who on a purple background transcribed their texts in letters of gold or silver, decorating them with painting. They could hardly stand up to comparison with, for instance, the *codex* of Rossano of the sixth century,[3] and its contemporary, the *codex* of Sinopus.[4]

THE MAJOR AND MINOR ARTS

The history of Western illumination gives us the only complete account in the history of art from the invasions until the Carolingian Renaissance. Without it, in fact, it would be even more difficult for us to imagine what were the major arts during that period. All traces of them have not been entirely lost, but they are so few, so widely dispersed, and so fragmentary that they suggest more than they tell us regarding the picture as a whole. Age and decay, holocausts, looting and the passage

[1] Middle of eighth century, Vatican Library.
[2] End of eighth century, Paris, Bibliothèque Nationale.
[3] Rossano, Calabria.
[4] Paris, Bibliothèque Nationale.

of time have left us few important vestiges of them. And to this should be added the fact that although the monasteries were not indifferent to works of art, in many places monastic poverty was disinclined to the use of precious materials.

As far as we can imagine it, the monastery was built in the form of a quadrangle formed by buildings on the four sides of a central court. On one side was the church, with an exterior door. The halls were large ones, for life was communal even at night. Porticos may have opened on to the court. But it is also a certainty that many monasteries were not built according to such a general plan and that the buildings were more irregularly constructed.

The Celtic monks lived in monasteries built of wood, which in fact was characteristic of them; they were known as *opus scotticum*. When they lacked wood they built with stone, and in default of that with earth. With their obstinate nationalism they refused even in this respect too closely to resemble the Gauls, who specialized in the use of rubble and mortar. In the fourth century the monastery of Candida Casa in Galloway was built of stone, but this was exceptional and was mentioned as such and accepted, because its founder was St Ninian.

The largest churches were no longer than a hundred feet, and even these were few, for they preferred to have several oratories scattered among the cells. These were buildings of a few yards in length or diameter, according to whether they were oval, in the shape of an inverted keel, or rounded, like beehives. The cenobites lived in cloisters of baked earth or wattle. At Clonmacnois, founded in 545 by St Ciaran on the banks of the Shannon, vestiges of five churches and a polygonal wall of 500 feet have been found. Elsewhere, at Maghera, Glendalough, remains of doors, windows, arches, entablatures and lintels reveal that the use of stone was allowed there. In the seventh century Kildare possessed frescoes, but nothing remains of these. On the other hand, stone crosses are very numerous: some are larger, some smaller, but they fall into two main classes. Either a cross was sculpted on a block of stone, surrounded by a disk, or else the arms of the cross were hollowed out from the material. The two most remarkable are those of Ruthwell, to the north of the Solway Firth in Scotland (around 665), and of Bewcastle in Northumbria (about 700). In Anglo-Saxon territory in the south, St Augustine had his cathedral of Canterbury built on the model of the Lateran. Both Benedict Biscop at Wearmouth and Wilfrid at Ripon built in the Roman style (*juxta ritum romanum*), and even sent to Gaul for master masons and glaziers.

Other objects deriving from the Celts have come down to us, such as chalices, patens, square reliquaries, made of wood covered in metal, pastoral crooks—the famous staves of the pilgrims—small bells for summoning the faithful, leather bags to contain relics and the liturgical books the monks took with them on their journeys. St Patrick's crook is famous, for it is known that he received it from the Lord and that it was destroyed by the heretics in the sixteenth century. The crook of a holy monk, preserved by the clan, was carried into battle like a lance, for protection and victory. The National Museum in Dublin contains the chalice of Ardagh and the little bell supposed to have been used by St Patrick.

According to the Merovingian records the churches of Gaul promised greater treasures. The church of the monastery of Ste Croix et St Vincent, built by Childebert between 552 and 559, later, St Germain des Prés, was described at the end of the tenth century by the author of the *Life* of St Doctrovée: 'It appears to us superfluous to describe the cunning arrangement of the windows, the precious marbles . . . the gilded hangings of the canopy, the splendour of the brilliantly coloured walls, the beauty of the pavement, decorated with mosaics. The roof of the edifice, of perfectly gilded bronze, and reflecting the rays of the sun, shone so dazzlingly that it was given the name of St Germain the Golden.' Fortunatus, St Radegunda's greedy friend, felt a similar admiration for Nantes cathedral: 'When the sun glows on the tin roof there are pictures there that seem to come alive as they reflect the burning rays of the sun in softer tones and seem to be moving with the sunrays.' We also learn from Fortunatus that there were mosaics at Tours, Autun, and Chalon-sur-Saône. Gregory of Tours gave us more precise information; as a good bishop he conscientiously took the measurements of his cathedral of St Martin—160 feet in length, 60 feet in width, 45 feet in height, 120 pillars, 52 windows. In 654 Jumièges included three cruciform churches, a chapel and two oratories, one of which was the cell in which its founder, St Philibert, had lived.

These accounts excite our imagination, but on examining the still remaining evidence we find it to be on a far more modest scale. In order to form an approximate and possibly erroneous idea of the monastic buildings of Merovingian Gaul we are obliged to turn to those buildings that have survived from those times, without distinguishing whether or not they were in fact monastic ones; a thoroughly unsatisfactory method. But we may in any event recall the fact that the Merovingians built simultaneously both in wood and stone, and that neither their architecture nor their sculpture underwent the regression that certain authors have claimed, for if the masons of Gaul had a high reputation this was because there were architects to give them employment. Apart from the scattered fragments discovered by archaeologists, such as foundations, lintels, cornices and diverse pieces of sculpture, which nearly all show Byzantine influences, the remaining buildings are small, few in number, and were rebuilt on the outside. They include, among others, the Oratory of St Victor at Marseilles (fifth century) and the chapel of St Laurent of Grenoble (sixth or eighth centuries). More important are the crypts of Jouarre, rebuilt during the eleventh, twelfth, and nineteenth centuries, described by Emile Mâle as 'the finest monument of Merovingian art that has come down to us'. And in comparison with the admiring descriptions given us by the contemporaneous writers this is indeed very little.

In the course of his stormy pilgrimages, St Columban, driven from Burgundy, had stopped at Ussy, on the banks of the Marne. He was welcomed by Anthaire, the local lord of the manor, and blessed his sons, Dado and Ado, who, having received the sign of the Cross, were bound to become monks sooner or later. About 630 Dado founded Rebais, and Ado founded Jouarre. The early foundations were merely a collection of huts. Jouarre was a dual monastery, and under the Abbess Théodechilde, the founder's niece, the community of nuns soon became larger than that of the monks. Shortly afterwards Agilbert, Théodechilde's brother and Bishop of Paris, retired to Jouarre where he built a crypt in honour of St Paul the Hermit, which was later completed by his cousin, Ebrégésile, Bishop of Meaux. Jouarre was the sole creation of a pious family.

Théodechilde's monastery, which was built of wood, was destroyed by fire at the end of the eighth century, but the crypt remained. This crypt of St Paul is a church measuring twenty-six metres by nine. It contains fine old marble columns and varied cornices of original workmanship, although not as deeply incised or well proportioned as the classical acanthus. Although vaulting was a general feature of Merovingian building, it appears that the upper part of this crypt was of timberwork, which at that period was known as *machina*.

The crypt of St Ebrégésile, dating from the early eighth century, was built a little later than its neighbour, and is inferior to it. At first it was meant only as an addition to it, but later on it was enlarged and also restored. Both these crypts were mortuary chapels. St Paul's contains thirteen tombs, seven of stone and six of plaster. The most remarkable of these is that of Théodechilde, who died towards 680, and in honour of the Mother Abbess the sculptor produced a masterpiece in vigour, precision, and proportions.

In Italy, where Roman and Byzantine architecture produced so many magnificent monuments, monastic architecture, if it existed at all at that period, left nothing definite behind. The monastery of St Saviour at Brescia does not give us an exact impression of it.

The monks of Visigoth Spain lived in huts. Among the remains of ecclesiastical architecture there the most famous monument is the Daurade of Toulouse (fifth century). Its name derives from the sparkling light with which its mosaics lit up the whole interior (*deaurate*, golden). St John the Baptist of Baños, constructed in 661, the church in the form of a Greek cross of San Pedro de la Nave, and the three churches of Terrassa near Barcelona—notable for the horseshoe arch, and in the sixth century containing mural paintings—can give us no more precise information regarding monastic art than the Daurade.

There exist numerous examples of the jeweller's art of the period. The Barbarians, who at the time of their migrations had little use for architecture, had a taste for the jewellery which had dazzled their ancestors who first came in touch with the East. When they became, if not yet civilized, domesticated, they retained their liking for plaques, fibulae (brooches), medallions, buckles and other ornaments. Their jewellers had a pronounced feeling for design, and in sockets soldered on to a basic plaque embedded either enamels, more or less precious stones, or simply, coloured glass. This was the so-called *cloisonné* technique, distinct from the *champlevé*, which they also used, in which the sockets containing the enamels were not soldered on to but embedded in the basic plaque. The clever combination of separate pieces combined in this way often produced harmonious blendings of colour. It was inevitable that the monks and Churchmen should adapt these methods to their liturgical vases. The treasure of Gourdon (Côte-d'Or) includes a crystal chalice and a tray of the sixth century. The reliquary of St Benoît sur Loire, of the seventh century, is of beaten metal. The chalice of Chelles, which has disappeared, but of which drawings are in existence, may have been the work of St Eloi.

Eloi was worthy of something better than the popular song about him. He was born towards 588, of a Gallico-Roman family, at Chaptelat in Limousin, and was a highly reputed goldsmith who worked for King Clotaire II in Paris. One day the king ordered from him a piece called *sella* in the account of it, and which was presumably made of gold and precious stones (*sellam urbane auro gemmisque fabricare*). Learned men have gravely discussed the question as to whether a *sella* was a saddle or a throne, but common sense suggests that a saddle of state, somewhat spikily encrusted, might not have provided the rider with a very comfortable seat, whilst a throne, which tradition would seem to indicate, would have been both more suitable and comfortable. Eloi, then, having received the precious metal with which to carry out his order, went to work, and on the day agreed produced not one, but two thrones. The king and court were amazed; for this extraordinary goldsmith had been provided with enough gold for one throne only; it was a marvel! But Eloi simply knew his trade and was aware of the fact that gold was too light a metal for the use to which he had been ordered to put it, but that if it were combined with a suitable alloy it would be strengthened. So that was what he did, probably quite deliberately, for he was a man of foresight as well as a good craftsman. His success won him the highest favour, for having produced the royal throne he was appointed to an episcopal see as bishop of Noyon-Tournai. During three successive reigns he remained a trusted counsellor and minister. Amongst a round twenty examples of the goldsmith's art attributed to him it is uncertain whether all of them came from his own workshop, although they certainly are all Merovingian in origin. The famous armchair of Dagobert, so-called, which has been attributed to him, was definitely not his work. Eloi was not a monk, although he did take great interest in the monks and his goldsmith's workshop was, naturally, taken over by Solignac, of which he was the founder. He died in 660.

WORLDLY GOODS

We can form an accurate picture of the material possessions of the great monasteries of the ninth century from certain important documents, the descriptions of St Riquier and St Gall in the polyptych of Irminion, Abbot of St Germain des Prés. Precise information regarding the Merovingian period and the early Carolingian is sparse, but when patiently and methodically collected as has been done for France by Mgr Lesne, it provides us with an overall picture of monastic properties.

Paradoxical as it may appear, the cenobites, whose profession was poverty, were condemned to a life of ease which might even become one of opulence. A hermit might live in sordid fashion, but a community, which only very occasionally was obliged to give evidence of collective heroism, could not live in total destitution without disintegrating. A minimum of well-being and security was required in order to keep a community going, to ensure that the offices were properly carried out and keep up morale. Intellectual activities alone, presuming that all the monks were employed in them, which was never the case, would not suffice for the purpose. Manual labour, imposed by the Rule, of which the principal aim was the training of the inmates, and secondarily, the assurance of their daily bread, was the only means of achieving this. But such labour could not be provided unless there were some place in which it might be performed, and it was therefore necessary for the monastery to possess a certain amount of land which, when well administered, would bear fruit and provide wealth. But in such cases another danger might threaten, for if they were too poor the monasteries might become debased, but if they were too rich run the risk of corruption. Even under the hairshirt and the habit, the members of those communities that were too well provided might fall victims to collective pride and the spirit of laziness (*otiositas*), those two perversions of the soul which, according to St Benedict, together with fatuous self-satisfaction, lay in wait for them. To preserve the will to poverty and humility in a rich abbey was a problem that called for every ounce of tact, thoughtfulness, and tenacity possessed by its superior. In the history of monasticism the fallibility of human nature only too often inclined the scales perilously to the wrong side. But we must also view this state of affairs according to the criteria of the times. Nobody in those days considered wealth to be a form of social injustice and in any case a part of it was devoted to works of charity and public good.

The earliest foundations were spread around the countrysides or in the forests, but from the fifth century onwards, for security reasons, they very often lay under the ramparts of cities, near to the cemeteries. The Celts revived the tradition of solitude, so much so that in the seventh century there were monasteries more or less everywhere.

As a rule a monastery was established as the result of a donation or gift. In the seventh century King Sigebert II granted the monks of Stavelot and Malmédy (near Liège) all the lands that spread for twelve miles around their cloisters. When the donor was a king his generosity cost him little; all he had to do was to select land at random from the immense domains that in the past had been seized from the Imperial treasury. If he were no more than a powerful overlord, whether a layman or an ecclesiastic, the gift still did not cost him much, for such lands were invariably either unproductive or uncultivated. Thus he could at one and the same time acquire at little price the satisfaction of enjoying his own generosity and a mortgage on eternal salvation.

Having built their chapel and laid down their huts, the few monks belonging to the foundation went to work in a manner that was heroic in a very different sense from the activities of the Egyptian semi-anchorites, who only used their fingers in making baskets. In Flanders they drained the valley of the Elnon. At Jumièges they became woodcutters. At Fulda Sturm's companions transformed the German forest into fertile land. And in Gaul St Wandrille, St Riquier, St Bertin and Luxeuil, among many others, were founded in similar fashion. All the monks of the early foundations were pioneers and only the labours of the Israelites in the desert can be compared to monastic labouring in its origins.

As soon as a monastery was securely established it was organized as a closed economic unit, having to live on and by its own produce. Apart from agricultural labourers a well-ordered house needed to have its own bakers, shoemakers, tailors, harnessmakers, wheelwrights, black-smiths and the rest of the necessary tradesmen. That was how St Benedict regarded the matter and in any case no other economic system was known at the time.

As the result of hard work, benefices, new acquisitions and eventually new donations, a monastery became a great landowning property, for at that time the ownership of land and produce was the only concrete evidence of power. A well-run monastery not only possessed the sur-rounding land, but also other properties (*villae*) more or less everywhere. At the beginning of the eighth century the land-ownership of the monks attained huge dimensions so that without exaggeration one may state that the largest part of the wealth of soil belonged to them. In Italy,for instance, where they owned less property than in Gaul, Bobbio, which in 643 contained around 150 monks, housed its community in ten buildings grouped around the church, each building containing several floors; in addition there were thirty single-storied buildings for the lay workers. It also owned twenty-eight farms in the immediate vicinity, whilst its other properties, further away, were important enough to require the services of seven parish churches. In England there were vast and numerous Church properties, and even more so in Germany and Gaul. In 787 St Wandrille possessed 4,624 parcels of land; if we reckon ten hectares to one parcel, which would seem to be the minimum, this would amount to 45,000 hectares (approx. 111,200 acres), more or less. And this was only the residue that was left over after the Caroling-ians had either confiscated or secularized monastic properties. In 734, in fact, Teutsindus, abbot of this self-same St Wandrille, the possessions of which amounted to around one hundred properties, distributed one-third of them amongst his family; Count Rathaire alone received twenty-nine of them. After Pippin the Short had taken a very large slice of them, the monks of St Denis obtained the restitution of forty-six places. However vexatious the royal demands may have been, there were, as might be said, some hefty slices left over.

These lands were as a rule better administered than those belonging to laymen. Nearly everywhere the economy was carefully controlled, and returns were good. The forests provided wood for building and heating, and under the oak-trees pigs, for which there was an enormous demand outside the monasteries, fed on acorns. Goats and sheep provided meat and skins; where the land had been reclaimed cows and horses—dedicated to St Julian by the Auvergnat peasants—cropped the lush meadows. Bees provided wax for Church candles and honey for sweetmeats. There was no lack of cereals, which were cut by sickle and trampled down by horses at threshing-time. There were apple and pear orchards and kitchen-gardens for raising beans, lentils, peas and turnips. The vines produced the Communion wine, of which a great deal was drunk, because both bread and wine were taken at Communion and also because nobody in those days, not even the monks, drank only water. The vine was cultivated as far north as Belgium, at St Peter of Ghent, not in vineries, as is still done today, but in the open air; the climate has certainly not changed, but in those days the Belgians did not mind drinking bad wine. The same was the case in Normandy, at St Wandrille, but elsewhere, in Burgundy for instance, a good wine gave a great deal of pleasure and sometimes even pride.

The monasteries, founded in poverty and containing few inmates, soon filled up; in the sixth and seventh centuries one or two hundred monks were the usual number, but some communities were much larger. To these figures must be added the many laymen who for one reason or another gravitated around the cloisters. A large property could not, as a matter of fact, be successfully worked by the monks alone. Most of them generally did their manual work indoors and nearly all the outdoor work was done by laymen.

This extra-mural work was organized on similar lines to the cultivation of the properties of the 'powerful' men of the time (*potentes*). The land was divided into two halves, the first of which was worked directly to the exclusive benefit of the owner (*indominicatum* or master's plot). This was the part that belonged exclusively to the *villa*. The *villa* was not a castle, but as M. Latouche has pointed out, more like a large farm in Beauce or Picardy, except that it was entirely self-supporting. The remainder was handed over to tenants, who developed it for their own profit, except for certain services and obligations, according to a method analagous to our own leaseholds. It was divided into tenures, the measure of which was the *manse* (from *maneo*, to live; hence the Provençal *mas*). The *manse* or hide, 'the basic cell of agrarian civilization',[1]

[1] A. Déléage.

was the area of land that in principle was thought necessary for the subsistence of a family. Bede described it as *'portio unius familae'*. At first the word referred to the dwelling itself, but later included the land around it. It originally appeared in the seventh century, but the situation has existed since the day when a family with a plough first settled on a bit of ground.[1]

The tenants, whether they were serfs, enfranchised slaves, or freemen, according to their condition, were attached to the soil and the fate of their own portion of it. They were bound by certain obligations to work directly in the service of the landowner, which was counted in days, two or three weekly. In this way the heavy work of the *indominicatum*—labour, sowing, harvesting, carting and vintage—was assured. The tenants spent their remaining time working the land allotted to them, on the produce of which further dues were required, mostly in kind, and often heavy. In 767 a tenant of Viterbo had to pay the following annual dues to Farfa: ten bushels of grain, forty measures of wine, twenty cartloads of hay, and two millstones, failing delivery of which he was without option fined one hundred gold sous, an exorbitant sum which must mean ruin to him. When, in addition, it became necessary, seasonal or annual wage-labourers were hired. They were, as was said, paid merely a few coppers and under no obligations; this was the first and very small-scale form of the prebend (*praebenda*).

At that period the man who was master of the soil was master of those who worked it. Such working conditions, which today would be regarded as unworthy, were then taken for granted. The serfs were part of the monastic 'family' and often better off there than in lay service. They were frequently set free and given small farms of their own. And in those anarchical times, when no one knew what the next day might bring, small independent landowners, of whom there were many, often endeavoured to place themselves and their goods under the protection of a monastery; whilst continuing to live in their villages they found it to their advantage to sacrifice a certain degree of their freedom. The possessions of a monastic centre might thus be increased by taking over their lots or even whole villages altogether.

Another source of revenue was mortgage. If a small independent landowner desperately needed money, yet was reluctant to borrow from a usurer at a rate of interest between twenty-five and fifty per cent, the administrator of the monastery might agree to make him a loan. The

---

[1] The word *'manse'* is not the same as *'mense'* (from *mensa*, table) which referred to the revenue of an abbey to the profit of a benefactor. The German, *Hufe*, and the English, hide, are the equivalents of the French *manse*.

amount lent him was then pledged, generally by a piece of land, of which the value was always higher than the amount loaned. During the entire loan period the monastery had a right to the land and to working it to its own advantage. Repayment could not be made in advance, for the lessor did not intend to be defrauded of his profits, nor, at least in principle, could it be postponed. If on the appointed day the debtor was insolvent, his pledge automatically and finally fell into the hands of the lessor. Thus the monastery ran no risks in the business and was always sure to benefit by it, as today might be the case in banking. On large loans the returns were from seven per cent to twelve per cent; on smaller sums, from twenty-five per cent to thirty per cent. The period allowed for repayment varied according to place and time, but was generally from one to nine years. These proceedings were permitted everywhere and, apparently, were not in contravention of the canonical laws forbidding usury.

There was obviously a very high surplus in production over the monastery's own requirements. To return to the case of Bobbio as an example—and it must again be emphasized that this was not one of the largest—in one year the monks in this establishment had the following surpluses for resale: 2,100 bushels of corn, 1,600 cartloads of hay, 2,700 litres of oil, 5,000 pigs, large and small cattle, to which must be added the production of around 650 farms, roughly 3,600 bushels of corn, 800 amphoras of wine and other products. St Benedict, who, although never anticipating such opulence, nevertheless foresaw that the monastery might produce a surplus, authorized the sale of such commodities, with, however, the restrictive clause that they should be disposed of at a lower rate than that charged by laymen. This suggestion, which does honour to his charity, would however raise problems that the Patriarch had not foreseen. If, as he did assume, the monastery would produce only a small surplus, to sell it at the lowest price would have been a benefit conferred on the poor of the immediate vicinity; but if, on the contrary, very large stocks were thrown on the market at an attractively low price to purchasers, they might cause the market price to collapse, since other producers, working at a lower profit margin, might be unable to face such competition. This is one of the many cases where charitable intentions may turn out to conflict with justice, and in this instance again the monasteries were condemned to acquiring large revenues.

Whether exchanges took place between the various estates in a given centre or with others at a distance from it, special agents who were known as negotiatores were required to handle them. As the roads were unsafe, they travelled in caravans, with an escort, but as the old Roman roads had never been kept up they preferred to go by water. Did the monks in fact open as many routes and build as many bridges as has been claimed? This would be a difficult question to answer, but it is at any rate certain that they possessed numerous fleets, and all the great rivers were at that time used as means of transport. The boats belonging to St Germain des Prés had the right of navigation on the Seine, the Marne, the Yonne, the Aisne and the Oise. In 651 Stavelot in Belgium even had two ports on the Loire, or more likely, two jetties.

The trading was also carried on under certain privileged conditions, another source of profits. Certain establishments had a monopoly of certain goods. As for the tax inspectors, and also the police, they were forbidden to examine any of the monastery's accounts, since it had none to render to them, in this respect enjoying special immunity. Nor, in many places, did it have to pay tolls, or market-tolls in the market places. In 753 Nonantola was not only exempt from market-tolls but also had a monopoly in merchandise.

Thus, what with enormous and easy production on the one hand, with immunities and exemptions on the other, the great monasteries plunged into riches, if one may say so, with both. There is nothing surprising therefore in the fact that centres such as St Martin of Tours, St Martin of Ligugé, St Philibert of Jumièges, St Denis of Paris and many others, enjoyed enough power and credit to produce their own coinage. This silver coinage, which in the seventh century was preferred to gold, was incidentally of a bad alloy but nevertheless constituted another form of exemption to the advantage of those interested and it also reveals to how low a state the central authority had fallen.

Mgr Lesne, who as a rule is reserved when making his careful analyses, has given a masterly description of the material situation of the monasteries at the beginning of the eighth century, and it is to be observed that he rightly also refers simultaneously to the episcopal as well as the monastic properties: 'The patrimony of the churches and the monasteries included everything that at that time might be owned by private individuals, and already a part of what was held by kings. Wealth flowed in waves through the hands of the clergy and the monks. Their treasury sufficed to pay all their current expenses, their buildings, their purchases, gradually becoming converted into landed property. And in ecclesiastical possessions land took the foremost place. The soil was the armature that upheld, enveloped, and enclosed all its other worldly goods. Harvests, vines, the forests that clothed it, the waters that lapped it and the roads that crossed it, the houses, farms, oratories and villages borne by it, the flocks that grazed on it and the oxen that tilled it, the men who cultivated it and whom it nourished, formed with and through it the basic goods of the churches. The clergy and the religious owned the meadows and woods, the rivers, roads and bridges; the pasturage and fishing rights, milling, toll-gathering and marketing. Either as serfs or free settlers the men of the estate also belonged to the church. It possessed the former and their mite as well, and owned the land which those in both groups occupied and could not leave. Apart from the freemen, who of right were under the patronage of the Church, all the men of the ecclesiastical *villae* came under the jurisdiction of the prelate. Such jurisdiction was possibly already conferred on him by the property rights of the Church over the villa and was confirmed by the privileges of immunity. This freed the bishops and abbots from all interference by officials of the crown, and made them the sole masters, after the king, of their lands. Exempt from tax-paying, they themselves raised taxes, imposed fines, and market dues which the revenue made over to them. Thus the ecclesiastical property had already acquired the general outlines of a little sovereign State. From this point of view it was the embryo from which, in the midst of a disintegrating society, was soon to develop the manorial Church, the most highly developed form of ecclesiastical landownership.'

But so many advantages could not be enjoyed without drawbacks. Firstly, the monasteries had to put up with their benefactors, kings, powerful laymen, bishops, from whose jurisdiction they were occasionally able to escape. Kings were particularly awkward protectors; choosing or even appointing abbots according to their own whims, they received from them money, horses, and arms, the quantity and quality of which they themselves sometimes suggested. Like the bishop, the abbot was expected to place himself at the disposal of the court, when required, by personal attendance on the ruler; as we observed, such sojourns were not at all to the liking of St Boniface. When travelling, the king had the right of lodging at the monastery, and such visits might be protracted ones. If he were well-disposed he might reward his hosts with a shower of presents and privileges that cost him nothing personally, but in any case a prolonged royal visit would bear very heavily on the monastic economy, since the entire court would accompany the king on his travels. Worse still, when the king wished to reward a layman for his services, he would purely and simply take his pick from among the monastic possessions; several properties were secularized thus by the first Carolingians. When family troubles were not settled by means of murder the weaker party was generally compelled to don the monk's habit, without, however, regulating his conduct accordingly. A distinguished abbot might be nominated ambassador, always, if he wished to succeed in his mission, at his own expense, including the cost of the customary gifts. Thus, at the beginning of 750, Pippin the Short ordered Fulrad, Abbot of St Denis, to Rome, to whisper in Pope Zachary's ear the necessary words that would appoint Pippin king of the Franks.

In the anarchical society of that period the monasteries all assumed certain responsibilities that in a modern society would be those of the State. The Church alone having to bear the entire weight of charity, the monks took over a very large part of it. This was fair enough, for as they had received so much it was right that they should make some return, and St Benedict had laid down that the brethren must contribute to the rehabilitation of the poor (*pauperes recreare*), as, like Christ Himself, they were to welcome the passing wayfarer.

And it is the fact that they fought hard to overcome the general poverty which in those days was as much a calamity as the plague. In this connection the Church founded a special charitable organization, known as the register. The *matricularii*, who by an ironical twist of history were in due course to become well-heeled churchwardens, were originally poor wretches inscribed on the charitable registers. They even formed a kind of brotherhood, which might hold certain lands that were managed on their behalf by the abbey that held the register. This apart, like today's beggars, they took up their stations at the church doors to beg from the congregation. Another form of monastic charity was the ransoming of prisoners. According to the customs of the time all prisoners were reduced to slavery, but when war ceased to provide a sufficient number of human beasts of burden slave-merchants took over the business; Great Britain and the Slavonic countries—hence the word 'slave'—provided them with a reserve supply. At that time the Church, although still permitting slavery, regarded it as a mission to endeavour to soften the lot of these unfortunates. St Caesarius, although he was by no means the only one to do so, provided ransom-money which he raised from the sale of the sacred vessels of his church. At Jumièges, St Philibert devoted one-tenth of the gifts he received to the ransoming of prisoners. St Eloi bought them out in lots of fifty or one hundred at a time.

Travellers and pilgrims used the monasteries as natural stages on their journeys. They were admitted to them with a certain degree of circumspection, as it was feared that they might meddle in the monastery's business. But once having satisfactorily replied to detailed questioning by the porter they were generously received. And the monasteries often provided a hospital next door to the guest-house. This was given the Greek name of *xenodochium*. In 667 Abbot Ansbert founded at Fontenelle a *xenodochium imbecillium et decrepitorum pauperum*, which was not an insane asylum, but a hospital for sick old paupers. Although hard-hit by secularizations, these works of charity did not, nevertheless, cease to exist.

Thus little by little settlements grew up around the monasteries that changed the demography of the landscapes. In Italy, where the cities had retained a certain degree of stability, this situation was less marked than in France and Germany. Around the *villae* lights appeared in the formerly deserted countryside. All names derived from *moutier* and *munster* (minster), point to monastic foundations. Elsewhere, outside the city gates and in the suburbs along the city walls, important settlements grew up, such as those of St Remy of Rheims, St Médard of Soissons, St Vincent of Paris (St Germain des Prés). All of these owe their origins to suburban monasteries.

The monastic economy of the period was still rudimentary and undeveloped, only its administration being superior to that of the lay economy. The spectacle of such enormous wealth is certainly an astounding one, and one cannot in this connection refrain from recalling the curses rained down on the rich by Our Lord, and the terrible words in which St Augustine denounced avarice as the root of all evil. And it is true that many monks did enjoy their worldly goods and that many of their administrators showed no mercy towards the unfortunate. Yet the fact still remains that in those hard times the monastic foundations employed and fed considerable populations, and that the poor and humble reckoned themselves fortunate if they were able to work or shelter beneath the abbatial crozier.

EPILOGUE

History is forever on the move and cannot be reversed. The facts and dates that we quote in order to refresh our memories refer only to an instant in time, and in time's constant flow they serve chiefly as landmarks. From this point of view the capture of Rome in 410 by Alaric and the Visigoths, and the accession of Charlemagne in 768 are merely two dates that the historian uses for convenience's sake, although he may still recall preceding events or occasionally anticipate those that followed.

For the Western world those three and a half centuries were a period of crisis during which civilization, gravely threatened, at first barely survived but later, not without heavy struggles, carved out a new way of advance.

In the midst of the existing general confusion the Church was a genuine stronghold. Its bishops preserved the cities at any rate to some extent, converted the heathens, organized the dioceses, and as far as was compatible with their pastoral duties, preserved a certain amount of culture. It is noteworthy that a large number of them progressed to their bishoprics from the monk's cell.

In the West the monastic world developed more or less haphazardly and as the result of individual initiatives, and in its origins was no more than a scattering of numbers similar to the Eastern colonies. In spite of his strong personality St Martin was unable to endow his efforts either with cohesion or permanence. In spite of its prestige Lérins did not survive. With all their many virtues the Celts did not possess the power of adaptation. Even at Monte Cassino St Benedict was wishing to do no more than experiment, and we have seen how at his death the number of Benedictine monasteries could be counted on the fingers of only one hand. It needed St Gregory the Great and his mission to Britain to open up horizons for the Benedictines that the Patriarch had not foreseen. Even this development would have been more restricted, or certainly occurred more slowly, had not St Wilfrid strengthened the bonds of spiritual unity between the Celts and the Romans, as St Aidan did with similar success between the Celts and Anglo-Saxons. The Christian settlements in the British Isles, Canterbury in the south, and Northumbria in the north, at that time brought to Benedictine monachism a degree of strength and power of development that it no longer possessed in Italy. It was from England that St Boniface set out to convert Germany, and his disciples, continuing St Columban's work on a more human basis, spread out over northern and eastern Gaul. Meanwhile the Lombards of Italy first permitted and then encouraged the Benedictine institution, and the Popes were preparing the ground for the time when Monte Cassino would again resume its leading role.

The work of civilization closely followed the lines of these developments. Having been greatly shaken by the disintegration of the Roman Empire, roughly handled by the Barbarians in course of migration and the Franks when they settled down, it was preserved thanks to the Anglo-Saxon monks who in close liaison with Rome developed the kernel of culture that was contained in the Rule of St Benedict. Canterbury, Lindisfarne, York, and, on the Continent, Echternach and Fulda, were the great centres from which enlightenment was to spread out over a part of Europe. Elsewhere, although southern Gaul, once the most highly civilized was no longer in the picture, Italy, thanks to Bobbio, was looking towards a fruitful future. Monasteries were spreading all over the place, and with them came religion and culture. The time was not far distant when Charlemagne and his successor, Louis the Pious, both of them seconded by St Benedict of Aniane were to impose the Rule of St Benedict on all monks, and give vigorous impetus to all monastic studies. In spite of the serious drawbacks of royal tutelage, in the ninth century Christian civilization was to enjoy a degree of fame which to a considerable extent was due to the contributions of the monks.

Thenceforward, we know, Western Christianity had found its destined path, yet in fact it was not altogether out of danger. In the south Islam had been contained and then gradually pushed back, yet it remained a danger in Spain, Sicily, and southern Italy. In 846 Moslem warriors profaned the tombs of the Apostles in Rome itself. To the east the Avars, who like the Huns were Turco-Tartars, the Hungarians and the Slavs, were all disturbingly on the move. 'The Norsemen' from Scandinavia, that matrix of invading hordes, seemed an even greater threat. They were thought to be pirates, whereas they were Vikings, i.e.

kings of the sea. From the end of the eighth century the Danes and Norwegians fell on England, Scotland, and Ireland, the latter having until then escaped invasion. And their invasions of western France, Lorraine, and Germany were every bit as devastating as those of the Barbarians of the fifth century. In 885, 700 of their ships, sailing up the Seine, besieged Paris. Yet although this long drawn-out crisis exhausted and ruined vast parts of the West, the essentials survived it; religion, many times menaced, was not destroyed, and civilization, although damaged in many places, recovered. Both now rested on sufficiently firm foundations to be able not only to resist the new Barbarians but to absorb them without tragic upheavals.

Towards the middle of the eighth century the situation was a promising one. The entire Western world had become a Catholic one, and this was thanks to the bishops, priests, and monks. On the plane of civilization, however, although it was to a large extent the creation of the monasteries, the picture was a less impressive one. Scribes, often without realizing the importance of having done so, had saved the essentials of classical literature and propagated Christian letters, whilst others among their brethren had been cultivating spiritual ground. Yet the results of their labours were still on a modest scale and no subsequent generation had produced men of the stature of a St Jerome or a St Augustine. St Bede himself, although he dominated his own period, was only a second-class intellect. Our monks preserved, taught, commented, but they did not create anything. Nevertheless they had grasped the essential point, which is that there can be no profound degree of religion without culture and that in order to create Christians it is not enough merely to immerse them in the baptismal font, but that it is also necessary to open their minds to a certain sense of human values which must be fertilized by the corresponding religious values.

At the same time they established a tradition, i.e. 'the living communication and progressive manifestation of a universal truth of which every age discovers a new aspect'. Securely grafted on to the tree of the Church they understood that although the tree itself remained the same, the composition of the soil in which it was rooted was different in the past and would also be different in the future. Thus it grew and constantly, imperceptibly renewed its growth according to the passing seasons, ever the same yet ever renewed, shedding its dead wood and ripening its fruits. Thus then were the monks. The Benedictine Order, which according to some of its critics lives in a stubborn state of nostalgia for the past, in the prime of its youth was in the vanguard of the great concepts of religion and culture, which it not only transmitted but directed towards the future. As M. Salvatorelli wrote: 'The Rule of St Benedict contained the nucleus of the burial of the old world and the bringing to light of a new world.' Before his time culture, insofar as it existed, was only beginning to feel its way forward; but after him, and to a great extent thanks to him, the Western world was beginning to become integrated as a whole, on a common basis of feeling, thinking, and living in a Christian and civilized world drawing its nourishment from the same sources. A new civilization was evolving, i.e. according to D. Schmidt, 'a social state that rested on material, intellectual, artistic and religious bases that offered men the possibilities of harmonious development'.

Yet this should not mislead us into regarding those conditions as idyllic. Once again we must repeat it—times were very hard indeed, and the monks themselves, in spite of the holiness and intelligence of a great many of them, had not yet all emerged from barbarism. As Henri Pirenne has rightly said, particularly in Gaul, which constituted the largest part of Christianity, they too were members of a society that was still in a state of barbarism, and although they had assumed the task of schooling the barbarian West, they were still working in a dawn which was only beginning to emerge from the darkness of night. Yet if we try to imagine what would have been the state of the Western world without the monks, during that lengthy age between the invasions and the end of the eighth century, we can without much difficulty estimate what would have been lost, both to the Church and to civilization.

CHRONOLOGICAL TABLES

N

	GENERAL EVENTS	MONKS	MONASTIC FOUNDATIONS
200		Origen (185–254)	
250	Invasion by Franks, Alamans and Goths	St Paul of Thebes, hermit (234–347) 270–275 St Anthony (251–351) in the desert. Anchorite life	
300	Emperor Constantine	305–306 St Anthony organizes the life of his disciples 307 Hilarion (c. 291–371) anchorite in Palestine c. 307 St Pachomus (286–346). Cenobitic life	307 Monastery of Tabennesis, founded by St Pachomus
325	Council of Nicaea		
350		358 St Basil (329 or 330–79) 360 Athanasius writes the life of St Anthony. St Martin of Tours (361–97) 373 St Ambrose (c. 340–97) Bishop of Milan. St Jerome (347–419). St Gregory of Nazianza (330–90). St Gregory of Nyssa (340–400). St John Chrysostom (c. 347–407)	c. 333 First monastery of cenobites in Palestine, founded by St Epiphanus 358 Monastery of Annesi, founded by St Basil 360 Ligugé founded by St Martin 372 Marmoutier, founded by St Martin

GENERAL EVENTS	MONKS	MONASTIC FOUNDATIONS
	382 Shenute (334–466) of Atripe	382 Atripe (white monastery, Egypt), founded by Shenute
	385 Translation of the Bible by St Jerome	
	386 Conversion of St Augustine (354–430)	
		388 Monastery of Tagaste, founded by Augustine
Emperor Theodosius	396 St Augustine Bishop of Hippo	c. 396 Monastic foundation by Augustine at Hippo
400		
The great invasions		
The Visigoths in Italy		
410 Seizure of Rome by Alaric	St Honoratius (c. 350–429)	410 Lérins Abbey founded by St Honoratius
	c. 412 Ascetism of St Simeon Stylites (c. 389–459)	
The Vandals in North Africa		
	Johannes Cassianus (John Cassian) (c. 350–434)	415 St Victor's Abbey at Marseilles, founded by John Cassian
Invasion of Great Britain by the Anglo-Saxons; fusion with the Britons	St Patrick (389–461)	c. 430 First foundations by St Patrick. First British monasteries
	St Hilary of Arles (c. 403–49) Bishop of Arles	444 Armagh monastery founded by St Patrick
450 Huns in Gaul		
476 End of the Western Roman Empire. Visigoths in Spain and Gaul. Apogee of the Byzantine Empire	St Brigid of Kildare	c. 490 Kildare Abbey, founded by St Brigid

GENERAL EVENTS	MONKS	MONASTIC FOUNDATIONS
496 Baptism of Clovis		
500 First Merovingians in Gaul	St Benedict of Nursia (c. 480–547)	c. 500 Abbey of Subiaco, founded by St Benedict
	502 St Caesarius (470–543), Primate of Arles	502 Abbey of St Caesarius at Arles founded by St Caesarius
		510 Abbey of St Germain d'Auxerre, founded by St Clotilde
		520 Clonard Abbey founded by St Finian
		c. 524 Abbey of Monte Cassino, founded by St Benedict
	537 Composition of the Benedictine Rule	
Frankish hegemony in the West		543–558 Abbey of St Croix St Vincent (St Germain des Prés), founded by Childebert I
550		550 Abbey of St Médard de Soissons, founded by Clotaire I
		c 550 Abbey of St Benigne de Dijon, founded by Gregory of Langres
	Cassiodorus (died in 578 or 580)	555 The Vivarium, founded by Cassiodorus
	St Comgall (516–601)	559 Bangor Abbey founded by Comgall
	St Brendan (484–577 or 583)	560 Clonfert Abbey founded by St Brendan
	St Columba (512–95 or 597)	563 Iona Abbey founded by St Columba
	St Radegunda (c. 520–87)	Monasteries of Kells and Durrow, founded by Columba

GENERAL EVENTS	MONKS	MONASTIC FOUNDATIONS
	573 Gregory of Tours (539–94), Bishop of Tours	
	c. 575 St Columban (c. 540–615) in Armorica	
		577 Destruction of Monte Cassino by the Lombards
		589 Abbey of St Martin d'Autun, founded by Brunhild
	590 St Gregory the Great (538–604) Pope	590 Luxeuil Abbey, founded by St Columban
Irish monks appear in Gaul	597 St Augustine of Canterbury (died in 605)	
	Isidore of Seville (560–636)	
600		601 Abbey of St Peter and St Paul of Canterbury, founded by St Augustine
		610 Westminster Abbey founded by St Mellitus
	St Gall (born between 532 and 550, died between 625 and 640)	c. 613 Hermitage of St Gall
		613 Abbey of Bobbio, founded by St Columban
		630 Jouarre Abbey, founded by Adon
		631 Abbey of Fleury sur Loire (St Benoît sur Loire) founded by Leodebold
632 Death of Mahomet	St Eloi (588–660)	632 Solignac Abbey, founded by St Eloi

GENERAL EVENTS	MONKS	MONASTIC FOUNDATIONS
634 Arab expansion	635 St Amandus (died in 676) Bishop of Maestricht	635 Lindisfarne Abbey, founded by Aidan
		636 Elnore Abbey, founded by St Amandus
	St Wandrille (died in 668)	649 Fontenelle Abbey (St Wandrille), founded by St Wandrille
	St Ouen (609–83)	649 Abbey of St Ouen de Rouen, founded by St Ouen
		650 Denis Abbey
650 Final conversion of the Lombards		654 Jumièges Abbey, founded by Philibert
	664 Synod of Whitby	664 Peterborough Abbey, founded by St Wilfrid
Byzantine decadence in Italy	St Wilfrid (634–709) spiritual unification of the Celts and Romans St Benedict-Biscop (628–90)	674 Wearmouth Abbey, founded by St Benedict-Biscop
	St Cuthbert (635–87)	682 Jarrow Abbey, founded by St Benedict-Biscop
Arabs in North Africa	690 St Willibrord (c. 658–739) evangelizes Friesland	
		695 Abbey of St Martin of Utrecht founded by St Willibrord
		696 Abbey of St Peter of Salzburg founded by the monk Rupert

GENERAL EVENTS	MONKS	MONASTIC FOUNDATIONS
700		
		703–708 Abbey of St Vincento di Volturno, founded by the Lombards
		708 Echternach Abbey, founded by St Willibrord
	709 Death of St Aldhelm St Pirmin, died in 753	
711 Arab conquest of Spain		
		720 Restoration of Monte Cassino by Petronax
		724 Reichnau Abbey, founded by St Pirmin
	731 Bede's 'Ecclesiastical History' (673–735)	
732 Charles Martel's victory over the Arabs at Poitiers		
		734 Murbach Abbey, founded by St Pirmin
	741 St Boniface reorganizes the Frankish church	741 Fulda Abbey, founded by St Boniface
750 Pippin the Short elected King of the Franks at Soissons		750 St Gall Abbey
		752 or 753 Nonantola Abbey, founded by Anselm

BIBLIOGRAPHY

The bibliography given below, except for a few older works that are quite indispensable, claims only to offer a selection from the very considerable recent literature. It was necessary, however, to cite a number of studies to be found in various journals or large ecclesiastical dictionaries, as they are important. Many of the texts have been issued in special editions, but most of them can be most conveniently consulted in Migne's *Patrologie grecque et latine* and *Monumenta Germaniae historica*.

A. GENERAL BIBLIOGRAPHY

I. GENERAL HISTORY

Collection CLIO: *Histoire de Rome*, A. PIGANIOL, Paris, 1939; *Le Monde féodal*, J. CALMETTE, Paris, 1942.

Collection GLOTZ: Histoire romaine, v. IV, *L'Empire romain de l'avènement des Sévères au concile de Nicée*, M. BESNIER, Paris, 1937; *L'Empire chrétien*, A. PIGANIOL, Paris, 1947; *Histoire du Moyen Age*, v. I: *Les Destinées de l'Empire en Occident de 395 à 888*, F. LOT, Chr. PFISTER, F. L. GANSHOF, Paris, 1940.

Collection HISTOIRE GÉNÉRALE DES CIVILISATIONS (M. CROUZET): *Rome et son Empire*, A. AYMARD et J. AUBOYER, Paris, 1954; *Le Moyen Age*, E. PERROY, Paris, 1955.

Collection PEUPLES ET CIVILISATIONS (L. HALPHEN and Ph. SAGNAC): *L'Empire romain*, E. ALBERTINI, Paris, 1938; *Les Barbares*, L. HALPHEN, Paris, 1940.

J. CALMETTE, *Le Moyen Age*, Paris, 1948.

C. DAWSON, *The Making of Europe*, London, 1932.

M. DEANESLY, *History of Early Medieval Europe* (476–911), London, 1960.

F. L. GANSHOF, *Le Moyen Age*, vol. I of *l'Histoire des Relations internationales*, P. RENOUVIN, Paris, 1953.

L. GENICOT, *Les Lignes de faîte du Moyen Age*, Paris, 1951.

R. LATOUCHE, *Textes d'Histoire médiévale* (5th–6th cent.), Paris, 1951.

J. PIRENNE, *Les Grands Courants de l'Histoire universelle*, Paris, 1951.

E. SALIN, *La Civilisation mérovingienne*, 4 vols., Paris, 1949–1959.
E. STEIN, *Histoire du Bas Empire*, 2 vols., Paris, 1949 and 1959 (French ed., important).

II. HISTORY OF THE CHURCH

F. CAYRÉ, *Précis de Patrologie*, v. II, Tournai, 1930.
DANIEL-ROPS, *L'Eglise des Apôtres et des Martyrs*, Paris, 1948; *L'Eglise des Temps barbares*, Paris, 1950.
L. DUCHESNE, *Histoire de l'Eglise*, 4 vols., to the end of the 6th cent., Paris, 1910–1925.
FLICHE et MARTIN, *Histoire de l'Eglise*, v. III: *De la paix constantinienne à la mort de Théodose*, J.-R. PALANQUE, G. BARDY, P. DE LABRIOLLE, Paris, 1945; v. IV: *De la mort de Théodose à l'élection de Grégoire le Grand*, P. DE LABRIOLLE, G. BARDY, G. DE PLINVAL, L. BRÉHIER, Paris, 1945; v. V: *Grégoire le Grand, les Etats barbares et la conquête arabe*, L. BRÉHIER et R. AIGRAIN, Paris, 1938.
Manuals: A. BOULANGER, A. DUFOURCQ, F. MOURRET, D. POULET.
Important articles in *Dictionnaire d'histoire et de géographie ecclésiastique*, *Dictionnaire de spiritualité*, *Dictionnaire de théologie catholique*, *Dictionnaire d'archéologie chrétienne et de liturgie*.
L. BOUYER, *La Spiritualité du Nouveau Testament et des Pères*, Paris, 1960.
D. J. LECLERCQ, D. Fr. VANDENBROUCKE, L. BOUYER, *La Spiritualité du Moyen Age*, Paris, 1961.

III. THE CHURCH AND CIVILIZATION

G. BARDY, *La Question des Langues dans l'Eglise ancienne*, v. I, Paris, 1948.
P. COURCELLE, *Les Lettres grecques en Occident de Macrobe à Cassiodore*, Paris, 1943.
E. R. CURTIUS, *La Littérature européenne et le Moyen Age latin*, Paris, 1956 (French ed.).
C. DAWSON, *Religion and the Rise of Western Culture*, London, 1950.
F. DRANE, *Christian school or sketch of education from the Christian Era to the Council of Trent*, London, 1924.
G. DE GHELLINCK, *La Littérature latine au Moyen Age*, v. I, Paris, 1939; *Patristique et Moyen Age*, 3 vols., Paris, 1946, 1947, 1948.
E. GILSON, *La Philosophie au Moyen Age*, Paris, 1944.
P. DE LABRIOLLE, *Histoire de la Littérature chrétienne*, 2 vols., Paris, 1947.
L. W. LAISTNER, *Intellectual heritage of the Early Middle Ages*, Itaca, 1957.
A. PUECH, *Histoire de la Littérature grecque chrétienne*, 3 vols., Paris, 1930.
E. K. RAND, *Founders of the Middle Ages*, Cambridge, 1928.
M. ROGER, *Les Lettres latines d'Ausone à Alcuin*, Paris, 1905.
G. SCHNUERER, *L'Eglise et la Civilisation*, v. I, Paris, 1933 (French ed.).

IV. STUDIES IN MONACHISM IN GENERAL

1. HISTORY
D. P. COUSIN, *Précis d'Histoire monastique*, Paris, 1959 (very important).

H. LECLERCQ, articles *Cénobitisme* and *Monachisme* in *Dictionnaire d'Archéologie chrétienne et de Liturgie.*

Moines, La Pierre-qui-Vire, 1953.

MONTALEMBERT, *Les Moines d'Occident,* 5 vols., Paris, 1863–1868.

D. Ph. SCHMITZ, *Histoire de l'Ordre de Saint Benoît,* 7 vols., Maredsous, 1942–1947 (very important).

2. SPECIAL STUDIES

D. U. BERLIÈRE, *L'Ordre monastique des origines au XIIIᵉ siècle,* Maredsous, 1923.

D. BESSE, *Les Moines de l'ancienne France,* Paris, 1906.

Centro italiano di studi sull'alto medioevo of Spoleto: *Il monachesimo nell'alto medioevo e la formazione della civiltà occidentale,* 1957.

3. MONASTIC SPIRITUALITY AND CULTURE

L. BOUYER, *Le Sens de la Vie monastique,* Turnhout, 1950.

D. J. LECLERCQ, *La Vie parfaite,* Turnhout, 1947; *L'Amour des Lettres et le Désir de Dieu,* Paris, 1957.

D. G. MORIN, *L'idéal monastique et la Vie chrétienne des premiers siècles,* Maredsous, 1921.

D. ROUSSEAU, *Monachisme et Vie religieuse d'après l'ancienne tradition de l'Eglise,* Chevetogne, 1957.

D. Fr. VANDENBROUCKE, *Le Moine dans l'Eglise du Christ,* Turnhout, 1947.

B. SPECIAL BIBLIOGRAPHY

Chapter I

1. CIVILIZATION

H. I. MARROU, *Culture, civilisation, décadence,* in *Revue de Synthèse,* XV, 1938; *Histoire de l'éducation dans l'Antiquité,* Paris, 1938; *Saint Augustin et la fin de la culture antique,* Paris, 1938.

A. J. TOYNBEE, *Civilization on Trial,* Oxford, 1948.

2. CHRISTIAN HUMANISM

E. GILSON, *L'Esprit de la Philosophie médiévale,* v. I, Paris, 1932; *Les Idées et les Lettres,* Paris, 1932; *Christianisme et Philosophie,* Paris, 1936.

J. MARITAIN, *Du régime temporel et de la liberté,* Paris, 1933; *Humanisme intégral,* Paris, 1936; *Religion et Culture,* Paris, 1948.

A. RENAUDET, *Définition de l'Humanisme,* in *Bibliothèque d'Humanisme et de Renaissance,* Paris, 1945.

3. MISSIONS

Bibliography of the question, pontifical documents, commentaries and works in *Parole et mission,* Feb., 1961.

Ch. DU MESNIL, *Les Missions,* Paris, 1948.

H. DE LUBAC, *Le Fondement théologique des Missions,* Paris, 1945; *Catholicisme,* Paris, 1947.

R. MILLOT, *L'Epopée missionnaire,* Paris, 1956.

4. HAGIOGRAPHY

R. AIGRAIN, *L.Hagiographie, ses sources, ses méthodes, son histoire*, Paris, 1953.

H. DELEHAYE, *Cinq Leçons sur la Méthode hagiographique*, Bruxelles, 1934; *Les Légendes hagiographiques*, Bruxelles, 1955.

Chapter II

1. THE DECLINE OF ROME

F. ALTHEIM, *Le Déclin du Monde antique*, Paris, 1953 (French trans.).

L. HOMO, *L'Empire romain*, Paris, 1930.

F. LOT, *La Fin du Monde antique et les Débuts du Moyen Age*, Paris, 1927.

H. St. L. B. MOSS, *Birth of the Middle Ages*, Oxford, 1935.

2. THE BARBARIANS

F. ALTHEIM, *Attila et les Huns*, Paris, 1952 (French ed.).

P. COURCELLE, *Histoire littéraire des grandes invasions*, Paris, 1948.

C. COURTOIS, *Les Vandales en Afrique*, Paris, 1955.

E. DEMOUGEOT, *Attila et les Gaules*, in *Mémoires de la Société d'agriculture, commerce, sciences et arts du département de la Marne*, 1958.

W. ENSSLIN, *Theodorich der Grosse*, Munich, 1947.

E.-F. GAUTIER, *Genséric*, Paris, 1932.

M. GORCE, *Clovis*, Paris, 1935.

R. GROUSSET, *L'Empire des Steppes*, Paris, 1939.

P. LAMMA, *Teodorico*, Brescia, 1951.

R. LATOUCHE, *Les Grandes Invasions et la crise de l'Occident au Ve siècle*, Paris, 1948.

F. LOT, *Les Invasions germaniques*, Paris, 1930; *La Naissance de la France*, Paris, 1948; *La France, des origines à la guerre de Cent Ans*, Paris, 1941.

P. RICHE, *Les Invasions barbares*, Paris, 1953.

R. SAFFET ATABINEN, *Esquisse d'une histoire rationnelle d'Attila dans les Gaules*, in *Mémoires de la Société d'agriculture, commerce, sciences et arts du département de la Marne*, 1957.

3. THE CHURCH AND THE BARBARIANS

G. BARDY, *L'Eglise et les derniers Romains*, Paris, 1948.

E. GRIFFE, *La Gaule, des origines chrétiennes à la fin du IVe siècle*, Paris, 1947.

A. LATREILLE, E. DELARUELLE, J.-R. PALANQUE, *Histoire du Catholicisme en France*, Vol. I, Paris, 1957.

E. MALE, *La Fin du Paganisme en Gaule et les plus anciennes basiliques chrétiennes*, Paris, 1950.

J.-R. PALANQUE, etc., *Le Christianisme et la Fin du Monde antique*, Lyon, 1943; *Le Christianisme et l'Occident barbare*, Paris, 1945.

J.-R. PALANQUE, *La Gaule chrétienne à l'époque franque*, in *Revue de l'histoire de l'Eglise de France*, 1952.

Chapter III

1. GENERAL STUDIES

J. et H. BREMOND, *Les Pères du désert*, 2 vols., Paris, 1925.

R. Draguet, *Les Pères du désert*, Paris, 1949.

A.-J. Festugière, *Les Moines d'Orient*, I *Culture et sainteté*, Paris, 1961.

Ph. Gobillot, *Les Origines du Monachisme chrétien et l'ancienne religion de l'Egypte*, in *Recherches de sciences religieuses*, Paris, 1920, 1921, 1922.

P. Ir. Hausherr, *Comment priaient les Pères*, in *Revue d'ascétique et de mystique*, Toulouse, 1956; *Direction spirituelle en Orient autrefois*, Rome, 1955.

J. Leroy, *Moines et Monastères d'Orient*, Paris, 1958.

P. Resch, *La doctrine ascétique des premiers maîtres égyptiens du IVe siècle*, Paris, 1931.

M. Viller and M. Olphe-Gaillard, article *Ascèse* in *Dictionnaire de spiritualité*.

P. Viller, *Martyre et Ascèse*, in *Revue d'ascétique et de mystique*, Toulouse, 1925.

2. ST ANTHONY

Arnaud d'Andilly, *La Vie et les Enseignements de Saint Antoine*, Ottawa-Montréal, 1947.

L. Bouyer, *Vie de Saint Antoine*, Saint-Wandrille, 1950 (important).

B. Lavaud, *Antoine le Grand, père des moines*, Lyon, 1943.

3. ST PACHOMUS

P. Ladeuze, *Etude sur saint Pachôme et le cénobitisme pachômien aux IVe et Ve siècles*, Paris, 1898.

Th. Lefort, *Les Premiers Monastères pachômiens*, in *Muséon*, 1939; *Vies coptes de Saint Pachôme et de ses premiers successeurs*, Louvain, 1943.

F. Nau, *Histoire de Saint Pachôme*, dans *Patrologie orientale*, Vol. IV, fasc. V, Paris.

4. SHENOUTE OF ATRIPE

H. Leclercq, article *Deir el Abiad*, in *Dictionnaire d'archéologie chrètienne et de liturgie*.

I. Leopold, *Shenouté von Atripé und die Entstehung des national-aegyptischen Christentums*, Leipzig, 1903.

5. MONACHISM IN SYRIA AND PALESTINE

H. Delehaye, *Saints stylites*, Paris, 1923; *Les stylites, saint Syméon et ses successeurs*, in *Revue des questions historiques*, 1895.

J. Lassus, *Sanctuaires chrétiens de Syrie*, Beyrouth, 1945.

H. Leclercq, article *Laures palestiniennes* and *Saba*, in *Dictionnaire d'archéologie chrétienne et de liturgie*.

J. Mattern, *A travers les villes mortes de Haute Syrie*, Beyrouth, 1945.

P. Peters, *Saint Syméon stylite et ses premiers historiens*, in *Analecta bollandiana*, 1943.

6. ST BASIL

P. Allard, *Saint Basile*, Paris, 1899.

D. Amand, *L'Ascèse monastique de Saint Basile*, Maredsous, 1948 (important).

E. Fleury, *Saint Grégoire de Nazianze et son temps*, Paris, 1930.

S. Giet, *Les Idées et l'Action sociale de Saint Basile*, Paris, 1941; *Sasimes, une méprise de Saint Basile*, Paris, 1941.

P. Humbertclaude, *La Doctrine ascétique de Saint Basile de Césarée*, Paris, 1930.
J. Rivière, *Saint Basile*, Paris, 1925.

7. ST JEROME
P. Antin, *Essai sur Saint Jérôme*, Paris, 1951.
J. Brochet, *Saint Jérôme et ses ennemis*, Paris, 1905.
F. Cavellera, *Saint Jérôme*, 2 vol., Paris, 1922 (important).
D. Gorce, *Saint Jérôme et la lecture sacrée dans le milieu ascétique romain*, Paris, 1925.
H. Leclercq, *Saint Jérôme*, Louvain, 1927.
P. Monceaux, *Saint Jérôme, sa jeunesse*, Paris, 1932.
J. Steinmann, *Saint Jérôme*, Paris, 1958.

Chapter IV

1. ST PAULINUS NOLA
A. Baudrillart, *Saint Paulin, évêque de Nole*, Paris, 1905.
G. Boissier, *La Fin du Paganisme*, Paris, 1891.
P. Courcelle, *Paulin de Nole et Saint Jérôme*, in *Revue des Etudes latines*, 1947.
P. de Labriolle, *La Correspondance d'Ausone et de saint Paulin de Nole*, Paris, 1910.
F. Lagrange, *Histoire de Saint Paulin de Nole*, 2 vols., Paris, 1882.

2. ST AUGUSTINE
G. Bardy, *Saint Augustin*, Paris, 1946.
G. Combes, *Saint Augustin et la culture classique*, Paris, 1927.
E. Gilson, *Introduction à l'Etude de Saint Augustin*, Paris, 1929.
H.-I. Marrou, *Saint Augustin et la fin de la culture antique*, Paris, 1938, followed by *Retractatio*, Paris, 1948; *Saint Augustin et l'Augustinisme*, Paris, 1955.
M. Mellet, *L'Itinéraire et l' Idéal monastique de Saint Augustin*, Paris, 1934.
N. Merlin, *Saint Augustin et la Vie monastique*, Albi, 1935.
G. de Plinval, *Pour connaître la pensée de saint Augustin*, Paris, 1954.

3. ST ISIDORE OF SEVILLE
J. Fontaine, *Isidore de Séville et la culture classique dans l'Espagne wisigothique*, 2 vols., Paris, 1958.
H. Leclercq, *L'Espagne chrétienne*, Paris, 1906.
Miscellanea Isidoriana, Homenaje a San Isidore de Sevilla en el XIII centenario de su muerte, Rome, 1936
B. Steilde, *Der heilige Isidor von Sevilla und die Westgoten*, in *Benediktinische Monatschrift*, 1936, pp. 425–34.

4. ST MARTIN
E.-Ch. Babut, *Saint Martin de Tours*, Paris, 1912, and refutation (indispensable) by P. Delehaye, *Saint Martin et Sulpice Sévère*, in *Analecta Bollandiana*, 1920.
H. Ghéon, *Saint Martin*, Paris, 1941.

P. LADOUË, *Saint Martin de Tours*, Paris, 1960.
P. MONCEAUX, *Saint Martin*, Paris, 1926.

5. LÉRINS

D. CAPPUYNS, article *Cassien* in *Dictionnaire d'Histoire et de Géographie ecclésiastique*.
O. CHADWICK, *John Cassian, A Study in Primitive Monachism*, Cambridge, 1950.
L. CHRISTIANI, *Jean Cassien*, Saint-Wandrille, 2 vols., 1946; *Lérins*, Saint-Wandrille, 1946.
A. MALNORY, *Saint Césaire, évêque d'Arles*, Paris, 1899.
H.-I. MARROU, *Jean Cassien à Marseille*, in *Revue du Moyen Age latin*, 1945.
M. OLPHE-GAILLARD, article *Cassien* in *Dictionnaire de Spiritualité*.
D. E. PICHERY, *Conférences de Cassien*, Paris, 1945, 1958, 1959 (important introduction).
G. DE PLINVAL, article *Césaire* in *Dictionnaire d'Histoire et de Géographie ecclésiastique*.

6. ST RADEGUNDA

R. AIGRAIN, *Sainte Radegonde*, Paris, 1916.
E. DELARUELLE, *Sainte Radegonde, son type de sainteté et la chrétienté de son temps*, in *Etudes mérovingiennes*, 1953.
G. MARIE, *Sainte Radegonde et le milieu monastique contemporain*, in *Etudes mérovingiennes*, Paris, 1953.

7. ST GREGORY OF TOURS

G. KURTH, *Etudes franques*, 2 vols., Bruxelles, 1919.
A. LATOUCHE, *Grégoire de Tours et les premiers historiens de la France*, in *Lettres d'humanité*, Paris, 1943.

8. SCHOOLS

H. LECLERCQ, article *Ecoles* in *Dictionnaire d'Archéologie chrétienne et de Liturgie*.
M. ROGER, and other authors cited in the section *L'Eglise et la Civilisation*

Chapter V

1. CELTS

H. HUBERT, *Les Celtes depuis l'époque de la Tène et la civilisation celtique*, Paris, 1950.
J. F. KENNEY, *The Sources for the Early History of Ireland*, I, New York, 1929.

2. MONACHISM

L. BIELER, *The Island of Scholars*, in *Revue du Moyen Age latin*, 1952.
DANIEL-ROPS, *Le Miracle irlandais*, Paris, 1956.
L. GOUGAUD, *Les Chrétientés celtiques*, Paris, 1911 (important).
P. GROSJEAN, *Notes d'hagiographie celtique*, in *Analecta Bollandiana*, Bruxelles, notably: Années 1944 and 1945 on St Patrick.

H. Leclercq, articles *Irlande* and *Celtique* in *Dictionnaire d'Archéologie chrétienne et de Liturgie*.

A. Lorcin, *La Vie scolaire dans les monastères d'Irlande du Ve au VIIIe siècle*, in *Revue du Moyen Age latin*, 1945.

E. Mac Neill, *St. Patrick, Apostle of Ireland*, London, 1934.

3. MIGRATIONS

G. Doble and L. Kerbiriou, *Les Saints bretons*, Brest, 1933.

T. Fowler, *Vita sancti Columbani*, Oxford, 1920 (important preface on St Columba).

L. Gougaud, *Les Saints irlandais hors d'Irlande*, Paris, 1936.

R. Largillère, *Les Saints et l'Organisation primitive de l'Armorique bretonne*, Rennes, 1925.

H. Leclercq, article *Migration bretonne* and *Iona*, in *Dictionnaire d'Archéologie chrétienne et de Liturgie*.

4. ST COLUMBAN OF LUXEUIL

M.-M. Dubois, *Saint Colomban*, Paris, 1950.

Mélanges colombaniens, Paris, 1951 (important).

M.-M. Rosier, *Dans la barbarie mérovingienne, saint Colomban*, Paris, 1950.

J. Roussel, *Saint Colomban*, Besançon, 1942.

Chapter VI

1. ST BENEDICT

La vie et les miracles du bienheureux Père saint Benoit, texte de saint Grégoire, Paris, 1952 (Bénédictins de Paris).

D. J. Chapman, *St Benedict and the Sixth Century*, London, 1929.

D. P. Delatte, *Commentaire de la Règle de Saint Benoît*, Paris, 1913 (important).

Ezio Franceschini, *La questione della Regola di san Benedetto*, in *Il monachesimo nell'alto medioevo e la formazione della civiltà occidentale*, Spoleto, 1957.

D. I. Herwegen, *Saint Benoît*, Paris, 1927 (French ed.).

D. Nesmy, *Saint Benoît et la Vie monastique*, Paris, 1959.

Card. Newman, *Historical Sketches* ('The Mission of St Benedict').

L. Salvatorelli, *San Benedetto e l'Italia del suo tempo*, Bari, 1929.

D. A. Savaton, *La Règle de saint Benoît*, Saint-Paul-de-Wisques, 1950.

Card. Schuster, *Saint Benoît et son Temps*, Paris, 1950.

2. CASSIODORUS

D. Cappuyns, article *Cassiodore* in *Dictionnaire d'Histoire et de Géographie ecclésiastique* (important).

P. Courcelle, *Les Lettres grecques en Occident; Le site du monastère de Cassiodore*, in *Mélanges d'archéologie et d'histoire ecclésiastique*, Rome, 1938.

A. Van de Vyver, *Cassiodore et son œuvre*, in *Speculum*, 1931; *Les Institutions de Cassiodore et la fondation du Vivarium*, in *Revue bénédictine*, Maredsous, 1941.

3. ST GREGORY THE GREAT

P. BATIFFOL, *Saint Grégoire le Grand*, Paris, 1908.

O. BERTOLINI, *Roma di fronte a Bisanzio e di Longobardi*, Bologna, 1941.

F. H. DUDDEN, *St Gregory the Great*, 2 vols., London, 1905.

D. J. FROGER, *Origines, histoire et restitution du chant grégorien*, in *Musique et liturgie*, Paris, 1950–1951.

H. DE LUBAC, *Saint Grégorie et la grammaire*, in *Recherches de sciences religieuses*, *Mémorial* 1960–1961, Paris.

H. I. MARROU, *Saint Grégoire le Grand*, in *La Vie spirituelle*, Paris, 1943.

G. PÉPE, *Le Moyen Age barbare en Italie*, Paris, 1956 (French ed.).

A. VALORI, *Gregorio Magno*, Turin, 1956.

4. ANGLO-SAXONS, CELTS AND LATINS

R. AIGRAIN, *L'Angleterre chrétienne et les Eglises celtiques*, in FLICHE and MARTIN.

F. CABROL, *L'Angleterre chrétienne avant les Normands*, Paris, 1909.

L. GOUGAUD, *Chrétientés celtiques*.

A. HUMBERT, article *Angleterre* in *Dictionnaire d'Histoire et de Géographie ecclésiastique*.

F. M. STENTON, *Anglo-Saxon England*, Oxford, 1950.

Chapter VII

1. MONASTIC CULTURE

E. S. DUCKETT, *Anglo-Saxon Saints and Scholars*, New York, 1948.

S. FLETCHER, *The Life and Work of St Wilfrid of Ripon*, Chichester, 1925.

L. GOUGAUD, article *Aidan* in *Dictionnaire d'Histoire et de Géographie ecclésiastique*.

L. W. LAISTNER, *Thought and Letters in Western Europe*, A.D. *500 to 900*, London, 1957.

H. LECLERCQ, article *Céolfrid*, in *Dictionnaire d'Archéologie chrétienne et de Liturgie*.

W. LEVISON, *England and the Continent in the Eighth Century*, Oxford, 1946.

J.-E. RABY, article *Bede* in *Dictionnaire d'Histoire et de Géographie ecclésiastique*.

W. REANY, *St Theodore of Canterbury*, St Louis, 1944.

2. MISSIONARIES

Bonifatius Gedenkgabe zum 1200 Todestag, Fulda, 1954.

M. COENS, *Saint Boniface et sa mission historique*, in *Analecta Bollandiana*, Brussels, 1955.

G. KURTH, *Saint Boniface*, Paris, 1913.

E. DE MOREAU, *Histoire de l'Eglise en Belgique*, v. I, 1945; *Saint Amand, apôtre de la Belgique et du nord de la France*, Louvain, 1942; *Saint Amand, le principal évangéliste de la Belgique*, Bruxelles, 1942; Article *Boniface* in *Dictionnaire d'Histoire et de Géographie ecclésiastique*.

Th. SCHIEFFER, *Winfrid-Bonifatius und die christlichen Grundlegung Europas*, Fribourg, 1954.

G.-H. VERBIST, *Saint Willibrord, apôtre des Pays-Bas et fondateur d'Echternach*, Louvain, 1939; *A l'aube des Pays-Bas, Saint Willibrord*, Bruxelles, 1953.

C. WAMPACH, *Sankt Willibrord, sein Leben und Lebenswerk*, Luxembourg, 1953.

3. ITALIAN MONASTERIES

G. CIMORELLI, *La badia di S. Vincenzo al Volturno*, Venafro, 1914. *Convegno di Studi storici per la celebrazione del 1200 anniversario di Nonantola*, in *Atti e memorie ... per le provincie modenesi*, Vol. 5, 1953.

M. DEL TREPPO, *Longobardi, Franchi et Papato in due secoli di storia vulturnese*, in *Archivo storico per le provincie napoletane*, 1953–1954.

V. FEDERICI, *L'origine del monastero di San Vincenzo secondo il prologo di Autperto*, in *Studi di storia in onore di Carlo Calisse*, Milan, 1940.

T. LECCISOTTI, *Le consequenze dell'invasione longobarda per l'antico monachesimo italiano*, in *Atti del 1° Congr. intern. di Studi longobardi*, Spoleto, 1952; *Aspetti e problemi del monachesimo in Italia*, in *Il monachesimo nell' alto medioevo e la formazione della civiltà occidentale*, Spoleto, 1957.

Card. SCHUSTER, *O'imperiale abbazia di Farfa*, Rome, 1921.

D. J. WINANDY, *Ambroise Autpert, moine et théologien*, Paris, 1953.

Chapter VIII

1. LITURGY

R. AIGRAIN, *Liturgia*, Paris, 1935.

L. BOUYER, *La Vie de la Liturgie*, Paris, 1956.

F. CABROL, *Les Origines de la Liturgie*, Paris, 1906; *Le Livre de la Prière antique*, Tours, 1919; *Les Livres de la Liturgie latine*, Paris, 1930; *La Messe en Occident*, Paris, 1932.

I.-H. DALMAIS, *Initiation à la Liturgie*, Paris, 1958.

L. DUCHESNE, *Les Origines du Culte chrétien*, Paris, 1925.

R. GUARDINI, *L'Esprit de la Liturgie*, Paris, 1935 (French trans.).

J.-A. JUNGMANN, *Missarium solemnia*, 3 vol., Paris, 1951, 1952, 1954 (French trans.).

H. LECLERCQ, numerous articles in *Dictionnaire d'Archéologie chrétienne et de Liturgie*, notably *Anamnèse, Anaphore, Canon, Elévation, Fraction, Kyrie eleison, Messe*.

A.-G. MARTIMORT, *L'Eglise en prière, Introduction à la Liturgie*, Paris, 1961.

E. NORDEN, *Die antike Kunstprosa*, 2 vols., Leipzig, 1898.

P. PARSCH, *The Liturgy of Mass*, London.

Card. SCHUSTER, *Liber sacramentorum*, 9 vols., Bruxelles, 1925–1933 (French trans.).

2. CHURCH MUSIC

R. AIGRAIN, *La Musique religieuse*, Paris, 1929.

S. CORBIN, *L'Eglise à la conquête de sa musique*, Paris, 1960.

A. GASTOUÉ, *L'Art grégorien*, Paris, 1910; *L'Eglise et la musique*, Paris, 1936.

D. A. Mocquereau, *Le Nombre musical grégorien*, 2 vols., Tournai, 1908.
N. Rousseau, *L'Ecole grégorienne de Solesmes*, Tournai, 1910.

3. SCRIPTORIUMS, LIBRARIES, MANUSCRIPTS
M. Audin, *Somme typographique*, Paris, 1947, v. I.
G. Battelli, *Lezioni di paleografia*, Vatican City, 1939.
H. Leclercq, article *Ecritures*, in *Dictionnaire d'Archéologie chrétienne et de Liturgie*.
E. Lesne, *Histoire de la propriété ecclésiastique en France*, v. IV, *Les livres, 'scriptoria' et bibliothèques*, Lille, 1938.
J. Mallon, R. Marichal, Ch. Perrat, *L'Ecriture latine, de la capitale romaine à la minuscule*, Paris, 1939.
R. Marichal, *Paléographie précaroline*, in *Scriptorium*, Bruxelles, 1955.
M. Prou, *Manuel de Paléographie latine et française*, Paris, 1924.

4. ILLUMINATIONS
R. Brunner, *The Art of Scriptorium at Luxeuil*, in *Speculum*, 1954.
Fr. Henry, *Art irlandais*, Dublin, 1954.
H. Leclercq, article *Miniature*, in *Dictionnaire d'Archéologie chrétienne et de Liturgie*.
E. Lesne, *Histoire de la propriété ecclésiastique en France*, v. IV.
F. Masaï, *Essai sur les origines de la miniature dite irlandaise*, Bruxelles, 1947; *Il monachesimo irlandese nei suoi rapporti col continente (arte)*, in *Il monachesimo nell'alto medioevo e la formazione della civiltà occidentale*, Spoleto, 1957.
L. Mazenod, *L'Art primitif en Suisse*, Geneva, 1942.
A. Michel, *Histoire générale de l'Art*, v. I, Paris, 1905.
C. Nordenfalk, *Le haut Moyen Age, du IVe au XIe siècle. L'enluminure*, Geneva, 1957 (important).
L. Reau, *Histoire de la Peinture au Moyen Age, La miniature*, Melun, 1946.
D. P. Salmon, *Le Lectionnaire de Luxeuil*, v. I and II, Rome, 1944–1953.
P. Toesca, *Storia dell'arte italiana*, v. I, *Il medioevo*, Turin, 1927.
E. H. Zimmermann, *Vor Karolingische Miniaturen*, Berlin, 1916.

5. MAJOR AND MINOR ARTS
L. Bréhier, *L'Art en France, des invasions barbares à l'époque romane*, Paris, 1930.
M. Durand-Lefebvre, *Art gallo-romain et Sculpture romane*, Paris, 1937.
L. Goucaud, *L'Art celtique chrétien*, Paris, 1911.
J. Hubert, *L'Art préroman*, Paris, 1938; *L'Architecture religieuse du haut Moyen Age en France*, Paris, 1952.
P. Lantier and J. Hubert, *Les Origines de l'Art français*, Paris, 1947.
E. Male, *La fin du paganisme en Gaule*.
R. Rey, *L'Art roman et ses origines, Archéologie préromane et romaine*, Paris, 1945.

6. TEMPORAL ACTIVITIES
P. Boissonnade, *Le Travail dans l'Europe chrétienne au Moyen Age*, Paris, 1921.
R. Grand, *L'Agriculture au Moyen Age*, Paris, 1950.

P. IMBART DE LA TOUR, *Des immunités commerciales accordées à l'Eglise du VIIe au IXe siècle*, Paris, 1896. (*Etudes d'histoire dédiées à Gabriel Monod.*)

Inspiration religieuse et structure médiévales, Collection 'Bases de l'humanisme', Paris, 1948.

R. LATOUCHE, *Les Origines de l'Economie occidentale*, Paris, 1956.

E. LESNE, *Histoire de la Propriété ecclésiastique en France*, v. I and VI, Lille, 1910 and 1943.

L. LEVILLAIN, *Etudes sur l'abbaye de Saint-Denis à l'époque mérovingienne*, *Bibliothèque de l'Ecole des Chartes*, No. 91, Paris, 1930.

INDEX

GEORGE ALLEN & UNWIN LTD
London: 40 Museum Street, W.C.1

Auckland: 24 Wyndham Street
Bombay: 15 Graham Road, Ballard Estate, Bombay 1
Bridgetown: P.O. Box 222
Buenos Aires: Escritorio 454-459, Florida 165
Calcutta: 17 Chittaranjan Avenue, Calcutta 13
Cape Town: 68 Shortmarket Street
Hong Kong: 44 Mody Road, Kowloon
Ibadan: P.O. Box 62
Karachi: Karachi Chambers, McLeod Road
Madras: Mohan Mansions, 38c Mount Road, Madras 6
Mexico: Villalongin 32-10, Piso, Mexico 5, D.F.
Nairobi: P.O. Box 4536
New Delhi: 13-14 Asaf Ali Road, New Delhi 1
São Paulo: Avenida 9 de Julho 1138-Ap. 51
Singapore: 36c Prinsep Street, Singapore 7
Sydney, N.S.W.: Bradbury House, 55 York Street
Tokyo: 10 Kanda-Ogawamachi, 3-Chome, Chiyoda-Ku
Toronto: 91 Wellington Street West, Toronto 1

JACQUES PIRENNE

THE TIDES OF HISTORY

VOLUME I. *From the beginnings to Islam*

'History,' the author writes in his Preface, 'is essentially continuity
and a unity; a continuity that goes on, without men being able to
escape it, from generation to generation, and which links our own
times to the most distant epochs; a unity, since in any society the life
of each man is bound up with the lives of all others, even as, in the
community of nations, the history of each nation develops, without
even being aware of it, as a part of the history of all the nations of
the universe. . . .'

Jacques Pirenne, the distinguished Belgian historian, and son of
the equally distinguished Henri Pirenne, has now completed a study
of universal history in seven volumes, covering the whole of civilization from the beginnings to the most recent events of the 1950's. The
first volume to be published in English, which ends with the advent
of Islam, includes all the civilizations of antiquity from the earliest
movements on the deltas of the Nile, the Indus, the Euphrates and
Tigris, through the histories of Ancient Egypt, Babylon, Assyria,
Persia, Greece, Rome and China and other parts of Asia. Gigantic in
its scope, this study is remarkable for its lucidity, its comprehensive-
ness and its great readability.

'If this opening instalment, which goes back to the dawn of
recorded time, be any indication, the work is destined to win a wide
readership in this country. The author does not confine himself to
wars and politics, as so many world histories do, but devotes much
attention to economics and the minutiae of everyday living. Moreover, he accords as much space to the Orient as to the West, thus
correcting a widespread imbalance found in most Western histories.
The translation by Lovett Edwards is first-rate.'—JOHN BARKHAM,
Saturday Review
Demy 8vo   *50s. net*

VOLUME II. *From the Expansion of Islam to the Treaties of Westphalia*

Throughout this comprehensive account of all the activities of civilized man—political, religious, social, commercial and artistic—during
this essential period of world history, Professor Pirenne's own philosophy of history emerges: he seeks the continuity of history, the
relationship between civilizations, the progress of humanity which is
not continuous but which can be perceived over the tides of growth,
decline and rebirth of civilizations.
Demy 8vo   *60s. net*

HISTORY OF MANKIND

CULTURAL AND SCIENTIFIC DEVELOPMENT

VOLUME I, PARTS ONE AND TWO

Prehistory and The Beginnings of Civilization

BY JACQUETTA HAWKES AND SIR LEONARD WOOLLEY

'The two distinguished authors have performed their tasks admirably
... this achievement of British scholarship deserves great praise. If
all succeeding volumes are as good and as readable, the International
Commission will have earned our thanks and our congratulations on
a major task, well-conceived and well-accomplished. . . .'—*The Times
Literary Supplement*

'the best available compendium of its subject. Both contributors have
provided clear and interesting panoramas; they muster a huge amount
of material without getting lost in the detail. The book is eminently
readable, and the plates, drawings and maps are all well chosen . . .
a highly valuable work, which reduces a vast field of history to manageable proportions.'—*Daily Worker*

'a magnificent, scholarly, well-written, definitive work: beautifully
illustrated with plates, diagrams, and line-drawings; copiously served
with maps; fairly representing opposite views in text or notes; and
citing all authorities. The bibliographies and indices are exhaustive.
The book itself is a tribute to British printers, papermakers and
binders: and for all its size, the pages are easy to read, and this
reviewer could scarcely find a misprint.'—*Economist*

'This magisterial survey by two of the leading authorities in their
respective fields, is balanced, lively, and informative, and the copious
plates illuminate the text.'—*Irish Times*

Small Royal 8vo   2nd Impression   *75s. net*

PART ONE. *Prehistory*

JACQUETTA HAWKES
Small Royal 8vo   *35s. net*

PART TWO. *The Beginnings of Civilization*

SIR LEONARD WOOLLEY
Small Royal 8vo   *42s. net*

GEORGE ALLEN AND UNWIN LTD